**The
Definitive
Object-
Oriented
Problem
Solver**

THE WAITE GROUP'S®

TURBO

PASCAL

HOW-TO

Gary Syck

WAITE GROUP PRESS
A Division of The Waite Group, Inc.
100 Shoreline Highway, Suite A-285
Mill Valley, CA 94941

Development Editor   *Mitchell Waite*
Content Editor   *Robert Lafore*
Design and Production   *Barbara Gelfand*
Cover Illustration   *Steve Epstein*
Text Illustration   *Pat Rogondino*
Production Coordination   *Merrill Peterson*
Production   *Karyn Kraft, Mary McDermott, Robin Purcell*
Editorial Director   *Scott Calamar*

ISBN: 1-878739-04-2

Printed in the United States of America

91 92 93 94 • 10 9 8 7 6 5 4 3 2 1

Library of Congress Cataloging-in-Publication Data

Syck, Gary
        The Waite Group's Turbo Pascal how-to : the definitive object-oriented
        problem-solver / Gary. -- 1st ed.
                    p. cm.
        Includes index.
        ISBN 1-878739-04-2
        1. Pascal (Computer program language) 2. Turbo Pascal (Computer program) 3. Object-oriented
        programming. I. Waite Group. II. Title. III. Title: Turbo Pascal how-to.
        QA76.73.P2S97 1991
        005.265--dc20   91-28267
                                                                                     CIP

TABLE OF CONTENTS

CONTENTS

Dear Reader:

Thank you for considering the purchase of *The Waite Group's Turbo Pascal How-To*. Readers have come to know products from The Waite Group for the care and quality we put in them. Let me tell you a little about our group and how we make our books.

It started in 1976 when I could not find a computer book that really taught me anything. The books that were available talked down to people, lacked illustrations and examples, were poorly laid out, and were written as if you already understood all the terminology. So I set out to write a good book about microcomputers. This was to be a special book—very graphic, with a friendly and casual style, and filled with examples. The result was an instant best-seller.

Over the years, I developed this approach into a "formula" (nothing really secret here, just a lot of hard work—I am a crazy man about technical accuracy and high-quality illustrations). I began to find writers who wanted to write books in this way. This led to co-authoring and then to multiple-author books and many more titles (over seventy titles currently on the market). As The Waite Group author base grew, I trained a group of editors to manage our products. We now have a team devoted to putting together the best possible book package and maintaining the high standard of our existing books.

THE
WAITE
GROUP

We think this book, *Turbo Pascal How-To,* is a good example of the things we will be doing at Waite Group Press. The first collective standard problem solver for Turbo Pascal, each solution provides a complete description that shows why the problem exists, how to solve it in code, dangers that can come up, and additional comments and enhancements. These solutions are not only practical, they teach you how to program in Pascal. You will find standard solutions in pure Turbo Pascal 6, TP 6 with objects, and Turbo Vision.

We hope you enjoy this and all the other books upcoming from Waite Group Press. If you wish to be on our mailing list, or if you have any comments to tell us after you have purchased and read the book, please fill out and send in detachable postpaid card.

Mitchell Waite

Mitchell Waite
President

100 Shoreline Highway   Suite A-285   Mill Valley   California   94941   415-331-0575   Fax 415-331-1075

FOREWORD

Almost anything you might say about Turbo Pascal will certainly be an understatement. It is one of the most successful and versatile languages in computer history.

As a learning language, Pascal has been around for awhile, but the implementation known as Turbo Pascal is barely a decade old. In that time, the language has spread worldwide—the United States, Europe, Asia, the Soviet Union, everywhere that MS-DOS computers are used—and it has dramatically changed the way that people use their computers and think about problem solving.

Borland's Turbo Pascal began as a $49 revolution in language software. The package included a thick paperback manual and a single (low-density) 5.25" floppy disk. Today, the Turbo Pascal package (priced at $149 but available for about $100) includes six manuals and six 3.5" floppy disks, each disk holding more than a megabyte of compressed files. Turbo Pascal Professional includes an integrated-debugger-editor, a profiler, a command-line compiler, a stand-alone debugger and an extensive online help system. Borland's new Turbo Pascal for Windows even gives you everything you need to develop Windows programs without Microsoft's intricate Windows (SDK) Software Development Kit. Turbo Pascal is now a complete software development system, ranking among the very best in the world.

The remarkable thing about the language is that it provides easy accessibility without sacrificing power. Think of an F-16 with training wheels. If you already know how to fly, you'll find it an exciting adventure and won't even notice the training wheels. If you're just starting out, it's reassuring to know that you can proceed at your own pace. You can climb into the cockpit without having to know what every single one of those little knobs and buttons mean. You can learn as you go.

To me, this is Turbo Pascal's strength—that you can use it at your own level of expertise. A beginner can start producing useful results almost immediately; anyone who can write a batch file or program in BASIC can write a simple Turbo Pascal program; but the more you use the language, the more it encourages you to expand your repertoire of programming skills.

It has been said that Turbo Pascal is the most democratic language in the world—almost all of its users have been self-taught, working entirely from manuals and after-market books like this one.

What makes this book special is its approach to problem solving.

The authors of most language texts take a wide overview and deal primarily with the principles of the language applied to very general problems—the emphasis is on the techniques of the language, rather than on the aspects of the problem. As a result, many dedicated Turbo Pascal users have shelves full of books that duplicate each other's information.

This book begins with the assumption that you already have some facility with the language, but that you would appreciate a reference that demonstrates how to solve specific tasks. This is it—a nuts-and-bolts guide. Its purpose is to provide applications and techniques that you can put to immediate use and shorten the time you spend reinventing low-level functions. It is a collection of all the best techniques that have been invented and lessons that have been learned since the language first appeared.

You can use this book as a toolbox full of useful routines to be plugged into your own programs, and you will certainly get your money's worth; but the real treasure here is the internal one: the more you use these tools, the more you will expand your own personal repertoire of programming techniques. You will become a more powerful programmer. And that's the best tool of all.

Of all of the books available to help you become more proficient in Turbo Pascal, this is one of the few that definitely deserves to be called a "must-have" book. I wish it—or something like it—had been available ten years ago.

David Gerrold
June 1991

David Gerrold is a contributing editor and columinst for PC Techniques Magazine. *In his spare time, he writes science fiction novels.*

PREFACE

This book is for the programmer who has learned Turbo Pascal and wants to create sophisticated programs. When you write an application using Turbo Pascal, you inevitably stumble across a question that begins "How do I..." To answer this question, you must know about Turbo Pascal, the IBM PC, and suitable algorithms. This book is a collection of these questions and the solutions used in actual applications.

The solutions combine information from several sources to give you the answer to your most commonly asked questions. To solve these problems yourself, you would need books on MS-DOS, PC BIOS, graphics, mathematics, and many more. We have extracted the relevant information from each of these subjects to give you just the answer you need.

This book covers all versions of Turbo Pascal, including the newest version 6. Version 6 comes with Turbo Vision, an object-oriented application framework for writing MS-DOS programs. We also focus in on solving problems using Borland's new Turbo Pascal for Windows, which allows you to develop programs for Microsoft Windows 3.

Each "How Do I..." entry presents a Turbo Pascal program that illustrates the solution. You can plug in the modular programs as we present them or modify the programs to meet your specific needs. Because these programs are meant to answer the questions completely, some are long and may be tedious to input. To save you this effort, you can order a companion disk from the Waite Group that includes all of the programs in this book.

This book is designed to be a reference for answering those "How do I..." questions. To get the answer you need, look in the chapter for the relevant category, then find a matching question. If your question does not match any of the questions in the chapter, you can read the "Description" sections to see if the question is similar to the one you want to answer. You can use most of the answers without knowledge of other answers in the book. You can refer to the questions indicated in the "See Also" section, however, to find helpful related information

The "Solution" and "Comments" sections give the answer to the question. The "Solution" section gives the theory behind the answer and a program that illustrates the answer. The "Comments" section gives information about how to run the program or use it in other programs.

The "Warnings" section points out possible dangers. Here you find information about possible memory conflicts or things to watch out for when modifying the routines. The "Warnings" section also gives cases in which the solution may not be appropriate.

The last section, "Enhancements", shows how you can improve or modify a solution for specific cases. Sometimes it shows how to avoid problems mentioned in the "Warnings" section.

This book has ten chapters. Chapter 1 contains questions about how Turbo Pascal programs interact with the user. It has solutions for writing to the screen, handling the keyboard, and creating sounds with the PC speaker. You can use these solutions to improve the user interface of your programs.

Chapter 2 concerns files and devices. The solutions here show you how to manipulate files, control printers, and use the serial port. If your program saves data or needs to send it to another computer or device, check out these solutions.

Chapter 3 is about mathematics. It starts simple, with routines for converting numbers to strings and back again. Then it covers complex numbers and matrices. Finally, it covers some questions about numerical analysis.

Chapter 4 shows how to handle strings using Turbo Pascal. There are solutions for searching and sorting strings, formatting strings, and compressing text data.

Chapter 5 gives solutions for interacting with MS-DOS and BIOS. These solutions show how to use the command line and MS-DOS environment variables, read the disk, and look at special MS-DOS and BIOS variables.

Chapter 6 shows what you can do with object-oriented programming. The solutions here show how object-oriented programming lets you create Turbo Pascal programs that are easy to modify and maintain. This chapter presents solutions that we build on later on in the book.

Chapter 7 contains solutions to graphics problems. It starts with simple plotting programs and moves all the way up to 3-D rendering with hidden line removal. There are also solutions for image enhancement.

Chapter 8 draws on computer science for its solutions. It covers basic data structures, commonly used formulas, and formula parsing.

Chapter 9 is a collection of Turbo Pascal utilities and routines. The solutions show how to make a complete user interface and handle text files.

Chapter 10 compares Borland's Turbo Vision library for MS-DOS text-mode applications to Borland's new Turbo Pascal for Windows. The solutions show how to create programs for each of these systems.

This book can be used in a few ways. We mentioned that in addition to being a problem solver, this book is set up to serve as a reference. You'll note that all program code is heavily commented, so you can improve your Turbo Pascal skills without having to read through long, ponderous tutorials. We take a "learn-by-doing" approach and explain our solutions in detail throughout.

Almost all of the code in this book is modular. Short examples illustrate simple "How Do I..." questions, and we build on these examples as the questions get more complex. You can actually plug these modules into your Turbo Pascal programs with a minimum of fuss and watch them work.

The Waite Group's Turbo Pascal How-To is the first in a new series of problem-solving books from the Waite Group. Please use the Satisfaction Report Card in the back of this book to tell us what you think of our approach.

For Erika

ACKNOWLEDGMENTS

The people of the Waite Group deserve most of the credit for making this book possible. I would like to give special thanks to Scott Calamar, Robert Lafore, and, of course, Mitchell Waite. Without their help and guidance, I would never have been able to put together a work of this scope.

I appreicate the assistance of Nan Borreson of Borland International for providing us with timely pre-release and final versions of Turbo Pascal 6 and Turbo Pascal for Windows.

I would also like to acknowledge my wife and daughter who had to put up with many evenings of neglect while I worked on this book. Their tolerance and understanding were above and beyond the call of duty.

ABOUT THE AUTHOR

Gary Syck lives and works in the Pacific Northwest. He began programming ten years ago in BASIC on PDP-8 computers. When Apple introduced the UCSD-p system, he learned Pascal. Now he uses Turbo Pascal, assembly language, and C to write database and communications programs. He is also the author of *The Waite Group's Turbo Assembler Bible*, published by Howard Sams.

1

INTERACTING WITH THE USER

All but a very few programs interact in some way with a human user. Even if they don't require user input, they display something on the screen. A clean, professional-looking screen is the face your program presents to the world. When users look at your program, they don't see the fancy algorithms and clever coding tricks you invented. They see the user interface. If the interface is difficult to use or not visually appealing, users will be put off by the program.

Turbo Pascal has excellent built-in tools for screen I/O. Because the CRT unit allows direct writing to video RAM, `Write` and `WriteLn` statements execute at lightning speed. The `TextColor` and `TextBackground` routines control the color of what you write, and the `Window` routine restricts output to a rectangular area on the screen. The `GotoXY` routine makes it easy to move the cursor, and `WhereX` and `WhereY` routines make it simple to check the cursor locations.

However, when you try to emulate commercial programs with pop-up windows and moving bar menus, you exceed the limits of the built-in video support. Turbo Pascal lets you put a pop-up window on the screen, but it won't restore the screen area that your pop-up window covered. Turbo Pascal routines allow you to move the cursor but not to hide it or change its shape. Here are some solutions that help you extend the video interface abilities built into Turbo Pascal.

SCREEN SOLUTIONS

To create the text image you see on your PC screen, the video interface reads a special area of memory. Your Turbo Pascal program can also read this memory area and write to it. The solutions in this section show you how to manipulate the screen by reading and writing to video memory. Solution 1.1 shows how to locate video memory and then fill regions of the screen with characters and attributes.

For monochrome video adapters the attribute of a character controls how it appears on the screen: normal, inverse, bold, or underlined. Other video adapters use the attribute to determine the color of the character. Solution 1.2 shows you how to modify just the character attributes on the screen to highlight different areas.

Once you know how to write to video memory, it is simple to also read it. This knowledge is useful in programs that temporarily overwrite portions of the screen. Solution 1.3 shows you how to save the screen image in memory, overwrite the screen, then restore the screen to its original state.

When your program overwrites an area on the screen, you want to make sure that the new text does not run into the text that is already there. One way to set off the new text is to put a box around it. Solution 1.4 shows how to draw a box on the screen by writing directly to screen memory.

Some programs let you look at a block of text that is larger than the screen. To see the parts that don't fit, you can press the arrow keys causing the text to scroll. A fast way to do the scrolling is to read the data on the screen and copy it to a new location. This technique is demonstrated in solution 1.5.

1.1   How do I...

Fill the screen (or part of it) with a particular character and attribute?

Description

The `clrscr` command fills the screen or current window with space characters in the current text color. However, you might want to fill the screen with some other character, and there are better ways to do so than using repeated `WriteLn` commands.

See Also

Solution

The video screen is stored in RAM as a series of 16-bit word values. The low byte of each word is the character to be displayed, and the high byte is the attribute to use. If you know the address of the video memory, you can store whatever you want in it. Figure 1-1 shows how video memory is organized.

Memory for 80x86 computers is divided into 64K blocks called segments. To address a given location in memory, you must specify the segment and the offset into that segment. Because segments can overlap in memory, you do not need to go 65536 bytes before starting a new segment. In fact, you can start a new segment every 16 bytes.

The segment for video RAM depends on the type of video card that is installed. You can infer this information from the video mode stored in the variable `TextMode`. If the video mode is 7, then the video card is a monochrome card, and the video memory is at segment $B000. If the mode is 2 or 3, then the video memory segment is $B800. All other modes mean that the card is not in text mode at all.

Once you know the segment of the video RAM, you must find the offset for the first screen position to fill. An obvious choice for the starting position is the cursor location. You can get this information by looking at the `WhereX` and `WhereY` variables. Here is the formula for converting this cursor position into an offset into video memory:

```
Offset := (( WhereY - 1 ) * 80 + WhereX - 1 ) * 2
```

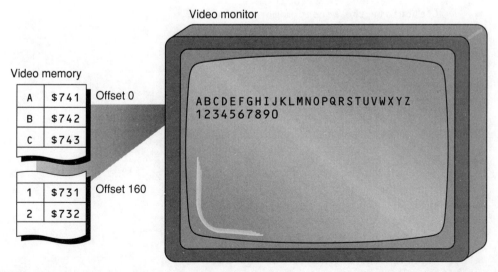

Figure 1-1 Video RAM

Once you know the segment and the offset of the screen location to change, you must tell Turbo Pascal to use that location. The `Ptr` function combines a segment and an offset into a pointer that can access the memory at the specified location. You can use the `^` operator to dereference (to access the data at the memory location indicated by the pointer) a function, and you can cast the data to the correct data type. So, a statement to store $0741 (the character 'A' in normal video) on a VGA card at `Offset` looks like this:

```
word( Ptr( $B800, Offset )^) := $0741;
```

The following program fills the screen with characters. It uses a function called `FillChars` that writes to video RAM.

```
{Program to fill the screen}
program FillScr;
uses Crt;

procedure FillChars( Data:word; Count:word );
var
Offset : word;                {The offset into screen memory}
        Segment : word;       {The segment for screen memory}
        ScrPtr : ^word;
begin
        {Calculate the offset}
        Offset := (( WhereY - 1 ) * 80 + WhereX - 1 ) * 2;
        {Find out what segment to use}
        if LastMode = 7 then
                Segment := $B000
        else
                Segment := $B800;
        {Calculate the screen memory pointer}
        ScrPtr := Ptr( Segment, Offset );
        {Loop Count times}
        while Count <> 0 do
        begin
                {Store the data}
                ScrPtr^ := Data;
                Inc( ScrPtr );
                {Decrement count}
                Dec( Count );
        end;
end;

var
   Ch : byte;
   Attr : byte;
   x, y : integer;
begin
     {Initialize the attribute and character}
     Attr := 0;
     Ch := 32;
```

```
for y:=1 to 25 do
        for x:=0 to 3 do
        begin
                GotoXY( x*20+1, y );
                FillChars( Attr SHL 8 + Ch, 20 );
                Inc( Attr );
                Inc( Ch );
        end;
    ReadLn;
end.
```

The `FillChars` procedure begins by computing the offset into the video segment for the current cursor location. Next, it gets the video mode to determine what segment to use. The `Ptr` function combines the segment and offset and puts the result in `ScrPtr`. The `while` loop counts the characters printed and exits when the requested number has been printed. After each character is stored in video memory, the `Inc` procedure increments the screen pointer. Because the pointer points to a word, Turbo Pascal knows that the pointer needs to be incremented by two.

The main program uses two loops to fill the screen with the character in `Ch` and the attribute in `Attr`. The outer loop goes through each line, and the inner loop puts four filled areas on the line. The expression `Attr SHL 8 + Ch` combines the attribute and character bytes into a word that `FillChar` can store in screen memory.

Comments

One useful side effect of using `FillChars` to fill the screen is that you can print to the last column on the last line without scrolling the screen. If you use `WriteLn` to write to the screen, the cursor advances to the position following the last character printed. Upon reaching the end of a line, the cursor moves to the first column on the next line. If the line is the last line, BIOS scrolls the screen up one line to make room for the cursor. Because `FillChar` does not move the cursor, it does not cause the screen to scroll.

Warnings

You need to watch out for several things when using routines, such as `FillChars`, that write directly to the screen memory. The first is the way some CGA cards work. These cards cannot display data at the same time that the video memory is being updated. The update creates screen interference that resembles snow. Programs that must work with CGA cards need an assembly-language routine that determines when it is safe to read or write to video memory.

Next, be careful whenever you are using pointer variables in Turbo Pascal. Under MS-DOS you can overwrite any location in the computer's memory when you use pointer variables. Although this feature allows programmers to write a routine such as FillChars, it also can cause problems. You are unlikely to get into trouble with the FillChar routine as it is written. If you change it, however, be sure that you know what values you assign to the pointer. If you have any doubt about a routine, use the debugger to check the value in a pointer variable before any damage is done.

Enhancements

One way to improve the performance of this routine is to code the loop in assembly language. For Turbo Pascal versions earlier than 6.0, you must look up the machine codes for the instructions in your routine and put them into an InLine statement. In version 6.0 you can use the asm directive to put assembly-code instructions into the program. A good source of information about assembly language and machine codes is *The Waite Group's Turbo Assembler Bible (Howard W. Sams, 1991)*.

The InLine version of the while loop looks like this:

```
InLine(
        $8B / $46 / < Segment /      {mov    ax, [bp + Segment]}
        $8E / $C0 /                  {mov    es, ax}
        $8B / $7E / < Offset /       {mov    di, [bp + Offset]}
        $8B / $4E / < Count /        {mov    cx, [bp + Count]}
        $8B / $46 / < Data /         {mov    ax, [bp + Data]}
        $FC /                        {cld}
        $F3 / $AB                    {rep stosw}
);
```

The asm version of the loop looks like this:

```
asm
        mov     ax, Segment          {Get the segment}
        mov     es, ax               {Put it in the ES register}
        mov     di, Offset           {Get the offset}
        mov     cx, Count            {Get the number of chars}
        mov     ax, Data             {Get the data to print}
        cld                          {Set direction to forward}
        rep     stosw                {Store the data}
end;
```

Change just the attribute of an area on the screen?

Description

Many programs change the appearance of the screen to signal what field of a data-entry screen should be filled in next. For example, a program may display default values in yellow, edited values in bright white, and the field being edited in inverse video. To accomplish this, you need a routine that changes screen attributes without affecting the text on the screen.

See Also

1.1   Filling screen areas with characters

Solution

The attribute byte is the high byte of each character word. To change the screen attributes, just modify odd-numbered bytes in screen memory. This program demonstrates the `SetAttrs` routine, which is similar to `FillChars` except that it changes only attribute bytes

```
{Program to fill the screen}
program FillScr;
uses Crt;

procedure SetAttr( Data:byte; Count:word );
var
   Offset : word;      {The offset into screen memory}
   Segment : word;     {The segment for screen memory}
   ScrPtr : ^byte;
begin
      {Calculate the offset}
      Offset := (( WhereY - 1 ) * 80 + WhereX - 1 ) * 2 + 1;
      {Find out what segment to use}
      if LastMode = 7 then
            Segment := $B000
      else
            Segment := $B800;
      {Calculate the screen memory pointer}
      ScrPtr := Ptr( Segment, Offset );
      while( Count <> 0 ) do
      begin
            {Store the data}
            ScrPtr^ := Data;
            Inc( ScrPtr, 2 );
            {Decrement count}
            Dec( Count );
      end;
end;
```

```
var
   Attr : byte;
   x, y, len : integer;
begin
   Randomize;
   {Initialize the attribute and character}
   repeat
       len := Random( 6 ) + 5;
       x := Random( 70 ) + 1;
       y := Random( 25 ) + 1;
       Attr := Random( 255 );
       GotoXY( x, y );
       SetAttr( Attr, len );
   until KeyPressed;
end.
```

SetAttr uses a byte pointer instead of the word pointer used in FillChar. This lets the routine address individual bytes instead of whole words. To affect attribute bytes, SetAttr adds 1 to the computed offset. Using a byte pointer also affects the Inc statement, which must be told to move ahead 2 bytes to the next character.

The main program generates random numbers to determine which area of the screen to change and which attribute to use. It keeps setting different attributes, without changing the text, until the user presses a key.

Comments

The attribute byte has two parts. The high nibble (upper four bits) determines the background color, and the low nibble determines the foreground color. For each of these nibbles, the high bit is a control bit. In the low nibble, it controls the intensity of the foreground color. In the high nibble, the high bit can control intensity or make the characters blink. The default mode is for the high bit to control blinking. See question 1.8 for a way to make this bit control the intensity of the background color.

Table 1-1 shows the color constants of the Crt unit. You can use two of these constants to make up an attribute byte, one for the background color and the other for the foreground. The formula for attributes is Background * 16 + foreground. Note that if you use one of the second eight values for the background you make the text blink. If you do want blinking characters, add the Blink constant.

Warnings

Take the same precautions with this routine as with the FillChars routine. The SetAttrs routine can cause snow, and you must be careful about overwriting areas of memory.

Constant Name	Value	Constant Name	Value
Black	0	LightBlue	9
Blue	1	LightGreen	10
Green	2	LightCyan	11
Cyan	3	LightRed	12
Red	4	LightMagenta	13
Magenta	5	Yellow	14
Brown	6	White	15
LightGray	7	Blink	16
DarkGray	8		

Table 1-1 Text color constants

Enhancements

This routine benefits from the same kind of assembly-language routine you saw in FillChars. You must make a few modifications to make sure that the routine doesn't overwrite the text portion. This new loop looks like this:

```
Inline(
    $8B / $46 / < Segment /      {mov    ax, [bp + Segment]}
    $8E / $C0 /                  {mov    es, ax}
    $8B / $7E / < Offset /       {mov    di, [bp + Offset]}
    $8B / $4E / < Count /        {mov    cx, [bp + Count]}
    $8B / $46 / < Data /         {mov    ax, [bp + Data]}
    $FC /                        {cld}
    $AA /                        {s1:    stosb}
    $47 /                        {inc di}
    $E2 / $FC                    {loop s1}
);
```

Instead of using rep stosw to store words, this routine uses a stosb instruction to store bytes. This routine does not use the rep prefix. In other words, all the bytes are not stored in a single instruction. Rather, this routine increments the di register and loops back to the stosb instruction. In this way, the routine skips over the character bytes in video memory.

1.3   How do I...

Save and restore areas of the screen?

Description

Some programs use a number of overlapping windows. When you move the top window, the window underneath becomes visible. To do this, you have to save a portion of the screen before you draw a window and then restore it when the window moves.

See Also

1.1   Filling screen areas with characters

1.4   Drawing boxes on the screen

Solution

First you must set aside a region of memory in which to store the screen data you want to save. To find out how much memory you need, count the number of rows and columns in the region to be saved. Then multiply the number of rows by the number of columns to get the number of characters in the region. Multiply this value by 2 to find out the number of bytes required.

Turbo Pascal programs can use an area of memory called the heap to store data items whose size must be computed at run time. A program calls GetMem to access a region of the heap. GetMem returns a pointer to the memory to tell the program where to store the data. When the program is done with the memory, it calls FreeMem to indicate that the memory can be used for something else. Figure 1-2 shows the memory used in a Turbo Pascal program, including the heap.

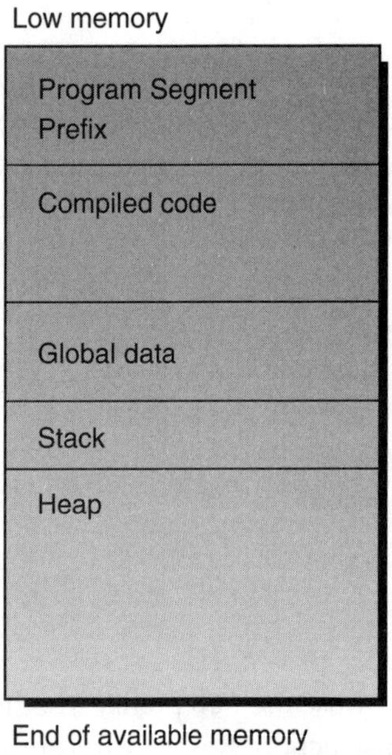

Once you allocate memory to hold the screen information, you can use the coordinates of the region to compute the address of the region in video memory. Then use the address to copy the data to the heap memory. When you need to restore the screen, reverse the copy process.

This program saves a region of the screen, fills it with spaces, waits for a keypress, then restores the original screen:

Low memory

Program Segment Prefix
Compiled code
Global data
Stack
Heap

End of available memory

Figure 1-2   Memory for Turbo Pascal programs

```
{Program to save and restore screen regions}
program SaveRest;
uses Crt;

{Function to save a region of the screen. Returns the number of bytes
used to save the region}
function SaveRect( RowCount, ColumnCount:integer
        ; var p:pointer ):word;
var
   SaveSize : word;
```

```
    ScrOff  : word;
    ScrData : ^word;
    SavePtr : ^word;
begin
    {Compute the offset of the upper-left corner}
    ScrOff := (( WhereY - 1 ) * 80 + WhereX - 1 ) * 2;
    {Find out what segment to use}
    if LastMode = 7 then
                ScrData := Ptr( $B000, ScrOff )
    else
                ScrData := Ptr( $B800, ScrOff );
    {Figure the number of bytes required}
    SaveSize := RowCount * ColumnCount * 2;
    {Allocate the memory to use}
    GetMem( SavePtr, SaveSize );
    p := SavePtr;
    while RowCount <> 0 do
    begin
        {Move one row from the screen to the heap}
        Move( ScrData^, SavePtr^, ColumnCount * 2 );
        {Go to the next line}
        Inc( SavePtr, longint(ColumnCount) );
        Inc( ScrData, 80 );
        Dec( RowCount );
    end;
    SaveRect := SaveSize;
end;

{Restore a previously saved region to the screen}
procedure RestRect( RowCount, ColumnCount:integer; p:pointer );
var
    ScrOff  : word;
    ScrData : ^word;
    SavePtr : ^word;
begin
    {Compute the offset of the upper left corner}
    ScrOff := (( WhereY - 1 ) * 80 + WhereX - 1 ) * 2;
    {Find out what segment to use}
    if LastMode = 7 then
                ScrData := Ptr( $B000, ScrOff )
    else
                ScrData := Ptr( $B800, ScrOff );
    SavePtr := p;
    while RowCount <> 0 do
    begin
        Move( SavePtr^, ScrData^, ColumnCount * 2 );
        Inc( SavePtr, longint( ColumnCount ) );
        Inc( ScrData, 80 );
        Dec( RowCount );
    end;
end;

var
    Size : integer;
```

```
    Region : pointer;
    i : integer;

begin
    GotoXY( 10, 10 );
    Size := SaveRect( 5, 40, Region );
    for i := 10 to 14 do
    begin
        GotoXY( 10, i );
        Write( '                              ' );
    end;
    ReadLn;
    GotoXY( 10, 10 );
    RestRect( 5, 40, Region );
    FreeMem( Region, Size );
    ReadLn;
end.
```

The SaveRect function starts by computing a pointer to the upper-left corner of the screen region. Next, it calculates the size of the region and allocates space on the heap for it. The while loop copies one row at a time from the screen to the heap memory. After a row is copied, the program uses Inc to increment the heap pointer by the size of a row and the screen pointer by 80 words (the size of a screen line). When the entire region is copied, SaveRect returns the size of the heap area. The routine that frees memory needs to know this value, so it is passed, along with the pointer, to that routine.

The RestRect procedure puts the data back on the screen. It computes the same pointers as for SaveRect, but instead of moving data from the screen to the heap, it moves data from the heap to the screen.

The main program uses SaveRect to save a region on the screen. Then it fills that region with spaces and waits for the user to press the Enter key. After that, the program restores the original screen. Finally, the program frees the heap memory before exiting.

Comments

Make sure that the restored region has the same number of rows and columns as the region you saved. There is no similar restriction on the location of the restored data. For this reason you can move text around the screen. This feature is demonstrated in the scroll routine in question 1.5.

Warnings

The cautions about snow and pointers apply here as well. In addition, these routines can get you into trouble by exhausting or fragmenting the heap.

The best way to avoid these problems is to make sure that you free up the memory blocks that you use.

Enhancements

A program that uses `SaveRect` and `RestRect` must keep track of the size of and pointer for each region. In addition, it must free each region when it is no longer needed. One way to keep all of this information straight is to encapsulate it in an object. Once you have done this, you need only tell the object what you want to do. You no longer have to keep track of such details as the size of the region. See Chapter 6 for more information about objects.

This program creates an object that saves and restores screen regions:

```
{Program to save and restore screen regions with objects}
program SaveRest;
uses Crt;

type
    Region = object
        SavedImage      : pointer;
        DataSize        : integer;
        X, Y            : integer;
        Rows, Cols      : integer;
        constructor Init( Xpos, Ypos, RCnt, CCnt : integer );
        procedure TextOut( XPos, YPos : integer; Text : string );
        procedure MoveReg( NewX, NewY : integer );
        destructor Done;
    end;

{Function to save a region of the screen. Returns the number of bytes
used to save the region}
function SaveRect( RowCount, ColumnCount:integer
        ; var p:pointer ):word;
var
    SaveSize    : word;
    ScrOff      : word;
    ScrData     : ^word;
    SavePtr     : ^word;
begin
    ScrOff := (( WhereY - 1 ) * 80 + WhereX - 1 ) * 2;
    {Find out what segment to use}
    if LastMode = 7 then
        ScrData := Ptr( $B000, ScrOff )
    else
        ScrData := Ptr( $B800, ScrOff );
    {Figure the number of bytes required}
    SaveSize := RowCount * ColumnCount * 2;
    {Allocate the memory to use}
    GetMem( SavePtr, SaveSize );
    p := SavePtr;
    while RowCount <> 0 do
    begin
```

```
            Move( ScrData^, SavePtr^, ColumnCount * 2 );
            Inc( SavePtr, longint( ColumnCount ) );
            Inc( ScrData, 80 );
            Dec( RowCount );
        end;
        SaveRect := SaveSize;
end;

{Restore a region to the screen}
procedure RestRect( RowCount, ColumnCount:integer; p:pointer );
var
   ScrOff   : word;
   ScrData  : ^word;
   SavePtr  : ^word;
begin
    ScrOff := (( WhereY - 1 ) * 80 + WhereX - 1 ) * 2;
    {Find out what segment to use}
    if LastMode = 7 then
        ScrData := Ptr( $B000, ScrOff )
    else
        ScrData := Ptr( $B800, ScrOff );
    SavePtr      := p;
    while RowCount <> 0 do
    begin
        Move( SavePtr^, ScrData^, ColumnCount * 2 );
        Inc( SavePtr, longint( ColumnCount ) );
        Inc( ScrData, 80 );
        Dec( RowCount );
    end;
end;

{Fill a region of the screen}
procedure FillChars( Data:word; Count:word );
var
    Offset  : word;         {The offset into screen memory}
    Segment : word;   {The segment for screen memory}
    ScrPtr : ^word;
begin
        {Calculate the offset}
        Offset := (( WhereY - 1 ) * 80 + WhereX - 1 ) * 2;
        {Find out what segment to use}
        if LastMode = 7 then
                Segment := $B000
        else
                Segment := $B800;
        {Loop Count times}
        {Calculate the screen memory pointer}
        ScrPtr := Ptr( Segment, Offset );
        while( Count <> 0 ) do
        begin
        {Store the data}
        ScrPtr^ := Data;
        Inc( ScrPtr );
```

```
          {Decrement count}
          Dec( Count );
        end;
end;

{Initialize a region object}
constructor Region.Init( Xpos, Ypos, RCnt, CCnt : integer );
var
   i : integer;
begin
    {Save coordinates}
    X := Xpos;
    Y := Ypos;
    Rows := RCnt;
    Cols := CCnt;
    {Save the screen image}
    GotoXY( X, Y );
    DataSize := SaveRect( Rows, Cols, SavedImage );
    for i := 1 to Rows do
    begin
        GotoXY( X, Y + i - 1 );
        FillChars( $0720, Cols );
    end;
end;

{Draw text in the region}
procedure Region.TextOut( XPos, YPos : integer; Text : string );
begin
    {Go to location in the region}
    GotoXY( X + XPos, Y + YPos );
    {Write the text}
    Write( Text );
end;

{Move the region to a new location}
procedure Region.MoveReg( NewX, NewY : integer );
var
   p : pointer;
   Size : integer;
begin
    {Save the current appearance of the region}
    GotoXY( X, Y );
    Size := SaveRect( Rows, Cols, p );
    {Put back old screen}
    RestRect( Rows, Cols, SavedImage );
    {Redraw at new location}
    GotoXY( NewX, NewY );
    RestRect( Rows, Cols, p );
    {Free temporary image memory}
    FreeMem( p, DataSize );
    X := NewX;
    Y := NewY;
end;
```

```
{Restore the screen and free the memory used}
destructor Region.Done;
begin
    GotoXY( X, Y );
    RestRect( Rows, Cols, SavedImage );
    FreeMem( SavedImage, DataSize );
end;

var
   Reg : ^Region;

begin
    {Make a new region}
    New( Reg, Init( 10, 10, 5, 40 ));
    {Put some text in the region}
    Reg^.TextOut( 1, 1, 'Test data' );
    ReadLn;
    {Move the region}
    Reg^.MoveReg( 20, 11 );
    ReadLn;
    {Get rid of the region}
    Dispose( Reg, Done );
end.
```

The type section of this program defines the Region object. Defining characteristics include the pointer to the data covered by the region, the location of the region and the size of the region. The type section also contains routines, called methods, that go with the object. Only the names of the routines appear in the object definition, the routines themselves appear later in the program.

You have seen the first three routines before in this chapter. The next four are the methods for the Region object. The Init method saves the information about the region, then uses SaveRect to save the information on the screen before filling the region with spaces. The TextOut method uses the location of the region and the user-specified offsets to compute where to write a string (presumably inside the region). The MoveReg method moves the region to a new location on the screen. The first step in moving a region is using SaveRect to save the current appearance of the region. Then, RestRect is used to restore the original screen data. Next, the saved region is restored at the new location, and the location variables are updated. Finally, the temporary region buffer is freed. The last method, called Done, restores the original screen data and frees the memory occupied by the image.

Draw a text-mode window frame on the screen?

Description

In programs that display more than one window on the screen, there must be a way to tell one window from another. An easy way to do this is to draw a box around the edge of the window. This solution shows how to use the FillChars routine and the built-in text graphics characters to draw boxes.

See Also

1.1   Filling screen areas with characters
1.3   Saving and restoring the screen

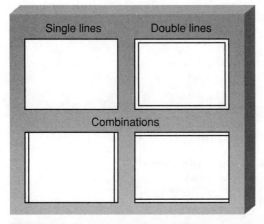

Figure 1-3 Line graphics boxes

Solution

Figure 1-3 shows some of the boxes that you can draw with the built-in text graphics character set available on PC-compatible computers. Programs that use the FillChar routine to put characters on the screen can draw all of these boxes. The corners and edges of these boxes are made up of special characters in the PC character set. Table 1-2 shows the characters you can use and the character value to pass to the FillChar routine.

Your program should define constants for the characters you use to draw boxes. Keep readability in mind: use "UpperLeft" instead of "$C9."

This program draws a box on the screen:

```
{Program to draw a box on the screen}
program box;
uses Crt;

{Define the drawing constants to use}
const
    UpperLeft  = $C9;
    LowerLeft  = $C8;
    UpperRight = $BB;
    LowerRight = $BC;
    Vertical   = $BA;
    Horizontal = $CD;
```

```pascal
procedure FillChars( Data:word; Count:word );
var
   Offset : word;        {The offset into screen memory}
   Segment : word;       {The segment for screen memory}
   ScrPtr : ^word;
begin
      {Calculate the offset}
      Offset := (( WhereY - 1 ) * 80 + WhereX - 1 ) * 2;
      {Find out what segment to use}
      if LastMode = 7 then
            Segment := $B000
      else
            Segment := $B800;
      {Calculate the screen memory pointer}
      ScrPtr := Ptr( Segment, Offset );
      {Loop Count times}
      while( Count <> 0 ) do
      begin
         {Store the data}
         ScrPtr^ := Data;
         Inc( ScrPtr );
         {Decrement count}
         Dec( Count );
      end;
end;

{Routine to draw a box with the upper-left corner at the current
 cursor location}
procedure DrawBox( RowCount, ColumnCount:integer );
var
    Attr : word;       {The attribute in the high byte}
    X    : integer;    {The left edge of the box}
begin
    Attr := TextAttr SHL 8;
    X := WhereX;
    {Draw the top edge of the box}
    FillChars( Attr + UpperLeft, 1 );
    GotoXY( X + 1, WhereY );
    FillChars( Attr + Horizontal, ColumnCount - 2 );
    GotoXY( X + ColumnCount - 1, WhereY );
    FillChars( Attr + UpperRight, 1 );
    {Draw the middle rows}
    while( RowCount > 2 ) do
    begin
        GotoXY( X, WhereY + 1 );
        FillChars( Attr + Vertical, 1 );
        GotoXY( X + 1, WhereY );
        FillChars(Attr + Ord( ' ' ), ColumnCount - 2 );
        GotoXY( X + ColumnCount - 1, WhereY );
        FillChars( Attr + Vertical, 1 );
        Dec( RowCount );
    end;
```

```
    GotoXY( X, WhereY + 1 );
    {Draw the bottom row}
    FillChars( Attr + LowerLeft, 1 );
    GotoXY( X + 1, WhereY );
    FillChars( Attr + Horizontal, ColumnCount - 2 );
    GotoXY( X + ColumnCount - 1, WhereY );
    FillChars( Attr + LowerRight, 1 );
end;

begin
    GotoXY( 10, 10 );
    DrawBox( 5, 40 );
    ReadLn;
end.
```

The DrawBox routine in this program draws a box in three basic steps. The first step is to draw the top line of the box, including the upper-left and upper-right corners. The next step is to draw the interior of the box. To do this, the routine loops through the middle rows of the box, drawing the left edge, spaces, and the right edge. The final step is to draw the bottom of the box, including the lower-left and lower-right corners.

Upper-left corner		Upper-right corner	
Character	Ordinal value	Character	Ordinal value
╔	$C9	╗	$BB
┌	$A9	┐	$AA
╒	$D5	╕	$B8
╓	$D6	╖	$B7
Lower-left corner		**Lower-right corner**	
Character	Ordinal value	Character	Ordinal value
╚	$C8	╝	$BC
└	$C0	┘	$D9
╘	$D4	╛	$BE
╙	$D3	╜	$BD
Vertical line		**Horizontal line**	
Character	Ordinal value	Character	Ordinal value
║	$BA	═	$CD
│	$B3	─	$C4

Table 1-2 Line-drawing characters

Comments

The `DrawBox` routine uses the current text attributes when it draws boxes. You can change the color by calling the Turbo Pascal procedures `TextColor` and `TextBackground`, as in this code fragment:

```
{Draw a blue box}
TextColor( Blue );    {Set the text color to blue}
GotoXY( 10, 10 );     {Go to the upper-left corner}
DrawBox( 5, 20 );     {Draw the box}
```

Warnings

Again, pay attention to the possible problems with snow and pointers. Also, you need to make sure that the box is actually on the screen. For instance, a box that is 20 columns wide and starts at column 70, does not fall inside the screen. If the box is near the bottom of the screen and is too tall to fit, `DrawBox` writes outside of the video memory with unpredictable results.

Enhancements

The regions in question 1.3 stand out better if you draw a box around them. This program shows how:

```
{Program to save and restore screen regions with objects}
program SaveRest;
uses Crt;

type
   Region = object
        SavedImage    : pointer;
        DataSize      : integer;
        X, Y          : integer;
        Rows, Cols    : integer;
        constructor Init( Xpos, Ypos, RCnt, CCnt : integer );
        procedure TextOut( XPos,YPos:integer; Text : string );
        procedure MoveReg( NewX, NewY : integer );
        destructor Done;
   end;

{Define the drawing constants to use}
const
    UpperLeft    = $C9;
    LowerLeft    = $C8;
    UpperRight   = $BB;
    LowerRight   = $BC;
    Vertical     = $BA;
    Horizontal   = $CD;

{Function to save a region of the screen. Returns the number of bytes
used to save the region}
function SaveRect( RowCount, ColumnCount:integer
     ; var p:pointer ):word;
```

```
var
   SaveSize    : word;
   ScrOff      : word;
   ScrData     : ^word;
   SavePtr     : ^word;
begin
   ScrOff      := (( WhereY - 1 ) * 80 + WhereX - 1 ) * 2;
   {Find out what segment to use}
   if LastMode = 7 then
   ScrData := Ptr( $B000, ScrOff )
   else
   ScrData := Ptr( $B800, ScrOff );
   {Figure the number of bytes required}
   SaveSize := RowCount * ColumnCount * 2;
   {Allocate the memory to use}
   GetMem( SavePtr, SaveSize );
   p := SavePtr;
   while RowCount <> 0 do
   begin
       Move( ScrData^, SavePtr^, ColumnCount * 2 );
       Inc( SavePtr, longint( ColumnCount ) );
       Inc( ScrData, 80 );
       Dec( RowCount );
   end;
   SaveRect := SaveSize;
end;


procedure RestRect( RowCount, ColumnCount:integer; p:pointer );
var
   ScrOff      : word;
   ScrData     : ^word;
   SavePtr     : ^word;
begin
   ScrOff      := (( WhereY - 1 ) * 80 + WhereX - 1 ) * 2;
   {Find out what segment to use}
   if LastMode = 7 then
       ScrData := Ptr( $B000, ScrOff )
   else
       ScrData := Ptr( $B800, ScrOff );
   SavePtr     := p;
   while RowCount <> 0 do
   begin
       Move( SavePtr^, ScrData^, ColumnCount * 2 );
       Inc( SavePtr, longint( ColumnCount ) );
       Inc( ScrData, 80 );
       Dec( RowCount );
   end;
end;


{Fill a region of the screen}
procedure FillChars( Data:word; Count:word );
var
Offset : word;          {The offset into screen memory}
```

```
        Segment : word;   {The segment for screen memory}
        ScrPtr : ^word;
begin
        {Calculate the offset}
        Offset := (( WhereY - 1 ) * 80 + WhereX - 1 ) * 2;
        {Find out what segment to use}
        if LastMode = 7 then
                Segment := $B000
        else
                Segment := $B800;
        {Loop Count times}
        {Calculate the screen memory pointer}
            ScrPtr := Ptr( Segment, Offset );
        while( Count <> 0 ) do
        begin
                {Store the data}
            ScrPtr^ := Data;
            Inc( ScrPtr );
            {Decrement count}
            Dec( Count );
        end;
end;


{Routine to draw a box with the upper-left corner at the current
 cursor location}
procedure DrawBox( RowCount, ColumnCount:integer );
var
    Attr  : word;           {The attribute in the high byte}
    X     : integer;        {The left edge of the box}
begin
    Attr := TextAttr * $100;
    X := WhereX;
    {Draw the top edge of the box}
    FillChars( Attr + UpperLeft, 1 );
    GotoXY( X + 1, WhereY );
    FillChars( Attr + Horizontal, ColumnCount - 2 );
    GotoXY( X + ColumnCount - 1, WhereY );
    FillChars( Attr + UpperRight, 1 );
    {Draw the middle rows}
    while( RowCount > 2 ) do
    begin
        GotoXY( X, WhereY + 1 );
        FillChars( Attr + Vertical, 1 );
        GotoXY( X + 1, WhereY );
        FillChars( Attr + Ord ( ' ' ), ColumnCount - 2 );
        GotoXY( X + ColumnCount - 1, WhereY);
        FillChars( Attr + Vertical, 1 );
        Dec( RowCount );
    end;
    GotoXY( X, WhereY + 1 );
    {Draw the bottom row}
    FillChars( Attr + LowerLeft, 1 );
    GotoXY( X + 1, WhereY );
```

```pascal
      FillChars( Attr + Horizontal, ColumnCount - 2 );
      GotoXY( X + ColumnCount - 1, WhereY );
      FillChars( Attr + LowerRight, 1 );
end;


{Initialize a region object}
constructor Region.Init( Xpos, Ypos, RCnt, CCnt : integer );
var
   i : integer;
begin
     {Save coordinates}
     X := Xpos;
     Y := Ypos;
     Rows := RCnt;
     Cols := CCnt;
     {Save the screen image}
     GotoXY( X, Y );
     DataSize := SaveRect( Rows, Cols, SavedImage );
     DrawBox( Rows, Cols );
end;

procedure Region.TextOut( XPos, YPos : integer; Text : string );
begin
     GotoXY( X + XPos, Y + YPos );
     Write( Text );
end;

procedure Region.MoveReg( NewX, NewY : integer );
var
   p : pointer;
   Size : integer;
begin
     {Save the current appearance of the region}
     GotoXY( X, Y );
     Size := SaveRect( Rows, Cols, p );
     {Put back old screen}
     RestRect( Rows, Cols, SavedImage );
     {Redraw at new location}
     GotoXY( NewX, NewY );
     RestRect( Rows, Cols, p );
     FreeMem( p, DataSize );
     X := NewX;
     Y := NewY;
end;

{Restore the screen and free the memory used}
destructor Region.Done;
begin
     GotoXY( X, Y );
     RestRect( Rows, Cols, SavedImage );
     FreeMem( SavedImage, DataSize );
end;
```

```
var
   Reg : ^Region;

begin
   New( Reg, Init( 10, 10, 5, 40 ));
   Reg^.TextOut( 1, 1, 'Test data' );
   ReadLn;
   Reg^.MoveReg( 20, 11 );
   ReadLn;
   Dispose( Reg, Done );
end.
```

This program includes the DrawBox routine shown before. The Init method calls DrawBox instead of clearing the region by filling it with spaces. The rest of the program is the same as the enhancement program in question 1.3.

1.5   How do I...

Scroll text in a text mode screen?

Description

When you use the WriteLn routine to generate lines on the screen and get to the bottom line, the block of text moves up one line to make room for a new line. This is the simplest type of scrolling. In some applications, you can scroll through the text in any direction, not just up. This solution shows you how to scroll up, down, left, and right.

See Also

1.3   Saving and restoring the screen

Solution

To create the effect of scrolling, you need to copy the data on one part of the screen to another part. After you move the screen data, you must fill in the part left empty. Figure 1-4 shows how this type of scrolling works.

In question 1.3, you learned some routines for saving and restoring the screen. You can use these same routines to move data around the screen. For example, to scroll the screen up, save the region from line two to the bottom of the screen, then move up one line and restore the region.

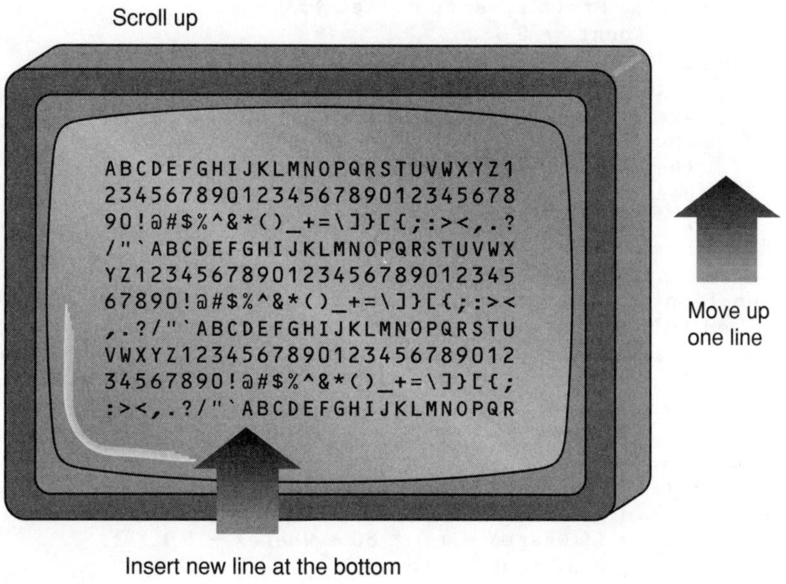

Scroll up

Move up
one line

Insert new line at the bottom

Figure 1-4 Scrolling

The following program uses `SaveRect` and `RestRect` to move data for scrolling. The data is from a 100-by-30 array of characters. Because the whole array does not fit on the screen, you must scroll to see it in its entirety.

```
{Scroll the screen}
program Scroll;
uses Crt;

procedure FillChars( Data:word; Count:word );
var
   Offset      : word;      {The offset into screen memory}
   Segment     : word;      {The segment for screen memory}
   ScrPtr      : ^word;
begin
   {Calculate the offset}
   Offset := (( WhereY - 1 ) * 80 + WhereX - 1 ) * 2;
   {Find out what segment to use}
   if LastMode = 7 then
      Segment := $B000
   else
      Segment := $B800;
   {Loop Count times}
   {Calculate the screen memory pointer}
```

```
    ScrPtr := Ptr( Segment, Offset );
    while( Count <> 0 ) do
    begin
        {Store the data}
        ScrPtr^ := Data;
        Inc( ScrPtr );
        {Decrement count}
        Dec( Count );
    end;
end;

{Function to save a region of the screen. Returns the number of bytes
   used to save the region}
function SaveRect( RowCount, ColumnCount:integer; var p:pointer ):word;
var
   SaveSize  : word;
   ScrOff    : word;
   ScrData   : ^word;
   SavePtr   : ^word;
begin
    ScrOff := (( WhereY - 1 ) * 80 + WhereX - 1 ) * 2;
    {Find out what segment to use}
    if LastMode = 7 then
        ScrData := Ptr( $B000, ScrOff )
    else
        ScrData := Ptr( $B800, ScrOff );
    {Figure the number of bytes required}
    SaveSize := RowCount * ColumnCount * 2;
    {Allocate the memory to use}
    GetMem( SavePtr, SaveSize );
    p := SavePtr;
    while RowCount <> 0 do
    begin
        Move( ScrData^, SavePtr^, ColumnCount * 2 );
        Inc( SavePtr, longint( ColumnCount) );
        Inc( ScrData, 80 );
        Dec( RowCount );
    end;
    SaveRect := SaveSize;
end;

procedure RestRect( RowCount, ColumnCount:integer; p:pointer );
var
   ScrOff  : word;
   ScrData : ^word;
   SavePtr : ^word;
begin
    ScrOff := (( WhereY - 1 ) * 80 + WhereX - 1 ) * 2;
    {Find out what segment to use}
    if LastMode = 7 then
        ScrData := Ptr( $B000, ScrOff )
    else
        ScrData := Ptr( $B800, ScrOff );
```

```
        SavePtr := p;
        while RowCount <> 0 do
        begin
            Move( SavePtr^, ScrData^, ColumnCount * 2 );
            Inc( SavePtr, longint( ColumnCount ) );
            Inc( ScrData, 80 );
            Dec( RowCount );
        end;
end;

var
    TextData : array [1..30] of array [1..100] of word;
    PosX, PosY : integer;
    X, Y, i : integer;
    Ch, Attr : byte;
    p : pointer;
    Size : integer;

{Move the data left}
procedure ScrollLeft;
begin
    {Check for the end of the array}
    if PosX <= 20 then
    begin
        {Move the position indicator}
        Inc( PosX );
        {Save all but the left edge of the screen}
        GotoXY( 2, 1 );
        Size := SaveRect( 25, 79, p );
        {Restore the region moved left}
        GotoXY( 1, 1 );
        RestRect( 25, 79, p );
        FreeMem( p, Size );
        {Get data from the array for the right edge}
        for y := 1 to 25 do
        begin
            GotoXY( 80, y );
            FillChars( TextData[Y][PosX + 79], 1 );
        end;
    end;
end;

{Move the data right}
procedure ScrollRight;
begin
    {Check for the edge of the array}
    if PosX > 0 then
    begin
        Dec( PosX );
        {Save all but the right edge}
        GotoXY( 1, 1 );
        Size := SaveRect( 25, 79, p );
        {Restore the region moved right}
```

```
            GotoXY( 2, 1 );
            RestRect( 25, 79, p );
            FreeMem( p, Size );
            {Get data for the left edge from the array}
            for y := 1 to 25 do
            begin
                GotoXY( 1, y );
                FillChars( TextData[Y][PosX], 1 );
            end;
        end;
end;

{Move the data up}
procedure ScrollUp;
begin
    {Check for the edge of the array}
    if PosY <= 5 then
    begin
        Inc( PosY );
        {Save all but the top line}
        GotoXY( 1, 2 );
        Size := SaveRect( 24, 80, p );
        GotoXY( 1, 1 );
        {Restore data up one line}
        RestRect( 24, 80, p );
        FreeMem( p, Size );
        {Get data for the bottom line from the buffer}
        for x := 1 to 80 do
        begin
            GotoXY( x, 25 );
            FillChars( TextData[PosY + 24][X], 1 );
        end;
    end;
end;

{Move the data down}
procedure ScrollDown;
begin
    if PosY > 0 then
    begin
        Dec( PosY );
        {Save all but the bottom line}
        GotoXY( 1, 1 );
        Size := SaveRect( 24, 80, p );
        {Restore moved down one line}
        GotoXY( 1, 2 );
        RestRect( 24, 80, p );
        FreeMem( p, Size );
        {Get data for the top line from the array}
        for x := 1 to 80 do
        begin
            GotoXY( x, 1 );
```

```
                FillChars( TextData[PosY][X], 1 );
            end;
        end;
end;

begin
    Ch := 32;
    Attr := 1;
    i := 9;
    {Fill the data array}
    for Y:= 1 to 30 do
        for X:= 1 to 100 do
        begin
            {Store the character}
            TextData[Y][X] := Attr SHL 8 + Ch;
            {Increment the character}
            Inc( Ch );
            {Keep it in the ASCII set}
            if Ch >= 127 then
                Ch := 32;
            {Count off 9 chars in the current attribute}
            Dec( i );
            if i <= 0 then
            begin
                i := 9;
                {go to the next attribute}
                Inc( Attr );
                {Stay out of blinking characters}
                if Attr >= 128 then
                    Attr := 1;
            end;
        end;
    {Display the array}
    for Y:= 1 to 25 do
        for X:= 1 to 80 do
        begin
            GotoXY( X, Y );
            FillChars( TextData[Y][X], 1 );
        end;
    {Move the array around}
    PosX := 1;
    PosY := 1;
    for i:= 1 to 20 do
        ScrollLeft;
    for i:= 1 to 5 do
        ScrollUp;
    for i:= 1 to 20 do
        ScrollRight;
    for i:= 1 to 5 do
        ScrollDown;
    ReadLn;
end.
```

The four scroll routines in this program each move the screen one line or column in the specified direction. The variables PosX and PosY contain the offset into the array for the upper-left corner of the screen. The first step is to check that the scroll does not cause movement beyond the edge of the array. If not, the scroll routines save all of the screen except for the edge in the direction of the scroll. Then the routine moves the cursor in the direction of the scroll and restores the data. The last step is to read data from the array to fill in the farthest line or column opposite the direction of the scroll.

Warnings

Again, the usual warnings about snow and pointers apply.

USING MS-DOS AND BIOS TO CONTROL THE SCREEN

One reason for going directly to video memory is that with the standard MS-DOS screen functions you can only output characters. You cannot move the cursor or change attributes, or perform any other advanced screen operations. To solve this problem, you can load a device driver that allows the screen to respond to ANSI standard screen commands. Then you can use the device driver to make sure that your program can run on a wide variety of computers. The problem is that if the device driver is not loaded, you cannot use the commands. Solution 1.6 shows how your program can test for the presence of the device driver so that it can decide how to do screen I/O.

PC-compatible computers achieve some of their compatibility by having a common set of low-level interface routines for the computer hardware. A compatible computer may have a different hardware video interface, but it must have the same software interface as other compatibles. This software interface is called the BIOS. You can access some computer features only through the BIOS. Modifying the cursor and changing the blinking attribute are two examples. Solutions 1.7 and 1.8 show you how.

1.6	How do I...

Test whether ANSI.SYS is in use?

Description

Many CRT capabilities, for instance, clearing the screen, are implemented in the Turbo Pascal CRT unit. The ANSI.SYS device driver transfers many of these capabilities to MS-DOS as screen output functions. The advantage of their residing in ANSI.SYS, and not the CRT, is that ANSI.SYS works on many MS-DOS computers, not just PC compatibles.

ANSI.SYS is available only if you install it when MS-DOS is booted. To install ANSI.SYS, you must include the instruction to load it in the file CONFIG.SYS, which is in the root directory, and reboot. Without this installation, programs that need ANSI.SYS do not work properly. This solution shows how a program can make sure ANSI.SYS is installed.

See Also

1.10   Clearing the keyboard buffer

1.13   Reading the extended keyboard

Solution

One ANSI.SYS function reports the position of the cursor. But if ANSI.SYS is not loaded, it cannot report anything. This is the key to writing a program that can tell whether ANSI.SYS is loaded. All you need to know is how to issue commands to ANSI.SYS and how to read the response.

ANSI.SYS receives commands from the stream of characters to be printed. Each command begins with an escape character (ASCII 27) so that ANSI.SYS can distinguish data to be printed from commands. Thus, to issue an ANSI.SYS command, you need only type the command. For example, to clear the screen use this write statement:

```
Write( #27, '[2J' );
```

If ANSI.SYS is installed, then the screen is cleared. If ANSI.SYS is not installed, then this statement prints the string "2J" at the current cursor location. Not only is the screen not cleared, but also the user sees mysterious characters on the screen. Because this test clears the screen when ANSI.SYS is installed, you need another procedure to clear the screen.

This statement prints the ANSI.SYS "get cursor position" command:

```
Write( #27, '[6n' );
```

The next problem is reading the result of this command. You may have guessed that since you issue ANSI.SYS commands by writing a string, you get a result by reading a string from the keyboard buffer. So, if you have a string variable named Result, you can use the following statement to get the result of the ANSI.SYS "get cursor position" command:

```
ReadLn( Result );
```

There are two problems with this approach. First, the ReadLn procedure echoes the characters read on the screen. Second, if ANSI.SYS is not installed, then the `ReadLn` procedure waits for the user to press the Enter key. Neither of these situations makes for a good user interface.

The answer is to use a routine that checks whether the keyboard buffer has recorded a keypress and, if so, reads it without echoing. Unfortunately, the Turbo Pascal functions that do this get their information from the BIOS. Because the BIOS is at a lower level than ANSI.SYS, it never sees the returned data. What you need is a routine that gets information about the keyboard buffer from MS-DOS:

```
{Returns the next key in the buffer or 0 if no key is ready}
function ReadKey : word;
var
    Reg                 : Registers;    {Used to transfer data with MS-DOS}
    KeyCode    :        Word;           {The value to return}
begin
    KeyCode := 0;                       {Start with the code for no key}
    Reg.AH := $0B;                      {Command to check keyboard}
    MsDos( Reg );                       {Call MS-DOS}
    if Reg.AL = $FF then                {If there is a key}
    begin
        Reg.AH := 7;                    {Command to read the key}
        MsDos( Reg );                   {Call MS-DOS}
            if Reg.AL = 0 then          {If it is a special key}
            begin
                MsDos( Reg );   {Get the next character}
                {Put it in the high byte of KeyCode}
                KeyCode := Word( Reg.AL ) * $100;
            end
            else
                KeyCode := Word( Reg.AL ); {Save the char}
    end;
    ReadKey := KeyCode;
end;
```

First, this function calls MS-DOS to see if a key has been pressed. The `MsDos` procedure and the `Registers` data type are in the DOS unit. If there is data in the keyboard buffer, then `ReadKey` calls MS-DOS again to get the key. If MS-DOS returns 0, the key is a special key, for instance, a function key. The next call to MS-DOS tells which of the special keys it is. In this case, the key is stored in the high byte of the return value. Ordinary keys are stored in the low byte of the return value. If there is no key, then the value returned is 0.

The keypresses that `ReadKey` looks for can be either keyboard-generated or driver-generated. The routine to test for the presence of ANSI.SYS uses the `ReadKey` function twice. The routine first calls the function to clear out the keyboard buffer, ensuring that the user hasn't pressed any keys that would interfere with the test. Then it calls the function a second time to see what the result of the "get cursor position" command is. The routine looks like this:

```
{Return TRUE if ANSI.SYS is loaded}
function IsAnsi : boolean;
var
   key  : word;
begin
    {Clear out the keyboard buffer}
    while ReadKey <> 0 do;
    {Issue the get cursor position command}
    write( #27, '[6n' );
    {Get the response string or no key}
    repeat
            key := ReadKey;
    until ( key = 0 ) OR ( key = 13 );
    {If it was no key then ANSI was not installed}
    if key = 0 then
    begin
        {Backspace over the ANSI command}
        write( #8, #8, #8, #8, '    ', #8, #8, #8, #8 );
        IsAnsi := FALSE;
    end
    else
        IsAnsi := TRUE;
end;
```

Comments

To test this routine, check your CONFIG.SYS file to determine if ANSI.SYS is installed. Look in the file for a line like this one:

```
device = ANSI.SYS
```

The line may be different from this one; common variations are NANSI.SYS and ZANSI.SYS. After checking the CONFIG.SYS file, you should write a program that uses the IsAnsi function. Here is a simple routine:

```
if IsAnsi = TRUE then
        write( #7 );  {Beep}
```

Enhancements

ANSI.SYS is often used to display fancy prompts. For example, try this prompt command after you load ANSI.SYS:

```
prompt $e[24;0H$_$e[44;37m$e[K$d  $p$_$e[46;30m$e[KCommand:
```

The $e signifies the escape character. This prompt command moves the cursor to the bottom of the screen, changes the screen colors, displays the data and the current directory, and prints "Command:". You can put a command like this in your AUTOEXEC.BAT file to set the prompt whenever you boot your computer. The problem is that if ANSI.SYS is not installed, the prompt will be mostly incomprehensible garbage. Again, you need a way to let the AUTOEXEC.BAT program know if ANSI.SYS is installed. A solution is to use the `IsAnsi` function in a program that sets the `errorlevel` flag, which can be tested in the AUTOEXEC.BAT program.

Here is the Pascal program to set the error level:

```
begin
     if IsAnsi = TRUE then{Check the IsAnsi function}
          Halt( 1 )               {If ANSI installed set errorlevel
                                   to 1}
     else
          Halt( 0 );              {Otherwise set errorlevel to 0}
end.
```

If the name of the program is ANSICHK.EXE then use this code in the AUTOEXEC.BAT file:

```
ANSICHK
IF ERRORLEVEL 1 GOTO AnsiYes
prompt $p$g
GOTO Done
:AnsiYes
prompt $e[24;0H$_$e[44;37m$e[K$d  $p$_$e[46;30m$e[KCommand:
:Done
```

This batch file code runs the `ANSICHK` program to set the `errorlevel` variable. Next, the batch file code checks for an error level of 1, indicating that the complex prompt is OK. Otherwise, it makes a much simpler prompt that does not require ANSI.SYS.

1.7   How do I...

Hide the cursor or change its shape?

Description

Some interfaces let the user choose an item from a list of items on the screen. Figure 1-5 shows an example of this interface. To pick an item, the user presses the arrow keys to move a highlighted bar from one item to the next, then presses Enter when the desired item is highlighted. In this case, the normal hardware generated cursor can be distracting and redundant. These interfaces should display the hardware cursor only when the user is supposed to type data. Some programs even display different cursors according to the type of data the user should input.

See Also

1.19   Handling numeric data entry

Solution

The video BIOS has a routine that tells you the location of the cursor and a 16-bit word that indicates the cursor shape. It also has a routine that lets you set the shape of the cursor. You can use the `Intr` routine from the Turbo Pascal `Dos` unit to access these BIOS routines.

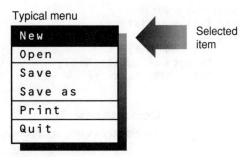

Typical menu

Selected item

Figure 1-5 Choosing items

Each character on the screen is made up of a matrix of pixels organized into rows and columns. When they refer to the cursor, the rows are called scan lines. The scan lines are numbered from the top to the bottom of the character. The low five bits of the high byte of the cursor-shape word give the scan line for the top of the cursor, and the low five bits of the low byte give the scan line for the bottom of the cursor. To make the cursor disappear, use a cursor shape whose top scan line lies below its bottom scan line.

This routine calls BIOS to get the current settings for the cursor, then it sets the cursor shape to $100 to make it disappear:

```
procedure CursorOff;
var Regs : Registers;
begin
    Regs.AH := 3;             {Read cursor position and shape command}
    Regs.BH := 0;             {Set video page zero}
    Intr( $10, Regs );        {Call BIOS}
    CursorShape := Regs.CX;   {Save the size}
    Regs.AH := 1;             {Set cursor shape command}
    Regs.CX := $100;          {Top scan line below bottom line}
    Intr( $10, Regs );        {Call BIOS}
end;
```

The type of the variable `Regs` is `Registers`, which is a structure defined in the `Dos` unit. The registers structure contains fields for each of the 80x86 registers. For more information about this structure and other aspects of MS-DOS and BIOS, see Chapter 5.

Note that this routine saves the cursor shape in the variable `CursorShape`, which should be defined as a global variable before this function is defined. This variable is important to the next routine, whose job is to restore the cursor to its previous shape:

```
procedure CursorOn;
var Regs : Registers;
begin
    Regs.AH := 1;                   {Set cursor shape command}
    Regs.CX := CursorShape;         {Use the old shape}
    Intr( $10, Regs );              {Call BIOS}
end;
```

Comments

To hide the cursor at the beginning of a program, call CursorOff. Data-input routines should start with a call to CursorOn and end with a call to CursorOff. Finally, call CursorOn before exiting the program. You can modify CursorOn, to make different cursors for different input field types by using different values for CursorShape.

Warnings

Be sure to turn the cursor back on before returning to DOS or spawning any other routines. Using the DOS command line without a cursor is more difficult than it sounds. You may want to write a program that forces the cursor on. Then, if a program changes the cursor, run the program to get the cursor back.

Enhancements

One way you can accidentally turn the cursor off for good is to call CursorOff twice in a row. After the second call, the blank cursor is stored in CursorShape. Now, calling CursorOn doesn't do you any good, because CursorShape contains the wrong (blank) value.

To get around this problem you can define a variable that keeps track of how many times the cursor has been turned off and allows you to reinstate the old cursor shape only if the cursor is visible. While you are at it, you can put the cursor code into an object that encapsulates all of the required routines and variables.

```
type
        Cursor = object;
                Shape   : word;
                OffCount : integer;
                procedure Init;             {initialize variables}
                procedure CursorOff;        {Turn the cursor off}
                procedure CursorOn;         {Turn the cursor back on}
                procedure CursorNotOff;     {Reduce the cursor off count}
        end;

procedure Cursor.Init;
begin
        Shape := 0;
```

```
        OffCount := 0;
end;

procedure Cursor.CursorOff;
begin
    if OffCount = 0 then
    begin
        Regs.AH := 3;          {Read cursor position and shape command}
        Regs.BH := 0;          {Set video page zero}
        Intr( $10, Regs );     {Call BIOS}
        Shape := Regs.CX;      {Save the size}
        Regs.AH := 1;          {Set cursor shape command}
        Regs.CX := $100;       {Top scan line below bottom line}
        Intr( $10, Regs );     {Call BIOS}
    end;
    Inc( OffCount );
end;

{Turn the cursor on no matter what}
procedure Cursor.CursorOn;
begin
    Regs.AH := 1;          {Set cursor shape command}
    Regs.CX := Shape;      {The saved shape}
    Intr( $10, Regs );     {Call BIOS}
    OffCount := 0;         {Indicate that the cursor is on}
end;

{Undo the work of cursor off}
procedure Cursor.CursorNotOff;
begin
    Dec( OffCount );
    {If the count went to 0 turn the cursor on}
    if( OffCount = 0 )
    begin
        Regs.AH := 1;          {Set cursor shape command}
        Regs.CX := Shape;      {The saved shape}
        Intr( $10, Regs );     {Call BIOS}
    end;
end;
```

The Cursor object has data fields for the size of the cursor and a counter
for the number of times the cursor was hidden. The Init method sets both
of these variables to 0.

The CursorOff and CursorNotOff methods turn the cursor off and on.
Before changing the cursor on the screen, these methods check the value of
their OffCount fields. If the value of OffCount in the CursorOff method is
0, the cursor size is saved in Shape and the screen cursor is hidden. At the
end of the CursorOff method, the OffCount field is incremented.
CursorNotOff decrements OffCount and checks to see if it is 0. When
OffCount is 0, CursorNotOff restores the cursor to the size saved in Shape.

You can use the `CursorOn` method to make sure the cursor is on, no matter what. It restores the cursor from `Shape` and sets `OffCount` to 0.

1.8   How do I...

Set up bright colors for background (that is, disable blinking)?

Description

When you use the Turbo Pascal procedure `TextBackground` to set the background color, you can choose from only half of the colors (8) that are available for the foreground color (16). If you choose the colors between `DarkGray` and `White`, you get blinking characters instead of the color you wanted. To get the extra colors, you need some way to disable the blinking.

See Also

1.6   Calling MS-DOS to test for ANSI.

Solution

The answer is in the BIOS Set Palette/Color Registers routine. This routine has a number of subfunctions, one of which sets the intensity/blink bit. This sounds like just the thing; all you need is a way to call BIOS routines. In question 1.7, you used the `MsDos` procedure from the DOS unit to call MS-DOS. The comparable function for BIOS routines is `Intr` (also in the DOS unit). The job of the `MsDos` routine is to load the registers with the passed values and do a software interrupt `$21`. `Intr` is slightly more complex in that it can do any software interrupt. This is needed because BIOS routines use a number of different interrupts.

The `Intr` function makes it simple to write a routine that disables blinking and gives you access to more colors.

```
procedure BlinkOff;
var Regs : Registers;        {Structure to pass registers back and forth}
begin
     Regs.AX := 1003h;       {Set the function and subfunction number}
     Regs.BL := 0;           {Turn off blinking}
     Intr( $10, Regs );      {Call BIOS interrupt $10}
end;
```

The function to reinstate blinking is similar, except that the variable `Regs.BL` should be set to 1 instead of 0.

Comments

Note that these functions affect blinking on all of the screen. There is no way to have hardware blinking (done by the video interface) and bright backgrounds on the same screen.

Enhancements

You can restore to a full-color screen by including a blinking procedure in your program. To do this, use the `SetAttrs` routine to change the visible attribute to invisible, like this:

```
procedure SoftBlink( Attr : byte ; Count : word );
var
      Invis : byte;
begin
      {Make an attribute byte with the same foreground
       and background}
      Invis := Attr DIV 16 + ( Attr DIV 16 ) * 16;
      while TRUE do
      begin
            {Make the field invisible}
            SetAttrs( Invis, Count );
            {Wait .5 seconds}
            Delay( 500 );
            {Make the field visible again}
            SetAttrs( Attr, Count );
            {and wait again}
            Delay( 500 );
      end;
end;
```

The loop in this procedure runs forever. First, it changes an attribute field so that the foreground is the same color as the background. This makes the field invisible. After waiting half a second, the routine restores visibility. A half a second later, the loop repeats again. See question 1.9 for a way to make this loop run only until the user presses a key.

KEYBOARD SOLUTIONS

Updating the screen is only half the job of designing a user interface for PC-compatibles. The other half is handling the keyboard. For simple applications you can use the Turbo Pascal routines `ReadLn` and `ReadKey`. These routines have a number of drawbacks that are addressed in the Solutions in this section.

Solution 1.9 shows how you can keep the computer busy while it is waiting for the user to press a key. Instead of waiting idly, the computer can perform background tasks while the user decides what key to press next.

On the other hand, while the computer is busy with some other task, such as reading the disk, the user's keypresses are stored in a buffer so that the computer can read them when it is ready. If the task that is taking up the computer's time generates an error, you may want to retract those keypresses. For example, suppose you are expecting the question, "OK to exit?" You press Y, expecting to leave the program. Instead, because of an error, the computer asks, "Data error. Delete file?" You may not want to answer yes here, but the Y keypress is already in the buffer. To handle this problem you can design your application to flush the keyboard buffer before it accepts a response to the error question. Solution 1.10 shows how to clear the keyboard buffer.

Solution 1.11 shows you how to do the opposite. Instead of clearing the keyboard buffer, you'll learn how to put characters into the buffer. Programs that run thereafter interpret the characters in the buffer as keypresses.

You can use the keys Shift, Ctrl, and Alt in combination with other keys to make *key chords*. Applications with many commands often use key chords to match to keystroke commands. Question 1.12 shows you how to use key chords by getting the status of the Shift key from BIOS. You also need to use special code to read the extra keys such as F11 and F12, on the enhanced keyboards. Solution 1.13 shows you how to do this.

The Break key generates a special interrupt that MS-DOS uses to stop the current program and return to the command processor. Of course, leaving a program unexpectedly can corrupt data files that have not been properly closed. Solution 1.14 shows you how to trap the Break key so that you can protect critical sections of your program.

The last solution in this section shows you how to notify your program immediately when a key is pressed or released. Programs such as Borland's Sidekick use this technique to watch for a *hot-key* that tells Sidekick to take control of the computer.

1.9 How do I...

Keep the computer busy while it waits for the user to press a key?

Description

The program in the enhancement section of question 1.8 is not very useful because it runs forever, simply causing characters to blink. This endless loop is impractical because it prevents the program from doing anything else. The loop would be more useful if the user's keypresses could interrupt it.

See Also

Solution

The Turbo Pascal function `KeyPressed` tells you if there is a keypress in the keyboard buffer. You can use this function in a loop that continues to run until the user presses a key. When the `KeyPressed` function detects a keypress, you can use `ReadKey` to find out what key was pressed.

This program causes an area of the screen to blink until the user presses the Enter key:

```
{Program to blink until the Enter key is pressed}
program Blink;
uses Crt;

procedure SetAttr( Data:byte; Count:word );
var
   Offset : word;      {The offset into screen memory}
   Segment : word;     {The segment for screen memory}
   ScrPtr : ^byte;
begin
     {Calculate the offset}
     Offset := (( WhereY - 1 ) * 80 + WhereX - 1 ) * 2 + 1;
     {Find out what segment to use}
     if LastMode = 7 then
            Segment := $B000
     else
            Segment := $B800;
     {Calculate the screen memory pointer}
     ScrPtr := Ptr( Segment, Offset );
     while( Count <> 0 ) do
     begin
            {Store the data}
        ScrPtr^ := Data;
        Inc( ScrPtr, 2 );
        {Decrement count}
        Dec( Count );
     end;
end;

function SoftBlink( Attr : byte ; Count : word ) : char;
var
     Invis : byte;
begin
     {Make an attribute byte with the same foreground
       and background}
     Invis := Attr DIV 16 + ( Attr DIV 16 ) * 16;
     while NOT KeyPressed do
     begin
```

```
                    {Make the field invisible}
                    SetAttr( Invis, Count );
                    {Wait .5 seconds}
                    Delay( 500 );
                    {Make the field visible again}
                    SetAttr( Attr, Count );
                    {and wait again}
                    Delay( 500 );
            end;
            SoftBlink := ReadKey;         {Get the key that was pressed}
    end;

    begin
        TextAttr := $07;
        ClrScr;
        GotoXY( 30, 1 );
        Write( 'The blinking screen' );
        GotoXY( 1, 1 );
        while SoftBlink( $71, 80 ) <> Chr( 13 ) do;
    end.
```

The SoftBlink routine periodically toggles the visible/invisible attribute of the screen area that blinks. (Recall that a character is invisible when the foreground and background colors are the same.) The condition in the while loop uses KeyPressed to test whether a key has been pressed. When KeyPress returns TRUE, the program exits the loop and reads the keypress in the buffer.

Comments

The loop in SoftBlink takes at least a second to run. So, you may have to wait a second after you press a key before the program exits the loop. If you are using this loop as your main keyboard input routine, the occasional delays may become annoying. The solution is to code the loop so that it tests for keys more often, as follows:

```
while NOT KeyPressed do
begin
                    {Make the field invisible}
                    SetAttr( Invis, Count );
                    if KeyPressed then
                            SetAttr( Attr, Count )
                    else
                    begin
                            {Wait .5 seconds}
                            Delay( 500 );
                            {Make the field visible again}
                            SetAttr( Attr, Count );
                            {and wait again}
                            if Not KeyPressed then
                                    Delay( 500 );
```

```
        end;
end;
```

This loop tests the keyboard before each `Delay` statement. This shortens the time that the user must wait to less than half a second. Note that if the user presses a key after the text becomes invisible, the program resets the attribute to make the text visible again.

Warnings

You must call the `ReadKey` function after the `KeyPressed` function detects a keypress, because the `KeyPressed` routine does not remove the key from the keyboard buffer. If your program does not read the key before entering the loop, the `KeyPressed` function returns TRUE right away, and the loop is never executed.

Enhancements

As you increase the number of tasks the computer must do while waiting for a keypress, you must add more and more calls to `KeyPressed`. This complicates the loop and slows it down. In addition, this routine does not detect presses of the Shift, Ctrl, or Alt keys because these keys do not generate a character by themselves. Instead, they modify the characters generated by other keys.

A user's keypress generates an interrupt. Your program can intercept this interrupt so that it can react as soon as the key is pressed. See question 1.14 for a way to handle keyboard interrupts.

1.10   How do I...

Clear the keyboard buffer?

Description

The program in question 1.6 relies on the data in the keyboard buffer to tell if ANSI.SYS is loaded. If there is data in this buffer (for example, if the user tried to type text) the `IsAnsi` function could return an incorrect result. To prevent this, you can use the `IsAlpha` function to clear the keyboard buffer before sending the ANSI "get cursor" command.

See Also

Solution

The IsAnsi function clears the keyboard buffer by reading keypresses until none are left. This loop, which uses the ReadKey and KeyPressed functions, does the job:

```
procedure FlushKeys;
var
        ch      : char;
begin
        while KeyPressed do      {While there is a key in the buffer}
            ch := ReadKey;       {Read the key}
end;
```

Because IsAnsi cannot use the CRT unit, the following loop looks more complex. In fact, the loop serves the same purposes, but it calls MS-DOS to do the jobs of the KeyPressed and ReadKey function:

```
procedure FlushKeys;
var
        Reg         : Registers;        {Used to transfer data with MS-DOS}
        ExitFlag    : boolean;          {TRUE when the buffer is clear}
begin
        ExitFlag := FALSE;
        repeat
        begin
            {This part is like KeyPressed}
            Reg.AH := $0B;          {Command to check keyboard}
            MsDos( Reg );           {Call MS-DOS}
            if Reg.AL = $FF then    {If there is a key}
            begin
                {This is like ReadKey}
                Reg.AH := 7;        {Command to read the key}
                MsDos( Reg );       {Call MS-DOS}
                if Reg.AL = 0 then  {If it is a special key}
                    MsDos( Reg );   {Get the next character}
            end;
            else
                ExitFlag := TRUE;
        end;
        until ExitFlag;
end;
```

Comments

You can choose one or the other of these routines according to the requirements of the rest of the program. The first loop uses the CRT unit, whereas the second requires the DOS unit.

Warnings

Whenever you use the MsDos procedure, be careful to set up the registers correctly. If, for example, you make a mistake loading the AH register, then MsDos calls a different MS-DOS function than you intended.

Enhancements

These functions do not flush the extended keys, such as F11, of the PC-AT. See question 1.12 for a way to test for and read these keys. Another way to make sure that all of the keys have been flushed is to modify the keyboard buffer pointer values in low memory. The main drawback to this technique is that it works only on highly IBM-compatible systems. It also does not work if a utility has taken over the keyboard interrupt and is storing keys in a different buffer.

This routine sets the keyboard buffer pointers to the beginning of the buffer:

```
procedure FlushKeys;
begin
     {Set the keyboard buffer tail to $1E}
     word( Ptr( $40, $1A )^ ) := $1E;
     {Set the keyboard buffer head to $1E}
     word( Ptr( $40, $1C )^ ) := $1E;
end;
```

| 1.11 | How do I... |

Stuff keys into the keyboard buffer?

Description

At some point in your program you may wish to call another program to perform some function. For example, you may need to allow the user to edit a large text buffer. Clearly it is best to let users call their favorite editor to do this task. The problem for users is that they need to exit your program, start the text editor, load the proper file, exit the text editor, and return to your program. As you will see in Chapter 5, you can easily start another program, but how do you tell this program what file to load? The answer is to stuff the keyboard buffer with the keys that instruct the program to load the appropriate file.

See Also

1.12   Using the keyboard BIOS
1.15   Detecting a keypress

Solution

The later versions of the XT BIOS and all newer BIOSs have a routine that makes stuffing the keyboard buffer easy. All you need to do is put the key code (as returned by GetKey) into the CX register and call the BIOS keyboard function number 5, as follows:

```
{Returns TRUE if the keyboard buffer is full}
function StuffIt( Key : word ) : boolean;
var
        Regs : Register;
begin
        Regs.AH := 5;          {The stuff a key routine}
        Regs.CX := Key;        {The key to stuff}
        Intr( $16, Regs );     {Call BIOS}
        StuffIt := boolean( Regs.AL );
end;
```

For systems with older BIOSs, you must stuff the keyboard buffer yourself. Be careful: You cannot allow the user to press a key while this routine is running because any keypress starts another routine that also stuffs the keyboard buffer. Having two routines updating the same buffer is a sure recipe for disaster. The easiest way to prevent this problem is to turn off interrupts while your routine is running. Without interrupts, the keyboard cannot get control of the computer.

This routine uses the machine-language instruction $FA (CLI) to turn off interrupts, then stuffs the keyboard buffer, and finally turns interrupts back on with a $FB (STI) instruction. It uses the information about the keyboard buffer in the BIOS data area to manipulate the buffer. The word at offset $1A is the offset of the next key to read. This routine uses the offset only to determine if the buffer is full. The word at offset $1C is the offset of the next available space in the buffer. This tells you where to put the character being stuffed. The words from offset $1E to $2C make up the keyboard buffer itself. The stuffed keys must be confined to this area.

```
{Returns TRUE if the keyboard buffer is full}
function StuffIt( Key : word ) : boolean;
var
        Regs : Register;
        Result : boolean;
        Head : word;           {The offset to stuff}
        Tail : word;           {The last possible location to stuff}
begin
        InLine( $FA );         {Turn off interrupts}
        {Find the buffer location just before the tail}
        Tail := word( Ptr( $40, $1C )^ ) - 2;
        if Tail = $1C then     {See if tail is below the beginning of
                                the buffer}
            Tail := $2C;       {Wrap to the top of the buffer}
        Head := word( Ptr( $40, $1A )^ );
        if Head = Tail then
                Result = TRUE
        else
        begin
                {Store the key in the buffer}
                word( Ptr( $40, Head )^ ) := Key;
```

```
            {Move head to the next location}
            Head := Head + 2;
            if Head = $2D then    {If past the end of the buffer}
                  Head := $1E;    {Wrap to the beginning}
            {Save the new head}
            word( Ptr( $40, $1A )^ ) := Head;
            Result := FALSE;
        end;
        InLine( $FB );                {Turn on interrupts}
        StuffIt := Result;
end;
```

The StuffIt routine starts by turning off interrupts to make sure that a key interrupt does not disrupt the keyboard queue. Next, StuffIt reads the Head and Tail pointers from the BIOS data area and compares them to see if there is any room in the keyboard buffer. If there is room, StuffIt puts the key into the keyboard buffer at the location indicated by the Head index. After putting the key in the buffer, StuffIt advances the Head index so that BIOS knows the key is in the buffer. Finally, StuffIt turns interrupts back on and returns a flag indicating if it successfully stuffed the key or not.

Comments

You can use this routine to return the last key read to the keyboard buffer. This is useful when you have a number of routines that monitor keypresses. Each routine determines from the last keypress whether to act on the keypress or pass it to the next routine. The basic structure of such a routine looks like this:

```
Key := GetKey;
if Key = MyKey then    {See if the key is interesting}
begin
        .                     {Operate on the key}
        .
        .
end
else
    StuffIt( Key );   {Put the key back}
```

Warnings

Be careful to watch the return value of this function. If it returns TRUE, then the keyboard buffer is full and the key is not stored. Another thing to watch out for is the use of special keypress-handling programs that bypass the keyboard buffer. If this is the case, storing keys in the keyboard buffer has no effect. Finally, be careful with any routine that turns off interrupts. The reason for turning interrupts off in this routine is to prevent the keyboard from generating an interrupt that would interfere with this routine. If you do not make sure that interrupts get turned back on, you cannot use the keyboard for anything. You will not even be able to reboot by pressing Ctrl-Alt-Del.

Enhancements

The keyboard buffer holds only 16 keys. This is not enough room to use this buffer to control other programs. You need a way to detect that the other program has read some of the keys, thus creating more room in the buffer. One way to do this is to create a interrupt handler that tries to insert a key into the buffer every time a clock tick occurs. In this example the keys to send are in a global array called SendKeys, and the index for the next key to send is called NextKey :

```
procedure KeyTick;
interrupt;                  {Make this an interrupt style procedure}
begin
        {See if there is a valid key to send}
        if SendKeys[NextKey] <> 0 then
        begin
                {Try to send the key}
                if NOT StuffIt( SendKeys[NextKey] ) then
                        {If the key went then go to the next key}
                        Inc( NextKey );
        end;
end;
```

To use this procedure you must make the clock interrupt vector point to the procedure. Whenever you set an interrupt vector you must keep the original vector so that you can restore it before the program exits. You can use the GetIntVec and SetIntVec procedures to do this as follows:

```
var
        OldTick : pointer;          {Place to store the old vector}

begin
        GetIntVec( $1C, OldTick );  {Get the clock interrupt vector}
        SetIntVec( $1C, @KeyTick ); {Point the vector at the new function}
        .                           {The rest of the program}
        .
        .
        SetIntVec( $1C, OldTick );  {Put back the original vector}
end;
```

See question 1.15 for more information on trapping interrupts.

1.12   How do I...

Read the Shift key status?

Description

Some programs use key combinations, such as [Left Shift]-F1, to signal commands. If you use the `ReadKey` function, you cannot distinguish this combination from [Right Shift]-F1. To tell them apart you need to read the state of the Shift keys.

See Also

1.13   Reading the extended keyboard

Solution

The BIOS interrupt `$16` includes a number of routines for reading the keyboard. Function number 2 returns the state of all of the Shift keys in the `AL` register. Table 1-3 shows the meanings of the bits in this register.

Bit	Mask value	Meaning
0	1	Right Shift key
1	2	Left Shift key
2	4	Ctrl key
3	8	Alt key
4	16	Scroll Lock enabled
5	32	Num Lock enabled
6	64	Caps Lock enabled
7	128	Insert enabled

Table 1-3 The Shift key status byte

This function uses the `Intr` procedure to get this byte:

```
function ShiftState : byte;
var
      Regs : Registers;
begin
      Regs.AH = 2;          {BIOS read shift state function number}
      Intr( $16, Regs );    {Call BIOS}
      ShiftState := Regs.AL;
end;
```

Comments

You can compare the mask values in table 1-3 with the value returned by ShiftState to see if the Shift key state matches a particular state. For example, to determine whether only the Right Shift key is pressed, use this statement:

```
if ShiftState = 1 then
    ...                    {This right shift key is down}
```

To detect combinations of keys, add the mask values of the keys to be tested. The following example checks whether the Alt key and the Ctrl key are pressed:

```
if ShiftState = 8 + 4 then
    ...                    {The Alt and Ctrl keys are pressed}
```

You can also use the mask values to test the value of a Shift key and ignore the rest of the Shift keys. To do so, use the AND operator in the condition to be tested.

```
if ( ShiftState AND 8 ) <> 0 then
    ...                    {The ALT key is down}
```

You can also use the AND operator to mask the Lock keys. This is useful because you want your program to work the same way regardless of the state of Num Lock and Scroll Lock. This statement masks the Lock keys and checks whether the Ctrl key has been pressed:

```
if ( ShiftState AND $F ) = 4 then
    ...                    {The Control key is down}
```

Warnings

This function tells you the state of the Shift keys only at the time that the function is called. If there is a backlog of keypresses in the keyboard buffer, you cannot determine what Shift state was in effect when the key was pressed.

1.13   How do I...

Use the extended keyboard?

Description

The PC-AT style keyboard includes a number of keys not found on older computers. Rather than just adding a few new key codes to the keyboard software, the designers of the AT chose to add two new BIOS keyboard functions for reading these extended keys. A program that uses the enhanced

Bit	Mask	Meaning
0	1	Carry flag
1	2	Unused
2	4	Parity flag
4	8	Unused
5	16	Auxiliary flag
6	32	Unused
7	64	Zero flag
8	128	Sign flag
9	256	Trap flag
10	512	Interrupt flag
11	1024	Direction flag
12	2048	Overflow flag
13	4096	Unused
14	8192	Unused
15	16384	Unused

Table 1-4 The Flags word

keyboard must be able to detect the presence of the extended keyboard and make the extra BIOS calls when required.

See Also

1.12   Using the keyboard BIOS

Solution

First, your program must check if the enhanced keyboard is being used. The BIOS data area includes a bit that tells which keyboard is attached. This statement checks that bit:

```
if ( byte( Ptr( $40,$96 )^ ) AND 16 ) <> 0 then
        ...             {The enhanced keyboard is attached}
```

Once you know that the enhanced keyboard is being used, you need to call the new BIOS keyboard functions. Function $11 detects the presence of a keypress in the buffer, and function $10 gets the keypress. Function $11 sets the zero flag if there is a keypress in the buffer. To find out the state of the zero flag, look at the Flags word in the Registers structure after the call to Intr. Table 1-4 shows the meanings of the bits in the Flags word.

The following function uses this information to call BIOS and return a Boolean value; TRUE indicates the presence of a keypress in the buffer:

```
function IsKey : boolean;
var
      Regs : Registers;
begin
      Regs.AH := $11;        {Test enhanced keyboard command}
      Intr( $16, Regs );     {Call BIOS}
      if ( Regs.Flags AND 64 ) <> 0 then {test the zero flag}
             IsKey := TRUE    {If zero flag is set there is a key}
      else
             IsKey := FALSE; {Otherwise there is no key}
end;
```

This function calls BIOS keyboard function $10 to read the key from the keyboard buffer:

```
function GetKey : word;
var
      Regs : Registers;
begin
      Regs.AH := $10;        {Read enhanced keyboard function}
      Intr( $16, Regs );     {Call BIOS}
      GetKey := Regs.AX;     {Return the key code}
end;
```

Comments

The value returned by the GetKey function has two parts. The high byte is the scan code for the key. The PC uses this code to distinguish each of the keys on the keyboard. The low byte of the word is the ASCII code for the key or a special code. The special codes are 0 or $E0; they indicate that the key is a function key, cursor-movement key, or the Alt key. These are the same keys that cause the ReadKey function to return 0. In most cases, the character following the 0 is the same as the high byte of the value from GetKey.

Warnings

These routines are safe as written, but if you decide to modify them, be careful when using the Intr procedure. The BIOS routines control all of the low-level functions in the computer; calling the wrong one can have disastrous results. Use a good reference on BIOS routines, such as *The Waite Group's MS-DOS Developer's Guide, 2nd edition*, when experimenting with these routines.

Enhancements

These routines let you determine the keyboard type and read the enhanced keyboard. What you really need are functions that will call the appropriate routines for the keyboard installed. This way you do not have to worry about these details every time you want to get a key. These routines solve this problem:

```
{Check if a key is in the buffer}
function IsKey : boolean;
var
      Regs : Registers;
begin
      if ( byte( Ptr( $40,$96 )^ ) AND 16 ) <> 0 then
            Regs.AH := $11        {Test enhanced keyboard command}
      else
            Regs.AH := $1;        {Test the regular keyboard}
      Intr( $16, Regs );    {Call BIOS}
      if ( Regs.Flags AND 64 ) <> 0 then {test the zero flag}
            IsKey := TRUE  {If zero flag is set there is a key}
      else
            IsKey := FALSE; {Otherwise there is no key}
end;

{Read a key from the keyboard buffer}
function GetKey : word;
var
      Regs : Registers;
begin
      if ( byte( Ptr( $40,$96 )^ ) AND 16 ) <> 0 then
            Regs.AH := $10        {Read enhanced keyboard command}
      else
            Regs.AH := $0;        {Read the regular keyboard}
      Intr( $16, Regs );          {Call BIOS}
      GetKey := Regs.AX;          {Return the key code}
end;
```

Both of these routines check the fifth bit in the byte at $40:$96. This is a byte in the BIOS data area that gives information about what devices are attached to the computer. If the bit is set, the enhanced keyboard is being used, and you must call BIOS keyboard functions $10 and $11 to read the keyboard or test for keys. If the bit is not set, an older keyboard is being used, and you must call the BIOS keyboard functions $0 and $1 .

1.14   How do I...

Disable the Break key?

Description

Before they exit, most programs call clean-up routines to put everything back the way it was before the program was run. For example, most programs do not want to leave the screen in 43/50 line mode after they exit. Cleaning up is not difficult; you simply put the clean-up code at the end of the program. One thing that can upset this procedure is the Break key. This key lets the user break out of the program at any time, bypassing the clean-up code and often leaving the computer in the wrong state.

See Also

1.13   Reading the extended keyboard

Solution

When the user presses the Break key, the PC generates an interrupt that tells MS-DOS when to shut down the program. The way to prevent this is to trap the break interrupt.

To trap the interrupt, use Turbo Pascal procedures `GetIntVec` and `SetIntVec`. `GetIntVec` gets the address of the procedure called whenever a given interrupt occurs. You tell it the interrupt number and the pointer variable that gets the address. You need `GetIntVec` to find out the address of the current interrupt handler. To get the vector for the break interrupt, use this statement:

```
GetIntVec( $1B, OldBreak );
```

`SetIntVec` sets the procedure called when the interrupt occurs. In a Turbo Pascal program, you create an interrupt procedure by including the keyword "`interrupt`" in the procedure definition, like this:

```
procedure MyBreak;
interrupt;
begin
end;
```

After defining this procedure, you can make it the break procedure by using `SetIntVec`, like this:

```
SetIntVec( $1B, @MyBreak );
```

Note the '`@`' before the procedure name. This operator tells the compiler to use the address of the procedure rather than calling the procedure and using the returned value. Because this is a procedure, no value is returned, so failing to use '`@`' causes a compiler error.

Because the break vector is redirected to a procedure that does nothing, MS-DOS does not get the word that the program should be stopped from this source. Another way MS-DOS detects a break is by looking at the keypresses in the keyboard buffer. Like any other key, the Break key generates a code that goes into the buffer. If a program calls MS-DOS to read keys from the buffer, MS-DOS will find the Break key code and stop the program. To avoid this problem, you can use the `GetKey` function you learned in question 1.13. This function bypasses MS-DOS and receives keypresses directly from BIOS. Thus, MS-DOS never detects the Break keypress.

You can use the fact that the Break key puts a code in the keyboard buffer to tell when the Break key was pressed. This way, you can do any needed clean-up before exiting. Part of the clean-up code should be a statement that restores the original break procedure like this one:

```
SetIntVect( $1B, OldBreak );
```

Comments

The `interrupt` keyword in the `MyBreak` procedure affects the code at the beginning and the end of the compiled procedure. At the beginning of the procedure, the compiler inserts code that pushes all the registers onto the stack, sets the `BP` register so that these values can be used as `var word` parameters, and sets the `DS` register so that it points to the data area for the program. For hardware interrupts, such as the break interrupt, you can omit the register parameters. For software interrupts, such as the MS-DOS interrupt `$21`, you need to check and possibly modify the registers. In this case, change the declaration to include the registers:

```
procedure MySoftInt(Flags,CS,IP,AX,BX,CX,DX,SI,DI,DS,ES,BP:word);
interrupt;
begin
       .    {Code that uses the registers like any other word
       .     variable}
       .
end;
```

The interrupt keyword also changes the code generated at the end of the procedure. This code pops all of the registers off the stack and then executes an `IRET` instruction. When the registers pop off the stack, they are set to the specified parameter values. The `var` keyword works like this with normal routines; `IRET` is a special return instruction for interrupt functions. It pops the flags off the stack before returning.

Warnings

Whenever you replace an interrupt vector, reinstate the original vector before your program exits. If you don't, and if an interrupt occurs after your program ends, the CPU jumps to the vector that you set to point to code in your program. This is fine while your program is in memory, but as soon as another program is loaded into that memory the interrupt jumps into the middle of that new program. This can cause all sorts of strange results.

Enhancements

There is no rule against having the break procedure perform some job. Although there are some restrictions on what kind of code can go in an interrupt procedure, there is nothing wrong with putting something in it. The restrictions reflect the fact that many routines cannot be called while they are already running. So, if the program calls MS-DOS and your interrupt also calls MS-DOS, you will get unpredictable results. The Turbo Pascal routines for input, output, and dynamic memory can create similar problems.

A useful thing to do when the user presses the Break key is to print a message indicating that the Break key does not work, if that is the case.

Although printing a string would seem to violate the rule about not using MS-DOS or I/O routines, you can safely use the MS-DOS routines with function numbers below 11h if no other routine is using them. The MS-DOS function to print a character is number 2, so all you have to do is avoid using the MS-DOS functions below in the rest of your program. The following routine shows how to print the string in the variable BreakStr when the user presses the Break key:

```
procedure MyBreak;
interrupt;
var
   Regs : registers;
   i : byte;
begin
   {for each character in the string}
   for i := 1 to byte( BreakStr[0] ) do
   begin
     {Call MS-DOS to print it}
     Regs.AH := 2;
     Regs.DL := byte( BreakStr[i] );
     MsDos( Regs );
   end;
end;
```

You can install this procedure as an interrupt service routine to handle interrupt $1B. Because you do not know the state of MS-DOS at the time of the interrupt, you can use only MS-DOS functions below $11. This routine uses function 2, which prints the character in the DL register. The procedure loops through the string to be printed, calling MS-DOS to print each character.

1.15   How do I...

Detect the pressing or release of any key, including Shift?

Description

The next time you see a program that says "Press any key to continue," try pressing the Shift key. In most programs nothing happens because the Shift key, by itself, does not generate a key code. You may not care about this picky inconsistency, but you have other reasons for wanting to detect when keys are pressed or released. For example, you may want a special screen to pop up when the user presses the Ctrl key and disappear when the user releases it.

See Also

Solution

Every time the user presses or releases a key, the keyboard controller generates an interrupt number 9. The solution for question 1.14 shows how to intercept interrupts. You can use that same procedure to make a routine that intercepts interrupt 9. The difference here is that you want to let the normal interrupt 9 function run and detect key presses as well.

The following program calls an interrupt handler that reads the keypress and beeps when the Space bar is pressed. It beeps at a higher frequency when the Space bar is released, then calls the original keyboard interrupt handler:

```
{This is a program to to intercept keyboard interupts}
program SitKey;
uses Dos, Crt;

var
  OldInt9 : pointer;                  {Place to save the real keyboard
                                       handler}

procedure MyInt9;                     {New int 9 handler}
interrupt;
var
  key : byte;                         {Stores the scan code for the key}
begin
    {This machine code reads the keyboard character port}
    InLine( $E4 / $60 );              {in al, 60h}
    {And stores the scan code in key}
    InLine( $88 /$46/ <key );         {mov [bp + key],al}
    {Test for Space bar pressed}
    if key = $39 then
    begin
        {If so beep}
        Sound( 144 );
        Delay( 100 );
        NoSound;
    end
    else
    {Otherwise, see if it is space bar released}
    if key = $B9 then
    begin
        {If so beep}
        Sound( 288 );
        Delay( 100 );
        NoSound;
    end;
```

```
    {Call the old interrupt procedure}
    InLine( $9C );              {pushf}
    InLine( $FF /$1E/ OldInt9 ); {call far ptr [OldInt9]}
end;

{Set up the keyboard interrupt handler}
begin
    {Get the old handler}
    GetIntVec( $9, OldInt9 );
    {Set the new handler}
    SetIntVec( $9, @MyInt9 );
    {wait for the Return key}
    ReadLn;
    {Restore the original handler}
    SetIntVec( $9, OldInt9 );
end.
```

First, the keyboard handler reads the data at port $60, the data port for keyboard information. The byte read is the scan code of the key that was pressed or released. The high bit of the byte tells if the key was pressed (0) or released (1). The scan code for the Space bar is $39. When it is released the code is $B9 or $39 + $86. These values are used in the if statements to determine whether the computer should beep and, if so, at what frequency. The last thing that the keyboard handler does is to call the original keyboard handler. Because the original handler is an interrupt routine, you must push the flags before the call to make the IRET at the end of the handler work properly.

The main body of this program is the standard code for placing and restoring an interrupt handler. Note the very important SetIntVec statement at the end of the program. If you omit this statement, everything will work fine until you load another program and press a key. At that time anything can happen.

Comments

When you use a routine like this one, you need to find the scan code for the key that starts your routine. You can look up this information in a technical reference on PCs, or you can write a routine that tells you the scan code of the key pressed. To do this, replace the if statements in the keyboard handler with this code:

```
if key < $80 then
begin
    Regs.AH := 2;              {MS-DOS print char}
    Regs.DL := Ord( '$' );     {Print a $}
    MsDos( Regs );             {Call MS-DOS}
    Regs.DL := key SHR 4;      {Get the high nibble of the code}
    {Turn into a hexadecimal digit}
```

```
   if Regs.DL < $A then
      Regs.DL := Regs.DL + $30
   else
      Regs.DL := Regs.DL - $A + Ord( 'A' );
   MsDos( Regs );
   {Do the same for the low nibble}
   Regs.DL := key AND $F;
   if Regs.DL < $A then
      Regs.DL := Regs.DL + $30
   else
      Regs.DL := Regs.DL - $A + Ord( 'A' );
   MsDos( Regs );
end;
```

Now, the routine prints the scan code of every key that you press. You can compute the code for the key release by adding $80 to the code printed by this program.

Warnings

Routines that intercept the keyboard handler are the most likely to lock up your system if you don't get them right. This problem is especially frustrating because you cannot use the debugger to find out what is going on. The reason is that the debugger also gets its commands from the keyboard. If you have replaced the keyboard handler with one that doesn't work, the debugger cannot get commands.

As with the interrupt handler in question 1.15, you cannot call MS-DOS or any of Turbo Pascal's I/O or heap management routines. Also, because interrupts are disabled while the interrupt handler is running, make sure that the routine doesn't take up too much machine time. If interrupts are disabled for too long a time, the MS-DOS clock will begin to lose time because it is not getting the clock interrupts that it needs to mark the passage of time.

Enhancements

This routine looks only at the key pressed. After it looks at the key, it calls the normal keyboard handler, which puts the keypress in the keyboard buffer. Keeping the key out of the buffer is a bit more complex than simply not calling the original handler.

If you do not call the normal keyboard handler, then you have to reset the interrupt controller chip. This chip ensures that high-priority interrupts are handled before lower-priority interrupts. To reset it, you send the value $20 to port number $20. Here are the InLine statements that do this job:

```
InLine( $B0 / $20 ); {mov    al,$20}
InLine( $E6 / $20 ); {out $20,al}
```

SOUND SOLUTIONS

Sound is often overlooked as an I/O technique. Its use is often limited to generating beeps that signal errors. But sounds can also be used to indicate that certain routines are being run, to alert the user to unusual situations, or simply to entertain. The next two solutions show how to make PC-compatible computers generate a variety of sounds. Solution 1.16 shows how to create various tones you can use to create beeps or melodies. Solution 1.17 shows how to create sounds effects.

1.16   How do I...

Make a sound at a given frequency?

Description

Sound is a useful way to get the user's attention. Many programs beep to signal an error. If your program has a routine that takes a long time to run, you can use a beep to tell the user that the routine has ended.

See Also

1.17   Making sound effects

Solution

Turbo Pascal has two routines for making sounds. The first is the `Sound` procedure, which turns on the speaker with a given tone. The second is the `NoSound` procedure, which turns off the speaker. The `Sound` procedure takes a single argument that tells what frequency to use. This code generates a tone of middle C tone for one second:

```
Sound( 262 ); {Turn on the speaker}
Delay( 100 ); {wait a second}
NoSound;      {turn the speaker off}
```

Comments

You can specify the duration of the beep in several ways. To generate a simple attention-getting beep, use the `Delay` procedure. Another way is to make the tone last as long as a keypress, from pressing to release.

Warnings

There is only one thing to watch for: Make sure that you turn the tone off. If you don't, the computer will make noise until you write a program to turn the sound off or you reboot.

Enhancements

By combining the sound procedures with the keyboard-intercept routines of question 1.16 you can make a simple computer organ program.

```
{This is a simple organ}
program Organ;
uses Dos, Crt;

var
   OldInt9 : pointer;
   SoundOn : boolean; {True while the organ is running}

procedure MyInt9;
interrupt;
var
   key : byte;
   Regs : Registers;
begin
    InLine( $E4 / $60 );        {in al, 60h}
    InLine( $88 / $46 / <key );  {mov [bp+key],al}
    {See if the key is ESC or 1 - 8}
    if ( Key >= 1 ) AND ( Key <= 9 ) then
    begin
        {Decide what note to play}
        case Key of
            1 : SoundOn := FALSE; {ESC - exit}
            2 : Sound( 262 ); {C}
            3 : Sound( 294 ); {D}
            4 : Sound( 330 ); {E}
            5 : Sound( 349 ); {F}
            6 : Sound( 392 ); {G}
            7 : Sound( 440 ); {A}
            8 : Sound( 494 ); {B}
            9 : Sound( 523 ); {C}
        end;
    end;
    {If a key goes up turn off the sound}
    if Key >= $80 then
        NoSound;
    {Reset the interrupt controller chip}
    InLine( $B0 / $20 );        {mov  al,20h}
    InLine( $E6 / $20 );        {out  20h,al}
end;

begin
    {Set the sound on flag}
    SoundOn := TRUE;
    {replace the keyboard interrupt}
    GetIntVec( $9, OldInt9 );
    SetIntVec( $9, @MyInt9 );
    {Wait until the sound variable becomes false}
    while SoundOn do;
    {return the original keyboard handler}
    SetIntVec( $9, OldInt9 );
end.
```

The keyboard handler for this program waits for the user to press either the Esc key, or one of the first eight number keys. The Esc key sets the SoundOn variable to FALSE, stopping the program. Any of the number keys start the sound at a different frequency. When any of the keys goes up, the sound stops.

Make sound effects?

Description
The PC can make a variety of sounds other than beeps. Although these sounds are not of hi-fi quality, they are fun to play with.

See Also
1.16   Making a tone

Solution
The sounds that the PC makes are generated by a chip that moves the speaker in and out. Unlike the speaker in a stereo, the PC speaker always moves the same amount. The clock chip is connected to this chip causing the speaker to move back and forth at regular intervals. This produces a nice tone. To get different sounds, you have to modify the intervals. This is called modifying the duty cycle of the signal. You can achieve a surprising variety of sounds this way.

The following program shows you how to control when the speaker moves in and when it moves out:

```
{Program to make sound effects}
program Effects;
Uses Key, Crt;

var
   Port61 : byte;          {The data on the speaker port}
   i : integer;            {variable for the delay loop}

begin
   {Read the status port}
   InLine( $E4/$61 );      {in al,$61}
   InLine( $A2/Port61 );   {mov [Port61], al}
   repeat
      {Clear the low two bits}
      Port61 := Port61 AND $FC; {Mask off low bits}
      {Move the speaker in}
```

```
    InLine( $A0/Port61 );         {mov  al, [Port61]}
    InLine( $E6/$61 );            {out  $61, al}
    {wait a little while}
    for i := 1 to 300 do;                  {Delay with bit off}
        {Set bit two}
        Port61 := Port61 OR 2;             {Toggle the speaker bit}
    {move the speaker out}
    InLine( $A0 / Port61 );       {mov  al, [Port61]}
    InLine( $E6 / $61 );          {out  $61}
    {wait a little while}
    for i := 1 to 300 do;                  {Delay with bit on}
  until NOT IsKey;
end.
```

This program uses inline assembly language to control the status port, which controls the built-in speaker. The first step is to clear the speaker bits in the status port to move the speaker in. Next, the program uses a for loop to wait for a short interval. After waiting, the program sets the bits in the status port to move the speaker back out. The program enters another delay loop before beginning the cycle all over again.

Comments

To make sound effects you need to vary the lengths of the two delay loops. Making both loops longer lowers the frequency of the tone. Changing one loop but not the other changes the duty cycle and thus the type of tone. You get really interesting results by constantly changing the duty cycle and frequency. For example, if you use random numbers for the delay values, you get a sound similar to static on the radio.

Sound is actually small variations in air pressure. By graphing the air pressure versus time, you can see a unique pattern for each sound. To approximate the sound with the PC speaker, move the speaker out whenever the pressure gets above the average pressure and move it in whenever the pressure is below the average.

You do not need to graph a sound to make interesting effects. Try different combinations of duty cycle and frequency changes until you get something interesting.

Warnings

This routine depends on the speed of the computer running it. You could use the Delay routine, but the minimum interval for this routine doesn't give you much range to play with. One alternative is to make a table of values to use for different computer speeds. Then you can select the correct table according to the type of computer you are using.

Enhancements

To determine the speed of a computer, use the timer interrupt. First, make a clock interrupt handler that sets a global flag, as follows:

```
procedure TickFlag;
interrupt;
begin
        TFlag := FALSE;
end;
```

The main routine must install this handler, set the TFlag variable to TRUE, wait for the flag value to become FALSE, set it back to TRUE, then start a loop that counts the number of iterations until TFlag is FALSE. The value of the counter times 18.2 (the number of timer ticks in a second) is the number of iterations possible in a second. This routine demonstrate this:

```
var
        OldTick : pointer;
        TFlag : boolean;
        Counter : longint;

begin
        GetIntVec( $1C, OldTick );  {Get the old handler}
        SetIntVec( $1C, @TickFlag );       {Put tickflag in}
        Counter := 0;
        TFlag := TRUE;
        while TFlag do;
        TFlag := TRUE;
        while TFlag do
                Inc( Counter );
        SetIntVec( $1C, OldTick );  {Put the handler back}
        {Multiply by 182 and divide by 10 to get the number of ticks
         per second}
        Counter := Counter * 182;
        Counter := Counter DIV 10;
        .                                {The rest of the program knows
        .                                 the speed of the computer}
        .
end.
```

The first statements in this program replace the clock tick interrupt service routine with the clock tick routine. Then the program sets TFlag to TRUE and waits for a clock tick to make TFlag FALSE. Next, the program sets TFlag to TRUE again and counts how many times the loop runs, waiting for TFlag to become FALSE again. This number is the number of counts per tick, which is multiplied by 18.2 to get the number of ticks per second. To avoid floating-point operations, the program multiplies by 182 and divides by 10 to get the same result as multiplying by 18.2.

PUTTING IT ALL TOGETHER

The last three solutions in this chapter show you how to put together several of the routines in this chapter to create data entry routines for use in your programs. Solution 1.18 shows how to put the routines you need into a unit to make them easy to add to other programs. The last two solutions use the routines in the unit to create formatted data entry fields. Solution 1.19 shows how to handle numeric input, and solution 1.20 shows how to create a more general formatted input routine.

1.18   How do I...

Make a screen I/O unit?

Description

Several of the programs in this chapter use the built-in Turbo Pascal units Crt and Dos. These units contain useful routines that become available when the unit is named in a uses statement. This solution shows how to create a unit that includes some of the routines presented in this chapter.

See Also:

1.1   Filling screen areas with characters

1.2   Changing screen attributes

1.13   Reading the extended keyboard

Solution

To create a unit you have to change the program statement at the beginning to a unit statement, and add interface and implementation directives. This is the syntax of the unit statement:

```
unit UnitName
```

The keyword unit tells the compiler that the program should be compiled as a unit. The UnitName is not used and is required only for historical reasons.

The next statement should be an interface directive. After the keyword interface, you must list all of the constants, types, variables, procedures, and functions that you want to make available to other routines.

After all of the interface declarations comes the implementation section. This section includes all of the constants, types, variables, procedures, and functions that are for use only in the unit. It also includes the code for the procedures and functions mentioned in the interface part.

Here is an example of a unit called ScreenIO that includes the FillChars and SetAttrs routines from earlier in this chapter:

```
{Screen IO unit}
unit ScreenIO;
interface
procedure FillChars( Data:word; Count:word );
procedure SetAttr( Data:byte; Count:word );

implementation
uses Crt;

{Copy characters to screen memory}
procedure FillChars( Data:word; Count:word );
var
   Offset : word;      {The offset into screen memory}
   Segment : word;     {The segment for screen memory}
   ScrPtr : ^word;
begin
     {Calculate the offset}
     Offset := (( WhereY - 1 ) * 80 + WhereX - 1 ) * 2;
     {Find out what segment to use}
     if LastMode = 7 then
             Segment := $B000
     else
             Segment := $B800;
     {Loop Count times}
     {Calculate the screen memory pointer}
     ScrPtr := Ptr( Segment, Offset );
     while( Count <> 0 ) do
     begin
             {Store the data}
        ScrPtr^ := Data;
        Inc( ScrPtr );
      {Decrement count}
      Dec( Count );
     end;
end;

{Set video attributes}
procedure SetAttr( Data:byte; Count:word );
var
   Offset : word;      {The offset into screen memory}
   Segment : word;     {The segment for screen memory}
   ScrPtr : ^byte;
begin
     {Calculate the offset}
     Offset := (( WhereY - 1 ) * 80 + WhereX - 1 ) * 2 + 1;
     { Find out what segment to use }
     if LastMode = 7 then
             Segment := $B000
     else
             Segment := $B800;
     {Calculate the screen memory pointer}
```

```
        ScrPtr := Ptr( Segment, Offset );
        while( Count <> 0 ) do
        begin
        {Store the data}
        ScrPtr^ := Data;
        Inc( ScrPtr, 2 );
        { Decrement count }
        Dec( Count );
        end;
end.
```

The interface section of this unit declares the procedures FillChars and SetAttrs. These functions are available to any program that uses the ScreenIO unit. The implementation section includes the code for the FillChars and SetAttrs routines. It also contains a statement to use the Crt unit. Because the Crt unit is included in the implementation section, it is available for use by routines in the unit. If the uses Crt statement is in the interface section, the Crt routines are available not only to this unit but also to any program that includes the ScreenIO unit.

Comments

Units can help organize large programs. Instead of making long source files that include all of the routines in the program, you can divide the program into units. If you need to update a routine you can work on just the unit with the routine without getting distracted by the rest of the program.

When you compile a unit, the compiler generates a file with a .TPU extension. Other programs can use this file without having to recompile it. If the program is long, you can save time by recompiling only the unit you are working on instead of the whole program.

Enhancements

You can expand the ScreenIO unit by adding whatever routines you wish. Most units include routines that have related uses. For example, the ScreenIO unit contains routines for I/O. It doesn't make sense to include a routine in it that computes compound interest, although it is not illegal to include it. There is no penalty for having too many routines in the unit. The compiler copies into the final program only those routines that the program needs.

The next two questions show two routines that you can add to the ScreenIO unit.

1.19 How do I...

Handle numeric data entry?

Description

The `ReadLn` function is okay for simple input, but it has several drawbacks. The major drawback is that if you type a nonnumeric key while `ReadLn` is looking for a number, you get a run-time error that stops the program.

See Also

1.13 Reading the extended keyboard

1.18 Make a **Screen I/O** unit

1.20 Making formatted data-entry fields

Solution

A numeric data-entry routine gets each keystroke and checks whether it is a command (such as backspace), a numeric digit, or any other key. The routine must also display the number as it is entered.

Here is a routine that you can add to the **ScreenIO** unit to do numeric data input:

```
{Do formatted numeric input}
function GetNumb( Len : integer; Attr : byte ) : integer;
var
        Data      : string;
        KPos      : integer;
        Key       : word;
        KeyCount  : integer;
begin
        {Set the selected text attribute}
        TextAttr := Attr;
        {Make a string the length of the field}
        Data := '';
        for KPos := 1 to Len do
                Data := Data + ' ';
        {Start with 0 digits in the field}
        KeyCount := 0;
        repeat
                {Write the data string}
                Write( Data );
                {Put the cursor at the rightmost position in the field}
                GotoXY( WhereX - 1, WhereY );
                {Get a key from the user}
                Key := GetKey AND $FF;
                {See if the key is a digit}
                if ( Key >= Ord( '0' )) AND ( Key <= Ord( '9' )) then
                begin
                        {If the field is full, beep}
                        if KeyCount = Len then
```

```
                begin
                        Sound( 244 );
                        Delay( 100 );
                        NoSound;
                end
                else
                begin
                        {Move all previous digits left one col}
                        for KPos := 1 to Len - 1 do
                                Data[KPos] := Data[KPos + 1];
                        {Put the new digit in at the left}
                        Data[KPos + 1] := char( Key );
                        Inc( KeyCount );
                end;
        end
        {See if the key was a backspace}
        else if Key = 8 then
        begin
                {If no digits to delete, beep}
                if KeyCount = 0 then
                begin
                        Sound( 244 );
                        Delay( 100 );
                        NoSound;
                end
                else
                begin
                        {Move all of the digits right one col}
                        KPos := Len;
                        while( KPos > 1 ) do
                        begin
                                Data[KPos] := Data[KPos - 1];
                                Dec( KPos );
                        end;
                        {Put a space at the beginning of the string}
                        Data[1] := ' ';
                        Dec( KeyCount );
                end;
        end
        {If the key is not the enter key, beep}
        else if Key <> $0D then
        begin
                Sound( 244 );
                Delay( 100 );
                NoSound;
        end;
        GotoXY( WhereX - Len + 1, WhereY );
    {Keep looping until the user presses enter}
    until Key = $0D;
    {Convert the string to a number}
    Val( Data, KPos, KeyCount );
    {Return the number}
    Get Numb := KPos;
end;
```

The first part of this routine sets up the text attribute to use and creates a string of spaces, called `Data`, that's as long as the input field. The `repeat-until` loop starts by displaying the string `Data` and positioning the cursor on the last character of the field. Next, the routine uses the `GetKey` function (see question 1.13) to get a key from the user. (Be sure to include the `GetKey` function in the implementation section of the unit.)

The `GetNumb` function tests the key pressed to see if it is a digit. If it is, `GetNumb` checks if there is room in the field for another digit. If not, the routine generates a beep (see question 1.16); otherwise, `GetNumb` shifts the characters in the field to the left and inserts the new digit at the end of the string.

If the key pressed is not a digit, `GetNumb` checks if it is a backspace. If the key is a backspace and there are digits in the field, `GetNumb` shifts the string to the right and inserts a space at the beginning of the string. Because the length of the string does not change, the digit at the left disappears.

The final test is whether the key is Enter. If not, the routine generates a beep; otherwise, the program exits the `repeat=while` loop. After the loop is done, `GetNumb` converts the string to a number by using Turbo Pascal's `Val` procedure.

Comments

The program that uses the `GetNumb` function must include `ScreenIO` in a `uses` statement. After that, you can use the functions in the unit as you would any other function. This program shows how to use the `GetNumb` function:

```
{This program does formatted data entry}
program DataForm;
uses Crt, ScreenIO;

var
        Numb        : integer;
        FormData    : string;

begin
        TextAttr := $7;
        ClrScr;
        GotoXY( 2, 3 );
        Write( 'Enter a number: ' );
        Numb := GetNumb( 10, $70 );
        Write( 'The number is: ', Numb );
end.
```

This program sets the normal screen attribute, clears the screen, and displays a prompt at column 2, row 3. Next it calls `GetNumb` to get a number from the user.

Enhancements

Many data-entry programs allow you to specify a default value for fields. This value appears when the routine is first called. The user who wants this value need only press the Enter key to accept the default. If you want to include this feature, change the declaration to something like this:

```
procedure GetNumb( Len:integer; Attr:byte; var Value:integer );
```

Then modify the code that initializes `Data` to put the default value in. Use the `Str` routine to convert the default number into a string, then use `Insert` to pad the string with spaces on the left.

```
Str( Value, Data );
while Length( Data ) < Len do
      Insert( ' ', Data, 1 );
```

Finally, change the last line to store the value in `Value` instead of returning it.

1.20 How do I...

Make formatted data-entry fields?

Description

Data-entry applications use not only numeric fields but also text fields, phone number fields, date fields, and so on. A generic data-entry field that can be used in all of these cases would be very useful.

See Also

1-19   Handling numeric data entry

Solution

The procedure below lets you specify a format field to describe how the field should look. Each character in the format string describes what happens in the corresponding position of the data field. An `'A'` indicates that any character can go in that position. A `'U'` is similar, except that alphabetic characters are converted to uppercase. An `'N'` means that only numeric digits can go in that position. Any other character in the format string is displayed, and no characters can be input in that position.

You can add this routine to the `ScreenIO` unit for use in programs that need to get data from the user:

```
{Get formatted data}
procedure GetData( FormStr : string; var Data : string );
var
```

```
    KPos            : integer;
    TData           : string;
    Key             : word;
    LeftCol         : integer;
    Row             : integer;
    NeverBefore     : boolean;
begin
    {Make the image of the field}
    TData := '';
    for KPos := 1 to Length( FormStr ) do
        {If a format character, get a char from the data string}
        if ( FormStr[KPos] = 'A' ) OR ( FormStr[KPos] = 'U' )
            OR ( FormStr[KPos] = 'N' ) then
        begin
            if KPos <= Length( Data ) then
                TData := TData + Data[KPos]
            else
                TData := TData + ' ';
        end
        else
            TData := TData + FormStr[KPos];
    KPos := 1;
    {Find the first editable character position}
    while Pos( FormStr[KPos], 'AUN' ) = 0 do
        Inc( KPos );
    {Initialize locations}
    LeftCol := WhereX;
    Row := WhereY;
    NeverBefore := TRUE;
    repeat
        {Write the field at the saved location}
        GotoXY( LeftCol, Row );
        Write( TData );
        {Position the cursor in the field}
        GotoXY( LeftCol + KPos - 1, Row );
        {Get a key}
        Key := GetKey;
        if Key = $4FE0 then {END key}
        begin
            {Move the cursor to the last editable position}
            KPos := Length( Data );
            while Pos( FormStr[KPos], 'AUN') = 0 do
                Dec( KPos );
        end
        else if Key = $47E0 then {HOME key}
        begin
            {Move the cursor to the first editable position}
            KPos := 1;
            while Pos( FormStr[KPos], 'AUN' ) = 0 do
                Inc( KPos );
        end
        else if Key = $4DE0 then {Right arrow}
        begin
```

```pascal
    {Move the cursor to the last editable position}
    repeat
        Inc( KPos )
    until ( KPos = Length( FormStr ))
        OR   ( Pos( FormStr[KPos], 'AUN' ) <> 0 );
    {If past the end, go to last position}
    if KPos = Length( FormStr ) then
        while Pos( FormStr[KPos], 'AUN' ) = 0 do
            Dec( KPos );
end
else if Key = $4BE0 then {Left arrow}
begin
    {Move cursor to previous editable position}
    repeat
        Dec( KPos );
    until ( KPos = 1 ) OR ( Pos( FormStr[KPos],'AUN' )<>0 );
    if KPos = 1 then
        repeat
            Inc( KPos )
        until ( KPos = Length( FormStr ))
            OR ( Pos( FormStr[KPos], 'AUN' ) <> 0 );
end
else if Key = $3920 then {Space}
begin
    {Insert a space in the field}
    TData[KPos] := Chr( Key );
    repeat
        Inc( KPos )
    until ( KPos = Length( FormStr ))
        OR   ( Pos( FormStr[KPos], 'AUN' ) <> 0 );
    if KPos = Length( FormStr ) then
        while Pos( FormStr[KPos], 'AUN' ) = 0 do
            Dec( KPos );
end
else if Key <> $1C0D then {Enter key}
begin
    Key := Key AND $FF;
    {See if looking for text}
    if ( FormStr[KPos] = 'A' )
        OR ( FormStr[KPos] = 'U' ) then
    begin
        {Check for alpha keys}
        if ((Key > = Ord( 'A' )) AND ( Key < = Ord( 'Z' )))
            OR (( Key> = Ord( 'a' ))
            AND ( Key< = Ord( 'z' ))) then
        begin
            {If first key, clear before inserting}
            if NeverBefore then
            begin
                for KPos:=1 to Length( FormStr ) do
                    if Pos( FormStr[KPos],'AUN' )
                        <>0 then
                        TData[KPos] := ' '
```

```
                    else
                        TData[KPos]
                               :=FormStr[KPos];
                    NeverBefore := FALSE;
                    KPos := 1;
                    while Pos( FormStr[KPos],'A' )=0 do
                        Inc( KPos );
                end;
                {If U typed, make the char uppercase}
                if FormStr[KPos] = 'U' then
                    TData[KPos]
                        :=Chr( Key AND ( NOT $20 ) )
                else
                    TData[KPos] := Chr( Key );
                {Go to the next editable char}
                repeat
                    Inc( KPos )
                until ( KPos = Length( FormStr ))
                    OR ( Pos( FormStr[KPos],'AUN' ) <> 0 );
                if KPos = Length( FormStr ) then
                    while Pos( FormStr[KPos],'AUN' )=0 do
                        Dec( KPos );
            end
            else {Not a legal key, beep}
            begin
                Sound( 244 );
                Delay( 100 );
                NoSound;
            end;
        end
        {See if looking for a digit}
        else if FormStr[KPos] = 'N' then
        begin
            {test for digits}
            if ( Key > = Ord( '0' )) AND ( Key < = Ord( '9' )) then
            begin
                {Insert the digit}
                TData[KPos] := Chr( Key );
                repeat
                    Inc( KPos )
                until ( KPos = Length( FormStr ))
                    OR ( Pos( FormStr[KPos],'AUN' ) <> 0 );
                if KPos = Length( FormStr ) then
                    while Pos( FormStr[KPos],'AUN' ) = 0 do
                        Dec( KPos );
            end
            else {Not a digit, beep}
            begin
                Sound( 244 );
                Delay( 100 );
                NoSound;
            end;
        end
```

```
        end;
    until Key = $1C0D; {Enter key}
    Data := TData;
end;
```

First, `GetData` creates the formatted input string by copying characters from the format string, replacing formatting characters with characters from the `Data` string.

In the `repeat-while` loop, `GetData` prints the formatted input string and positions the cursor at the current location in the field. Next, it uses the `GetKey` function to get a key from the user. It tests whether the key is one of the editing keys, such as Home or End. If the key is an editing key, `GetData` moves the cursor to the indicated position, making sure that it's in an editable position.

If the key is not an editing key, `GetData` checks the format string to see if the character should be an alphabetic character or a numeric digit. Then, `GetData` checks the key to see if it is of the correct type. If so, it adds the key to the input string and advances the cursor to the next editable position.

When the user presses the Enter key, the program exits the `repeat-while` loop. The last step is to copy the input string to the `Data` string.

Comments

Table 1-5 shows some common fields that you can use with this routine.

String	Purpose
NN/NN/NN	Dates
NN-UUU-NN	Alternate date format (12-JAN-90)
(NNN) NNN-NNNN	Phone numbers
NNNNN AAAAAAAAAAAAAA	US street address

Table 1.5 Common format strings

This program shows how to use the `GetData` routine:

```
{This program does formatted data entry}
program DataForm;
uses Crt, ScreenIO;

var
    Numb        : integer;
    FormData    : string;

begin
```

```
        TextAttr := $7;
        ClrScr;
        {Set up the default data string}
        FormData := '<asdf-QWER.1234>';
        Write( 'Enter a string: ' );
        {Do formatted input}
        GetData( '<AAAA-UUUU.NNNN>', FormData );
        Write( 'The result is: ', FormData );
end.
```

The preceding program creates the string FormData to hold the data to input. Then it calls GetData to get the formatted data. The format string shows the three different formatting characters.

Warnings

Make sure that the format string that you use has some editable characters in it. If not, the GetData procedure hangs when it tries to find the first editable character.

Enhancements

As soon as you begin using this procedure, you will start to think of other things that it could do for you. For example, you can design the code for 'MM' so that it accepts only integers from 1 to 12, for use in date format strings.

2

FILES
AND
DEVICES

2

One of the most useful things a computer can do is to store and retrieve data. The data can be database information, text files, programs, and so on. To manipulate data, most applications need some way of interacting with files. For block devices, such as disk drives, you need to look at file and directory names in addition to manipulating the files themselves. This chapter shows you how to use Turbo Pascal to find out what files are on your disks, as well as how to copy, move, find, create, and delete files.

Once you know how to use the file system, you can move on to working with the data in the files. Turbo Pascal has several routines for reading and writing files. The examples in this chapter show you how to choose the functions that will give you the best performance. In addition, you will see how to structure a file for improved data access.

MS-DOS considers printers, modems, and similar devices special files. This simplifies the I/O system because all devices work the same way. All you need to know is how to use the file I/O routines and what device name to use to access any device that is installed. The second part of this chapter shows you how to use the printer device driver to send data to the printer. You'll also learn how to format the data neatly on the page.

The last part of the chapter deals with the serial port. The serial port device driver for MS-DOS works well for sending data but it can lose characters when receiving data at high speeds. The examples in this section show you how to get the best performance from the MS-DOS serial device driver.

FILES

Despite the importance of files in MS-DOS computers, Turbo Pascal provides only a few limited routines for using files. The reason is that huge libraries would be needed to provide all of the possible routines for text files, graphics files, databases, executable files, and others. Instead, Turbo Pascal includes a carefully chosen set of file routines you can use to make routines for all types of files.

The solutions in this section show some ways to use these routines. Solutions 2.1 and 2.2 show you how to copy or move files from one directory to another. These routines demonstrate how files are opened, read, written, and closed in Turbo Pascal programs.

The next four solutions show you how to find out what files and directories are available on the computer. Solutions 2.3 and 2.4 show how to use the Turbo Pascal routines that read directories. Solution 2.5 combines the previous solutions into a single file-management program. This program shows lists of files and lets you enter commands to manipulate the files. Solution 2.6 shows you how to search directories for a specific file.

The last three solutions in this section show how to manipulate the contents of files. Solution 2.7 shows how you can speed up file operations by using memory buffers. Solutions 2.8 and 2.9 show how to make database files with variable length records and an index system.

2.1   How do I...

Copy a file with a Turbo Pascal program?

Description

To save the user from having to decipher MS-DOS commands, many applications come with install programs that copy files from the distribution diskettes to the user's hard disk. Other programs copy a file to a backup file before letting the user edit the original file. Both of these programs require a procedure that copies one file to another.

See Also

2.5   Using the file manager
2.7   Using buffers to speed file operations

Solution

Copying a file is simply a matter of reading the data in one file and writing it back to another file. To make sure that the destination file exactly matches the source file, you should use the `BlockRead` and `BlockWrite` procedures with a record size of 1 byte. Using these procedures prevents any translations of the data, and a record size of 1 byte ensures that files of any size can be read.

This procedure performs the copy:

```
{Copy a file to the file or directory in DestName}
procedure CopyFile( SrcName, DestName : string );
var
   Source : file;
   Destination : file;
   Buffer : array[1..1024] of byte;
   ReadCnt : word;
   WriteCnt : word;
   PName : PathStr;
   DName : DirStr;
   FName : NameStr;
   EName : ExtStr;
{$I-}
begin
   {Open the source file for reading}
   Assign( Source, SrcName );
   Reset( Source, 1 );
   {Make sure the file opened OK}
   if IOResult <> 0 then
      WriteLn( 'The source file does not exist' )
   else
   begin
      {If the dest file is a directory}
      if DestName[Length(DestName)] = '\' then
      begin
         {Get the parts of the source filename}
         PName := SrcName;
         FSplit( PName, DName, FName, EName );
         {Add the filename and extension to the dest file}
         DestName := DestName + FName + EName;
      end;
      {Assign and open the destination file for writing}
      Assign( Destination, DestName );
      ReWrite( Destination, 1 );
      {Copy the file}
      repeat
         BlockRead( Source,Buffer,sizeof( Buffer ),ReadCnt );
         BlockWrite(Destination,Buffer,ReadCnt,WriteCnt);
      until ( ReadCnt = 0 ) OR ( WriteCnt <> ReadCnt );
      Close( Destination );
      Close( Source );
   end;
end;
{$I+}
```

This procedure uses the `{$I-}` directive to turn off automatic I/O error handling. Without this directive, file errors, such as opening a file that does not exist, cause a run-time error that stops the program. The {$I-} directive tells Turbo Pascal to record any errors in the variable IOResult and continue with the rest of the program.

The first step in copying the file is to open the source file for reading. Before you can open any file in a Turbo Pascal program, you must associate the filename with a file type variable. The CopyFile procedure uses the Assign procedure to associate the source filename with the variable Source. Next it uses the Turbo Pascal Reset procedure to open the file for reading. The second argument of the Reset procedure is the number of bytes in a record. Because you do not know the size of records in the file, this routine sets the record size to one byte.

If the Reset routine cannot find the filename associated with Source, it puts an error code in IOResult. CopyFile first checks for an error and prints a message if there is one. If the source file was successfully opened, then CopyFile tries to open the destination file.

Before it opens the destination file, CopyFile checks if the name of the destination file ends in a backslash ('\'). The backslash indicates that the destination file is a directory and that the source filename should be added to the destination name to make the complete destination filename.

The Assign procedure associates the destination file name with the variable Destination. This file must be created, or replaced if it exists, so the Turbo Pascal ReWrite procedure is used instead of Reset.

The data is copied in a repeat-while loop containing the Turbo Pascal routines BlockRead and BlockWrite. The BlockRead statement uses the sizeof function to get the size of the array Buffer (1024 bytes). When the program reads the last block of data from the file, it will contain less than 1024 bytes. BlockRead puts the actual number of bytes read in the variable ReadCnt. This variable is passed to BlockWrite to specify the number of bytes to write. It is also used to determine when all of the file has been copied.

After the data is copied, the source and destination files are closed to tell MS-DOS that the program is finished with the files so that it can write the directory information for the files to the disk.

Comments

You can include this routine in a Turbo Pascal unit of file I/O routines. Then you can use it in programs by adding the name of the unit to the uses statement. The solution for question 2.5 shows one use of the copy routine.

Warnings

This routine cannot deal with trying to write to a directory, overwriting an existing file, or filling up the disk. Since I/O error handling is turned off by the {$I-} directive, file errors are not displayed.

Enhancements

The larger the buffer, the faster this routine runs. The reason is that a larger buffer means fewer calls to BlockRead and BlockWrite. The trade-off, of course, is that a larger buffer leaves less room for other things in memory.

If you are using this routine to back up files on floppy disks, there is another way to improve performance. It is simply this: Don't copy the file if the destination file has the same time/date stamp as the source file. The time date stamps are identical if the source file has not been changed since the last time the file was copied.

To test this condition, add the variables CopyOK : boolean, SFTime : Longint, and DFTime and substitute this code for the rewrite procedure call:

```
CopyOK := TRUE;
Reset( Destination, 1 )            {Try to open an existing file}
if IOResult = 0 then               {The file exists}
begin
     GetTime( Destination, DFTime );
     GetTime( Source, SFTime );
     if SFTime <= DFTime then       {If source is older}
          CopyOK := FALSE;              {Don't copy}
     else                          {Otherwise create the file}
          Rewrite( Destination, 1 );
     if CopyOK then
          { Put the copy loop here }
     end;
```

In this routine the Turbo Pascal procedure GetTime gets the MS-DOS time stamp from the source and destination files. If the source file is older than or the same age as the destination file, then the program sets the variable CopyOK to FALSE. CopyOK is used to determine whether or not the copy should be made.

Move a file to another directory with a Turbo Pascal program?

Description
To get a file from one directory to another you can copy the file, then delete the source file. A more efficient way is to leave the file where it is on the disk and move the directory entry from the source directory to the destination directory.

See Also
2.1   Copying files
2.5   Using the file manager

Solution
The MS-DOS Rename routine moves a file from one directory to another if the paths of the source and destination files are different. Turbo Pascal includes the Rename procedure to call the MS-DOS rename routine. To use this Turbo Pascal procedure to move a file you must assign a file variable to the source file and create a string variable that includes the new path and the name of the file. The following code shows you how:

```
procedure MoveFile( FileName, DestPath : string );
var
   DPath : PathStr;          {The name of the final file}
   DDir : DirStr;            {The directory part of the source}
   DName : NameStr;          {The name part of the source}
   DExt : ExtStr;            {The extension part of the source}
   FHand : file;             {File variable for the source}
begin
   {Associate the source file}
   Assign( FHand, FileName );
   {Make sure there is a '\' at the end of the
    destination path}
   if DestPath[Length( DestPath )] <> '\' then
      DestPath := DestPath + '\';
   {Get the parts of the source filename}
   FSplit( FileName, DDir, DName, DExt );
   {Add the filename to the destination path}
   DPath := DestPath + DName + DExt;
   Rename( FHand, DPath );
end;
```

MoveFile moves the file given in FileName to the directory in DestPath. The Turbo Pascal Rename procedure requires that you associate the file to be renamed with a `file` type variable. For this reason, `MoveFile` first uses `Assign` to associate the filename with the variable `FHand`. The next step is to make the final name for the file.

Figure 2-1 shows the various parts of an MS-DOS pathname. The destination name for the `MoveFile` routine consists of the `DestPath` supplied by the calling routine and the filename portion of the source filename. This name, along with the `FHand` variable, is passed to `Rename`, which actually moves the file.

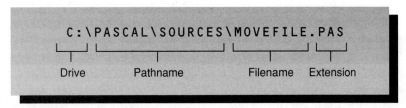

Figure 2-1 The parts of a filename

Comments

You should add `MoveFile` to the file I/O unit you started in question 2.1. The program in question 2.5 shows you how to use `MoveFile` in a program.

Warnings

This routine does not check if the file already exists in the destination directory. If so, you get a run-time error that stops the program.

Enhancements

`MoveFile` will not move a file from one drive to another. The reason is that a file on a disk must appear in a directory on that disk. The Turbo Pascal `Rename` procedure moves only the directory entry from one directory to another, it does not move the file. To move a file from one drive to another, you have to copy it. The following function shows how to check if the source file and the destination file are on the same drive. The file manager in question 2.5 uses this information to determine if it should use `MoveFile` or `CopyFile` to move a file.

```
function SameDrive( Source, Dest : string ) : boolean;
var
      FullSrc : string;
```

```
        FullDest : string;
begin
        {Get a fully qualified path for the source}
        FullSrc := FExpand( Source );
        {And for the destination}
        FullDest := FExpand( Dest );
        {Return the result of comparing the first letters}
        SameDrive := FullSrc[1] = FullDest[1];
end;
```

The Turbo Pascal function FExpand makes sure that the filename string is the complete path for the file. For example, if you use just a filename with routines such as Assign and Rename, Turbo Pascal assumes that you want the file with that name in the current directory. In this case, FExpand adds the name of the current directory to the beginning of the filename. In the preceding function, FExpand makes sure that the filename includes the letter of the drive containing the file. SameDrive compares the drive letters of the two drives and returns the result of that comparison.

2.3   How do I...

List files with a Turbo Pascal program?

Description

Many programs need to know the names of all the files that are available. One reason is to make a list to show to the user. Another reason is to perform some operation on all of the files in the directory, for instance search all of the files for a text string, compress all files, or translate the files to a new format.

See Also

2.5   Using the file manager

Solution

The Turbo Pascal procedures FindFirst and FindNext make it easy to look at all of the files in a directory, as this procedure shows:

```
procedure ListFiles( Pattern : string );
var
   DirInfo : SearchRec;
   Name : string[20];
begin
    FindFirst( Pattern, AnyFile, DirInfo ); {Get the first file}
    while DosError = 0 do          {While there is a file}
    begin
```

```
      Name := DirInfo.Name;        {Get the name of the file}
                                    {And pad it with spaces}
      while Length( Name ) < 20 do
          Name := Name + ' ';
                                    {Display the name and file size}
      WriteLn( Name, DirInfo.Size );
      FindNext( DirInfo );         {Get the next file}
   end;
end;
```

First, ListFiles calls the Turbo Pascal procedure FindFirst to get the first file in the directory that matches the pattern. The pattern is a string that may contain the MS-DOS wildcard characters "*" and "?" The asterisk matches any number of characters in the file name and the question mark matches a single character.

The while loop tests the variable DosError, which is set by FindFirst and FindNext to tell when all of the files have been found. Inside the while loop, ListFiles gets the filename from the structure set up in FindFirst and FindNext.

Comments

The FindFirst and FindNext procedures use a structure called SearchRec defined in the DOS unit. This structure contains information about the last file found and the state of the file search. This is its format:

```
type
      SearchRec = record
             Fill          : array[1..21] of byte;
             Attr          : byte;
             Time          : longint;
             Size          : longint;
             Name          : string[12];
      end;
```

In this structure, Fill is miscellaneous information used by MS-DOS. Attr contains flags that tell what type of file it is. Time is the time the file was created. Size is the size of the file in bytes, and Name is the name of the file.

You can search for files with only certain attributes by modifying the value of the second argument to FindFirst. The values to pass to FindFirst match those that can be found in the Attr field of the SearchRec record. Here are the constants you can use:

```
const
      ReadOnly     = $1;
      Hidden = $2;
      SysFile      = $4;
```

```
VolumeID      = $8;
Directory     = $10;
Archive       = $20;
AnyFile       = $3F;
```

Notice that there is no constant for regular files. The reason is that the search always includes regular files. If you want to look only at files with a particular attribute, you must check the attribute field of the SearchRec record before accepting the file.

Warnings

The file search routines require that the SearchRec structure not be changed from one call to the next. If you use these routines, be sure that you do not modify the SearchRec structure yourself.

Enhancements

By making the FileList procedure recursive you can make it list all of the files in the current directory and any subdirectories. A recursive routine is one that calls itself to do its job. For example, when the ListFiles routine encounters a subdirectory while searching the directory, it can change to the subdirectory, then call itself to find the files in the subdirectory.

This function uses recursion to list all of the files on a disk:

```
procedure ListSubdirs( Pattern : string; Level : integer );
var
        DirInfo : SearchRec;
        Name : string[20];
        i : integer;
        PatLen : integer;
begin
        FindFirst( Pattern, AnyFile, DirInfo ); {Get the first file}
        PatLen := Length( Pattern ) - 2;{Where to put sub-dir names}
        while DosError = 0 do
        begin
                {Format the file name}
                Name := DirInfo.Name;
                while Length( Name ) < 20 do
                        Name := Name + ' ';
                {Print tabs for the level}
                for i := 0 to Level do
                    Write( Chr( 9 ));
                {Print the name and the file size}
                WriteLn( Name, DirInfo.Size );
                {See if the file is a subdirectory}
                if (( DirInfo.Attr AND Directory ) <> 0 ) AND
                        ( DirInfo.Name[1] <> '.' ) then
```

```
begin
        {If so, insert the directory name}
        Name := DirInfo.Name + '\';
        Insert( Name, Pattern, PatLen );
        {And call recursively}
        ListSubdirs( Pattern, Level + 1 );
        {After listing remove the subdir name}
        Delete( Pattern, PatLen, Length( Name ));
    end;
    FindNext( DirInfo );
  end;
end;
```

ListSubDirs uses the same basic procedure to read directories as ListFile does. Code has been added to keep track of the name of the directory being searched and to call itself recursively to search subdirectories.

The Pattern argument includes the pathname of the directory to search. When ListSubDirs comes to a directory, it uses the Turbo Pascal routine Insert to insert the name of the subdirectory into the pattern just before the "*.*". It uses this new pattern when it calls itself to list the subdirectory. After listing the subdirectory, the Turbo Pascal routine Delete removes the subdirectory name from the pattern so that it can be used with the next subdirectory.

2.4   How do I...

List all available disk drives with a Turbo Pascal program?

Description
Install programs often provide a list of drives and let the user pick one. It would be counterproductive to present a list of drives containing devices that did not actually exist. Because different computers can have different numbers of drives installed, (in a network, a single computer can have different numbers of drives at different times) programs that list the drives need to be able to ask MS-DOS what drives are available.

See Also
2.3   Listing files
2.5   Using the file manager

Solution

MS-DOS has a built-in routine to give the number of drives on the computer. This routine is unreliable because it never reports a number less than five. Also, certain networks do not report all of the network drives to MS-DOS, and these are not included in the count. To find out which drives exist, you have to check each of the possible drives to see if it is really there.

The easiest way to check for the presence of a drive is to attempt to make it the current drive. The MS-DOS change drive routine checks low-level device drivers to see if the drive really exists. If the drive does not exist, the change drive routine fails, and there is no change in which drive is designated as current. So, all you have to do is try to make each of the possible drives the current drive and see if any change takes place. This procedure uses this technique to print a list of drives:

```
procedure ListDrives;
var
    CurDrive : byte;
    TestDrive : byte;
    Regs : Registers;
begin
    Regs.AH := $19;          {Get current disk drive}
    MsDos( Regs );
    CurDrive := Regs.AL;
    for TestDrive := 0 to 25 do
    begin
        Regs.AH := $E;       {Select a new current drive}
        Regs.DL := TestDrive;
        MsDos( Regs );
        Regs.AH := $19;
        MsDos( Regs );
        if TestDrive = Regs.AL then
            WriteLn( Chr( TestDrive + Ord( 'A' )), ':' );
    end;
    Regs.AH := $E;
    Regs.DL := CurDrive;
    MsDos( Regs );
end;
```

The MS-DOS routine number $19 gets the current disk drive. The drive number is returned in the AL register. Drive number 0 is drive A:, 1 is drive B:, 2 is C:, and so on. The drive number of the current drive is stored in CurDrive. This way you can return to this drive after running the routine.

The MS-DOS routine number $E selects a new current drive. The drive number to test goes in the AL register. If the drive does not exist, the status of the current drive will not change. To see if the drive really changed, ListDrives calls MS-DOS routine $19 to get the current drive. If the result of routine $19 is the same as that of routine $E, the drive exists.

Warnings

This procedure tells you only if the device driver for the selected drive is operating. It does not tell you if the drive can actually be used. The drive may require a diskette, the drive door may be open, or the drive may be off-line for some reason. You have to perform further tests to tell if the drive is actually ready for I/O.

Enhancements

On systems with only one floppy drive, drive B: is actually drive A:. This lets you copy a file from one floppy to another as if you had two floppy drives. The big drawback to this feature is that if your program uses drive B:, the operating system prints "Please insert disk for drive B:" on your nicely formatted screen. If you know that drive B: is mapped to drive A: you can avoid using drive B: and thus avoid the message. Replace the `WriteLn` statement with this statement block to see the current drive mappings:

```
begin
    {Display the drive name}
    Write( Chr( TestDrive + Ord( 'A' )), ':' );
    {Call MS-DOS to find the mapping}
    Regs.AX := $440E;
    Regs.BL := TestDrive + 1;
    MsDos( Regs );
        {If the drive is mapped, print the mapping}
        if Regs.AL <> 0 then
        Write( ' Map ',Chr( Regs.AL+Ord( 'A' ) - 1 ), ':' );
    WriteLn;
end;
```

This routine uses MS-DOS routine `$44` subfunction `$E` (Show drive mapping) to see if a drive is mapped to another. If this routine returns 0, the drive is mapped; otherwise, the value returned specifies the drive to which the current drive is mapped.

2.5   How do I...

Make a file-management program?

Description

A number of commercial utility programs let you look at directories and manipulate files. Perhaps you have used one of these programs and found that it is missing a feature or two that would make it more useful to you. If so, you can pester the software author until your feature is added, or you can write your own file manager and add whatever features you like.

See Also

Solution

The following program is a crude example of a file manager. It can show files from different directories, copy and rename files, and delete selected files. You can use it as a starting point to design your own full-featured file manager.

This program assumes that you have put the routines from questions 1.3 into a Turbo Pascal unit called FileIO.

```
{This is a simple file-management program}
program FileMan;
uses Scr, Crt, Dos, FileIO;

var
        Cmnd : char;
        Running : boolean;
        FirstFile : integer;

{Write the file information on the screen}
procedure ShowFiles;
var
        FileRec : SearchRec; {Record for FindFirst/FindNext}
        Line : integer;        {The line to write on}
        FileCnt : integer;    {The number of files found}
        DirCnt : integer;     {The number of directories found}
        DataSize : longint;   {The total size of all the files}
        CurDir : string;      {The current directory}
begin
        {Blank out all of the fields}
        for Line := 6 to 21 do
        begin
                GotoXY( 3, Line );
                FillChars( $720, 75 );
        end;
        GotoXY( 22, 2 );
        Write( '                        ' );
        GotoXY( 10, 3 );
        Write( '       ' );
        GotoXY( 33, 3 );
        Write( '        ' );
        GotoXY( 52, 3 );
        Write( '        ' );
    GotoXY( 66, 3 );
    Write( '          ' );
```

```
{Find the first file}
FindFirst( '*.*', AnyFile, FileRec );
Line := 6;
FileCnt := 0;
DirCnt := 0;
DataSize := 0;
{While there are more files}
while DosError = 0 do
begin
    {Count directories and files}
    if (FileRec.Attr AND Directory) <> 0 then
       Inc( DirCnt )
     else
       Inc( FileCnt );
    {Keep track of the total size}
    DataSize := DataSize + FileRec.Size;
    {If not at the bottom of the screen and
    past the first file number}
    if ( Line < 22 ) AND (( FileCnt+DirCnt ) >= FirstFile ) then
    begin
       {Write the filename}
       GotoXY( 3, Line );
       Write( FileRec.Name );
       {Write the file size}
       GotoXY( 20, Line );
       Write( FileRec.Size );
       {Write the data and time stamp}
       GotoXY( 30, Line );
       {Month}
       Write(( FileRec.Time SHR 21 ) AND $F : 2, '/' );
       {Day}
       Write( (FileRec.Time SHR 16 ) AND $1F : 2, '/' );
       {Year}
       Write( (FileRec.Time SHR 25 ) + 80 : 2, ' ' );
       {Hour}
       Write( (FileRec.Time SHR 11 ) AND $1F : 2, ':' );
       {Minute}
       Write(( FileRec.Time SHR 5 ) AND $3F : 2, ':' );
       {Second}
       Write(( FileRec.Time AND $1F ) * 2 : 2 );
       {Write the file attributes}
       GotoXY( 50, Line );
       if ( FileRec.Attr AND ReadOnly ) <> 0 then
          Write( 'R ' );
       if ( FileRec.Attr AND Hidden ) <> 0 then
          Write( 'H ' );
       if ( FileRec.Attr AND SysFile ) <> 0 then
          Write( 'S ' );
       if ( FileRec.Attr AND VolumeID ) <> 0 then
         Write( 'V ' );
      if ( FileRec.Attr AND Directory ) <> 0 then
         Write( 'D ' );
```

```
            if ( FileRec.Attr AND Archive ) <> 0 then
               Write( 'A ' );
            Inc( Line );
      end;
      FindNext( FileRec );
      end;
         {Get the current directory}
         GetDir( 0, CurDir );
         TextAttr := $F;
         GotoXY( 22, 2 );
         Write( CurDir );
         GotoXY( 10, 3 );
         Write( FileCnt );
         GotoXY( 33, 3 );
         Write( DirCnt );
         GotoXY( 52, 3 );
         Write( DataSize );
         GotoXY( 66, 3 );
         Write( DiskSize( 0 ));
         TextAttr := $7;
end;

{Write the static text on the screen}
procedure ShowBack;
begin
         ClrScr;
         GotoXY( 1, 1 );
         DrawBox( 25, 80 );
         GotoXY( 33, 1 );
         Write( ' File Manager ' );
         GotoXY( 3, 2 );
         Write( 'Current directory: ' );
         GotoXY( 3, 3 );
         Write( 'Files:       Subdirectories:       ' );
         Write( 'Bytes used:        Disk:' );
         GotoXY( 1, 4 );
         Write( Chr( $CC ));
         FillChars( ( TextAttr * 256 + $CD ), 77 );
         Write( Chr( $B9 ));
         GotoXY( 5, 5 );
         Write( 'Name         Size      ' );
         Write( 'Date/time stamp     Attributes' );
         GotoXY( 1, 22 );
         Write( Chr( $CC ));
         FillChars( ( TextAttr * 256 + $CD ), 77 );
         Write( Chr( $B9 ));
         GotoXY( 3, 23 );
         Write( 'Copy Rename Delete Set directory ' );
         Write( 'Next page Previous page Quit' );
         GotoXY( 3, 23 );
         SetAttrs( $F, 1 );
         GotoXY( 8, 23 );
         SetAttrs( $F, 1 );
```

```
        GotoXY( 15, 23 );
        SetAttrs( $F, 1 );
        GotoXY( 22, 23 );
        SetAttrs( $F, 1 );
        GotoXY( 36, 23 );
        SetAttrs( $F, 1 );
        GotoXY( 46, 23 );
        SetAttrs( $F, 1 );
        GotoXY( 60, 23 );
        SetAttrs( $F, 1 );
        GotoXY( 3, 24 );
end;

{Get filenames and copy the file}
procedure CopyIt;
var
   SourceName : string;
   DestName : string;
begin
    GotoXY( 3, 24 );
    Write( 'Filename:       ' );
    GotoXY( 14, 24 );
    ReadLn( SourceName );
    GotoXY( 3, 24 );
    Write( 'Destination: ' );
    GotoXY( 16, 24 );
    ReadLn( DestName );
    CopyFile( SourceName, DestName );
    FirstFile := 0;
end;

{Get the filenames and rename the file}
procedure RenameIt;
var
   SourceName : string;
   DestName : string;
   FHand : file;
begin
    GotoXY( 3, 24 );
    Write( 'Filename:       ' );
    GotoXY( 14, 24 );
    ReadLn( SourceName );
    GotoXY( 3, 24 );
    Write( 'New name:        ' );
    GotoXY( 13, 24 );
    ReadLn( DestName );
    Assign( FHand, SourceName );
    Rename( FHand, DestName );
    FirstFile := 0;
end;

{Get a filename and delete it}
procedure DeleteIt;
```

```
var
   FileName : string;
   Regs : registers;
begin
      GotoXY( 3, 24 );
      Write( 'Filename:                              ' );
      GotoXY( 14, 24 );
      ReadLn( FileName );
      FileName := FileName + Chr( 0 );
      Regs.AH := $41;  {MS-DOS delete file function}
      Regs.DS := Seg( FileName );
      Regs.DX := Ofs( FileName ) + 1;
      MsDos( Regs );
      FirstFile := 0;
end;

{Get a directory name and set the current directory}
procedure NewDir;
var
   DirName : string;
begin
      GotoXY( 3, 24 );
      Write( 'Directory:                             ' );
      GotoXY( 14, 24 );
      ReadLn( DirName );
      ChDir( DirName );
      FirstFile := 0;
end;

{Main Program}
begin
    {Draw the background}
    ShowBack;
    FirstFile := 0;
    ShowFiles;
    Running := TRUE;
    while Running do
    begin
       {Get a command from the user}
       GotoXY( 3, 24 );
       Write( 'Command:                           ' );
       GotoXY( 12, 24 );
       ReadLn( Cmnd );
       {Find out what command}
       case Cmnd of
              'C', 'c' : CopyIt;
              'R', 'r' : RenameIt;
              'D', 'd' : DeleteIt;
              'S', 's' : NewDir;
              'N', 'n' : FirstFile := FirstFile + 15;
              'P', 'p' : FirstFile := FirstFile - 15;
              'Q', 'q' : Running := FALSE;
       end;
```

```
    {Repaint the file information}
    ShowFiles;
  end;
end.
```

Despite the size of this listing, it is really quite simple. The first procedure, ShowFiles, prints a list of files from the current directory and some summary information about the directory. Then next procedure, ShowBack, prints all of the static text for the display. These procedures use some of the screen-handling routines from Chapter 1. They have been combined into a unit called Scr. If you do not want to make this unit you can enter the required routines into this file. Figure 2-2 shows the screen after these two procedures are called.

Skip down to the main routine to see the overall logic of the program. The while loop in the main routine gets commands from the user, decodes the command, and calls the routine to execute the command. This loop runs until the user selects the Quit command.

The first command is the Copy command, which calls the procedure CopyIt. This procedure asks the user for the name of the source and destination files, then uses the CopyFile procedure from question 2.1 to copy the file.

```
============================ File Manager ============================
 Current directory: C:\TPHOWTO
 Files: 40    Subdirectories: 2     Bytes used: 555589   Disk: 21309440

    Name        Size      Date/time stamp       Attributes

 ,               0        8/30/90   20:53: 8    D
 ..              0        8/30/90   20:53: 8    D
 CHAP01.DOC    134144     9/24/90   22:18:48    A
 WAITE.DOC      40960     9/ 9/90   16: 8:38    A
 FILEMAN.PAS     7292     9/29/90   16:26:56    A
 MENU.PAS        4698     9/ 8/90   15:58:58    A
 CHAP02.DOC    123392     10/ 7/90  12:49: 6    A
 TERMINAL.PAS     847     10/ 6/90  16:21:48    A
 CHAP10.DOC     20480     9/ 9/90   18:26: 6    A
 ISANSI.PAS      1600     9/18/90   23: 9:10    A
 DATAFORM.PAS    5105     9/24/90   20:42:44    A
 ISANSI.EXE      2320     9/18/90   20:17: 4    A
 CHAPTERX.DOC    1536     9/16/90   16:27: 8    A
 CHAP02.BAK    123392     10/ 7/90  12:47:14    A
 OUTLINE.DOC     8704     9/29/90   14:53:46    A
 CHAP04.DOC      1536     9/16/90   16:27: 8    A

 Copy Rename Delete Set directory Next page Previous page Quit
 Command
```

Figure 2-2 The file manager screen

The RenameIt procedure works the same way as the CopyIt function, but instead of calling CopyFile at the end, it calls Rename. Of course, you cannot pass two filenames to Rename, and so the source file is associated with the file variable FHand.

The next command is Delete, which calls DeleteIt. The procedure uses the MS-DOS file delete routine to delete the file. The trick here is to make the string into an ASCIIZ string as required by MS-DOS. The first step is to append a 0 to the end of the string. This statement does the job:

```
FileName := FileName + Chr( 0 );
```

Next, you have to put the address of the text portion of the string variable into the DS and DX registers. The text portion of a Pascal string is one byte greater than the address of the string.

The last procedure is NewDir. This procedure gets a directory name and uses the Turbo Pascal procedure ChDir to change to that directory.

The last two commands change the portion of the directory that is displayed. The global variable FirstFile tells ShowFiles the number of the first file to display. By changing this number, you can change the list of files on the screen.

Warnings

This program has no tests for I/O errors or nonsense input. It is entirely up to users to make sure they don't delete or overwrite an important file.

Enhancements

The purpose of this program is to get you started designing a file-management program. You can add features according to your needs. Some possibilities are drop-down menus (see Chapter 9), a cursor to select files from the list, a way to select several files to be acted upon, and more commands.

One feature you can add easily is a way to remember the current directory when the program starts and restore it when the program exits. To do this, you need to add a new global string variable to hold the directory name.

```
var
      HomeDir : string;
```

Then call the GetDir procedure at the beginning of the program.

```
GetDir( 0, HomeDir );
```

The 0 tells the GetDir procedure to use the current disk drive. At the end of the program, use the ChDir procedure to restore the directory.

```
ChDir( HomeDir );
```

2.6   How do I...

Search the path for a file with a Turbo Pascal program?

Description

Many programs need parameter files that hold information about options. A critical decision you must make is where on the user's disk to put the parameter file. One simple solution is to put the file in the same directory as the application program. This solution shows how you can find such files by searching PATH just as MS-DOS does when it loads programs.

See Also

2.3   Listing files

5.3   Displaying memory blocks

Solution

Turbo Pascal has two functions that make searching the path easy. The first is GetEnv, which returns MS-DOS environment strings such as PATH. The second is FSearch, which searches a list of directories for a file. The following routine uses these functions to find a file:

```
uses Dos;

function SearchPath( FileName : string ) : string;
begin
      SearchPath := FSearch( FileName, GetEnv( 'PATH' ));
end;
```

Here, the GetEnv function returns the path string from the MS-DOS environment, which is then passed to FSearch along with the filename to look for.

Comments

The string returned by SearchPath is the MS-DOS path that contains the file, concatenated with the filename. For example, if the file MYUTIL.EXE is in the directory C:\UTILS, the result is C:\UTILS\MYUTIL.EXE. If the file is not in any of the directories, then the string is empty.

Warnings

The Turbo Pascal FSearch function searches the current directory before looking at the rest of the path. This may not be a problem, but be aware of this when you use this function.

Enhancements

If this routine does not find the file, you may want to expand the scope of the search. The following routine uses a modified version of the `ListFiles` routine in question 2.3 to search the entire disk for the file:

```
function FindFile( FileName,Pattern:string; Level:integer ):string;
var
   DirInfo : SearchRec;
   Name : string;
   i : integer;
   PatLen : integer;
   FileFound : boolean;
begin
   FileFound := FALSE;
   FindFirst( Pattern, AnyFile, DirInfo ); {Get the first file}
   PatLen := Length( Pattern ) - 2; {Where to put subdir names}
   DosError = 0 ) AND ( NOT FileFound ) do
   begin
       {See if the file is a subdirectory}
       if (( DirInfo.Attr AND Directory ) <> 0 ) AND
          ( DirInfo.Name[1] <> '.' ) then
       begin
           {If so, insert the directory name}
           Name := DirInfo.Name + '\';
           Insert( Name, Pattern, PatLen );
           {And call recursively}
           Name := FindFile( FileName, Pattern, Level + 1 );
           if Name = '' then
              Delete( Pattern, PatLen, Length( Name ))
           else
           begin
              Pattern := Name;
              FileFound := TRUE;
           end;
       end
       else if DirInfo.Name = FileName then
       FileFound := TRUE;
       FindNext( DirInfo );
   end;
   {If the file is found return the pattern}
   if FileFound then
      FindFile := Pattern
   else
      FindFile := '';
end;
```

The difference between this routine and the one in question 2.3 is that, instead of writing the names of all of the files found, this routine checks whether the file matches the supplied name. When the matching file is found, `FindFile` sets the `FileFound` flag to indicate that the search is over. The `FileFound` flag is tested in the main loop so that the program can exit when the file is found.

2.7   How do I...

Use buffers to speed file operations in Turbo Pascal programs?

Description

Turbo Pascal uses an internal 128-byte buffer for Text type files. When your program reads the file, Turbo Pascal gets a 128-byte piece of the file and puts it in this buffer. Because of the way MS-DOS formats disks, it can read much larger amounts of data in about the same time that it can read 128 bytes. The actual time depends on how the disk was formatted and how the file is arranged on the disk. Buffers of about 4096 bytes consistently give much better performance than programs that use smaller buffers.

See Also

2.1   Copying files

Solution

To replace the Turbo Pascal text file buffers with larger buffers you must use `file` type variables in the `Assign` statement instead of `text` type variables. When you do this, you lose the ability to read lines from the file with routines such as `ReadLn`. This solution shows you how to write a routine that you can use in place of `ReadLn` for files with large buffers.

You can think of a buffer as a window into a file. (See figure 2-3). The buffer shows a portion of the whole file. To keep track of what you are looking at, you need to include some other variables that tell you how much and what part of the file is in the buffer.

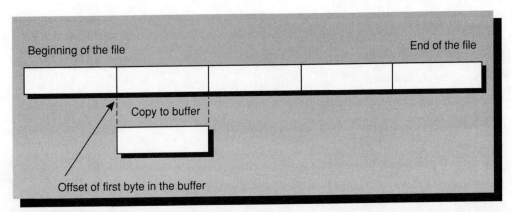

Figure 2-3 A buffer as a window into a file

Before reading or writing the data in the buffer, you must be sure that the buffer contains the part of the file you want to see. If the buffer does not contain the required data, you must read new data from the file into the buffer.

Using object-oriented programming is a good way to organize all of the data and code required for reading and writing buffered files. The key is to use an object that represents a file. This object keeps track of all of the data required and allows you to manipulate file contents, for instance, to read or write a line. You don't need to worry about the fact that this is a buffered file; the object handles such details.

The following routine creates an object to read and write buffered text files:

```
{This is the file I/O unit}
unit FileIO;
interface
type
   BufferedFile = Object
        Name : string;
        Handle : file;
        Dirty : boolean;
        Buffer : array [0..4095] of byte;
        Size : word;
        First : longint;
        FileOffset : longint;
        constructor Init( FileName : string );
        function ReadLine : string;
        procedure WriteLine( Line : string );
        procedure FileSeek( Position : longint );
        function IsEOF : boolean;
        destructor Done;
   end;

implementation

{$I-}
{Initialize the file object}
constructor BufferedFile.Init( FileName : string );
begin
    Name := FileName;
    Assign( Handle, FileName );
    {Open the file if it exists}
    Reset( Handle, 1 );
    {If the file does not exist, create it}
    if IOResult <> 0 then
      ReWrite( Handle, 1 );
    {Put some data into the buffer}
    BlockRead( Handle, Buffer, sizeof( Buffer ), Size );
    Dirty := False;
    First := 0;
```

```
      FileOffset := 0;
end;

{Read a line from the file}
function BufferedFile.ReadLine : string;
var
   TmpStr : string;
   i : integer;
   Result : word;
begin
    {Initialize the string variable}
    TmpStr := '';
    {Get the offset into the buffer}
    i := FileOffset - First;
    {while not at the end of the file or the end of the string}
    while ( Not IsEOF ) AND ( Buffer[i] <> 13 ) do
    begin
        {while not at the end of the buffer or the string}
        while ( i < Size ) AND ( Buffer[i] <> 13 ) do
        begin
            TmpStr := TmpStr + Chr( Buffer[i] );
            Inc( i );
        end;
        {See if at the end of the buffer}
        if i >= Size then
        begin
            {If the buffer is dirty, write it}
            if Dirty then
            begin
                Seek( Handle, First );
                BlockWrite( Handle, Buffer, Size, Result );
            end;
            {Compute the address of the buffer}
            First := First + Size;
            {Read the new buffer}
            Seek( Handle, First );
            BlockRead( Handle,Buffer, sizeof( Buffer ), Size );
            Dirty := False;
            i := 0;
        end;
    end;
    {If at the end of the line, skip the CR and the LF}
    if Buffer[i] = 13 then
       i := i + 2;
    {Compute the new file position}
    FileOffset := First + i;
    ReadLine := TmpStr;
end;

{Write a line to the file}
procedure BufferedFile.WriteLine( Line : string );
var
   i, j : integer;
```

```
    Result : word;
begin
    {Make an index into the buffer}
    i := FileOffset - First;
    j := 1;
    while j < Ord( Line[0] ) do
    begin
        Dirty := True;
        {Copy line to the buffer}
        while ( i<Size ) AND ( j<Ord( Line[0] )) do
        begin
            Buffer[i] := Ord( Line[j] );
            Inc( i );
            Inc( j );
        end;
        {See if at the end of the buffer}
        if i >= Size then
        begin
            {Write the buffer to the file}
            Seek( Handle, First );
            BlockWrite( Handle, Buffer, Size, Result );
            {Compute the address of the buffer}
            First := First + Size;
            {Read the new buffer}
            Seek( Handle, First );
            BlockRead( Handle,Buffer,sizeof( Buffer ),Size );
            Dirty := False;
            i := 0;
        end;
    end;
end;

{Go to a certain location in the file}
procedure BufferedFile.FileSeek( Position : longint );
var
   Result : word;
begin
    {Set fileoffset to the new position}
    FileOffset := Position;
    {See if the position is in the buffer}
    if ( FileOffset < First ) OR ( FileOffset > First + Size ) then
    begin
        {Compute the location of a buffer containing the position}
        First:=( FileOffset DIV sizeof( Buffer ))*sizeof
        ( Buffer );
        {If the buffer is changed, write it}
        if Dirty then
        begin
            Seek( Handle, First );
            BlockWrite( Handle, Buffer, Size, Result );
        end;
        {Read the new buffer}
        Seek( Handle, First );
```

```
        BlockRead( Handle, Buffer, sizeof( Buffer ), Size );
        Dirty := False;
    end;
end;

{Return true when at the end of the file}
function BufferedFile.IsEOF : boolean;
begin
    {See if at the end of the last buffer}
    if ( Size < sizeof( Buffer ))
      AND ( FileOffset - First = Size ) then
      IsEOF := True
    else
      IsEOF := False;
end;

{Flush the buffer and close the file}
destructor BufferedFile.Done;
var
   Result : word;
begin
    {If the buffer is dirty, write it}
    if Dirty then
    begin
        Seek( Handle, First );
        BlockWrite( Handle, Buffer, Size, Result );
    end;
    {Close the file}
    Close( Handle );
end;
{$I+}
end.
```

The BufferedFile object keeps track of all of the required information about the file, such as the name of the file, the File variable to use, and the buffer. The information about the buffer includes the data for the buffer, the location of the buffer in the file, and a flag to indicate when the data in the buffer has been changed but not written to the disk.

The first method in the BufferedFile object is the Init, which opens the file and reads the first part of the file into the buffer. After the Init method opens the file and initializes the object fields, you can use the other methods to read and write the file.

The ReadLine method gets a line of data from the file via the buffer. It starts copying characters from the buffer to the string variable TmpStr until either the whole line is copied or the end of the buffer is reached. If the end of the buffer has been reached, the ReadLine method writes the current buffer. If the data in the buffer has been changed, then it reads the next buffer from the file. When a complete line is copied, the FileOffset pointer is advanced to the beginning of the next line.

To write data to the file, use the `WriteLine` method. This method copies a line of data from a string variable to the buffer. If the string goes beyond the end of the buffer, the buffer is written to the file. After copying the string to the file, the `Dirty` flag is set so that other routines know that the buffer needs to be written.

The `FileSeek` and `IsEOF` methods change and test the position in the file for the next read or write. `FileSeek` changes the `FileOffset` pointer to a specified value. It also makes sure that the current buffer includes the file position indicated by the new `FileOffset` value. `IsEOF` checks if the `FileOffset` pointer is at the end of the file. It works by checking whether the buffer is the last one and whether `FileOffset` points to the last location in this buffer.

Comments

To use this object, begin by including the `FileIO` unit in your program. Then you can declare a `BufferedFile` object variable for the file to use. The first method you should use is `Init`, which opens the file and initializes the fields for the object. Then you can use the other methods as needed to read and write the file. When you are done with the file, call the `Done` method to write the buffer and close the file.

The following program shows how to use the `BufferedFile` object to make a simple text-file display program:

```
{This is a program to display text files}
program display;
uses Scr, Crt, ScreenIO, FileIO;

var
   ListFile : BufferedFile;
   TopLine : longint;
   Running : boolean;
   Cmnd : integer;
   HitBottom : boolean;

{Show the part of the text file}
procedure ShowScreen;
var
   Line    : integer;
   TextLine : string;
begin
    TextAttr := 7;
    Line := 1;
    ListFile.FileSeek( TopLine );
    while ( Line <= 24 ) AND ( NOT ListFile.IsEOF ) do
    begin
        GotoXY( 1, Line );
        TextLine := ListFile.ReadLine;
```

```
          if Ord( TextLine[0] ) > 80 then
             TextLine[0] := Chr( 80 );
          while Ord(TextLine[0]) < 80 do
              TextLine := TextLine + ' ';
          Write( TextLine );
          Inc( Line );
      end;
      HitBottom := ListFile.IsEOF;
end;

{Move the top of screen pointer forward one line}
procedure Forward;
var
   TmpStr : string;
begin
     if NOT HitBottom then
     begin
         {Go to the top of the screen}
         ListFile.FileSeek( TopLine );
         {Move forward one line}
         TmpStr := ListFile.ReadLine;
         {Remember the new location}
         TopLine := ListFile.FileOffset;
     end;
end;

{Move the top of screen backward one line}
procedure Backward;
var
   LastPos : longint;
   TmpStr : string;
begin
     if TopLine > 0 then
     begin
         if TopLine > 100 then
            ListFile.FileSeek( TopLine - 100 )
         else
            ListFile.FileSeek( 0 );
         repeat
             LastPos := ListFile.FileOffset;
             TmpStr := ListFile.ReadLine;
         until ListFile.FileOffset = TopLine;
         TopLine := LastPos;
     end;
end;

begin
    {Open the file and load the buffers}
    ListFile.Init( ParamStr( 1 ));
    TopLine := 0;
    HitBottom := False;
    {Get commands}
    Running := True;
```

```
    while Running do
    begin
        {Show a screen full of the file}
        ShowScreen;
        {Show the prompt}
        TextAttr := $F;
        GotoXY( 1, 25 );
        write( 'Command: ' );
        {Get a key from the user}
        Cmnd := GetKey;
        case Cmnd of
            $1071, $11B : Running := FALSE;
            $50E0 : Forward;
            $48E0 : Backward;
        else
            write( Cmnd );
        end;
    end;
end.
```

The first procedure in this program, ShowScreen, uses a BufferedFile object to read 24 lines from the file and write them on the screen. It uses the variable TopLine to indicate the position in the file of the first line. When all of the lines are written, ShowScreen checks whether the end of the file has been reached. If so, it sets the HitBottom flag to TRUE.

The Forward procedure advances the TopLine variable by one line. To do this, it uses the FileSeek method to go to the current TopLine position, then reads a line, and finally copies the new file position to TopLine.

The third procedure, Backward, moves the TopLine variable back one line. It uses FileSeek to move back enough bytes to ensure that it is past the previous line. Then Backward uses ReadLine to read forward until it gets back to the position of TopLine. At this point, the position of the last line read is the new location of TopLine.

The main program gets a filename from the command line (see question 5.2) and uses the name to initialize the BufferedFile object ListFile. Then it gets keys from the user to see what to do. The user can press the Up Arrow and Down Arrow keys to move around in the file, or press the Esc key to end the program. Before exiting, the program calls the Done method to close the file.

Warning

When you write to a BufferedFile object, the data stays in memory until the object needs to load a new buffer or the program calls the Done method. If your program does not call the Done method or crashes before calling it, you can lose all of the data in the buffer. In the preceding examples, this can be as much as 4096 bytes.

Read/write/append a file with variable-length records in Turbo Pascal programs?

Description

It is simple to read and write fixed-length, random-access records with Turbo Pascal. You can set the record size in the `Reset` or `Rewrite` statement and then use `Seek` to go to the record number. To compute the location of the record in the file, Turbo Pascal multiplies the record length by the record number. If the records are of variable length, you cannot directly compute the address of any record in the file. This solution shows how to find records by adding a record table to the database file.

See Also

2.9   Indexing files

Solution

To use a database with variable-length records, you need to know where each record starts and how long it is. You can keep all of this information in a simple table at the beginning of the file. To find a given record, you look it

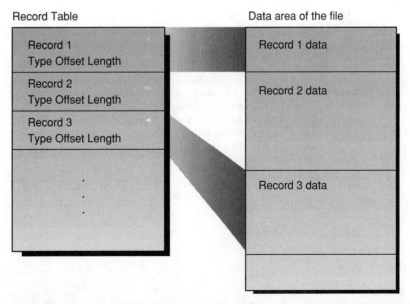

Figure 2-4 File with a table and variable-length records

up in the table and get the starting position and length of the record. Figure 2-4 shows a file laid out this way.

When creating a variable-length record, the program begins by looking for an unused entry in the table. Then, the program puts the location of the new record into the previously unused table entry. While searching for an unused entry, the program can also look for a deleted record that is large enough to hold the new record. If it doesn't find a suitable deleted record, the program puts the record at the end of the file.

The following unit implements an object that describes a data file with records of variable length:

```
{Random-access file I/O unit}
unit RandFile;
interface
type
    {An entry in the record table}
    TabEntry = record
            RecType : byte;
            RecSize : integer;
            RecOffset : longint;
    end;

    {The file object}
    VFilePtr = ^VariableFile;
    VariableFile = object
        Table : array [0..511] of TabEntry;
        First : longint;
        TableAt : longint;
        TabDirty : boolean;
        NextTab : longint;
        Handle : file;
        NewFile : boolean;
        constructor Init( FileName : string );
        function AddRec( var Rec; Len : integer ) : longint;
        procedure ReadRec( var Rec; RecNo : longint );
        procedure WriteRec( var Rec; RecNo : longint );
        procedure DelRec( RecNo : longint );
        procedure ChangeTable( RecNo : longint );
        destructor Done;
    end;

implementation

const
    UNUSED  = 1;
    DELETED = 2;
    ACTIVE  = 3;

{$I-}
{Initialize the variable record file object}
```

```
constructor VariableFile.Init( FileName : string );
var
   i : integer;
begin
    {Associate the filename with a handle}
    Assign( Handle, FileName );
    {Try for existing file}
    Reset( Handle, 1 );
    {if error, create the file}
    if IOResult <> 0 then
    begin
        ReWrite( Handle, 1 );
        {Create a new table}
        NextTab := -1;
        for i:=0 to 511 do
            Table[i].RecType := UNUSED;
        {Write the new table to the file}
        BlockWrite( Handle, NextTab, sizeof( longint ));
        BlockWrite( Handle, Table, sizeof( Table ));
        NewFile := True;
    end
    else       {The file exists}
    begin
        {Read the record table from the file}
        BlockRead( Handle, NextTab, sizeof( longint ));
        BlockRead( Handle, Table, sizeof( Table ));
        NewFile := False;
    end;
    TableAt := 0;
    First := 0;
    TabDirty := False;
end;
{$I+}

{Add a new record to the file}
function VariableFile.AddRec( var Rec; Len:integer ):longint;
var
   i, j : integer;
   RecFound : boolean;
   RecAt : longint;
begin
    {Look for an available entry}
    RecAt := -1;
    RecFound := False;
    i := 0;
    while Not RecFound do
    begin
        {When an unused record is found, use it}
        if Table[i].RecType = UNUSED then
        begin
            {Make entry for the new record}
            Table[i].RecType := ACTIVE;
            Table[i].RecSize := Len;
```

```
            if RecAt = -1 then
               Table[i].RecOffset := FileSize( Handle )
            else
                Table[i].RecOffset := RecAt;
            RecFound := True;
            TabDirty := True;
         end
         {If a suitable deleted record has not been found, check
         deleted records}
         else if ( Table[i].RecType=DELETED ) AND ( RecAt=-1 ) then
         begin
            {If the deleted record has exactly the right size, use it}
            if Table[i].RecSize = Len then
            begin
                Table[i].RecType := ACTIVE;
                RecFound := True;
                TabDirty := True;
            end
            {If the deleted record is larger, use the space}
            else if Table[i].RecSize < Len then
            begin
                {Reduce the size of the deleted record by
                the size of the new record}
                Table[i].RecSize := Table[i].RecSize - Len;
                {Save the location of the available space}
                RecAt := Table[i].RecOffset+Table[i].RecSize;
            end;
            {If an entry has not been found, go to the next entry}
            if Not RecFound then
            begin
                Inc( i );
                if i >= 512 then
                   ChangeTable( First + 512 );
            end;
         end
         else
         begin
            Inc( i );
            if i >= 512 then
               ChangeTable( First + 512 );
         end;
      end;
   {Write the new record to the file}
   Seek( Handle, Table[i].RecOffset );
   BlockWrite( Handle, Rec, Len );
   AddRec := First + i;
end;

{Read a record from the file}
procedure VariableFile.ReadRec( var Rec; RecNo : longint );
var
   i : integer;
begin
```

```
    {Be sure that the correct table is loaded}
    ChangeTable( RecNo );
    {Compute the index into the table}
    i := RecNo - First;
    {Verify that the record exists before reading}
    if Table[i].RecType = ACTIVE then
    begin
        Seek( Handle, Table[i].RecOffset );
        BlockRead( Handle,Rec,Table[i].RecSize );
    end;
end;

{Write a record to the file}
procedure VariableFile.WriteRec( var Rec; RecNo : longint );
var
   i : integer;
begin
    {Be sure that the correct table is loaded}
    ChangeTable( RecNo );
    {Compute the index into the table}
    i := RecNo - First;
    {Verify that the record exists before writing}
    if Table[i].RecType = ACTIVE then
    begin
        Seek( Handle, Table[i].RecOffset );
        BlockWrite( Handle,Rec,Table[i].RecSize );
    end;
end;

{Delete a record from the file}
procedure VariableFile.DelRec( RecNo : longint );
var
   i : integer;
begin
    {Load the correct table}
    ChangeTable( RecNo );
    i := RecNo - First;
    {Mark the record as deleted}
    if Table[i].RecType = ACTIVE then
       Table[i].RecType := DELETED;
end;

{Load the table for the indicated record}
procedure VariableFile.ChangeTable( RecNo : longint );
var
   i : integer;
begin
    {If the record number is less than the beginning of the
    current table}
    if RecNo < First then
    begin
        {If the table has changed write it}
        if TabDirty then
```

```
        begin
            Seek( Handle, TableAt );
            BlockWrite( Handle, NextTab, sizeof( longint ));
            BlockWrite( Handle, Table, sizeof( Table ));
            TabDirty := False;
        end;
        {Read the first table for the file}
        First := 0;
        TableAt := 0;
        Seek( Handle, TableAt );
        BlockRead( Handle, NextTab, sizeof( longint ));
        BlockRead( Handle, Table, sizeof( Table ));
    end;
    {See if the record is beyond the end of the table}
    while ( RecNo >= First + 512 ) AND ( NextTab <> -1 ) do
    begin
        {Write the table if it changed}
        if TabDirty then
        begin
            Seek( Handle, TableAt );
            BlockWrite( Handle, NextTab, sizeof( longint ));
            BlockWrite( Handle, Table, sizeof( Table ));
            TabDirty := False;
        end;
        {Load the next table in the chain}
        Seek( Handle, NextTab );
        TableAt := NextTab;
        First := First + 512;
        BlockRead( Handle, NextTab, sizeof( longint ));
        BlockRead( Handle, Table, sizeof( Table ));
    end;
    {Check for past the end of the last table}
    if RecNo >= First + 512 then
    begin
        {Create a new table at the end of the file}
        NextTab := FileSize( Handle );
        Seek( Handle, TableAt );
        BlockWrite( Handle, NextTab, sizeof( longint ));
        BlockWrite( Handle, Table, sizeof( Table ));
        TabDirty := False;
        for i:= 0 to 511 do
            Table[i].RecType := UNUSED;
        TableAt := NextTab;
        NextTab := -1;
        Seek( Handle, TableAt );
        BlockWrite( Handle, NextTab, sizeof( longint ));
        BlockWrite( Handle, Table, sizeof( Table ));
    end;
end;

{Close the database}
destructor VariableFile.Done;
begin
```

```
    {If the table changed, write it}
    if TabDirty then
    begin
        Seek( Handle, TableAt );
        BlockWrite( Handle, NextTab, sizeof( longint ));
        BlockWrite( Handle, Table, sizeof( Table ));
        TabDirty := False;
    end;
    Close( Handle );
end;
```

The methods for this object let programs create, delete, read, and write variable-length records to a file. The `Init` method opens the data file and initializes the variables for the object. First, `Init` tries to open an existing file. If that fails, it uses the Turbo Pascal procedure `ReWrite` to create a new file. When `Init` creates a file, it also creates a new record table and writes it at the beginning of the file. If the file already exists, `Init` reads the table at the beginning of the file.

The `AddRec` method creates a new record of any length in the file. The `while` loop in this method looks at each entry in the record table to find an available place in the table for the new entry, and space in the file for the data. `AddRec` checks each entry to see if it is unused or if it contained a deleted record. If the entry is unused, `AddRec` uses the entry for the new record. If the entry contained a deleted record, `AddRec` looks at the record size to see if it is greater than or equal to the size of the new record. If the size is sufficient, `AddRec` uses that entry for the new record.

If the deleted record is larger than the new record, `AddRec` uses enough of the deleted record to hold the new record. In this case, the deleted entry is changed to show the new size of the deleted record, and the location of the deleted record is stored in `RecAt` so that it will be used when an unused entry is found.

The `while` loop keeps searching until it finds an unused entry. If it gets to the end of the table in memory, it uses the `ChangeTable` method to load the next table. When a table is written to the file, the program also writes the offset in the file of the next table. `ChangeTable` uses these offsets to search through the file for the correct table. The last table has a next table offset of -1. When `ChangeTable` sees this -1, it creates a new table at the end of the file.

The `ReadRec` and `WriteRec` methods start by calling `ChangeRec` to make sure that the table that holds the entry for the record to be read or written is in memory. Next they check the entry in the table to make sure that the record is active, then they read or write the record, as appropriate. The `DeleteRec` method differs from the `ReadRec` and `WriteRec` methods in that it marks the entry as deleted instead of reading or writing the record.

Comments

The `RandFile` unit makes using a file with records of random length as easy as using a file with records of fixed length. The first step is to use the `Init` method to open the file, then use `AddRec`, `ReadRec`, and `WriteRec` to manipulate the records in the file. When the program is finished with the file, it calls the `Done` method to close the file. This program shows how the `RandFile` unit works:

```pascal
{Program to demonstrate variable-length record files}
program FileDemo;
uses RandFile;

var
   DataFile : VariableFile;
   TmpStr : string;
   DataStr : string;
   RecNo : longint;

begin
    {Open the file}
    DataFile.Init( 'sample.dat' );
    repeat
        {Get a command}
        Write( 'Enter command N)ew, R)ead, D)elete, E)xit: ' );
        ReadLn( TmpStr );
        if Length( TmpStr ) <> 0 then
        begin
            if ( TmpStr[1] = 'N' ) OR ( TmpStr[1] = 'n' ) then
            begin
                {Get the data to save}
                Write( 'Enter text: ' );
                ReadLn( DataStr );
                {Add a new record holding the data}
                RecNo := DataFile.AddRec( DataStr
                    , Length( DataStr ) + 1 );
                {Show the record number}
                WriteLn( 'Created record number ', RecNo );
            end
            else if ( TmpStr[1]='R' ) OR ( TmpStr[1]='r' ) then
            begin
                Write( 'Enter record number: ' );
                ReadLn( RecNo );
                {Read the requested file}
                DataFile.ReadRec( DataStr, RecNo );
                WriteLn( 'The data is: ', DataStr );
            end
            else if ( TmpStr[1]='D' ) OR ( TmpStr[1]='d' ) then
            begin
                Write( 'Enter record number: ' );
                ReadLn( RecNo );
                {Delete the record}
```

```
            DataFile.DelRec( RecNo );
        end;
    end;
    until ( TmpStr[1] = 'E' ) OR ( TmpStr[1]='e' );
    DataFile.Done;
end.
```

The Init method opens the file sample.dat, then FileDemo gets user commands to see what records should be created, read, and deleted. The repeat-until loop gets single-letter user commands until the user enters an E, for exit. The records used in this program are user-entered strings.

Warnings

The current record table remains in memory until a new table is needed or until the Done method closes the file. If you don't call the Done method, changes made to the table are not saved. The table is the only way of knowing where records begin and end in the file; if the table is incorrect, the file is unusable.

When a record is deleted, the space it occupied is still in the middle of the disk space occupied by the file. That space is used again when you create a record that is the same size or smaller. When you delete a small record its space may never be used again because no record will fit in it. You may have several kilobytes of unusable space scattered throughout the file's disk space; this is called *fragmentation*. If your program often creates and deletes records from a file, you may want to write a utility that reads the records from the active file and adds them to a less active file. Then you can erase the active file to recover the disk space.

2.9   How do I...

Create an indexed file with Turbo Pascal?

Description

When a database reaches a certain size, it is no longer practical to look at every record in the file to find a particular one. You need a way to look up records according to a key word, phrase, or number. This solution shows how to create index records in a file with records of variable length. These index records contain keys and record numbers you use to look up the record that matches the key.

See Also

2.8   Creating a variable-length database file

Solution

One way to make an index is simply to make a list of all of the keys with the record numbers. To look up a record, a program searches the list until it finds the key. The drawback to this technique is that it takes time to search long lists. In a list of 5000 records the average search takes about four minutes if the average time it takes to test a key is one-tenth of a second.

To reduce the search time for a key, you need to eliminate some of the searches. Solution 4.3 shows how to use a binary search to reduce the average number of tests in a 5000-entry list to less than 13. To perform a binary search, however, the computer must sort the list. Because it takes time to sort the list, there may be no time savings at all.

The idea behind the binary search is to divide the list in half, then search only the half that contains the key. By continuing to divide the list in half, you can quickly eliminate most of the keys without actually looking at them. You can narrow the search even quicker by dividing the list into many pieces, and finding a way to search only the piece with the required key. The program in this solution divides the list of keys into several parts, then makes a list of the starting keys for each part. If the new list is too long to fit into a memory buffer, it is divided in the same way as the original list, and yet another list of pointers is created. This process is repeated until the pointer list is small enough to fit in the buffer. Figure 2-5 shows this structure.

If the buffer can hold a list of 10 keys and there are 5000 keys in the file, the tree structure is three levels deep. Each level can be searched in an aver-

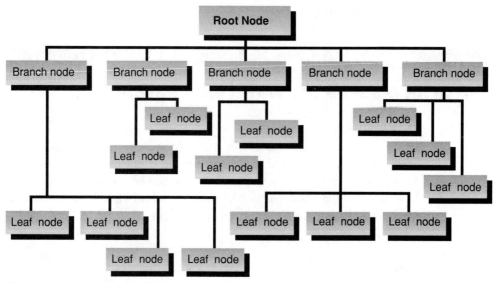

Figure 2-5 A tree of keys

age of five comparisons, and so it takes an average of 15 comparisons to find a key. Because only 30 items need to be resorted (each of the three 10-item lists) when you add a new record, this technique is much faster than the binary search.

The following unit implements an object that represents a tree of key records. This unit should be in the same source file as the file-handling unit from question 2.8. The file-handling routines from question 2.8 are used to store the nodes used in this object.

```
{Random access file I/O unit}
unit RandFile;
interface
   BTreeBase = record
           KeySize : integer;
           RootNode : longint;
   end;
   BTreeNode = record
           ParentNode : longint;
           KeyCnt : integer;
           NodeType : byte;
           KeyBlock : array [0..504] of byte;
   end;
   BTree = object
       DataFile : VFilePtr;
       Base : BTreeBase;
       NodeNumb : longint;
       CurNode : BTreeNode;
       constructor Init( FilePtr : VFilePtr; KSize : integer );
       procedure AddKey( Key : string; RecNo : longint );
       function LookUp( Key : string ) : longint;
       procedure NewKey( Key : string; Recno : longint );
       procedure GetKeyRec( index : integer;
               var Key : string; var RecNo : longint );
       procedure SetKeyRec( index : integer;
               Key : string; RecNo : longint );
       procedure DelKey( Key : string );
   end;
implementation

const
   LEAF = 1;
   BRANCH = 2;

var
   TmpBlock : BTreeNode;        {Scrap key tree node}

{Initialize an index tree}
constructor BTree.Init( FilePtr : VFilePtr; KSize : integer );
var
   RecNo : longint;
begin
```

```
    DataFile := FilePtr;
    if FilePtr^.NewFile then
    begin
        {Get the first record in the file}
        RecNo := FilePtr^.AddRec( Base, sizeof( Base ));
        CurNode.ParentNode := -1;
        CurNode.KeyCnt := 0;
        CurNode.NodeType := LEAF;
        Base.KeySize := KSize;
        {Create the root node}
        Base.RootNode
              :=FilePtr^.AddRec( CurNode, sizeof( CurNode ));
        FilePtr^.WriteRec( Base, 0 );
    end
    else
    begin
        FilePtr^.ReadRec( Base, 0 );
        FilePtr^.ReadRec( CurNode, Base.RootNode );
    end;
    NodeNumb := Base.RootNode;
end;

{Add a new key to the index tree}
procedure BTree.AddKey( Key : string; RecNo : longint );
var
   LastNode : longint;
   i : integer;
   TmpStr : string;
   TmpNode : longint;
   Found : boolean;
begin
    {Make sure that the root node is in memory}
    LastNode := -1;
    if Base.RootNode <> NodeNumb then
    begin
        DataFile^.ReadRec( CurNode, Base.RootNode );
        NodeNumb := Base.RootNode;
    end;
    {Find the correct leaf node for this key}
    while CurNode.NodeType <> LEAF do
    begin
        {Check each entry in the node}
        i := 0;
        Found := False;
        while ( i < CurNode.KeyCnt ) AND ( Not Found ) do
        begin
            {Get the key from the node}
            GetKeyRec( i, TmpStr, TmpNode );
            {Exit when the node key is greater than the search key}
            if TmpStr > Key then
               Found := True
            else
               Inc( i );
```

```
        end;
        {Back up to the last key less than the key
        we are looking for}
        if i > 0 then
        begin
           Dec( i );
           GetKeyRec( i, TmpStr, TmpNode );
        end;
        {Go to the indicated node}
        LastNode := NodeNumb;
        DataFile^.ReadRec( CurNode, TmpNode );
        NodeNumb := TmpNode;
        {Make sure parent links are correct}
        if CurNode.ParentNode <> LastNode then
        begin
            CurNode.ParentNode := LastNode;
            DataFile^.WriteRec( CurNode, NodeNumb );
        end;
    end;
    {Put the new key into the current block}
    NewKey( Key, RecNo );
end;

{Insert a key record into the specified node, return location}
function InsertRec( var TmpBlock : BTreeNode
        ; Key : string; RecNo : longint; KeySize : integer ) : integer;
var
   Found : boolean;
   i : integer;
   TmpStr : string;
   TmpNode : longint;
   KeyRecLen : integer;
begin
    {Compute the length of a key record}
    KeyRecLen := KeySize + sizeof( longint );
    InsertRec := i;
    i := 0;
    Found := False;
    {Look for the spot to insert the key}
    while ( i < TmpBlock.KeyCnt ) AND ( Not Found ) do
    begin
        {Get key data}
        Move( TmpBlock.KeyBlock[i * KeyRecLen], TmpStr,
            KeySize );
        Move( TmpBlock.KeyBlock[i * KeyRecLen + KeySize]
            , TmpNode
            , sizeof( longint ));
        if TmpStr > Key then
           Found := True
        else
           Inc( i );
    end;
    {Open a space for the new key}
```

```
    if i < TmpBlock.KeyCnt then
    Move( TmpBlock.KeyBlock[ i* KeyRecLen]
        , TmpBlock.KeyBlock[( i + 1 ) * KeyRecLen]
        , ( TmpBlock.KeyCnt- i )*KeyRecLen );
    {Save the new key record}
    Move( Key, TmpBlock.KeyBlock[i * KeyRecLen], KeyRecLen );
    Move( RecNo
        , TmpBlock.KeyBlock[i * KeyRecLen + KeySize]
        , sizeof( longint ));
    Inc( TmpBlock.KeyCnt );
    InsertRec := i;
end;

{Add a key to the current node, splitting if needed}
procedure BTree.NewKey( Key : string; Recno : longint );
var
  MaxKeys : integer;
  KeyRecLen : integer;
  i, Split : integer;
  LastNode : longint;
  TmpNode : longint;
  TmpStr : string;
  Found : boolean;
begin
    KeyRecLen := Base.KeySize + sizeof( longint );
    MaxKeys := sizeof( CurNode.KeyBlock ) DIV KeyRecLen;
    {See if the node is not full}
    if MaxKeys > CurNode.KeyCnt then
    begin
        {Put the new key into the node}
        i := InsertRec( CurNode, Key, RecNo, Base.KeySize );
        DataFile^.WriteRec( CurNode, NodeNumb );
        {If the  first item changed, fix the parent}
        while ( i = 0 )  AND ( CurNode.ParentNode <> -1 ) do
        begin
            LastNode := NodeNumb;
            {Go to the parent node}
            NodeNumb := CurNode.ParentNode;
            DataFile^.ReadRec( CurNode, NodeNumb );
            {Search for the node entry}
            i := 0;
            Found := False;
            while ( i < CurNode.KeyCnt ) AND ( Not Found ) do
            begin
                GetKeyRec( i, TmpStr, TmpNode );
                {Compare node numbers to find the matching entry}
                if TmpNode = LastNode then
                begin
                    {Change the entry}
                    SetKeyRec( i, Key, TmpNode );
                    DataFile^.WriteRec( CurNode, NodeNumb );
                    Found := True;
                end;
```

```
        end;
      end;
end
else {Split the node}
begin
    {Make the second node}
    TmpBlock := CurNode;
    Split := MaxKeys DIV 2;
    Move( TmpBlock.KeyBlock[Split*KeyRecLen]
          , TmpBlock.KeyBlock[0]
          , ( TmpBlock.KeyCnt - Split ) * KeyRecLen );
    TmpBlock.KeyCnt := TmpBlock.KeyCnt - Split;
    CurNode.KeyCnt := Split;
    {Get the key at the split}
    Move( TmpBlock.KeyBlock[0], TmpStr, Base.KeySize );
    {See if in the first or second block}
    if TmpStr >= Key then
       i := InsertRec( CurNode,Key,RecNo,Base.KeySize )
    else
       i := InsertRec( TmpBlock,Key,RecNo,Base.KeySize );
    {Write the modified node}
    DataFile^.WriteRec( CurNode, NodeNumb );
    {Add a new node for the second half}
    TmpNode:=DataFile^.AddRec( TmpBlock,sizeof( TmpBlock ));
    {If this was the root node, create a parent}
    if CurNode.ParentNode = -1 then
    begin
        CurNode.NodeType := BRANCH;
        CurNode.KeyCnt := 2;
        {Fix the node pointer for the first node}
        Move( NodeNumb
              , CurNode.KeyBlock[Base.KeySize]
              , sizeof( longint ));
        {Add a pointer for the second node}
        Move( TmpBlock.KeyBlock[0]
              , CurNode.KeyBlock[KeyRecLen]
              , Base.KeySize );
        Move( TmpNode
              , CurNode.KeyBlock[KeyRecLen+Base.KeySize]
              , sizeof( longint ));
        NodeNumb := DataFile^.AddRec( CurNode
                  , sizeof( CurNode ));
        Base.RootNode := NodeNumb;
        DataFile^.WriteRec( Base, 0 );
    end
    else {Add an entry to the parent node}
    begin
        {Load the parent node}
        NodeNumb := CurNode.ParentNode;
        DataFile^.ReadRec( CurNode, NodeNumb );
        {Add the new key to the parent block}
        Move( TmpBlock.KeyBlock[0], TmpStr, Base.KeySize );
        NewKey( TmpStr, TmpNode );
```

```
        end;
     end;
end;

{Find a key in the index tree}
function BTree.LookUp( Key : string ) : longint;
var
   i : integer;
   TmpStr : string;
   TmpNode : longint;
   Found : boolean;
begin
    if Base.RootNode <> NodeNumb then
    begin
        DataFile^.ReadRec( CurNode, Base.RootNode );
        NodeNumb := Base.RootNode;
    end;
    {Find the correct leaf node for this key}
    while CurNode.NodeType <> LEAF do
    begin
        i := 0;
        Found := False;
        {Search for the first key greater than the target key}
        while ( i < CurNode.KeyCnt ) AND ( Not Found ) do
        begin
            GetKeyRec( i, TmpStr, TmpNode );
            if TmpStr > Key then
              Found := True
            else
                Inc( i );
        end;
        if i > 0 then
        begin
          Dec( i );
          GetKeyRec( i, TmpStr, TmpNode );
        end;
        {Read the indicated node}
        DataFile^.ReadRec( CurNode, TmpNode );
        NodeNumb := TmpNode;
    end;
    {Search the leaf node for the key}
    i := 0;
    Found := False;
    while ( i < CurNode.KeyCnt ) AND (Not Found ) do
    begin
        GetKeyRec( i, TmpStr, TmpNode );
        if TmpStr >= Key then
          Found := True
        else
            Inc( i );
    end;
    {Return the record number for an exact match}
    if TmpStr = Key then
```

```
        LookUp := TmpNode
    else {Return closest match with negative sign}
    begin
        GetKeyRec( i - 1, TmpStr, TmpNode );
        LookUp := - TmpNode;
    end
end;

{Get a key record from the current node}
procedure BTree.GetKeyRec( index : integer;
    var Key : string; var RecNo : longint );
var
  Pos : integer;
begin
    Pos := index * (Base.KeySize + sizeof( longint ));
    Move( CurNode.KeyBlock[Pos], Key, Base.KeySize );
    Move( CurNode.KeyBlock[Pos + Base.KeySize]
            , RecNo, sizeof( longint ));
end;

{Set a key record in the current node}
procedure BTree.SetKeyRec( index : integer;
    Key : string; RecNo : longint );
var
  Pos : integer;
begin
    Pos := index * ( Base.KeySize + sizeof( longint ));
    Move( Key, CurNode.KeyBlock[Pos], Base.KeySize );
    Move( RecNo, CurNode.KeyBlock[Pos+Base.KeySize]
            , sizeof( longint));
end;

{Remove a key from an index tree}
procedure BTree.DelKey( Key : string );
var
  i : integer;
  TmpStr : string;
  TmpNode : longint;
  KeyRecLen : integer;
  Found : boolean;
begin
    if Base.RootNode <> NodeNumb then
    begin
        DataFile^.ReadRec( CurNode, Base.RootNode );
        NodeNumb := Base.RootNode;
    end;
    {Find the correct leaf node for this key}
    while CurNode.NodeType <> LEAF do
    begin
        i := 0;
        Found := False;
        while ( i < CurNode.KeyCnt ) AND ( Not Found ) do
        begin
```

```
            GetKeyRec( i, TmpStr, TmpNode );
            if TmpStr > Key then
               Found := True
            else
                Inc( i );
        end;
        if i > 0 then
        begin
          Dec( i );
          GetKeyRec( i, TmpStr, TmpNode );
        end;
        DataFile^.ReadRec( CurNode, TmpNode );
        NodeNumb := TmpNode;
    end;
    i := 0;
    Found := False;
    while ( i < CurNode.KeyCnt ) AND ( Not Found ) do
    begin
        GetKeyRec( i, TmpStr, TmpNode );
        if TmpStr >= Key then
           Found := True
        else
            Inc( i );
    end;
    {if a match found, delete it}
    if TmpStr = Key then
    begin
        KeyRecLen := Base.KeySize + sizeof( longint );
        if i+1 < CurNode.KeyCnt then
          Move( CurNode.KeyBlock[( i+1 ) * KeyRecLen]
             , CurNode.KeyBlock[i * KeyRecLen]
             , ( CurNode.KeyCnt-i ) * KeyRecLen );
        Dec( CurNode.KeyCnt );
        DataFile^.WriteRec( CurNode, NodeNumb );
    end;
end;

end.
```

The record BTreeNode shows the format of each node in the tree of keys. The NodeType field tells you whether the node is a branch node or a leaf node. In branch nodes, the numbers that go with each key are the record numbers of other nodes; in leaf nodes, the numbers are the record numbers of a data record. The ParentNode field lets the AddKey method work its way back down the tree when it needs to update parent nodes. KeyCnt is the number of keys in the node, and KeyBlock is the keys and record numbers in the node.

KeyBlock is an unstructured array of bytes allowing different key files to have keys of different sizes. The methods GetKeyRec and SetKeyRec let programs read and write individual key records in the KeyBlock.

The `AddKey` method puts a new key in the tree. The first step is to find the leaf node of the key to be added. The search begins at the root node of the tree. `AddKey` searches the sorted key list in the node to find the last key that is less than the search key. The record number of that key is the next node to read. The process continues until `AddKey` finds a leaf node. `AddKey` inserts the new key into the leaf node just before the first key greater than the search key. This keeps the node in sorted order. If the key is inserted into the first spot in the node, the parent node must be updated. This ensures that each entry in a parent node is the first entry in the child nodes.

`AddKey` also modifies the parent node if the child node is full. In this case, it splits the child node into two nodes of equal size. The key at the beginning of the resulting second node is inserted into the parent node. This operation is recursive because adding a node to the parent may fill it, requiring the parent node to be split as well.

The `LookUp` method searches in just the same way as the `Addkey` method does to find the leaf node containing the key. If it doesn't find the key, `LookUp` returns a negative number whose magnitude is the record number of the closest match. The `DelKey` method looks up keys in just the same manner as `AddKey` and `LookUp`. Then it removes the key from the node.

Comments

Before using `BTree` objects, you must initialize a `VariableFile` object in which the `BTree` object can store nodes. The first thing that you should do with a `VariableFile` object that contains a `BTree` is to call the `BTree.Init` method. The reason is that the first record in the file must be the base record of the `BTree` object; otherwise, the `BTree` object cannot find the record when it needs it.

The following program shows how to create and use a data file that uses keys to find records:

```
{Program to demonstrate index files}
program FileDemo;
uses RandFile;

var
   DataFile : VariableFile;
   IndxFile : BTree;
   TmpStr : string;
   DataStr : string;
   RecNo : longint;

begin
   DataFile.Init( 'index.dat' );
```

```
    IndxFile.Init( @DataFile, 50 );
    repeat
        Write( 'Enter command N)ew, R)ead, D)elete, E)xit: ' );
        ReadLn( TmpStr );
        if Length( TmpStr ) <> 0 then
        begin
            if ( TmpStr[1] = 'N' ) OR ( TmpStr[1] = 'n' ) then
            begin
                Write( 'Enter text: ' );
                ReadLn( DataStr );
                RecNo := DataFile.AddRec( DataStr
                    , Length( DataStr ) + 1 );
                WriteLn( 'Created record number ', RecNo );
                Write( 'Enter key: ' );
                ReadLn( DataStr );
                IndxFile.AddKey( DataStr, RecNo );
            end
            else if ( TmpStr[1] = 'R' ) OR ( TmpStr[1] = 'r' ) then
            begin
                Write( 'Enter key: ' );
                ReadLn( DataStr );
                RecNo := IndxFile.LookUp( DataStr );
                if RecNo > 0 then
                begin
                    DataFile.ReadRec( DataStr, RecNo );
                    WriteLn( 'The data is: ', DataStr );
                end
                else
                    WriteLn( 'No Data found' );
            end
            else if ( TmpStr[1] = 'D' ) OR ( TmpStr[1] = 'd' ) then
            begin
                Write( 'Enter key: ' );
                ReadLn( DataStr );
                RecNo := IndxFile.LookUp( DataStr );
                DataFile.DelRec( RecNo );
                IndxFile.DelKey( DataStr );
            end;
        end;
    until ( TmpStr[1] = 'E' ) OR ( TmpStr[1] = 'e' );
    DataFile.Done;
end.
```

Unlike the program in question 2.8, this one asks the user to enter a key. When users create a record, they enter a key that AddKey adds to the BTree object. To read or delete a record, the user enters the key for the record, and the program uses the lookup method to find the record number.

PRINTERS

2.10   How do I...

Send a page of text to the printer with Turbo Pascal?

Description

One way to send text to a printer is to open the print device driver as a file and use the Turbo Pascal `Write` procedure to write the data to the printer. The drawbacks to this technique have to do with the limits of a sheet of paper. Your print routine should ensure proper margins all around the text. Also, when printing a long line, you should break the line between words, not in the middle of words. This solution shows how to create margins around printed text and split lines at word boundaries.

See Also

2.7   Using buffers to speed file operations

2.12   Checking if printer is ready

Solution

Most printers can use a monospaced font for printing text. Each character in a monospaced font takes up the same amount of space on the page. This makes it easy to compute the number of characters and lines you can fit on a page. For example, if your printer prints 10 characters per inch horizontally and 6 lines per inch vertically, you can fit 85 characters per line and 66 lines on a standard 8.5"-by-11" sheet of paper. To allow for margins, you can subtract characters from these dimensions to arrive at the size of the printed area.

To create a top margin, a program prints linefeed characters at the top of the page. It creates the left margin by printing spaces before each line. The program creates a right margin by printing only the precomputed number of characters per line or less. The bottom margin is created by sending a formfeed after the precomputed number of lines is printed.

The program in this solution reads a text file into a buffer, 1024 bytes at a time. It copies characters from this buffer until it gets a whole word. Then it checks whether that word, if printed, would go beyond the end of the line. If not, the program prints the word by writing to the Lst device defined in the Turbo Pascal unit Printer. If the word is too long, the program prints a carriage return and linefeed to move to the next line before printing the word.

```
{This program sends a file to the printer}
program PFILE;
uses Printer;

var
   Buffer : array[1..1024] of byte;
   BuffSize: integer;
   BuffPoint : integer;
   Ch : byte;
   CurLine : integer;
   CurCol : integer;
   PageNumb : integer;
   FileRec : file;
   NextWord : string;
   Running : boolean;
   WordState : integer;
   TextCnt : integer;

const
    PageLines = 66;
    PageCols = 80;

begin
    {Open the text file specified}
    Assign( FileRec, ParamStr( 1 ));
    Reset( FileRec, 1 );
    {Initialize page position variables}
    CurLine := 0;
    CurCol := 0;
    PageNumb := 1;
    {Initialize buffer variables}
    BuffPoint := 1025;
    BuffSize := 1024;
    Running := TRUE;
    while Running do
    begin
        {If at the bottom of a page}
        if CurLine = PageLines - 6 then
        begin
            {Send form feed}
            write( Lst, Chr( 13 ), Chr( 12 ));
            CurLine := 0;
        end;
        {If at the top of a page}
        if CurLine = 0 then
        begin
            {Print page number and advance three lines}
            FillChar( NextWord, PageCols DIV 2, ' ' );
            NextWord[0] := char( PageCols DIV 2 - 1 );
            write( Lst, NextWord, PageNumb, Chr( 10 )
                    , Chr( 10 ), Chr( 10 ), Chr( 13 ) );
            Inc( PageNumb );
            CurLine := 4;
```

```
end;
{Prepare to read a word from the buffer}
WordState := 1;
NextWord := '';
TextCnt := 0;
{While not at the end of a word}
while Running AND ( WordState <> 3 ) do
begin
    {See if more data from the file is needed}
    if BuffPoint = BuffSize + 1 then
    begin
        if BuffSize <> 1024 then
          Running := FALSE
        else
        begin
          BlockRead( FileRec, Buffer, 1024, BuffSize );
          BuffPoint := 1;
        end;
    end;
    if Running then
    begin
        {Get the next character from the buffer}
        Ch := Buffer[BuffPoint];
        {If white space}
        if ( Ch = 32 ) OR ( Ch = 9 ) OR ( Ch = 13 )
          OR ( Ch = 10 ) then
        begin
            {Go to state 2}
            if WordState = 1 then
              WordState := 2
            else if ch=10 then {End the word on LF}
                WordState := 3;
            {Add the white space to the word}
            NextWord := NextWord + Chr( Ch );
            Inc( BuffPoint );
        end
        else {Non-white space}
        begin
            {If in state 2, we have a word}
            if WordState = 2 then
              WordState := 3
            else {Otherwise add to the word}
            begin
                NextWord := NextWord + Chr( Ch );
                Inc( BuffPoint );
                Inc( TextCnt );
            end;
        end;
    end;
end;
{See if the word fits on the line}
if (TextCnt <= PageCols)
  AND ( CurCol + TextCnt >= PageCols ) then
```

```
    begin
        write( Lst, Chr( 13 ), Chr( 10 ));
        Inc( CurLine );
        CurCol := 0;
    end;
    {Write the word}
    Write( Lst, NextWord );
    if NextWord[Length( NextWord )] = Chr( 10 ) then
    begin
        Inc( CurLine );
        CurCol := 0;
    end;
    CurCol := CurCol + Length( NextWord );
  end;
  Write( Lst, Chr( 13 ), Chr( 12 ));
  Close( FileRec );
end.
```

Before printing the first line on a page, this program prints the page number at the top of the page and three linefeeds, creating the top margin. After printing all but three of the available lines, the program sends a formfeed to go to the next page, creating the bottom margin.

The left margin is made by aligning the paper so that the left limit of the print head is indented from the left edge of the paper. If this is not possible with your printer, you need to print spaces before each line.

You need to make sure that the line breaks between words, not in the middle of a word. To break lines on a word boundary, the program copies a word at a time from the file buffer. All of the white space following the word is considered part of the word. If the current position on the line plus the length of the word minus the white space are less than the width of the line, the word is printed. Otherwise, the program sends a carriage return and a line-feed before printing the word.

Warnings

Many programs format the text into word-wrapped lines before writing the text to a file by adding carriage returns and linefeeds to each line. If this is the case, and the margins are smaller than those in this program, it breaks each line again. The result is a page with a single word on every other line. Similar problems can occur when the file contains embedded formfeeds to signal page breaks.

If the format of text files created by other applications is compatible with your printer, you can copy the file to the printer, and you don't need to use this program. Otherwise, you will have to write another program to remove the formatting before using this program to format the file.

Enhancements

The program PFILE assumes that your printer is using a monospaced font. If you look closely at the text type in this book, you will see that each character has a different width. This is called a proportional font. Printers using proportional fonts move the print head a distance that is proportional to the width of the character just printed. For example, the print head moves a small distance after printing an *i*, and the print head moves farther after printing a *w*. Also notice that in some character combinations, such as *Va* and *fi*, the characters overlap slightly. These combinations are called *kerned pairs* or *ligatures*, respectively.

If your printer is set up to print proportional fonts and kerned pairs, you have to be more sophisticated about how you measure the length of each word and the line. In this case, make the PageCols variable use some other unit besides characters. For example, if you use 1/100ths of a inch, an 8.5"-by-11" sheet of paper is 850 units wide. Then you need a table that gives the width of each character in the printer's character set. The printer manufacturer may supply this information, or you can determine it experimentally. To avoid having to make exact measurements of small characters, print several characters in a row, measure the row, and divide by the number of characters.

Kerning requires another table that contains all of the ligatures in the printer's character set. This table should give the width of the complete ligature. When you add character widths to determine the length of the word, you must check the kerning table first to see if any two adjacent characters in the word make up a ligature. If so, use the ligature width; otherwise, use the widths of the two individual characters.

This technique is not easy; you must know the exact dimensions of each character used by your printer. Microsoft Windows programs can get information about fonts by asking Windows for *font metrics*. The problem is that the Windows font must match the printer font exactly; otherwise, a Windows program cannot format the text properly. If you have used different fonts with Windows word processors you may have seen the effects of incorrect font metrics.

2.11   How do I...

Print forms with Turbo Pascal?

Description

When you send output to a monitor, you can display data at any screen location, and in any order. Most printers do not give you these options. The data at the top left of the page must be printed first, and you must continue from left to right and top to bottom.

Another problem is lining up the printer with the preprinted blanks on printed forms. This is especially frustrating when you try to print forms that are not designed for use with computer printers.

See Also

2.10   Sending data to printer

2.12   Checking if printer is ready

Solution

The first step to printing a form is to collect all of the data to print. The following code segment defines the data structures used for this:

```
type
    Field = record
        Row   : integer;              {The row for the data}
        Col   : integer;              {The column}
        Text  : string[40];           {The text to print}
    end;
    Form = array[1..100] of Field;    {An array of fields}
```

A program can fill in the fields of a `Form` array to indicate what data should be printed. It can do this in any convenient order because the procedure to print the fields sorts them before printing. Then the procedure sends commands to the printer to position the paper and print head before printing each of the fields. The commands are specific to the HP LaserJet and DeskJet printers.

```
procedure PrintForm( var Data : Form; Count : integer );
var
   i, j, h : integer;
   v : Field;
begin
    {Shell sort the fields}
    h := 1;
    repeat
        h := 3 * h + 1;
    until h > Count;
    repeat
```

```
       h := h DIV 3;
       for i := h + 1 to Count do
       begin
           v := Data[i];
           j := i;
           while (( Data[j - h].Row > v.Row ) OR
               (( Data[j - h].Row = v.Row ) AND
               ( Data[j - h].Col > v.Col ))) AND
               ( j > h ) do
           begin
               Data[j] := Data[j - h];
               j := j - h;
           end;
           Data[j] := v;
       end
    until h = 1;
    {Print the sorted fields}
    for i := 1 to Count do
    begin
        {Move to the specified row}
        Write( Lst, Chr( 27 ), '&a', Data[i].Row,'R' );
        {Move to the specified column}
        Write( Lst, Chr( 27 ), '&a', Data[i].Col,'C' );
        {Print the data}
        Write( Lst, Data[i].Text );
    end;
    {Send a CR and a formfeed}
    Write( Lst, Chr( 13 ), Chr( 12 ) );
end;
```

Comments

This procedure uses a shell sort, which is similar to the familiar bubble sort except that instead of comparing items that are next to each other it compares items that are at various intervals from each other. The interval is large at first and decreases as the sort progresses. For this reason, items can be moved in big steps during early stages of the sort. As the interval decreases, items are moved to precisely where they belong. This sort is easy to implement and efficient enough for this purpose.

Once the array is sorted, it is a simple matter to print each of the fields. This routine uses the positioning commands of Hewlett-Packard's Printer Command Language (PCL) to move from one field to another. An alternative is to keep track of the last position printed and print enough linefeeds and spaces to move the print head to the next field.

Warnings

This routine does not check to see if fields overlap. Different printers react differently to overlapping fields. Many simply print the second field on top of the first, creating an illegible mess. Others do not allow you to move the print head backward on the line. In this case, the two fields are printed one after the other. The program that puts data in the `Form` array should make sure that the printed fields fit on the form and that they do not overlap.

Enhancements

On forms not designed for computer printers, the lines where data is supposed to go are often placed where the print head can't move. Or your computer output may be designed to be printed eight lines per inch, and your printer may print at six lines per inch. To solve problems like these, you have to be creative in moving the print head.

The first step is to express your row and column parameters in units that are more precise than lines and characters. For example, you could specify the position in 1/300ths of an inch. Now that you can specify the position more accurately, you need a way to tell the printer where to print. This is where the creativity comes into play. Check your printer's programming manual to see what positioning commands are available. HP's PCL includes commands for moving the print head 1/300th of an inch at a time.

Other printers have commands to change the line pitch or to advance half a line. You can use combinations of these commands to move the print head as close as possible to the desired position.

2.12   How do I...

Check whether the printer is ready?

Description

It takes time for the computer to get the data ready to print, and printing itself is often slow. Most people like to leave the computer while it performs these tasks. It can be very frustrating to come back after awhile only to find that, because the printer was off or not online, nothing was printed. This solution is a routine that checks if the printer is ready before you send data to be printed.

See Also

1.12   Using the keyboard BIOS

Solution

BIOS uses interrupt $17 to communicate with printers connected to parallel ports. The three functions for this interrupt are: send a character (AH = 0), reset the printer (AH = 1), and check the status. All three of these routines

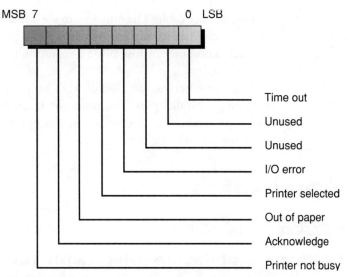

MSB 7   0 LSB

Time out

Unused

Unused

I/O error

Printer selected

Out of paper

Acknowledge

Printer not busy

Figure 2-6 Format of the printer status byte

return the status of the printer in the AH register. Figure 2-6 shows the format of this status byte.

The program in this section uses this BIOS call to check on the printer:

```
{Find the status of the printer}
program printer;
uses Dos;

var
   Regs : registers;
begin
    Regs.AH := 2;                    {Get printer status}
    Regs.DX := 0;                    {Use LPT1:}
    Intr( $17, Regs );               {Call BIOS}
    if ( Regs.AH AND $10 ) = 0 then
        WriteLn( 'The printer is not ready' );
end.
```

Comments

You can make this routine into a function that returns the status, or you could just put this code into your program before your printing routine. You may want to use some of the other status bits to tell the user why the printer is unavailable. This saves users the trouble of checking all of the possibilities.

Warnings

In certain cases, this routine returns incorrect information. It won't work correctly with printers that don't supply the paper-out and deselected signals in the interface cable. The only way to see if this kind of printer is ready is to send it a character and see if the character is acknowledged. A similar case exists for computers whose BIOS does not fully support the Get Printer status function.

The printer status BIOS calls work only for printers connected to the computer's parallel port. You must check serial printers by looking at the line-status registers on the serial port. See questions 2.13 and 2.14 for more information on using serial ports.

SERIAL PORTS

2.13   How do I...

Make a serial device driver with Turbo Pascal?

Description

The MS-DOS device driver for serial ports (COM1) does a good job of sending data, but it can lose data sent at high speeds. You could write a Turbo Pascal program to overcome this difficulty, but then you would not be able to use the Turbo Pascal procedures Read and Write with the serial port. This solution shows how to write a Turbo Pascal text device driver that allows you to access your serial port as a standard device.

See Also

2.14   Making a simple terminal emulator

8.2   Using ring buffers

Solution

Turbo Pascal device drivers consist of six routines contained in a Turbo Pascal unit. The header for this unit must show the name of the initialization procedure in the interface section. The initialization procedure works like the Assign procedure for normal text files. It also puts the address of the other device driver routines into the Text structure. The structure of the unit looks like this:

```
{This is a serial port device driver}
unit Serial;
interface
uses Dos;
procedure AssignCom( var F: Text; IOPort, Baud, WordSize : word;
Parity : char; Stops : word );
implementation
```

```
{$R-,S-}

{Global variables}

{$F+}  {All these routines must be "far"}
{Support routines}

{Read routine}

{Write routine}

{Flush routine}

{Close routine}

{Ignore routine}

{Open routine}

{$F-}

{Initialization procedure}

end.
```

The initialization routine, AssignCom, sets up the Text structure for the serial device and initializes the serial port for a given I/O port, baud rate, word size, parity, and number of stop bits. The I/O port is the number of the first I/O port used by the desired serial port. For COM1 this port is usually $3F8 and for COM2 it is $2F8. The rest are standard serial parameters, which must match those of the device connected to the serial port.

```
procedure AssignCom( var F: Text; IOPort, Baud, WordSize : word;
Parity : char; Stops : word );
var
   Divisor : word;
   Params : word;
begin
   {Initialize the TextRec structure}
   with TextRec( F ) do
   begin
      {Set the handle to -1 ( Closed state )}
      Handle := $FFFF;
      {Mark the device as closed}
      Mode := fmClosed;
      {Set the size of the buffer used}
      BufSize := Sizeof( Buffer );
      {Save the location of the buffer}
      BufPtr := @Buffer;
      {Save the address of the open device function}
      OpenFunc := @ComOpen;
      {Make the name blank}
```

```
        Name[0] := #0;
    end;
    {Save the IOPort in a global variable}
    ComPort := IOPort;
    {Determine the divisor to use for the desired baud rate}
    case Baud of
        110    : Divisor := $417;
        150    : Divisor := $300;
        300    : Divisor := $180;
        600    : Divisor := $C0;
        1200   : Divisor := $60;
        2400   : Divisor := $30;
        4800   : Divisor := $18;
        9600   : Divisor := $C;
        19200  : Divisor := $6;
        38400  : Divisor := $3;
    end;
    {Make the parameter byte to send to the UART}
    Params := WordSize - 5 + Stops * 4;
    case Parity of
        'E' : Params := Params + $18;
        'O' : Params := Params + $8;
    end;
    {Send the baud rate divisor and parameters to the UART}
    Port[IOPort + 3] := Port[IOPort + 3] OR $80;
    Port[IOPort] := Byte( Divisor AND $FF );
    Port[IOPort + 1] := Byte( Divisor DIV $FF );
    Port[IOPort + 3] := Params;
end;
```

The AssignCom procedure puts the address of the device open routine, ComOpen, into the Text structure. When your program calls the Turbo Pascal Reset or Rewrite procedures, they in turn call the ComOpen routine. The ComOpen routine finishes setting up the serial port by defining a serial interrupt handler and telling the serial port to generate interrupts when it receives a character. It also sets up the flush, I/O, and close routines for the device.

```
{Open routine}
function ComOpen( var F: TextRec ): integer;
begin
    {Finish setting up the Text structure}
    with F do
    begin
        {If this is a Reset operation}
        if Mode = fmInput then
        begin
            {Make the I/O function read the port}
            InOutFunc := @ComInput;
            FlushFunc := @ComIgnore;
            {Set up the serial data interrupt}
            Head := 0;
```

```
            Tail := 0;
            GetIntVec( $C, OldVect );
            SetIntVec( $C, @ComInt );
            Port[ComPort + 4] := $F;
            Port[ComPort + 1] := 1;
            Port[$21] := Port[$21] AND $EF;
            {Make the close function clean up the interrupt}
            CloseFunc := @ComClose;
        end
        else   {Must be a Rewrite operation}
        begin
            Mode := fmOutput;
            {Make the I/O function send data}
            InOutFunc := @ComOutput;
            FlushFunc := @ComOutput;
            {The close function does nothing}
            CloseFunc := @ComIgnore;
        end;
    end;
    ComOpen := 0;
end;
```

When calling the open routine, the Reset procedure sets up a serial interrupt service routine. This routine is called whenever the serial chip receives a character. (See question 1.14 for more information on interrupt service routines.) The serial interrupt service routine puts the character into a ring buffer, where the read routine can access it. (See question 8.2 for more information on ring buffers.)

```
{Global data}
var
   ComPort : word;
   IntBuffer : array[0..4095] of char;
   Head, Tail : integer;
   OldVect : pointer;

{Intercept serial interrupts}
procedure ComInt;
interrupt;
begin
    {Get the character}
    IntBuffer[Head] := Char( Port[ComPort] );
    Head := ( Head + 1 ) AND $FFF;          {Adjust the Head pointer}
    Port[$20] := $20;                       {Send EOI}
end;
```

The Turbo Pascal Read and ReadLn procedures first call the flush function to see if there is a flush operation to be performed, then they call the I/O routine to get the data. In this device driver, the flush function does nothing. The I/O routine for reading was set to ComRead in the open routine. When data comes in at the serial port, the serial interrupt service routine puts the data into the ring buffer. The `ComRead` function checks the ring buffer to see if there is any data available and if so returns in the `Text` structure the data it finds in the buffer.

```
{Used for closing output files and flushing input files}
function ComIgnore( var F: TextRec ): integer;
begin
    ComIgnore := 0;
end;

{Get input data from the ring buffer}
function ComInput( var F: TextRec ) : integer;
var
  P : word;
begin
    with F do
    begin
        P := 0;
        {See if there is any data and there is room in
        the buffer}
        while ( Head <> Tail ) AND ( P < BufSize ) do
        begin
            {Get the data}
            BufPtr^[P] := IntBuffer[Tail];
            {Advance the tail pointer}
            Tail := ( Tail + 1 ) AND $FFF;
            {Advance the buffer index}
            Inc( P );
        end;
        BufPos := 0;
        {Return the amount of data read}
        Bufend := P;
    end;
    ComInput := 0;
end;
```

The `Write` and `WriteLn` procedures first call the flush routine. Then, if the buffer is full, `Write` or `WriteLn` calls the write routine. For this driver, the open routine sets the flush routine to `ComOutput`. The `ComOutput` routine sends all of the data in the buffer to the serial port one byte at a time.

```
function ComOutput( var F: TextRec ): integer;
var
  P : word;
begin
    with F do
    begin
        P := 0;
        while P < BufPos do
        begin
            {Wait for the port to get ready}
            while ( Port[ComPort + 5] AND $20 ) = 0 do;
```

```
            Port[ComPort] := Byte( BufPtr^[P] );
            Inc( P );
        end;
        BufPos := 0;
    end;
    ComOutput := 0;
end;
```

If the file was opened for reading, the open routine sets the serial interrupt vector to the serial interrupt service routine. When the program is done
with the serial port, you must restore the serial interrupt vector to its original
value. The close routine takes care of this job.

```
function ComClose( var F: TextRec ): integer;
begin
    with F do
    begin
        {Mask serial interrupts at the 8259 chip}
        Port[$21] := Port[$21] OR $10;
        {Restore the original interrupt vector}
        SetIntVec( $C, OldVect );
    end;
    ComClose := 0;
end;
```

Comments

To use this unit, put all of the pieces into a file, as indicated by the unit
template at the beginning. The order of routines is important; make sure
that routines are defined before they are referenced. Also be sure to include
the compiler directives {$F+} and {$F-} around all of the routines except
AssignCom. This makes sure that the addresses of the functions are far
pointers, as required by the Text structure.

Warnings

This unit changes the serial interrupt vector when the device is opened for
writing. Any program that changes an interrupt vector must restore it before
it exits. By changing the vector, you cause the processor to jump to a certain
program location whenever that interrupt occurs. If the program exits with
the processor in this condition and another interrupt occurs, the processor
jumps to the now-missing code. The best that you can hope for in this situation is that the computer will crash. To prevent this, be sure that you call
the Close routine before the program exits.

Enhancements

Some devices that you can connect to the serial port may send more than
4096 bytes before your program can read them from the ring buffer. If this

happens, the program behaves as if the 4096 bytes were never received. You can often direct these devices to stop sending data by sending a Ctrl-S (ASCII $13) character. Then, after some data is read from the buffer, you can send a Ctrl-Q (ASCII $11) to tell the device to resume sending.

To implement this system, you need to know how much data is in the buffer. Because the pointers move around the ring buffer, the head pointer may be behind the tail pointer. The following statement checks for this condition in calculating the amount of data in the buffer:

```
if Head < Tail then
      Size := 4096 + Head - Tail
else
      Size := Head - Tail;
```

When the size approaches the limit of the buffer, the interrupt service routine must send a Ctrl-S directive, as follows:

```
if Size > 4090 then
begin
      {Wait for the port to get ready}
      while ( Port[ComPort + 5] AND $20 ) = 0 do;
      Port[ComPort] := $13;
      DataStopped := True;
end;
```

The amount of space you must leave in the buffer depends on the baud rate and the time elapsed after one character is sent and the next is received. If you are losing data, then you should try a smaller number in place of 4090.

After you read some data from the ring buffer, you need to send the Ctrl-Q directive to restart the sending of data. To do this, add this code to the ComRead function:

```
if DataStopped then
begin
      {Wait for the port to get ready}
      while ( Port[ComPort + 5] AND $20 ) = 0 do;
      Port[ComPort] := $11;
      DataStopped := False;
end;
```

2.14   How do I...

Make a simple terminal emulator with Turbo Pascal?

Description

Many people are using their computers to communicate with information services and electronic bulletin boards. To take advantage of these services all you need is a modem and a program that makes your computer act like a terminal, called a *terminal emulator*. This solution uses the serial device driver from question 2.13 to make a simple terminal emulator.

See Also

1.10   Clearing the keyboard buffer
2.13   Making a serial device driver

Solution

The terminal emulator is simply a loop that tests for data from the keyboard or from the serial port. If the data comes from the serial port, it is sent to the screen; if it is from the keyboard, it is sent to the serial port.

The serial driver from question 2.13 and the keyboard routines from question 1.10 simplify the program.

```
{This is a simple terminal emulator}
program Terminal;
uses serial, key;

var
   Com1In : text;      {Serial input device}
   Com1Out : text;     {Serial output device}
   Done : boolean;     {FALSE while the program is running}
   KeyIn : word;       {The key pressed}
   Ch : char;          {The character received from the serial port}

begin
   {Initialize the input and output channels}
   AssignCom( Com1In, $3F8, 1200, 7, 'E', 1 );
   AssignCom( Com1Out, $3F8, 1200, 7, 'E', 1 );
   {Open the serial port for reading}
   Reset( Com1In );
   {And for writing}
   ReWrite( Com1Out );
   Done := FALSE;
   repeat
      {See if a key is pressed}
      if IsKey then
      begin
         {If so, get the key}
         KeyIn := GetKey;
```

```
            {If it is F1 exit the program}
            if( KeyIn = 15104 ) then
                  Done := TRUE
            else
                  {Otherwise send the key}
                  write( Com1Out, Chr( KeyIn AND $FF ));
      end;
            {See if there is data at the serial port}
            if NOT Eof( Com1In ) then
      begin
            {If so read it}
      Read( Com1In, Ch );
            {And display it on the screen}
            write( Ch );
      end;
   until Done;
   {Close the serial port}
   Close( Com1In );
   Close( Com1Out );
end.
```

Comments

Make sure that the parameters in the AssignCom statements match those of the computer at the other end of the serial link. The two most common settings are 7, E, 1 (7 data bits, even parity, and one stop bit), as shown here, or 8, N, 1 (8 data bits, no parity, and one stop bit). The baud rate can be any of several values; check with the administrator of the host computer before attempting to connect. If the parameters do not match, the screen will be filled with incomprehensible symbols.

Warnings

Because this program uses the serial driver from question 2.13, make sure to call the Close routine to close the port at the end of the program. If the user presses the Break key while the program is running, however, the program exits without calling the close routine. See question 1.14 for a way to intercept the Break key.

Enhancements

Most computer systems that you can access via the serial port echo each character that they receive from the terminal. This program capitalizes on this feature to ensure that you see what you type. This feature is associated with computers that use full duplex serial lines. Some systems use half duplex lines, which require the terminal to handle the echoing of typed characters.

It is easy to adapt this program to handle half duplex systems. Simply add a screen Write statement after the serial port Write statement, as follows:

```
write( Chr( KeyIn AND $FF ));
```

MATHEMATICAL

OPERATIONS

3

he first electronic computers were designed to solve the mathematical problems of computing the trajectory of artillery shells. Even today, a common use of powerful supercomputers is to solve the differential equations used to simulate ocean currents or predict the weather. Many of the problems solved with microcomputers also require mathematical computations.

This chapter shows how to use Turbo Pascal to work on a variety of mathematical problems. Solutions 3.1 through 3.4 show you how to convert strings into numbers and numbers back into strings. The next section (solutions 3.5 and 3.6) shows you how to solve problems in statistics and probability and work with lists of numbers. You will find out all the ways to shuffle the list, including a random shuffling. Solution 3.7 shows you how to perform basic statistical computations: mean (average), median (the middle value), mode (the most common value), and standard deviation (the average distance of each value from the mean). Statisticians use these computations to characterize long lists of data.

Turbo Pascal can do computations with several different types of numbers, such as integers and real numbers. Solutions 3.8 through 3.10 show how to manipulate another kind of number called *complex numbers*. These numbers are made up of both real numbers and so-called *imaginary numbers*. Imaginary numbers allow mathematicians to solve equations containing the square root of a negative number. Complex numbers are commonly used by electrical engineers and mathematicians who generate fractal images. You will learn how to create a complex number object, which makes using complex numbers as easy as using integers and real numbers.

Solutions 3.11 to 3.13 cover the topic of matrices. Matrices are used to manipulate graphic images and solve simultaneous equations. In many dialects of BASIC and FORTRAN, matrices are an essential element of the language. The matrix object given here brings this power to Turbo Pascal.

The final part of this chapter (solutions 3.14 to 3.17) deals with numerical analysis. It shows how to find common denominators, roots, and powers of numbers. It also shows how to use numerical methods to find the roots of equations. The last question in the chapter deals with a technique for calculating the value of π. The technique shows how you can (given enough time) break the record for calculating the most digits for this number.

CONVERSIONS

Before a program can use numeric data it needs a way to get that data into its variables. When the computations are done, the program needs a way to display the results. You can use the Turbo Pascal routines `WriteLn` and `ReadLn` for numeric I/O *only* as long as you use decimal numbers. But some programs use binary and hexadecimal numbers in addition to decimal numbers. To perform I/O with binary and hexadecimal numbers, you must convert numbers to strings and strings to numbers using the required number base. The first four solutions show you how to do these and other numeric conversions.

3.1   How do I...

Convert a number to a string of hexadecimal digits with Turbo Pascal?

Description
Programs that display the contents of a computer's memory most often display output in hexadecimal format. Hexadecimal numbers are convenient for displaying data bytes because a byte fits evenly into two hexadecimal digits.

See Also
3.2   Converting a number to a binary string
3.3   Converting a hexadecimal string to a number
3.4   Converting a binary string to a number

Solution

The first step in converting an integer to a string of hexadecimal digits is to find a way to fetch the digits of a number one at a time. Because each hexadecimal digit is exactly four bits long, you can isolate them by shifting and using the AND operator.

The second step is to find the ASCII character for each four-bit digit. If the digit is between 0 and 9, then the characters range from '0' (ASCII $30) to '9' (ASCII $39). For numeric digits from 10 to 15, use the characters 'A' (ASCII $45) to 'F' (ASCII $4A).

This procedure converts an integer to a string and stores the result in a string:

```
procedure HexString( Number : integer; var Result: string );
var
    Tmp : integer;          {Holds digits from the number}
    i : integer;            {Which digit is being converted}
begin
    for i := 1 to 4 do      {Do each digit}
    begin
        Tmp := Number AND $F;      {Get a digit}
        Number := Number SHR 4;    {Move everything 1 hexadecimal digit
                                    right}
        if Tmp >= 10 then          {See what characters to use}
           Result[5 - i] := Chr( Tmp - 10 + Ord( 'A' ))
        else
            Result[5 - i] := Chr( Tmp + Ord( '0' ));
    end;
    Result[0] := Chr( 4 );         {Set the length of the string}
end;
```

Comments

To display a number in hexadecimal format, simply call the following procedure and then print the resulting string, as follows:

```
var
    Numb : integer;     {Holds number to convert to a string}
    Str  : string;      {The resulting string}

begin
    .
    .                   {Get a number to print}
    .
    HexString( Numb, Str );
    Write( 'The number is: ', Str );
end.
```

Warnings

HexString does not distinguish between positive and negative numbers. Most programs that print hexadecimal numbers do not need to be concerned with negative numbers. If your program must use minus signs for hexadecimal numbers, see the enhanced routine below.

Enhancements

The fact that each hexadecimal digit fits neatly into four bits simplifies HexString. If you need to make strings of numbers in other bases, such as base 10 or base 3, you need some other way to fetch each digit from the number. The following shows how to convert a number to a string using any radix:

```
{Program to convert numbers to any base}
program base;

const
    Digits : string = '0123456789ABCDEF';

procedure Numb2String( Numb : integer; var Result : string
        ; Radix : integer );
var
   Index : integer;
   TmpStr : string;
   MinusFlag : boolean;
begin
    Index := 1;
    {If the number is negative}
    if Numb < 0 then
    begin
        {Set the minus flag}
        MinusFlag := True;
        {Make the number positive}
        Numb := - Numb;
    end
    else
        MinusFlag := False;
    {Get the least significant digit and remove it from the number}
    while Numb > 0 do
    begin
        {Get the least significant digit}
        TmpStr[Index] := Digits[(Numb MOD Radix) + 1];
        {Remove the digit from the number}
        Numb := Numb DIV Radix;
        Inc( Index );
    end;
    {If the number was negative, put a minus sign in the result}
    if MinusFlag then
       Result := '-'
    else
        Result := '';
    {Reverse the digits}
    while Index > 1 do
```

```
    begin
        Dec( Index );
        Result := Result + TmpStr[Index];
    end;
end;

var
    Number : integer;
    NumbBase : integer;
    ResString : string;

begin
    Write( 'Enter the number to convert: ' );
    ReadLn( Number );
    Write( 'Enter base for the conversion: ' );
    ReadLn( NumbBase );
    Numb2String( Number, ResString, NumbBase );
    Write( 'The result is: ', ResString );
    ReadLn;
end.
```

The procedure `Numb2String` converts an integer to a string of the base given in `Radix`. The loop in `Numb2String` divides the number by the radix and puts the remainder into `TmpStr`. When the number is divided down to 0, the second loop reverses the digits as it copies them from `TmpStr` to `Result`.

3.2   How do I...

Convert an integer to a string of binary digits with Turbo Pascal?

Description

Some of the status information stored in the PC's memory is in the form of 1-bit flags collected into a byte or word. One way for a program to display this information is to print the byte or word as a string of binary digits. The user can easily see what bits are set and what bits are not.

See Also

3.1   Converting a number to a hexadecimal string

3.3   Converting a hexadecimal string to a number

3.4   Converting a binary string to a number

Solution

This solution is very similar to solution 3.1. In this case, the size of a digit is only 1 bit, and the characters are limited to '0' and '1'. Here is the routine:

```
procedure BinString( Number : integer; var Result : string );
var
   i : integer;         {What bit to convert}
begin
   for i := 15 downto 0 do  {Go from most to least significant
                              bit}
   begin
      {If the bit is set store a 1}
      if ( Number AND ( 1 SHL i )) <> 0 then
         Result[16 - i] := '1'
      else {Otherwise store a 0}
         Result[16 - i] := '0';
   end;
   {Set the length of the string}
   Result[0] := Chr(16);
end;
```

Warnings

Like the routine in question 3.1, this one does not distinguish negative numbers from positive ones. Another thing to watch for is the size of the string you pass to the routine. Passing a string that is shorter than 16 characters can cause errors later in the program.

Enhancements

See question 3.1

3.3   How do I...

Convert a string of hexadecimal digits to an integer with Turbo Pascal?

Description

When a program uses hexadecimal numbers in its output, it can expect the user to use hexadecimal numbers for input. If this is the case, you need a routine to convert the hexadecimal input to a number.

See Also

3.1   Converting a number to a hexadecimal string
3.2   Converting a number to a binary string
3.4   Converting a binary string to a number

Solution

The first step in converting a string of hexadecimal digits to a number is to convert an ASCII character to a digit. If the character is between '0' and '9', it is converted to a number from 0 to 9. If the character is between 'A' and 'F' then it is converted to a number from 10 to 15.

As each digit is added, digits already in the number shift left to accommodate the new digit. When all of the digits are converted, the number is returned to the calling routine.

```
function FromHex( Number : string ):integer;
var
   i : integer;              {Index to the digit being converted}
   Result : integer; {Intermediate results}
begin
    Result := 0;              {Start with 0}
    for i := 1 to Length( Number ) do
    begin
       {Get a digit and put it in result}
       if Ord( Number[i] ) >= Ord( 'A' ) then
             Result := (Result SHL 4 )
                   + Ord( Number[i] ) - Ord( 'A' ) + 10
         else
             Result := ( Result SHL 4 )
                   + Ord( Number[i] ) - Ord( '0' );
    end;
    {Return the result}
    FromHex := Result;
end;
```

Comments

FromHex can convert a string of from one to four digits to an integer. It automatically computes the correct place value for each digit by shifting digits from the right end of the integer.

To see how this works, consider the hexadecimal number $2AF. The FromHex function examines this number one digit at a time. After adding the first digit to the result, it gets the result $2. Before it adds the next digit, the function shifts the result, yielding $20. Then it adds in the digit, yielding $2A. FromHex repeats these steps for each digit in the string.

Warnings

FromHex tries to convert every character in the string even when the result no longer fits in an integer. For example, if you enter the string '12345', the '1' is shifted left, making the final result 2345.

Enhancements

The enhancement for question 3.1 shows how to convert a number to a string for any base. This routine converts a string of any base to an integer:

```
function String2Number( Data : string
     ; Radix : integer ):integer;
```

```
var
        i : integer;
        Result : integer;
begin
        Result := 0;
        for i := 1 to Length( Data ) do
        begin
                {Get a digit and put it in result}
                if Ord( Data[i] ) >= Ord( 'A' ) then
                        Result := ( Result * Radix )
                                + Ord( Data[i] ) - Ord( 'A' ) + 10
                else
                        Result := ( Result * Radix )
                                + Ord( Data[i] ) - Ord( '0' );
        end;
        String2Number := Result;
end;
```

3.4   How do I...

Convert a string of binary digits to a number in Turbo Pascal?

Description

It is not common for users to enter binary numbers. If your program calls for this input, however, you need a routine to convert the binary string to a number.

See Also

3.1   Converting a number to a hexadecimal string
3.2   Converting a number to a binary string
3.3   Converting a hexadecimal string to a number

Solution

This solution is similar to solution 3.3. The difference is that there is no need to convert a character to a digit. You simply need to determine if the character is a '1' or a '0'.

```
function FromBin( Number : string ): integer;
var
   i : integer;              {The bit to test}
   Result : integer;         {The number in the string}
begin
    Result := 0;             {Start at 0}
    {Look at each digit in the string}
    for i := 1 to Length( Number ) do
    begin
       { If the digit is a '1' put a 1 in the result}
```

```
      if Number[i] = '1' then
         Result := ( Result SHL 1 ) + 1
      else  {Otherwise put a 0 in the result}
         Result := ( Result SHL 1 );
   end;
   FromBin := Result;
end;
```

Comments

This routine uses the same shifting technique as in question 3.3. Of course, for binary numbers, you need to shift only one bit at a time.

Warnings

This routine performs no error checking on the string. If the user enters any character other than a '1', the program treats it as if it were a '0'.

Enhancements

See question 3.3.

STATISTICS AND PROBABILITY

Blaise Pascal, for whom the Pascal language is named, is famous for the development of the mathematics of probability. He developed much of the theory of how to determine the probability of different types of events. The first step in determining the probability of a given event is to find the number of possible events. For example, to determine to probability of drawing a royal flush from a deck of cards you need to determine the number of possible ways the deck can be shuffled (about 8.0658×10^{67}) and then divide by the number of shuffles that give a royal flush (about 1.0344×10^{60}).

The next two solutions are practical applications of combinational theory. The first one shows how to generate a randomly ordered array, and the second shows how to generate all of the possible combinations of data in an array.

For some data sets, you do not want to consider all of the possible combinations. For example, suppose you give a test to a class of 30 students, who can each receive a score from 1 to 100. In theory there are many possible outcomes, but many of these are unlikely. Generally, the scores will cluster, with a few students getting higher-than-average scores and a few students getting lower-than-average scores, while most students get average scores. In this case the probabilities are less important than the mean, median, and mode of the data set. The solution to question 3.7 shows how to calculate and use statistical data.

3.5   How do I...

Shuffle an ordered array?

Description
Scrambling the order of records in an array has a number of uses. An obvious application is simulating games for which you shuffle a deck of cards. Graphics programs, too, use this technique. To create "dissolve" effects, you scramble the order in which the program displays pixels. Another use is to find optimum ways of combining large numbers of items. If the number of combinations is too large to allow every combination to be tested, you can try a smaller number of random combinations and hope to hit upon one that is good enough. This solution shows how to generate a randomly ordered list.

See Also
3.6   Finding the permutations of an array
3.7   Testing random numbers

Solution
You cannot shuffle an array by simply using random numbers to get the index for each item. As the array is filled in, the chance of getting an index that has already been used increases. If you design the routine to keep trying when an index is duplicated, there is no guarantee that the routine will ever finish.

Instead of trying to stuff each item into a random location, you can swap each item with an item at a random index. This way, you can guarantee that the routine ends after going through the array once. It is not a problem if the random number routine generates the same random number twice, because the value already at that location is moved before the new value is copied to the location.

This program initializes an array of records that represent a deck of cards:

```
program Shuffle;

type
   {Each card in the array is type Cards}
   Cards = record
      Value : integer;
      Suit : integer;
   end;

var
   Deck : Array [1..52] of Cards;        {The deck}
```

```
    v, s, 1 : integer;
    Value : array [1..13] of string[10];      {The card value names}
    Suit : array [1..4] of string[10];        {The card suit names}
    TmpCard : Cards;                           {Temp card for swapping}
    Jumble : Index;                            {The index for swapping}
begin
    {Initialize card names}
    Value[1] := 'ACE';
    Value[2] := '2';
    Value[3] := '3';
    Value[4] := '4';
    Value[5] := '5';
    Value[6] := '6';
    Value[7] := '7';
    Value[8] := '8';
    Value[9] := '9';
    Value[10] := '10';
    Value[11] := 'JACK';
    Value[12] := 'QUEEN';
    Value[13] := 'KING';
    Suit[1] := 'HEARTS';
    Suit[2] := 'CLUBS';
    Suit[3] := 'DIAMONDS';
    Suit[4] := 'SPADES';
    {Initialize the deck}
    i := 1;
    for v := 1 to 13 do
        for s := 1 to 4 do
        begin
            Deck[i].Value := v;
            Deck[i].Suit := s;
            Inc( i );
        end;
    {Display the cards in the deck}
    for i := 1 to 52 do
        writeln( Value[Deck[i].Value], ' of ',
            Suit[Deck[i].Suit] );
    ReadLn;
    {Shuffle the deck}
    Randomize;               {Make sure this is a random sequence}
    for i := 1 to 52 do      {For each card}
    begin
        v := Random( 52 ) + 1;      {Get the card to swap with}
        TmpCard := Deck[i];         {Swap cards}
        Deck[i] := Deck[v];
        Deck[v] := TmpCard;
    end;
    {Show the shuffled deck}
    for i := 1 to 52 do
        writeln( Value[Deck[i].Value], ' of ',
            Suit[Deck[i].Suit] );
    ReadLn;
end.
```

Comments

This program uses the Turbo Pascal routines `Randomize` and `Random` to get random numbers for the shuffle algorithm. The `Random` function uses a formula to generate numbers that appear to be random (called *pseudorandom* numbers). It uses the previous random number as part of the formula for the next random number. Because the random sequence is the result of a formula, `Random` always gives the same sequence if you use the same initial value. The `Randomize` procedure uses the time-of-day clock to make sure that a different initial value is used each time the program runs.

3.6   How do I...

Find the permutations of an array?

Description

A task well suited for computers is finding the most efficient use of resources. For example, suppose an air freight company must find the way of loading packages that makes the most efficient use of aircraft space. If you simply load the planes in any order, you may find that you have 2 cubic feet of space left in each of four airplanes. If the next package to be shipped occupies 3 cubic feet, you need another airplane. But suppose there is a 1-cubic-foot package in one of the airplanes. You can transfer that package to another plane, leaving 1 cubic foot in one plane and 3 cubic feet in another. Of course, it is better to know this before you load the airplanes, or else the 1-cubic-foot box may be at the back of the airplane, and you'll have to unload and reload the plane.

One way to solve this problem is to create an array that describes all of the packages to be shipped, then look at each of the possible orderings of this array to find the one that results in the most efficient use of the available resources.

See Also

3.5   Making a random ordering

Solution

You can use recursion to simplify the problem of finding all of the possible orderings of an array. The smallest array has two items. This array has two possible orderings: 1, 2 and 2, 1. A three-item array is a two-item array plus the third item. If you put each of the three items in the first position and generate the possible orderings for the other two, you get the six possible orderings:

```
        1, 2, 3
        1, 3, 2
        2, 1, 3
        2, 3, 1
        3, 1, 2
        3, 2, 1
```

For four-item arrays, put each of the four items in the first position and use the same algorithm to order the remaining three items. This gives the 24 possible orderings of four items.

This routine implements the algorithm:

```
procedure Permute( var Data : Index; Count, Max : integer );
var
   i, j: integer;
   Swap : integer;
begin
   {For each of the items in the array}
   for i := 1 to Count - 1 do
   begin
      {Swap one of the numbers into last position}
      Swap := Data[Count];
      Data[Count] := Data[i];
      Data[i] := Swap;
      {If there are at least two items in the array}
      if Count > 1 then
      begin
            {Find the orderings for all but the last item in
             the array}
            Permute( Data, Count - 1, Max );
            {Show the array}
            for j := 1 to Max do
                Write( Data[j] );
            WriteLn;
        end;
   end;
   {Put the array back to the original order}
   Swap := Data[1];
   for i := 1 to Count - 1 do
      Data[i] := Data[i + 1];
   Data[Count] := Swap;
   {If there are at least two items in the array}
   if Count > 1 then
   begin
      {Find the orderings for all but the last item in the array}
      Permute( Data, Count - 1, Max );
      {Show the final ordering}
      if Count = Max then
      begin
            for i := 1 to Max do
                Write( Data[i] );
            WriteLn;
```

```
      end;
    end;
end;
```

Comments

This routine puts each number in the last position in the array and calls itself to get the orderings of all but the last item. This technique simplifies the routine because each subordering uses just the first few items in the array.

When the routine finds a new ordering, it prints the array. If your program is searching for an optimum pattern, then you must replace the `Write` loops with a call to a pattern-evaluation routine.

Warnings

The final step in this routine puts the array back in its original order. This step is very important because each recursive call uses the same array. If you do not restore the order of the array, then the routine does not know which values it had already put at the end of the array. The result is that you get the same ordering more than once and skip some orderings altogether.

3.7   How do I...

Find the mean, median, mode, and standard deviation of a data set?

Description

Most people are familiar with the mean (average) of a data set. Statisticians go a step further and use four numbers to characterize a data set. If you give a group of people a test, most of the test scores will be close to the mean. As the scores get further from the mean (above or below), the number of people getting those scores decreases. This is called a "normal" distribution.

The median is the value that is halfway between the highest and lowest value in the data set. If the median is close to the mean, then the highest and lowest values are the same distance from the mean. This is a sign that the distribution is normal.

The mode is the value that occurs most often in the data set. In a normal distribution, this value is near the mean and mode of the data set. Some data sets may have more than one modal value. This indicates that there may have been more than one influence in the backgrounds or training of the test subjects.

The standard deviation is the average distance of the scores from the mean. A small standard deviation in test scores indicates that the test sub-

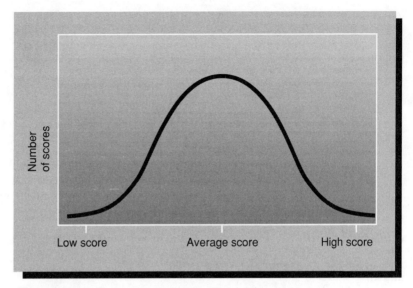

Figure 3-1 The normal-distribution bell curve

jects have similar backgrounds and have received similar training in the subject matter. A large standard deviation in test scores shows that the subjects have received uneven training in the subject matter.

A small standard deviation and low mean in test scores indicate that the students are well trained but the test is too hard. In this case, the test scores may be scaled up by some factor. This is called "grading on the curve" because of the bell-shaped curve created when you plot test scores against the number of people who got that score in a normal distribution (see Figure 3-1).

A large standard deviation indicates that the students have not been well trained in the subject matter. This tells the educator that a review is needed to bring the entire class up to speed on the material.

See Also

2.11 Sorting data

4.2 Sorting string

Solution

The mean is easy to calculate: Simply add all of the data items and divide by the number of items in the list.

```
type
      DataArray = array[1..100] of integer;

function Mean( var Data : DataArray; Count : integer ) : integer;
```

```
var
        i : integer;
        Total : integer;
begin
        {Add all of the data items}
        Total := 0;
        for i := 1 to Count do
                Total := Total + Data[i];
        Mean := Total DIV Count;    {Divide by the number of items}
end;
```

To calculate the median, you need to search the data for the highest and lowest values. If the data is sorted, then you need to look at only the first and last values in the array. Because sorting the array also helps you find the mode, it is a good idea to sort the array before continuing.

```
procedure SortData( var Data : DataArray; Count : integer );
var
   i, j, h, v : integer;
begin
    {Shell sort the array}
    h := 1;
    repeat
        h := 3 * h + 1;
    until h > Count;
    repeat
        h := h DIV 3;
        for i := h + 1 to Count do
        begin
            v := Data[i];
            j := i;
            while Data[j - h] > v do
            begin
                Data[j] := Data[j - h];
                j := j - h;
            end;
            Data[j] := v;
        end
    until h = 1;
end;
```

Because the list is sorted, finding the median is simple. Here is the median function:

```
function Median( Data : DataArray; Count : integer ): Median;
begin
        Median := ( Data[1] + Data[Count] ) DIV 2;
end;
```

To find the mode, you need to count the number of items that have the same value and keep track of the longest run of values. This function does the job:

```
function Mode( Data : DataArray; Count : integer ) : integer;
var
   i, j : integer;
   ModeVal : integer;
   ModeCnt : integer;
begin
   ModeCnt := 0;
   i := 1;
   while i < Count do
   begin
      {Count how many items in a row are the same}
      j := i + 1;
      while ( j <= Count ) AND ( Data[i] = Data[j] ) do
           Inc( j );
      {See if the run is greater than the greatest}
      if j - i > ModeCnt then
      begin
         ModeCnt := j - i;
         ModeVal := Data[i];
      end;
      {Go to the next different data item}
      i := i + j;
   end;
   Mode := ModeVal;
end;
```

The routine for calculating the standard deviation is similar to the routine for calculating the mean. Instead of adding the data values, it adds the absolute value of the difference between the data item and the mean.

```
function Deviation( Data : DataArray; Count : integer ) : integer;
var
   Average : integer;
   Dist : integer;
   i : integer;
begin
   {Get the mean}
   Average := Mean( Data, Count );
   {Sum the distances from the mean}
   Dist := 0;
   for i := 1 to Count do
      Dist := Dist + Abs( Average - Data[i] );
   {Divide by the count for the standard deviation}
   Deviation := Dist DIV Count;
end;
```

Comments

Here is a program that uses these routines to calculate the characteristics of an array of random values:

```
var
   i : integer;
```

```
    Data : DataArray;

begin
    Randomize;
    for i := 1 to 100 do
        Data[i] := Random( 100 );
    SortData( Data, 100 );
    WriteLn( 'The mean is: ', Mean( Data, 100 ));
    WriteLn( 'The median is: ', Median( Data, 100 ));
    WriteLn( 'The mode is: ', Mode( Data, 100 ));
    WriteLn( 'The standard deviation is: ',
            Deviation( Data, 100 ));
    ReadLn;
end.
```

One property of a good random-number generator is that it yields evenly distributed numbers. For example, if 100 numbers from the set 1–100 are being generated, the mean and median should be close to 50, and the standard deviation should be close to 25. The mode can be any value, because there should not be more than two of any number. You can use this information to test the reliability of your random-number generator. If your program returns values much different from these, there is something wrong with the random-number generator.

Warnings

When you add a large number of integers, you run the risk of overflowing the integer variables used. If there is a chance that the sum of the values in the data set will be more than 32,767, consider using a `longint` to hold the sum for the `Mean` function.

COMPLEX NUMBERS

Complex numbers are used in several kinds of mathematical formulas, including those used in generating fractal images and in electrical engineering. Some languages, such as FORTRAN, let you declare a variable of type `Complex` to manipulate complex numbers. Up to now, Pascal has not had this feature. But you can create a complex-number object that makes complex numbers almost as easy to use as any other number type.

Create a complex-number object?

Description

The routines in this question show how to create a complex-number object, including a number of methods for performing simple mathematical operations on complex numbers. In a traditional program, every part of the program that uses complex numbers has to know about the records and functions for complex numbers. This solution shows you how to create a complex-number object that encapsulates these details. In your program, you simply call the method that does the desired operation.

See Also

3.9   Multiplying and dividing complex numbers

3.10   Raising complex numbers to a power

Solution

Because many different programs use complex numbers, it makes sense to put the complex-number object into a unit. The interface portion of the unit includes the definition of the complex-number object.

```
type
   CplxNumb = object
        RealPart, ImaginaryPart : real;
        procedure Load( RP, IP : real );
        procedure Equal( CNumb : CplxNumb );
        procedure Add( CNumb : CplxNumb );
        procedure Subtract( CNumb : CplxNumb );
        procedure Print;
   end;
```

The variables `RealPart` and `ImaginaryPart` hold the two parts of the complex number. You can initialize these variables by using the `Load` method, which is defined in the implementation section of the unit.

```
procedure CplxNumb.Load( RP, IP : real );
begin
    RealPart := RP;
    ImaginaryPart := IP;
end;
```

You use `Equal` method to set one complex number equal to another, as follows:

```
procedure CplxNumb.Equal( CNumb : CplxNumb );
begin
    RealPart := CNumb.RealPart;
```

```
      ImaginaryPart := CNumb.ImaginaryPart;
end;
```

To add two complex numbers, you add the real parts and then add the imaginary parts. To subtract them, you subtract the real parts and then the imaginary parts. These methods add and subtract complex numbers:

```
Procedure CplxNumb.Add( CNumb : CplxNumb );
begin
    RealPart := RealPart + CNumb.RealPart;
    ImaginaryPart := ImaginaryPart + CNumb.ImaginaryPart;
end;

procedure CplxNumb.Subtract( CNumb : CplxNumb );
begin
    RealPart := RealPart - CNumb.RealPart;
    ImaginaryPart := ImaginaryPart - CNumb.ImaginaryPart;
end;
```

The last method lets you display complex numbers on the screen:

```
procedure CplxNumb.Print;
begin
    Write( RealPart, ' + ', ImaginaryPart, 'i' );
end;
```

Comments

Complex-number objects hide the details of how complex numbers work, leaving you free to concentrate on the algorithm that uses them. If the algorithm calls for the addition of two complex numbers, you don't have to remember how to do it. Simply use this:

```
CNumb1.Add( CNumb2 );
```

Warnings

The real numbers used in the complex-number object can range from 2.9×10^{-39} to 1.7×10^{38}. This range is adequate for many calculations, but many applications require the wider ranges provided by the Single, Double, and Extended types.

Using Real type variables ensures that these routines work in the default configuration of Turbo Pascal. When you use other floating-point types, you need to include the {$N+} directive to use the 8087 floating- point routines. You do not need an 8087 to run programs that are compiled this way; you can simply include the {$E+} directive in the program to use the software floating-point emulator.

Enhancements

See questions 3.9 and 3.10 for other complex-number methods.

Include multiply and divide methods in the complex-number object?

Description

One advantage of object-oriented programming is the ease with which you can add features to an object. By simply adding methods, you can add features to any object.

See Also

Solution

To multiply the complex number `a + bi` by the complex number `c + di` use this formula:

```
ac - bd + (ad + bc)i
```

The difference between `ac` and `bd` is the real part of the final result, and the sum of `ad` and `bc` is the imaginary part. You can translate this into Turbo Pascal as follows:

```
procedure CplxNumb.Multiply( CNumb : CplxNumb );
begin
    RealPart := RealPart * CNumb.RealPart
          - ImaginaryPart * CNumb.ImaginaryPart;
    ImaginaryPart := RealPart * CNumb.ImaginaryPart
          + CNumb.RealPart * ImaginaryPart;
end;
```

The formula for dividing two complex numbers is more complicated. Here it is:

```
(ac + bd) / (c² + d²) + (cb - ad) i / (c² + d²)
```

If you are mathematically ambitious, you can derive this formula. Start with this fraction:

$$\frac{a + bi}{c + di}$$

Then try to remove all imaginary terms from the denominator. (Hint: multiply the numerator and the denominator by `c - di`) Once this formula is converted to Pascal, it looks like this:

```
procedure CplxNumb.Divide( CNumb : CplxNumb );
var
```

```
    Tmp1, Tmp2 : real;
begin
    Tmp1 := CNumb.RealPart * CNumb.RealPart
            + CNumb.ImaginaryPart * CNumb.ImaginaryPart
    Tmp2 := (RealPart * CNumb.RealPart
          + ImaginaryPart * CNumb.ImaginaryPart) / Tmp1;
    ImaginaryPart := (ImaginaryPart * CNumb.RealPart
          + RealPart * CNumb.ImaginaryPart) / Tmp1;
        Real Part: = Tmp2;
end;
```

Comments

You should include both of these methods in the implementation section of the complex-number unit. In addition, you need to include definitions of these functions to the definition of the complex-number object. Here is the expanded complex-number object:

```
type
    CplxNumb = object
            RealPart, ImaginaryPart : real;
            procedure Load( RP, IP : real );
            procedure Equal( CNumb : CplxNumb );
            procedure Add( CNumb : CplxNumb );
            procedure Subtract( CNumb : CplxNumb );
            procedure Print;
            procedure Multiply( CNumb : CplxNumb );
            procedure Divide( CNumb : CplxNumb );
    end;
```

Warnings

Whenever a program divides numbers, you have to consider the possibility of division by 0. The preceding divide method suffers from this possibility. If either of the real parts or either of the imaginary parts is 0, then your program attempts division by 0. Carefully analyze the complex numbers that your program may use before you use this divide method.

Enhancement

See question 3.10 for more complex-number methods.

3.10   How do I...

Include methods to do exponential calculations with complex numbers in Turbo Pascal?

Description

This is the formula for creating a popular fractal, known as the Mandelbrot set:

```
f(Z) = Z² + C
```

In this formula, z and c are complex numbers. You compute z^2 by multiplying z by itself. Not all fractals are this easy to compute. For instance, some fractals raise z to an imaginary or complex power. You need a general way to raise a complex number to any power.

See Also

3.8   Creating a complex-number object

3.9   Multiplying and dividing complex numbers

Solution

The answer to the problem of raising a complex number to any power involves logarithms. In the days before computers, engineers used logarithms to make complex calculations. When raising a number to some power, engineers would look up the logarithms of both of the numbers, multiply the logarithms together, and finally look up the value of the result in the table to find the answer. This was so much simpler than previous methods for calculating these results that Johannes Kepler, the famous astronomer, claimed that logarithms more than doubled the life of an astronomer.

The computer makes the process even easier. In Turbo Pascal you need only one statement to raise a real number to any real power. Here it is:

```
Result := Exp( Ln( Numb1 ) * Ln( Numb2 ));
```

In this statement, `Numb1` is the number to be raised to the power given by `Numb2`.

To raise a complex number to any power, you have to find its logarithm. After that, you can raise a complex number to any power as easily as a real number. Here is the formula for computing the logarithm of a complex number:

```
Ln(r) + θi
```

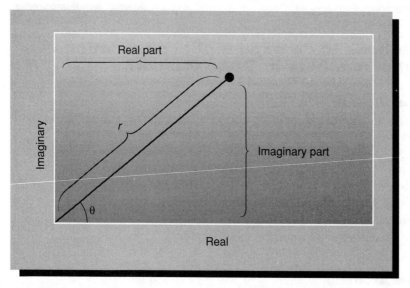

Figure 3-2 Representing a complex number as a point

To see how this formula relates to complex numbers, you must realize that complex numbers can represent a point on a graph. The x-coordinate of this point is the real part of the number, and the y-coordinate is the imaginary part. Figure 3-2 shows that this point can also be defined by the angle θ and distance r.

Some basic trigonometry gives the formulas for calculating θ and r:

```
  = arctan( realpart / imaginarypart )
r = sqrt( realpart² + imaginarypart² )
```

You can plug these values into the formula Ln + θ, which gives the logarithm of the complex number. This function calculates θ for all possible complex numbers:

```
function Angle( RealPart, ImaginaryPart : real ) : real;
var
      Th : real;
begin
      if ImaginaryPart <> 0.0 then        {Don't divide by 0}
      begin
          Th := Arctan( RealPart/ImaginaryPart );
          {Adjust for what quadrant contains the point}
          if ImaginaryPart < 0.0 then
            if RealPart < 0.0 then
                  Th := Th + Pi * -1
            else
                  Th := Th + Pi;
```

```
          end
          else    {If ImaginaryPart is 0 there are
                   only 2 possible angles}
             if RealPart < 0.0 then
                 Th := -Pi / 2.0
             else
                 Th := Pi / 2.0;
end;
```

You can use this function to calculate the logarithm, as in this method:

```
procedure CplxNumb.CLn;
var
   Tmp : real;
begin
   {Calculate r }
   Tmp := Ln( Sqrt( RealPart * RealPart
              + ImaginaryPart * ImaginaryPart ));
   {Calculate θ}
   ImaginaryPart := Angle( ImaginaryPart, RealPart );
   RealPart := Tmp;
end;
```

After you have manipulated the logarithms, you have to find out what number the result represents. For real numbers, you use the Exp function to do this job. For complex numbers, use this method:

```
procedure CplxNumb.CExp;
var
   Tmp : real;
begin
   Tmp := Exp( RealPart ) * Cos( ImaginaryPart );
   ImaginaryPart := Exp( RealPart ) * Sin( ImaginaryPart );
   RealPart := Tmp;
end;
```

Now you have all of the tools you need to create a method that raises a complex number to any power. Here it is:

```
procedure CplxNumb.Power( CNumb : CplxNumb );
begin
   CLn;                     {Calculate the logarithm of the complex
                             number}
   Multiply( CNumb );       {Multiply by the exponent CNumb}
   CExp;                    {Get the final result}
end;
```

Comments

You can use a similar routine to calculate the value of a complex number raised to a real power, but that is not necessary. If you set the imaginary part of the complex power to 0, you can use the Power method as written.

Warnings

The mathematics used in these routines is more complex than that used in many routines. If you modify them, be sure that the routines still use the appropriate formulas.

Enhancements

The last three solutions by no means exhaust the possible methods that you could use with complex numbers. Your application may require special calculations, and if so you may want to write special methods for them. You may also want to include methods that are more specific than the general methods in this book. For example, if you need to raise a complex number only to a specific power, you may be able to write a method that is more efficient than the general Power method given here.

MATRICES

A matrix is a two-dimensional array of numbers. Computer programs can use matrices to store a group of related data items. If you know a little math, you can also use matrices to translate graphical coordinates, process images, and solve simultaneous equations.

3.11   How do I...

Create a matrix object with Turbo Pascal?

Description

When you use a matrix, you have to keep track of the width and height of the matrix as well as the matrix elements. A matrix object encapsulates all of this information and so you don't have to worry about setting the values correctly each time you need to use a matrix.

See Also

3.12   Transposing rows and columns in a matrix

3.13   Using matrices to solve simultaneous equations

Solution

The main problem to solve before implementing a matrix class is how to manage memory. Simply defining a two-dimensional array with enough space for the largest possible matrix is wasteful when the average matrix size is smaller than the largest possible matrix. For example, consider this array:

is smaller than the largest possible matrix. For example, consider this array:

```
var
     Data : array[1..100,1..100] of real;
```

The Data array uses 60,000 bytes of storage (100 × 100 × 6 bytes per real number). This is just under the 65,536-byte limit for arrays, and is large enough for most applications. If the matrix you are using is only 50 × 25, there are 58,200 bytes (60,000 − 50 × 25 × 6) wasted in the Data array.

Another problem is how to handle a 200 × 50 matrix. This matrix uses the same amount of memory as data, but the first index goes past the limit for that index. Trying to access an element at, say, [125,21] would cause a run-time error.

To get around these problems you must write your own memory-management routines to store the matrix data. The first step is to allocate enough memory to hold the matrix data for a single matrix. The amount of memory required is equal to the number of rows times the number of columns times the number of bytes in a single cell. The method shown below uses the GetMem procedure to get the memory to store the matrix:

```
constructor Mat.Init( MaxRows, MaxCols : integer );
var
   r, c : integer;
begin
   {Save the dimensions of the matrix}
   Rows := MaxRows;
   Cols := MaxCols;
   GetMem( Data, MaxRows * MaxCols * Sizeof( Real ));
   {Initialize all of the cells to 0.0}
   for r := 1 to Rows do
      for c := 1 to Cols do
         SetCell( r, c, 0.0 );
end;
```

When a program calls the Init method, it saves the dimensions of the matrix, allocates memory for the matrix data, and sets all of the matrix cells to 0. Init uses the SetCell method to put a 0 in each cell. SetCell computes the position of the cell in the memory array and copies the number to the cell.

```
{Set a particular cell to a value}
procedure Mat.SetCell( Row, Col : integer; Item : real );
var
   SegPart, OffPart : word;
begin
   {Find the address of the cell}
   SegPart := integer( longint( Data ) SHR 16 );
   OffPart := integer( longint( Data ) AND $FFFF )
         + (( Row - 1 ) * Cols + Col - 1 ) * Sizeof( Real );
   {Copy the data into the cell}
```

```
      Real( Ptr( SegPart, OffPart )^ ) := Item;
end;
```

To set a cell, this routine must calculate the address of the cell. Figure 3-3 shows how to calculate the offset into the matrix array for a cell. This offset is added to the offset of the allocated memory to give the address of the cell.

The method to get the data in a cell is similar to the SetCell method:

```
{Get the data from a particular cell}
function Mat.GetCell( Row, Col : integer ) : real;
var
   SegPart, OffPart : word;
begin
    SegPart := integer( longint( Data ) SHR 16 );
    OffPart := integer( longint( Data ) AND $FFFF )
           + (( Row - 1 ) * Cols + Col - 1 ) * Sizeof( Real );
    GetCell := real( Ptr( SegPart, OffPart )^ );
end;
```

The difference is that instead of copying data to the cell, this method reads the data out of the cell.

Any object that allocates memory must have a method to release the memory when the object is no longer needed. This method is called a destructor. The destructor for this object calls FreeMem to release the memory used by the matrix:

```
destructor Mat.Done;
begin
    FreeMem( Data, Rows * Cols * Sizeof( Real ));
end;
```

To make a matrix unit for use in other programs, put the preceding routines into the implementation part of the unit. The interface part contains the definition of the object.

```
type
   Mat = object
      Rows, Cols : integer;
      Data : ^real;
      constructor Init( MaxRows, MaxCols : integer );
      procedure SetCell( Row, Col : integer; Item : real );
      function GetCell( Row, Col : integer ) : real;
      procedure ShowIt;
      destructor Done; virtual;
   end;
```

Note that this definition includes a method that has not been presented yet. This is the ShowIt method, which displays the information in the matrix on the screen:

```
procedure Mat.ShowIt;
var
```

```
  r, c : integer;
begin
    for r := 1 to Rows do
    begin
        for c := 1 to Cols do
            Write( Self.GetCell( r, c ) : 8 : 3, ' ' );
        WriteLn;
    end;
end;
```

This method uses the `GetCell` method to get each cell and display it on the screen. At the end of each row, it writes an end-of-line character to format the matrix properly.

Comments

Although matrices have many interesting mathematical properties, they are also convenient for storing data. Any program that uses double subscripted (two-dimensional) arrays can use the matrix class instead. The main factor in determining whether to use arrays or matrices is whether you know the dimensions of the data before run-time. If you know the dimensions when you write the program, arrays are a faster, easier solution. Otherwise, the memory savings of matrices may make up for their slower performance.

Warnings

The methods presented here do not check matrix limits. Before you use them, make sure that the arguments to methods such as `GetCell` and `SetCell` are within the matrix limits. For some programs, you may want to modify the methods so that they check matrix limits. This will, of course, degrade the performance of the routines.

Enhancements

See questions 3.12 and 3.13 for some other methods you can include in the matrix object.

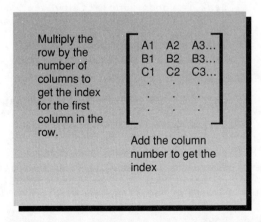

Figure 3-3 Calculating cell offsets

3.12   How do I...

Make a transpose method for the matrix class?

Description

Figure 3-4 shows how to swap the rows and columns of a matrix to transpose it. Transposing a matrix is useful when you want to multiply two matrices. You can multiply two matrices only if the number of rows in one matrix is the same as the number of columns in the other matrix.

See Also

3.11   Creating a matrix object

Solution

Transposing is a bit more complicated than just moving the cells around. You must also exchange the Rows and Cols fields. This procedure allocates a new memory block to hold the transposed matrix, copies the cells, and changes the fields in the matrix object:

```
procedure Mat.Transpose;
var
   NewData : ^integer;
   Seg1, Off1, Seg2, Off2 : Word;
   r, c : integer;
begin
    {Allocate a new memory block}
    GetMem( NewData, Rows * Cols * Sizeof( Real ) );
    {Get the address of the matrix}
    Seg1 := word( longint( Data ) SHR 16 );
    Off1 := word( longint( Data ) AND $FFFF );
       {And the address of the new matrix}
    Seg2 := word( longint( NewData ) SHR 16 );
    Off2 := word( longint( NewData ) AND $FFFF );
    {Transpose the cells}
    for r := 0 to rows - 1 do
       for c := 0 to cols - 1 do
       begin
          Real( Ptr( Seg2,Off2+( c*( Cols+1 )+r ) * Sizeof( Real ))^)
                    := Real( Ptr( Seg1, Off1 )^ );
          Off1 := Off1 + Sizeof( Real );
       end;
    {Free the memory in the old matrix}
    FreeMem( Data, Rows * Cols * Sizeof( Real ));
    {Save the new address in the object}
    pointer( Data ) := pointer( NewData );
       {Swap the dimensions}
    r := Rows;
    Rows := Cols;
```

```
    Cols := r;
end;
```

Comments
Note that this procedure does not use the `GetCell` and `SetCell` methods, saving one multiplication and two calls for each cell. The performance benefits of this kind of optimization increase as the size of the matrices grows. Any routine that deals with a large number of cells can benefit from similar refinements.

Warnings
All of the cell coordinates used in this routine are within the bounds of the arrays used, but you can still get into trouble with it. The problem is that there must be enough memory on the heap to hold a second copy of the matrix while the matrix is being transposed. If there is not, you will get a run-time error.

Enhancements
See question 3.13 for another method for the matrix class.

3.13 How do I...

Solve simultaneous equations with matrices?

Description
You can easily solve an equation with a single variable by using algebraic or numerical methods. When there is more than one variable in the equation you cannot find the values for the variables because there is more than a single solution. If you have as many equations as you have variables, you can often combine these equations to find the values of each of the variables.

The technique used here was developed by the mathematician Carl Gauss (1777-1855). It is another case of an algorithm that was discovered long before there were computers to use it.

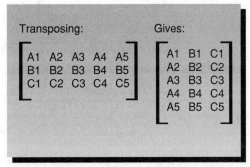

Figure 3-4 Transposing a matrix

See Also

3.16   Finding roots of equations

Solution

The first step in solving a set of simultaneous equations is to represent them with a matrix. Consider the following three equations:

```
3x +  4y + 8z = -1
6x -  6y - 10z =  7
9x + 10y + 14z = -8
```

You can make a matrix of the coefficients of these equations that looks like this:

$$\begin{vmatrix} 3 & 4 & 8 & -1 \\ 6 & -6 & -10 & 7 \\ 9 & 10 & 14 & -8 \end{vmatrix}$$

You can multipy any row in the matrix by a constant and not affect the result. You can also add two rows together without affecting the result. A procedure called Gaussian elimination uses these two facts to solve the equations. The first step is to get a zero in the first column of the second row. Multiplying the first row by –2 and adding it to the second row does the trick. Next you need to get two zeros into the first two columns of the third row. To do this you can multiply the first row by –3 and add it from the third row, then multiply the third row by 7 and subtract it from the second row. After you have done these manipulations the matrix looks like this:

$$\begin{vmatrix} 3 & 4 & 8 & -1 \\ 6 & -14 & -26 & -5 \\ 0 & 0 & -44 & -30 \end{vmatrix}$$

The last step is to put these new coefficients back into the equations and solve them. If you work up from the last equation you get the following:

```
-44z=-30 or z = 0.682
-14y -26z =-5 or y = 1.623 (Use 0.682 for z)
3 ^x + 4y +8z = -1 or x = -4.316 (Use 0.682 for z and 1.623 for y)
```

This method shows how to do these operations in Turbo Pascal:

```pascal
procedure Mat.Gauss;
var
   i, j, k, max : integer;
   tmp : real;
begin
   for i := 1 to Rows do
   begin
      {Find the row below the current row with the highest
      absolute value in the cell on the diagonal}
```

```
        max := i;
        for j := i + 1 to Rows do
            if abs( Self.GetCell( j, i ))
                > abs( Self.GetCell( max, i )) then
                max := j;
        {Swap the current row with the max row}
        if i <> max then
            for k := i to Cols do
            begin
                tmp := Self.GetCell( i, k );
                Self.SetCell( i, k, Self.GetCell( max, k ));
                Self.SetCell( max, k, tmp );
            end;
        {Reduce cells under the diagonal to 0}
        tmp := Self.GetCell( i, i );
        for j := i + 1 to Rows do
            for k := Cols downto i do
                Self.SetCell( j, k, Self.GetCell( j, k )
                    -Self.GetCell( i,k ) * Self.GetCell( j, i )
                    / tmp );
    end;
    {Do substitute phase}
    for j := Rows downto 1 do
    begin
        tmp := 0.0;
        if j < Rows then
            for k := j + 1 to Rows do
                tmp := tmp + Self.GetCell( j, k )
                    * Self.GetCell( k, Cols )
        else
            k := j;
        Self.SetCell( j,Cols, ( Self.GetCell( j, Cols ) - tmp )
            / Self.GetCell( j, j ));
    end;
end;
```

Comments

The routine presented is slightly more complex than the procedure described. The reason is that if the cell on the diagonal is 0, the elimination loop will divide by 0. To prevent this, the routine searches for the row with the highest absolute value in the cell where the column number matches the row number. Then it swaps the current row with the row it found. If any of the rows do not have a 0 in the diagonal column, this swap prevents the division by 0.

Warnings

Some combinations of equations cannot be solved. This routine make no effort to detect this situation. Instead, it divides by 0 if there is no solution. You can add code to test for a division by 0 in the two statements that do division. When the routine is about to divide by 0, you should return a flag that indicates that the equations could not be solved.

Due to the number of calculations involved, rounding-off errors can be a real problem. If possible, choose equations that have widely different coefficients for any variable in each of the equations.

Enhancements

You can include many other methods in the matrix object. For example, matrices can be added, subtracted, multiplied, and divided. These two methods show how to add and subtract matrices:

```
procedure Mat.Add( MData : Mat );
var
   r, c : integer;
begin
    for r := 1 to Rows do
    begin
       for c := 1 to Cols do
          Self.SetCell( r, c, Self.GetCell( r, c )
             + MData.GetCell( r, c ));
       WriteLn;
    end;
end;

procedure Mat.Subtract( MData : Mat );
var
   r, c : integer;
begin
    for r := 1 to Rows do
    begin
       for c := 1 to Cols do
          Self.SetCell( r, c, Self.GetCell( r, c )
             - MData.GetCell( r, c ));
       WriteLn;
    end;
end;
```

In both of these routines, each cell in one matrix is combined with the corresponding cell in the other matrix. Note that you cannot add or subtract matrices unless their dimensions are identical.

ELEMENTARY ANALYSIS

This section contains a number of miscellaneous mathematical functions. Solution 3.14 shows you how to find the greatest common divisor of two integers. The greatest common divisor is useful in reducing fractions to their lowest terms and in solving certain equations. Solution 3.15 shows several ways to find roots and powers of numbers. This is important for evaluating mathematical expressions. You cannot solve some equations simply by evaluating an expression. For example, there is no simple formula for finding the value of x in this equation:

$$x^3 + x^2 - x - 12 = 0$$

Solution 3.16 shows a way to solve these types of equations.

The last solution shows how to calculate the value of π. Although programs do not need to calculate π, the solution is included because this is a well-known mathematical application of computers.

Find the greatest common divisor of two integers?

Description

The scientific notation that Turbo Pascal uses to display numbers is not the most intuitive way to display numbers. Some programs should display a number such as 1.33333 as 1 1/3. To display fractions properly, you have to find their lowest terms. To do that, you need to find the greatest common divisor of the numerator and the denominator. Euclid included the technique for finding the greatest common divisor in a book written about 300 B.C.

Solution

The program to find the greatest common divisor of two numbers uses the Mod operator. This operator gives the remainder after one number is divided by another. For example, after executing the statement

```
X := 45 Mod 18
```

X contains the value 9. If a number evenly divides another, the Mod operator returns 0, as in the case of 18 Mod 9. This routine ends when the Mod operator returns 0, which signals that the previous divisor is the greatest common divisor. So, the greatest common divisor of 45 and 18 is 9.

This routine shows the algorithm in Turbo Pascal:

```
function Great( Numb1, Numb2 : integer ) : integer;
var
   Tmp : integer;
begin
   {Make sure the second number is greater than the first}
   if Numb1 > Numb2 then
   begin
      Tmp := Numb1;
```

```
        Numb1 := Numb2;
        Numb2 := Tmp;
    end;
    {Find the remainder after dividing the numbers}
    Tmp := Numb2 MOD Numb1;
    {Keep doing this until the remainder is 0}
    while Tmp <> 0 do
    begin
        Numb2 := Numb1;
        Numb1 := Tmp;
        Tmp := Numb2 MOD Numb1;
    end;
    {Return the result}
    Great := Numb1;
end;
```

Comments

The following program uses the preceding function to reduce the fraction 18/45 to its lowest terms and print the result:

```
var
        GCD : integer;
begin
        GCD := Great( 18, 45 );
        WriteLn( 18 DIV GCD, '/', 45 DIV GCD );
end.
```

This program gets the greatest common divisor of the two numbers, then it divides each number by the greatest common divisor before printing the results.

3.15 How do I...

Find roots and powers of numbers?

Description

Before you can evaluate exponential equations, you need a way to raise a number to any power. This includes fractional powers, which are, in fact, roots of the number.

See Also

3.10 Raising complex numbers to a power

Solution

You can use repeated multiplications to raise a number to a power. This technique has two drawbacks. First, the technique is very slow when the exponents are large. Second, it does not work when the exponent is a fraction.

You can use logarithms to calculate the result of raising any real number to any real power. The product of the logarithms of two numbers gives the logarithm of the result of the exponentiation, as in this Pascal expression:

```
Result := Exp( Ln( Number ) * Ln( Power ));
```

This expression raises `Number` to `Power`. The `Ln` function gets the logarithm for each of the arguments, and the `Exp` function converts the resulting logarithm to a regular number.

Calculating the root of a number is the same as raising the number to a fractional power. For example, to get the cube root of a number, raise it to the 1/3 power. This Pascal expression does the job:

```
Result := Exp( Ln( Number ) * Ln( 0.333333 ));
```

Comments

You could put these expressions in functions to clarify the purpose of the expression. Doing so has an effect on performance. Because the functions are so short, there is not a big savings in memory space by using functions unless you use the expression many times. Also, the extra call to the function takes up time, which can be considerable if the calculation occurs in a loop that is executed many times. Examine the needs of your program carefully before deciding how to implement the expressions.

Warnings

The `Ln` and `Exp` functions use long formulas to get their results. The need to find the roots or powers of many numbers slows program execution noticeably.

Formulas that use exponents can generate very large numbers. It is easy to get numeric overflows. Be sure to use a floating-point format that is large enough not only for the input data and the results but also for any intermediate values.

Enhancements

One way to keep the performance up is to write special routines for certain exponentiations that you use often in your program. You can "hard code" the logarithm of the exponent in the routine to save one call to `Ln`. Also, you can write special code for certain exponentiations. For example, this routine raises a number to the fifth power:

```
function Power5( Numb : real ) : real;
var
```

```
        Part : real;
begin
        Part := Numb * Numb; {Compute Numb squared}
        Power5 := Part * Part * Numb;
end;
```

Notice that the preceding routine performs only three multiplications to raise a number to the fifth power. It is also faster than the Ln/Exp technique.

3.16   How do I...

Find roots of equations?

Description

In question 3.13 you saw how to solve equations with several variables. The equations used were linear, that is, none of the variables could have an exponent. This solution shows a technique for solving equations with one variable raised to one or more powers.

See Also

3.15   Finding roots and powers of numbers

Solution

The first step in solving a nonlinear equation is to use algebra to get it into standard form. An equation is in standard form if each of the terms with the same exponent are added together and a 0 appears on the right side of the equal sign. This is an example of an equation in standard form:

$$x^2 + 3x - 4 = 0$$

You can express this equation as a function that returns the result of substituting some value for x:

```
function Eval( x : real ) : real;
begin
        Eval := x * x + 3 * x - 4;
end;
```

One way to find the value of x that gives 0 as a result is to try various real numbers until the result is 0. This search can take a long time; a better way is required. To get a clue about how to do this, look at Figure 3-5. The graph in this figure shows the possible values of x and the results of the Eval function. The root corresponds to the point where the curve crosses the x-axis.

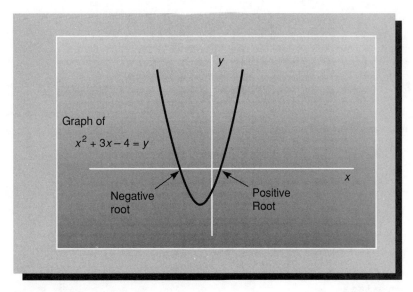

Figure 3-5 Graph of an equation

Note the points A and B on the graph. These points represent initial guesses about the root of the equation. The guesses do not have to be very accurate; they simply have to generate points on opposite sides of the x-axis. A line drawn between the points A and B will cross the x-axis somewhere near the root. A line drawn perpendicular to the x-axis will cross the curve at some point. This point represents the next guess to try. Use it instead of the point that is on the same side of the x-axis.

This Turbo Pascal program implements this technique:

```
{This program solves nonlinear equations}
program roots;

{Evaluate the function x^2 + 3x - 4}
function Eval( x : real ) : real;
begin
    Eval := x * x + 3.0 * x - 4.0;
end;

var
   LoGuess, HiGuess, NextGuess : real;
   LoVal, HiVal, NextVal : real;

begin
   LoGuess := 0.0;                    {Make initial guesses}
   HiGuess := 100.0;
   LoVal := Eval( LoGuess );          {Evaluate both points}
```

```
   HiVal := Eval( HiGuess );
   {If the points are not on opposite sides of the x-axis
       there is no solution in the interval}
   if (( LoVal < 0.0 ) AND ( HiVal < 0.0 ))
      OR (( LoVal > 0.0 ) AND ( HiVal > 0.0 )) then
      WriteLn( 'No solution' )
   else
   begin
      repeat
          {Compute where the line crosses the x-axis}
          NextGuess := LoGuess + ( LoGuess - HiGuess ) * LoVal
                 / ( LoVal - HiVal );
          { Evaluate the new point }
          NextVal := Eval( NextGuess );
          {See what point to replace}
          if ( LoVal < 0.0 ) AND ( NextVal < 0.0 ) then
          begin
             LoGuess := NextGuess;
             LoVal := NextVal;
          end
          else
          begin
             HiGuess := NextGuess;
             HiVal := NextVal;
          end;
      {Keep trying until very close to the root}
      until Abs( NextVal ) < 0.0000001;
      WriteLn( 'The root is: ', NextGuess );
   end;
   ReadLn;
end.
```

Comments

This program zeros in on the root very quickly, even when the guesses are way off. If you look back at the graph of the curve, you can see that this equations has two roots. This technique can find only one root at a time; to find the second root, you have to use a separate set of initial guesses.

In many programs you can use "hard-coded" guesses to find the roots of the equations. In other programs, you may have to let the computer make the initial guesses. One way to do this is to have the computer try real numbers a certain interval apart, looking for a pair that yields points straddling the x-axis. Obviously, anything that reduces the number of guesses improves the efficiency of the code.

Warnings

Rounding errors can make it difficult to get the exact value of a root. For this reason, the until statement does not check for a value of 0. Instead, it checks whether the result is close to 0. If you require more accuracy, make the number in this statement smaller.

Enhancements
You can use this function to evaluate most equations:

```
Type
      CoArray : array[1..20] of real;

function Eval( var Coeff : CoArray; cnt : integer; x : real ) : real;
var
   Result : real;
   Xpart : real;
begin
    Result := Coeff[cnt];
    Xpart := x;
    Dec( cnt );
    while cnt <> 0 do
    begin
        Result := Result + Coeff[cnt] * Xpart;
        Xpart := Xpart * x;      {Raise x to the next power}
        Dec( cnt );
    end;
    Eval := Result;
end;
```

To use this function you must make an array of the coefficients of the equation. If a particular term is missing, the coefficient should be 0. For example, to evaluate the equation:

$$x^4 - 14x^2 + 3x - 10$$

make an array containing: 4, 0, -14, 3, -10. The function starts by setting the result to the last coefficient. Then it adds each of the terms, working backward. The reason for working backward is that each term includes the next higher power of x.

3.17   How do I...

Calculate the value of π?

Description
Every few years someone breaks the record for calculating the number of digits of π. These days, this effort requires very powerful computers that apparently have nothing better to do. This routine shows one equation that calculates π.

See Also

3.16   Finding roots of equations

Solution

This solution is based on the following equation:

$$\pi = \frac{4}{1} - \frac{4}{3} + \frac{4}{5} - \frac{4}{7} \ldots \frac{4}{N}$$

This example shows how to evaluate this series in Pascal:

```
{This is a program to calculate pi}
program pi;
{These options are required to use the extended data type}
{$N+}
{$E+}
var
   Result : Extended;
   Sign : Extended;
   Denom : Extended;
   i : integer;

begin
    Result := 0.0;
    Denom := 1.0;
    Sign := 4.0;
    while Denom < 1.0E20 do
    begin
        Result := Result + Sign / Denom;
        Denom := Denom + 2.0;
        Sign := Sign * -1.0;
    end;
    WriteLn( Result );
    ReadLn;
end.
```

The variable `Result` contains the value calculated so far. Each time through the loop, it gets closer to the actual value of π. `Denom` holds the denominator of the next term to add to the result. It is also used to terminate the loop. If you have more time and want a more accurate result, increase the maximum number for `Demon` in the `While` statement. The last variable is `Sign`, which contains either 4 or -4, according to whether it is an even term or an odd term.

Comments

The number of digits in the result depends on the number of times that the loop runs. Of course, you cannot generate more digits than will fit in the data type you are using. To get more digits you need to create a new data type. This data type does not have to be complete; the ability to add, subtract, and divide is sufficient.

Warnings

This routine takes quite a bit of time to generate a result. It was chosen not for speed but for ease of coding. You may want to put this line inside the loop to show that something is really happening.

```
Write( Chr($13), Result );
```

Enhancements

Many mathematical texts contain one or more formulas that can be used to generate π. By experimenting you can find expressions that are faster or use simpler calculations. One good source for more information about π is the book *A History of* π by Petr Beckmann.

4

STRING

MANIPULATION

4

strings are an important data type. String variables, hold data that is displayed on the screen and store data for later retrieval, as in databases. Because they are so common, it is important to have a number of efficient string-handling routines in your programing library.

This chapter gives you a good start on a string-routine library. It begins with some of the most common things to do with strings: searching and sorting. You'll learn several routines to find and sort strings quickly. You may be surprised to find that you can improve on the performance of the obvious "brute force" searching algorithms.

In users' minds, a program is only as good as its interface. No matter how clever or quick the underlying programming is, users judge a program by what they can see. That is why the second section describes routines for formatting strings. These routines let you make strings appear just the way you want on the screen.

The last section is important for programs that use large numbers of strings. It describes two methods for fitting more strings into less memory. The first method is to store strings in a table. It saves memory by finding duplicate strings and replacing them with a single one. The second technique is to look for redundant information in each string and then compress it.

SEARCHING AND SORTING

One way to implement the search command in word processors is to compare each character of the search string with each character of the text until a match is found. Although this approach works, it becomes very time consuming as the size of the text file grows. Solution 4.1 shows a more efficient way to solve this problem.

Database applications use lists of string-variables to store information such as names or addresses. When the time comes to display this data, most programs provide a way to print the information in alphabetical order. This requires the ability to sort the list of strings. Solution 4.2 shows how to do the sort. It also brings up some points about making this sort efficient.

Databases also have the ability to find one record out of a large list of records. Solution 4.3 shows a technique for searching the lists of data for a given string. You'll learn how to use a binary search to locate the desired string very quickly.

4.1   How do I...

Find one string in another with Turbo Pascal?

Description

The most obvious way to see if one string contains another is to compare the search string against a text or target string, starting at the first character. If the first character does not match, then move to the second character and compare again. This "brute force" approach works and is easy to implement. This solution shows a more efficient way to solve the problem.

See Also

4.3   Searching lists of strings

Solution

The key to increasing the performance of the string search is to reduce the number of comparisons. Still, you must make sure that you do not miss the string you are looking for. Figure 4-1 shows the Boyer-Moore algorithm for comparing strings. The search begins with the last character in the search string. If this character does not match the corresponding character in the target text, and the character in the target string does not occur in the search string, the search can advance by the number of characters in the search string. Thus, after just one comparison, you can eliminate as many characters as there are in the search string.

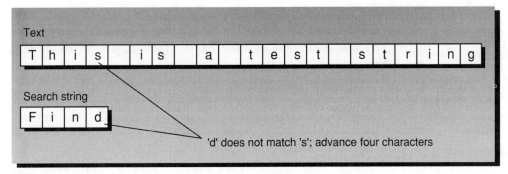

'd' does not match 's'; advance four characters

Figure 4-1 The Boyer-Moore algorithm for comparing strings

The next case to look at is what happens when the last character in the search string does not match, and the character in the target text appears in another position in the search string. In this case the search string is advanced until the matching characters line up (see Figure 4-2).

Determining whether the search string contains the character in the target text requires more comparisons, which slows the routine. To prevent these extra comparisons, the Boyer-Moore algorithm uses a precomputed array of numbers that tells, how many characters to skip for any character in the target text. The position in the array is the ASCII value of a character. For all characters that are not in the search string, the corresponding array element is the length of the search string. If the character is in the search string, the number is the length of the search string minus the position of that character in the search string. If the character appears more than once, the rightmost position is used. When a character in the search string does

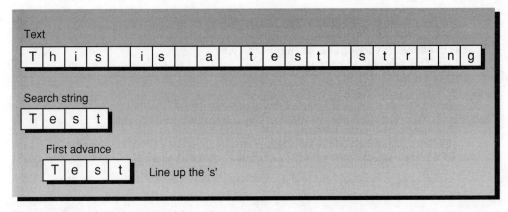

Line up the 's'

Figure 4-2 Aligning matching characters

not match a character in the target text, the character from the target text is used as an index into the array to get the number of characters to skip.

Here is a program that uses the Boyer-Moore algorithm to locate a substring in a file:

```
{Boyer-Moore string search program}
program boyer;

var
   Skip : array[0..127] of byte;        {Number of chars to skip}
   FileName : string;                   {Name of the file to search}
   FHand : Text;                        {The text file being searched}
   FileLine : string;                   {A line from the file}
   SrchStr : string;                    {String to look for}

procedure MakeArray( Pattern : string );
var
   StrLen : integer;
   i : integer;
begin
     {Get the length of the search string}
     StrLen := Length( Pattern );
     {Fill the skip array with the length of the search string}
     for i := 0 to 127 do
         Skip[i] := StrLen;
     {Adjust the values for characters that occur
     in the search string}
     for i := 1 to StrLen do
         Skip[Ord( Pattern[i] )] := StrLen - i;
end;

{Look for the pattern in the Text string}
function Search( Text, Pattern : string ) : integer;
var
   i, j : integer;
   TxtLen, PatLen : integer;
begin
    PatLen := Length( Pattern );
    TxtLen := Length( Text );
    {Initialize the compare pointers to the
    end of the search string}
    i := PatLen;
    j := PatLen;
    {Loop until all text is searched or a match is found}
    repeat
      {Compare the characters}
      if Text[i] = Pattern[j] then
      {If they match, check the previous characters}
      begin
            Dec( i );
            Dec( j );
```

```
            end
            else    {Otherwise, use the skip array to see
                    how far to advance the search string}
            begin
                if PatLen - j + 1 > Skip[Ord( Text[i] )] then
                    i := i + PatLen - j + 1
                else
                    i := i + Skip[Ord( Text[i] )];
                j := PatLen;
            end;
        until ( j<1 ) or ( i > TxtLen );
        Search := i + 1;
end;

{Get a filename and search string, then use Boyer-Moore to
search the file}
begin
    Write( 'Enter the filename: ' );
    ReadLn( FileName );
    Assign( FHand, FileName );
    Reset( FHand );
    Write( 'Enter the search string: ' );
    ReadLn( SrchStr );
    MakeArray( SrchStr );
    while NOT EOF( FHand ) do
    begin
        ReadLn( FHand, FileLine );
        if Search( FileLine,SrchStr ) < Length( FileLine ) then
            WriteLn( FileLine );
    end;
    Close( FHand );
    ReadLn;
end.
```

The first procedure in this program fills the skip array with the number of characters that the search string should be advanced for each possible character in the target text. The first loop fills in each element of the array with the length of the search string. The next loop goes through the search string and, for each character, sets the entry in the skip array to the distance between the character and the end of the search string.

The next function, Search, uses the skip array to see if the search string is in the target text. The main loop in this routine compares characters from the search string with characters from the target text. When the characters do not match, the character in the target text is used as an offset into the skip array. The value from the skip array is used to move the search string forward. The loop continues until the entire target text has been searched, or all of the characters in the search string have been successfully compared with the target text.

The main routine in the program prompts the user for a filename and the search string. It opens the file for reading and uses the search string to make a `skip` array. The loop reads each line from the file and passes it to the `Search` function. If the search string is in the line, the routine prints the line on the screen.

Comments

Some implementations of the Boyer-Moore algorithm include the `MakeArray` step in the `Search` function. Although this is more convenient, it degrades performance. If you make this a separate step, your program can use the search string many times without rebuilding the array.

Warnings

The `Search` function uses many of the characters in the target text as offsets into the `skip` array. This is okay as long as the target text contains only standard ASCII characters. If the target text contains characters with ordinal values greater than 127 (such as the IBM line-drawing characters), you get a run-time error when you call `Search`.

To get around this problem you can enlarge the `skip` array and modify the `MakeArray` routine to fill the enlarged array. This, of course, makes `MakeArray` slower, reducing the performance advantage of this algorithm.

Enhancements

You can increase the overall performance of this algorithm by modifying the `MakeArray` routine. One way to speed it up is to restrict the allowable characters and shorten the `skip` array. For example, if you don't need to make case-sensitive searches and you don't want to search for punctuation, you can write a function to reduce the character set to 27 items, as follows:

```
function GetIndex( ch : character ) : integer;
begin
        {See if the character is an uppercase letter}
        if ( Ord( ch>=Ord( 'A' )) AND ( Ord( ch )<=Ord( 'Z' )) then
                GetIndex := Ord( ch ) - Ord( 'A' ) + 1
        {See if the character is a lowercase letter}
        else if ( Ord( ch )>=Ord( 'a' )) AND ( Ord( ch )<=Ord( 'z' )) then
                GetIndex := Ord( ch ) - Ord( 'a' ) + 1
        {All other characters are converted to a 27}
        else
                GetIndex := 27;
end;
```

Now, use this function when accessing the `skip` array, as in this example:

```
Skip[ GetIndex( Pattern[i] )] := Strlen - 1;
```

Be sure to change both the `MakeArray` function and the `Search` function.

Sort strings into dictionary order with Turbo Pascal?

Description

The order in which characters occur in a character set is called the collating sequence. If you use the ASCII collating sequence to determine the order of a set of strings, you will find all of the lowercase characters grouped together. If you want to put the strings in dictionary order, you have to define a new collating sequence that puts each lowercase letter next to its corresponding uppercase letter.

See Also

4.6   Making a string all uppercase

2.11   Printing forms (uses the shell sort)

Solution

You can use the shell sort routine from question 2.11 to sort strings. The shell sort compares two items and, if they are not in the correct order, swaps the items. This works as easily for strings as it does for numbers. If you compare two Turbo Pascal strings with the greater-than operator (>) the ASCII collating sequence is used to make the comparison. Because the goal of this solution is to sort the strings alphabetically, you need a new function that compares strings according to dictionary order.

First, this new string-comparison function should compare the first characters in each string without regard to case. If the characters are different, that difference tells which string occurs later. If the characters are the same, the function case compares to see which string occurs later.

The following program uses a shell sort to sort a file into dictionary order:

```
{This is a program to sort strings}
program strsort;

type
    SList  = array[1..50] of string;

function Compare( Strng1, Strng2 : string ) : integer;
var
   i : integer;
begin
    i := 1;
    Strng1 := Strng1 + Chr( 0 );
    Strng2 := Strng2 + Chr( 0 );
    {Look for the first character that does not match}
    while ( i < Length( Strng1 )) AND ( Strng1[i] = Strng2[i] ) do
```

```
        Inc( i );
    if UpCase( Strng1[i] ) = UpCase( Strng2[i] ) then
    begin
        if Strng1[i] = Strng2[i] then
            Compare := 0
        else if Strng1[i] < Strng2[i] then
            Compare := -1
        else
            Compare := 1;
    end
    else if UpCase( Strng1[i] ) < UpCase( Strng2[i] ) then
        Compare := -1
    else
        Compare := 1;

end;

{Use shell sort to sort the list}
procedure SortList( var Data :SList; Count : integer );
var
   i, j, h : integer;
   v : string[40];
begin
    {Compute the size of the first shell}
    h := 1;
    repeat
        h := 3 * h + 1;
    until h > Count;
    repeat
       {Make the next smaller shell}
       h := h DIV 3;
       {Compare the strings at the edges of the shell}
       for i := h + 1 to Count do
       begin
           v := Data[i];
           j := i;
           {If the strings are out of order, swap them}
           while ( Compare( Data[j - h], v ) = 1) AND ( j>h ) do
           begin
               Data[j] := Data[j - h];
               j := j - h;
           end;
           Data[j] := v;
       end
    until h = 1;
end;

var
   Strngs : SList;
   i : integer;
   StrCnt : integer;

begin
```

```
    StrCnt := 0;
    repeat
        Inc( StrCnt );
        Write( 'Enter string: ' );
        ReadLn( Strngs[StrCnt] );
    until Strngs[StrCnt] = 'done';
    Dec( StrCnt );
    if StrCnt > 0 then
    begin
        SortList( Strngs, StrCnt );
        for i := 1 to StrCnt do
            WriteLn( Strngs[i] );
    end;
    ReadLn;
end.
```

The Compare function begins by looking for the first character that is different in the two strings. This character determines which string occurs later. To determine dictionary order, the Compare function compares the uppercase versions of the two characters. If the uppercase versions are the same, it checks the lowercase version to fine-tune the ordering. In other words, a comparison between "a" and "b" yields the same result regardless of case. When comparing an "a" with an "A," Compare puts the uppercase letter first.

The SortList function does the actual sorting. This function is a slightly modified version of the sort shown in question 2.11. The heart of this routine is the call to Compare, which determines if two strings need to be swapped. By changing this call, you can change the order of the sort. For example, if you test to see if the result of the comparison is -1, the list is sorted in reverse order.

The main program prompts the user for a number of strings. After entering all of the strings to sort, the user enters the string "done." After that, the program calls SortList, then prints the strings in sorted order.

Comment

You can easily change this program into an MS-DOS "filter" program to sort lists. A filter program takes input from the standard input device (the keyboard) and sends output to the standard output device (the screen). You can use the command line operators <, >, and | with filters to change the standard input and output devices. For instance, use < to copy the contents of a file to the standard input, > to copy the output of a program to a file, and | to copy the output of one program to the input of another program.

To convert the sort program to a filter, simply remove the Write('Enter string: '); statement. This statement puts unwanted data in the standard output. To sort all of the lines in a file, you can use a program like this:

```
strsort < file.txt > sortfile.txt
```

The file `file.txt` starts with the strings to sort. The last line in this file should be the string "done." When the program ends, the sorted list is in the file `sortfile.txt`.

Warnings

The `Compare` routine modifies the strings that it compares by adding a Ctrl-@ to the end of the string. Make sure that there is enough space in the string to accommodate the extra character.

Enhancements

There is not much you can do to improve the comparison algorithm, but you can improve the sort in a number of ways. One improvement is to make an array of indexes to the array of strings and swap indexes instead of swapping strings. Figure 4-3 shows how this works. This can save quite a bit of time: swapping indexes takes only three moves, whereas swapping strings takes as many moves as there are characters in the string.

4.3   How do I...

Search a list of strings with Turbo Pascal?

Description

A list of strings may contain keys to a database or a list of commands, prompts, and so on. The longer the list, the longer it takes to find one of the strings in the list. This question shows an efficient way to search the list.

See Also

4.2   Sorting strings

4.7   Using string tables

Solution

When the list of strings is sorted, you can use a binary search to find a particular item. This search is based on the fact that if the string you are looking for occurs earlier than ("is less than") a string in the table, the search string must be earlier in the sorted array than the current string in the list. So, if you start the search at the string in the middle of the list, you eliminate half of the possible strings with a single comparison. Then, you repeat this opera-

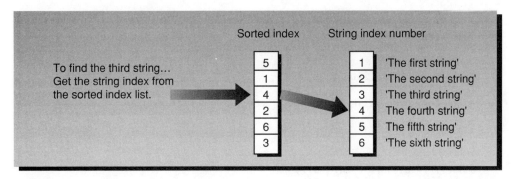

Figure 4-3 Sorting string indexes

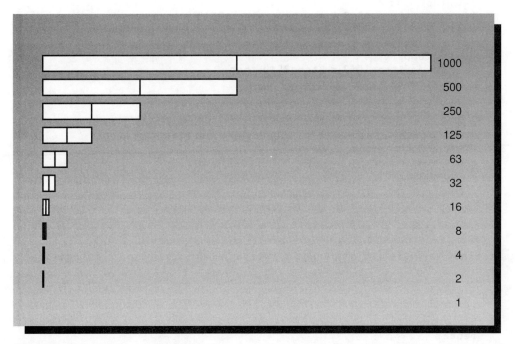

Figure 4-4 A binary search

tion with the half that contains the string. Continue halving the list until only one string is left. This is the string you are looking for. Figure 4-4 shows how you can search a 1000-item list with no more than ten comparisons.

This program uses a binary search to search a list of strings entered by the user:

```
{This is a program to search strings}
program strsrch;

type
   SList  = array[1..50] of string;

function Compare( Strng1, Strng2 : string ) : integer;
var
   i : integer;
begin
   i := 1;
   Strng1 := Strng1 + Chr( 0 );
   Strng2 := Strng2 + Chr( 0 );
   {Look for the first character that does not match}
   while ( i < Length(Strng1 )) AND ( Strng1[i] = Strng2[i] ) do
        Inc( i );
   if UpCase( Strng1[i] ) = UpCase( Strng2[i] ) then
   begin
      if Strng1[i] = Strng2[i] then
          Compare := 0
      else if Strng1[i] < Strng2[i] then
          Compare := -1
      else
          Compare := 1;
   end
   else if UpCase( Strng1[i] ) < UpCase( Strng2[i] ) then
      Compare := -1
   else
      Compare := 1;

end;

{Find the string in the list}
function
StrFind( var Data :SList; Count : integer; Test : string ) : integer;
var
   mid, hi, lo: integer;
begin
   lo := 1;
   hi := Count;
   repeat
      {Find the middle of the list}
      mid := ( hi + lo ) DIV 2;
      {Compare the search string to the current string}
      if Compare( Test, Data[mid] ) = -1 then
          hi := mid - 1
      else
          lo := mid + 1;
   until ( Compare( Test, Data[mid] ) = 0 ) OR ( lo > hi );
   {Return the index of the matching string,
    or -1 for no match}
   if lo > hi then
      StrFind := mid
```

```
    else
        StrFind := -1;
end;

var
   Strngs : SList;          {The list of strings to search}
   i : integer;             {Index into the list}
   StrCnt : integer;        {The number of strings in the list}
   SrchStr : string;        {The string to find}

begin
    StrCnt := 0;
    {Note: the strings must be entered in sorted order}
    repeat
        Inc( StrCnt );
        Write( 'Enter string: ' );
        ReadLn( Strngs[StrCnt] );
    until Strngs[StrCnt] = 'done';
    Dec( StrCnt );
    if StrCnt > 0 then
    begin
        Write( 'Enter search string: ' );
        ReadLn( SrchStr );
        WriteLn( 'Match at line: ', StrFind( Strngs, StrCnt
                 , SrchStr ));
    end;
    ReadLn;
end.
```

The comparison function is identical to the one in question 4.2. This is important, because a binary search is impossible unless the list is sorted. If you use some other comparison function to sort the data, you must use that comparison function in the binary search.

The function StrFind does the binary search. The first statement in the loop calculates the index of the string in the middle of the list. Then the search string is compared to the string in the middle of the list. If the search string occurs earlier than the middle string, the list end-points are set to the first half of the list. Otherwise, the end-points are set to the second half of the list. The process is repeated until a match is found or the length of the sublist being examined becomes 0 or negative.

The last step is to return the index of the matching string or -1 if no match was found.

Comments

You can use the sort filter described in question 4.2 to provide the input for this program. Just use the sort program to create a sorted version of the file to search, then add the string 'done' and the search string to the end of the file. Then enter a command like this one:

```
strsrch < sortlist.txt
```

The binary search always finds the string within $\log_2$(Array size). A quick way to estimate this value is to convert the number of items in the array to a binary number (see question 3.2), then count from the right to the leftmost 1-bit and add 1. For example, if your list has 21,451 items, convert 21,451 to a binary number: 101001111001011. Counting and adding one gives 16. This means that you can find any string in a list of 21,451 items with 16 or fewer comparisons.

Warnings

This algorithm will not work unless the list of items is sorted. Sorting the list may take longer than doing a sequential search in the first place. If possible, leave the list sorted so that you do not have to sort it before each search.

Enhancements

It is not always possible to keep a list sorted at all times. In a database of people, for example, it is not practical to re-sort the list every time you add a person to the list. Fortunately, you do not have to have the whole list sorted to get reasonable performance from your search routine. If you leave the first part of the list sorted and add new strings to the end of the list, you can use a composite search to find strings.

A composite search is actually two searches in one. First it does a binary search of the sorted part of the list. Then, if the string is not found, it searches the unsorted part sequentially. This function shows how to do this:

```pascal
function CompSearch( var Data :SList; SCnt, Count : integer;
        Test : string ) : integer;
var
        i : integer;
begin
        {Search the sorted portion}
        i := Search( Data, SCnt, Test );
        {If the record is not found search the rest of the array}
        if i = -1 then
        begin
            i := SCnt + 1;
            while ( i <= Count ) AND Compare( Data[i], Test ) <> 0 do
                    Inc( i );
            if (i > Count )   {If not record found}
                    i := -1;
        end;
        {Return the index found}
        CompSearch := i;
end;
```

FORMATTING

If you want to display a string on the screen or print it on paper, the first thing to decide is where on the screen or paper the string should appear. If you know the length of the string, it is easy to make the string begin and end at just the right points on the page or screen. Often, however, you do not know the length of the string, and so the computer must decide where to place the string. Solution 4.4 shows how to add spaces to a string to left-, right-, or center-justify it in the available space.

Many programs receive data from other programs or from formatted data-entry fields. This data may have formatting spaces at either end of the string. Solution 4.5 shows how to remove these spaces. After trimming the spaces, you can store a string in less space and compare it with other trimmed strings.

Users enter data in many creative ways: capitalization, spacing, and spelling can all vary. This variation makes it hard for a program to determine if the string entered is the same as one entered before. The simplest variation to deal with is differences in capitalization. You can eliminate this difference before comparing strings by converting all of the characters in each string to uppercase. Solution 4.6 illustrates this procedure.

4.4   How do I...

Left-, right-, and center-justify strings with Turbo Pascal?

Description

The screen area in which to display string data is limited. This question deals with ways of placing the string in that area.

See Also

1.20   Making formatted data-entry fields
4.5   Trimming formatting characters

Solution

Placing a string at a certain location in a field is simply a matter of adding the correct number of spaces at the correct point in the string. Figure 4-5 shows how to add spaces to justify a string. The following routine shows how to left-justify text in Turbo Pascal. It adds spaces at the end until the string is long enough to fill the field.

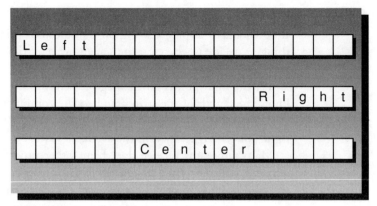

Figure 4-5 Justifying strings

```
procedure LeftJust( var Str : string; len : integer );
begin
    while Length( Str ) < len do
        Str := Str + ' ';
end;
```

The routine to right-justify a string is a bit more complex because it has to move the text in the string to make room for the spaces. Here is that routine:

```
procedure RightJust( var Str : string; len : integer );
var
  i : integer;
begin
    {Move the string to the right}
    for i := Length( Str ) downto 1 do
      Str[i + len - Length( Str )] := Str[i];
    {Fill in the left side with spaces}
    for i := 1 to len - Length( Str ) do
      Str[i] := ' ';
    {Set the length of the string to the length of the field}
    Str[0] := Chr( len );
end;
```

The first loop in this procedure moves the characters to the end of the field. Note that it starts with the last character in the string. This is so that routine won't overwrite a character that has not been moved yet. The second loop copies spaces into the beginning of the new string. The last step is to modify the length of the string by changing the byte at offset 0.

To place a string in the center of a field, you must put half of the spaces needed to fill the field to the right of the string and the other half to the left of the string. You can do this by calling the LeftJust and RightJust procedures, as follows:

```
procedure CenterJust( var Str : string; len : integer );
begin
    LeftJust( Str, ( len - Length( Str )) DIV 2 + Length( Str ));
    RightJust( Str, len );
end;
```

Comments

Typically, you use the `CenterJust` routine to place a title at the top of the screen, the `RightJust` routine to display data strings, and the `LeftJust` routine to display data. For example, to print the title "Data-entry screen" in the middle of the top line of the screen, you might use this code:

```
Title := 'Data-entry screen';
CenterJust( Title, 80 );
GotoXY( 1, 1 );
Write( Title );
```

Warnings

These routines do not check whether strings are larger than the allotted field. In many cases this is not a problem because the data comes from fixed-length fields in a database or from formatted screen entry. If you cannot guarantee that the strings will fit, you should add code to truncate the string at the beginning of each of these routines:

```
if Length( Str ) > len then
    Str[0] := Chr( len );
```

Enhancements

The string-formatting routines in this question can be an important part of a data field object class. A data field object class makes it easy to create data-entry screens. This program shows how to make a simple data-entry screen that includes right-, left-, and center-justified fields:

```
{This program shows how to use justified fields}
program DataEntry;
{StrJust is a unit that contains the routines described in this
 question}
uses crt, StrJust;

type
    Fields = object
            Text : string;                {The data in the field}
            Row, Col : integer;           {The location of the field}
            Len : integer;                {The size of the field}
            constructor Init( Default : string;
                    RPos, CPos, FLen : integer );
            procedure Show; virtual;
            procedure Input; virtual;
    end;
```

```
    LeftField = Object( Fields )
        procedure Show; virtual;
    end;
    RightField = Object( Fields )
        procedure Show; virtual;
    end;

{Initialize the data fields for a field object}
constructor Fields.Init( Default : string; RPos, CPos, FLen : integer );
begin
    Text := Default;
    Row := RPos;
    Col := CPos;
    Len := FLen;
end;

{The default way to show a field (uses center justification)}
procedure Fields.Show;
var
   Tmp : string;
begin
    {Make a copy of the string}
    Tmp := Text;
    {Justify it}
    CenterJust( Tmp, Len );
    {And display it on the screen}
    Gotoxy( Col, Row );
    Write( Tmp );
end;

{Get data from the user}
procedure Fields.Input;
var
   ch : char;
begin
    repeat
        Show;                     {Show the data field}
        ch := ReadKey;            {Get a key}
        if ch = Chr( 8 ) then     {If backspace}
           Text[0] := Chr( Ord(Text[0] ) - 1)
        else if ch <> Chr( 13 ) then {if not enter}
            Text := Text + ch;    {Add the char to the string}
    until ch = Chr( 13 );         {Loop until enter key}
end;

{Show right justified fields}
procedure RightField.Show;
var
   Tmp : string;
begin
    {Make a copy of the string}
    Tmp := Text;
    {Justify it}
```

```
      RightJust( Tmp, Len );
      {Position the cursor}
      Gotoxy( Col, Row );
      {Write the justified string}
      Write( Tmp );
end;

{Show left justified fields}
procedure LeftField.Show;
var
   Tmp : string;
begin
      {Make a copy of the string}
      Tmp := Text;
      {Justify it}
      LeftJust( Tmp, Len );
      {Position the cursor}
      Gotoxy( Col, Row );
      {Write the justified string}
      Write( Tmp );
      {Put the cursor at the end of the string}
      Gotoxy( Col + Length( Text ), Row );
end;

var
   Fld1 : Fields;          {Sample center justified field}
   Fld2 : LeftField;       {Sample left justified field}
   Fld3 : RightField;      {Sample right justified field}

begin
      ClrScr;
      Fld1.Init( 'A sample data entry screen', 1, 1, 80 );
      Fld1.Show;
      Fld2.Init( 'Left justified field', 3, 5, 40 );
      Fld2.Show;
      Fld3.Init( 'Right justified field', 5, 5, 40 );
      Fld3.Show;
      {Loop until Fld3 contains the word 'done'}
      while Fld3.Text <> 'done' do
      begin
         Fld2.Input;
         Fld3.Input;
      end;
end.
```

Three object types are defined in the type section. The first object is the base class for the other types. It includes the methods for initializing the object, displaying center-justified fields, and allowing data input. The objects LeftField and RightField change only the Show method to handle different justification.

The Input method accepts user keystrokes that cause changes to the field data. Input modifies the data for its object and then calls the Show method for that object to display the data. This is why the show methods use the virtual keyword, which tells the compiler to generate code that decides what function to use at run time.

All that is left for the program to do is to initialize the fields and get input for the data-entry fields. Notice that the first field is simply a title; it is not included in the input loop. You exclude other fields from the loop to create prompts and messages. The input loop just calls the input method for each field until the last field contains the string "done."

4.5   How do I...

Trim padding characters with Turbo Pascal?

Description
One problem with using the justification routines in question 4.4 is that the extra spaces become part of the field of data. This solution shows how to remove those spaces to recover the original data.

See Also
1.20   Making formatted data-entry fields

4.4   Justifying strings

Solution
This routine trims all of the spaces at the beginning and the end of the text portion of the string:

```
procedure Trim( var Str : string );
var
   First, Last, i : integer;
begin
    First := 1;
    {Search for the first character that is not a space}
    while ( First < Length( Str )) AND ( Str[First] = ' ' ) do
        Inc( First );
    Last := Length( Str );
    {Search for the last character that is not a space}
    while ( Last > 1 ) AND ( Str[Last] = ' ' ) do
        Dec( Last );
    {Move the string to the left}
    for i := First to Last do
       Str[i - First + 1] := Str[i];
    {Adjust the length of the string}
    Str[0] := Chr( Last - First + 1 );
end;
```

The first loop in this procedure finds the first nonspace character in the string. The second loop searches backward for the last nonspace character in the string. The third loop copies the characters between those two values to the beginning of the string. The last step is to adjust the length of the string to reflect the fact that it no longer contains the spaces.

Comment

This routine is especially useful in programs that deal with formatted data. Data-entry routines often add spaces to display data properly as the user is entering it. When the user indicates that the data is all entered, the spaces must be removed.

Warnings

This routine removes spaces from the beginning and the end of the string, even if the data had spaces in it before it was justified. In most cases this is okay, since spaces usually are not significant in data strings. If your program must preserve spaces, you need to add code that keeps track of how many spaces should be preserved.

4.6   How do I...

Convert a string to uppercase with Turbo Pascal?

Description

Turbo Pascal includes the UpCase function for converting a character to uppercase. This routine goes a step farther by allowing you to capitalize every character in a string.

See Also

4.2   Sorting strings

4.3   Searching lists of strings

Solution

This procedure passes each character in the string to the UpCase function, which capitalizes the character.

```
procedure UpStr( var Str : string );
var
    i : integer;
begin
    for i := 1 to Length( Str ) do
        Str[i] := UpCase( Str[i] );
end;
```

Comments

This procedure is handy with such routines as StrFind, the string-search routine in question 4.3. If the user is not concerned about case, then you can make every character in the array and the search string uppercase. In this way, strings with the same letters match, regardless of the case.

The following routine uses UpStr to capitalize all of the characters of strings in an array for use with StrFind:

```
procedure UpLst( Data : SList; Count : integer );
var
        i : integer;
begin
        for i := 1 to Count do
                UpStr( Data[i] );
end;
```

SAVING MEMORY

It seems that there is always more data than there is memory to hold it. Your computer dealer is always glad to sell you a larger hard drive or more RAM, but it would be nice if you could make the available storage hold more data instead. The two solutions in this section show you how to squeeze a few more strings into memory or disk storage.

Solution 4.7 shows how to eliminate redundant strings by using a string table. Strings tables are lists of strings used in a program. A program can reference a string by using the index of the string in the table. For example, in a database you can store string table indexes in the data records instead of a string for a field such as a name field. If there are several records for people named "Smith," you save 4 bytes for each record (6 bytes for the string versus 2 bytes for an integer.)

Solution 4.8 shows how to compress a string by using Huffman encoding. You compress the strings by encoding each character with the fewest possible bits. This technique can compress text files by 20% to 30%.

4.7	How do I...

Create and use a string table with Turbo Pascal?

Description

String tables let you keep all of the strings in a program in one place. One advantage of a string table is that you can easily avoid having multiple copies of a single string. This saves space because each routine that uses the string can use an integer instead of a string array to represent the string.

See Also

4.2   Sorting strings

Solution

The following functions make up a string table object class. Here is the definition for this class:

```
type
    Entry = record              {Each entry in the string table}
        UseCnt : integer;       {Number of times this string was added}
        Data : ^string;         {The string}
    end;

    StrTable = object
        Table : array[1..256] of Entry;
        StrCnt : integer;       {Total entries}
        procedure Init;
        function AddStr( Str : string ) : integer;
        procedure DeleteStr( Numb : integer );
        procedure WriteStr( Numb : integer );
    end;
```

The first method for this class initializes the string table. The only variable that you need to initialize is strCnt, which contains the total number of strings.

```
procedure StrTable.Init;
begin
    StrCnt := 0;
end;
```

Once the object is initialized, you can begin adding strings to it. The AddStr method for adding a string to the table begins by searching for a matching string in the table. If the string is already in the table, AddStr increments the usage count for that string and returns the string number. If the string does not exist, AddStr adds it to the table.

```
{Add a new string to the string table}
function StrTable.AddStr( Str : string ) : integer;
var
    Indx : integer;
    Available : integer;
begin
    Indx := 1;
    Available := StrCnt + 1;
    {Search the string table for a matching string and
    an available spot in the table}
    while ( Indx < StrCnt ) AND ( Str <> Table[Indx].Data^ ) do
    begin
        {If the string is not being used, its
        table spot is available}
```

```
         if Table[Indx].UseCnt = 0 then
            Available := Indx;
         Inc( Indx );
      end;
      {If the string was in the table}
      if Indx < StrCnt then
      begin
         {increment the use count}
         Inc( Table[Indx].UseCnt );
         AddStr := Indx;
      end
      else {The string is not in the table}
      begin
         {If a string is available use it}
         if Available <= StrCnt then
            FreeMem( Table[Available].Data
              , Length( Table[Available].Data^ ) + 1 )
         else {Otherwise add the string to the end of the table}
            Inc( StrCnt );
         {Allocate memory for the string}
         GetMem( Table[Available].Data, Length( Str ) + 1 );
         {Copy the string to the table}
         Table[Available].Data^ := Str;
         {Initialize the use count}
         Table[Available].UseCnt := 1;
         AddStr := Available;
      end;
end;
```

The first loop goes through all of the strings in the table, looking for one that matches. It also searches for any deleted strings. A string is considered deleted if the use count is 0. If the string exists, the `AddStr` method increments the use count for that string. Otherwise, it adds the string to the list by either using one of the deleted entries or by adding the string to the end of the list.

The next method deletes a string. The string must be deleted as many times as it was added before it is actually removed from the list. For this reason, `DeleteStr` only decrements the use count. When the use count becomes 0, the string is removed from the list, making room for new strings.

```
procedure StrTable.DeleteStr( Numb : integer );
begin
   if Table[Numb].UseCnt > 0 then
      Dec( Table[Numb].UseCnt );
end;
```

The final method prints a string from the table. This is simply a matter of looking up the string at the indicated index and printing it.

```
procedure StrTable.WriteStr( Numb : integer );
begin
```

```
    if Table[Numb].UseCnt > 0 then
        Write( Table[Numb].Data^ );
end;
```

Comments
Table like this one are often used to store prompts and error messages, eliminating redundant messages. A string table is also useful if your program is translated into a foreign language. The reason is that your program uses integers to represent strings. To translate the program, you must change only the module that loads the strings into the string table.

String tables also help you make efficient use of database memory. In this case, you add each field to the string table and save the number returned by AddStr in the record. For this reason, you do not have to store each instance of a field that is the same in several records. Of course, you must save the entries from the string table along with the data, so that you can reconstruct the records.

Warnings
Because these routines use the heap, there is a limit on the amount of string data that you can store and the number of entries that you can create. If you use these routines to handle large amounts of data, you should add code to test limits and handle the exceeding of limits.

Enhancements
The biggest performance limitation of these routines is the time it takes to search for a string. You can improve performance by applying the search techniques discussed in question 4.3. Be careful if you sort the list, because routines in your program may be using the index numbers that were valid before the sort. In this case, you should sort an array of indexes that can be used when you search the list.

4.8   How do I...

Compress strings with Huffman encoding in Turbo Pascal?

Description
Most strings take up more space than they really need. For example, if the string contains only alphabetic characters, each character needs only 6 of the 8 bits used. This solution shows not only how to reduce the number of bits

used in the string but also how to compute the optimum number of bits required for each character.

See Also

9.7   Compressing files

Solution

The key to this technique is to use the fewest possible bits for the most commonly used characters. For example, in the string "test data", the most common character is "t". You can encode the "t" as 11, using only 2 bits. The next most common character is "a", which you can encode as 01. The characters "e", "s", "(space)", and "d" are equally common; you can encode them as 100, 101, 001, and 0001, respectively. Thus, the encoded string is 1110010111001000101101, and you use only 23 bits for a string that ordinarily occupies 72 bits. The string can be decoded because none of the codes begins with any of the other codes. In this example, the first two 1's must be a "t" because none of the other characters starts with "11".

As you may have guessed, the hard part is determining the optimum codes to use for each character. One way to generate codes is to use a tree similar to the one in Figure 4-6.

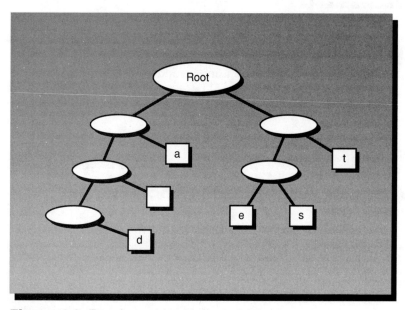

Figure 4-6 Tree for making Huffman codes

The character code gives the path from the root of this tree to the character. Each digit in the Huffman code tells whether to go left or right as you move down the tree. To convert a Huffman code to a character, start at the root, then move to the left child if the first digit of the code is a 0 and the right child if it is a 1. Keep getting digits from the code and moving down the tree until you get to a character node. The next digit in the Huffman-encoded string is the first digit of the next character.

To convert a character to its Huffman code, you must start at the character and work your way up to the root. The tree must include parent pointers for each node so that the encoding routine can move from child to parent node back to the root. The parent pointer tells what node is the parent of the current node and also indicates whether the node is the left or right child of the parent node. Because the conversion process works up the tree, the bits are in reverse order. You must restore the correct order before outputting the code.

These routines show how to encode and decode strings in Turbo Pascal:

```
{Encode a string using a Huffman tree}
procedure Encode( var Str : string );
var
   i : integer;
   NodeNumb : integer;
   OutStr : string;
   CharNumb : integer;
   BitNumb : byte;
   Code : byte;
   CodeBit : byte;
begin
    {Set the initial location for outputting bits}
    CharNumb := 1;
    BitNumb := 7;
    {Initialize the current character}
    OutStr[1] := Chr( 0 );
    {Go through each character in the string}
    for i := 1 to Length( Str ) do
    begin
        {The first node matches the ASCII code for the char}
        NodeNumb := Ord( Str[i] );
        {Initialize variables that will define the code}
        CodeBit := 0;
        Code := 0;
        {Go until you get to the root node}
        while NodeNumb <> List[1] do
        begin
            {If the field contains a positive value set a
            bit in the code}
            if Tree[NodeNumb].Parent > 0 then
                Code := Code OR ( 1 SHL CodeBit );
            {Go to the next bit}
```

```
            Inc( CodeBit );
            {Go to the parent node}
                NodeNumb := Abs( Tree[NodeNumb].Parent );
        end;
        {Copy the bits from the code to the output string}
        while CodeBit > 0 do
        begin
            Dec( CodeBit );
            if ( Code AND ( 1 SHL CodeBit )) <> 0 then
              OutStr[CharNumb]
                  := Chr( Ord( OutStr[CharNumb] )
                OR ( 1 SHL BitNumb ));
            if BitNumb > 0 then
              Dec( BitNumb )
            else
            begin
                Inc( CharNumb );
                BitNumb := 7;
                OutStr[CharNumb] := Chr( 0 );
            end;
        end;
    end;
    {Set the size of the output string}
    OutStr[0] := Chr( CharNumb );
    {Copy it to the caller's string}
    Str := OutStr;
end;

{Decode a string using a Huffman tree}
procedure Decode( var Str : string );
var
   CharNumb : integer;
   BitNumb : byte;
   OutStr : string;
   NodeNumb : integer;
begin
    {Initialize the output string}
    OutStr := '';
    {The next two variables point to the next bit in the
    encoded string}
    CharNumb := 1;
    BitNumb := 7;
    {Go until decoding a period}
    while OutStr[Length(OutStr)] <> '.' do
    begin
        NodeNumb := List[1]; {Start at the root}
        {When the node numbers get down to the character set
        the character has been decoded}
        while NodeNumb > 128 do
        begin
            {If the bit is set go left, otherwise go right}
            if ( Ord( Str[CharNumb] ) AND ( 1 SHL BitNumb ))= 0 then
                NodeNumb := Tree[NodeNumb].Right
```

```
else
        NodeNumb := Tree[NodeNumb].Left;
     {Go to the next bit in the encoded string}
     if BitNumb > 0 then
           Dec( BitNumb )
     else
     begin
           Inc( CharNumb );
           BitNumb := 7;
      end;
   end;
   {Add the character to the output string}
   OutStr := OutStr + Chr( NodeNumb );
 end;
 {Copy the output string to the caller's string}
 Str := OutStr;
end;
```

The variables `CharNumb` and `BitNumb` identify the current bit in the encoded string. `CharNumb` is the current character in the string, and `BitNumb` is the number of the bit being changed or examined. `BitNumb` starts at 7 to indicate the most significant bit.

The main loop in the `Encode` procedure encodes each character in the source string. It does this by working its way up the tree to the root node, recording in the variable `Code` the turns it takes to get there. When the character is completely encoded, the bits are copied from `Code` to the output string. When all of the characters have been encoded, the output string is copied to `Str`, which is the string provided by the calling routine.

The decode routine works its way through the encoded string one bit at a time. It begins at the root of the tree and works its way down according to the bits in the encoded string. When it gets to one of the terminal nodes, it has found a character. The routine copies this character to the output string and goes back to the root node to get the next character.

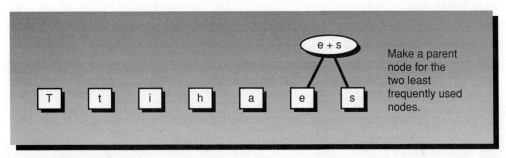

Figure 4-7 Building the Huffman tree

David Huffman discovered the technique for making the tree from a list of frequencie of characters (see Figure 4-7). The tree begins as a group of unconnected nodes, one for each character in the string to be compressed. The algorithm finds the two least frequently used characters and creates a parent node whose frequency is the sum of the frequencies of the two characters. This new node replaces its two child nodes in the frequency table. Then the algorithm repeats the search for least frequently used characters, and combines them into a new parent node. This process of creating parent nodes continues until the root node is created.

Here are some of the global variables used in building the tree:

```
{Huffman code compression}
program Huff;

type
    Node = record           {Each node in the tree}
        Freq : integer;     {The frequency for the character}
        Parent : integer;   {The parent of this node}
        Left : integer;     {The left child of this node}
        Right : integer;    {The right child}
    end;

var
    Tree : Array[1..256] of Node;       {The huffman tree}
    List : Array[1..128] of integer;    {A list of indexes into
                                        the tree}
```

Tree is the tree used to encode and decode strings. The first 128 entries in the array are the character set used in the string to be compressed. The first step in creating the tree is to initialize the first 128 entries in the tree with the frequencies of the characters in the string to be encoded. At the same time List is initialized to indexes into the tree. Next, the entries in List are sorted in decreasing order of frequency. This sort routine is a modified version of the shell sort used earlier in this book.

```
{Sort the list of indexes based on frequency}
procedure SortList;
var
    i, j, h : integer;
    Tmp : integer;
begin
    {h does not need to be calculated because the length of the
     list is known ( 128 bytes )}
    h := 364;
    repeat
        h := h DIV 3;
        for i := h + 1 to 128 do
        begin
            Tmp := List[i];
```

```
                j := i;
                {Compare the tree entries}
                while ( Tree[List[j - h]].Freq < Tree[Tmp].Freq )
                    AND (j > h) do
                begin { But swap indexes }
                    List[j] := List[j - h];
                    j := j - h;
                end;
                List[j] := Tmp;
        end
    until h = 1;
end;
```

This routine makes entries in `Tree` according to Huffman's algorithm. It keeps the list of indexes sorted so that the last two entries in the list always point to those nodes in `Tree` with the lowest frequencies. When the list is reduced to a single item, that item points to the root of `Tree`.

```
procedure MakeTree( Str : string );
var
    i : integer;
    ListCnt : integer;
    TreeCnt : integer;
    NewFreq : integer;
begin
    {Initialize Tree and List}
    for i := 1 to 128 do
    begin
        Tree[i].Freq := 0;
        Tree[i].Parent := -1;
        List[i] := i;
    end;
    {Calculate the frequencies}
    for i := 1 to Length( Str ) do
        Inc( Tree[Ord( Str[i] )].Freq );
    SortList;
    ListCnt := 128;
    {Back up to non-zero frequency}
    while ( ListCnt > 0 ) AND ( Tree[List[ListCnt]].Freq = 0 ) do
        Dec( ListCnt );
    TreeCnt := 128;
    while ListCnt > 1 do
    begin
        {Make a new node in the tree for the sum of the two
        least frequent items}
        Inc( TreeCnt );
        NewFreq := Tree[List[ListCnt]].Freq
                + Tree[List[ListCnt - 1]].Freq;
        Tree[TreeCnt].Freq := NewFreq;
        Tree[TreeCnt].Parent := -1;
        Tree[TreeCnt].Left := List[ListCnt];
        Tree[TreeCnt].Right := List[ListCnt - 1];
        Tree[List[ListCnt - 1]].Parent := -TreeCnt;
```

```
        Tree[List[ListCnt]].Parent := TreeCnt;
        Dec( ListCnt );
        {Sort the new node into list}
        i := ListCnt;
        while ( i > 1 ) AND ( NewFreq > Tree[List[i - 1]].Freq ) do
        begin
            List[i] := List[i - 1];
            Dec( i );
        end;
        List[i] := TreeCnt;
    end;
end;
```

Comments

There are two steps to encoding a string. First, make the tree by calling MakeTree to make a tree from the string to compress. Second, call Encode to compress the string. This code fragment shows how this works:

```
Sample := 'This is a test string.'
MakeTree( Sample );
Encode( Sample );
```

The encoded string is now in the string Sample. Note the period at the end of the string. This character marks the end of the string during decoding. You can use any character for this purpose, as long as you modify the test in the Decode procedure.

As long as the tree has not been changed, you can decode the string by simply calling Decode. This converts the string in Sample back to the original string. Make sure that the tree used to encode a string is the same one used to decode the string. So, if you save the encoded string, you must also save the tree.

Warnings

Together, the encoding tree and the encoded string might take up more memory than the original string. The higher the ratio of string length to different characters used, the better the performance of this algorithm.

Enhancements

You do not need to make a separate tree for each string that you compress. The only requirements are that the tree include all of the characters that you intend to encode and that you use the same tree to decode a string as you used to encode it. You can modify the MakeTree routine to generate frequencies for a large number of strings and generate the tree from that data. Then you can use that tree to encode each of the strings. Although the individual compressions may not be as efficient, the overall compression may be improved because of the fewer number of trees.

If you can make certain assumptions about the data to be compressed, you can vastly improve the performance of this algorithm. For example, if you know that the data is text, then you can make a tree according to the frequency of characters in the English language. This saves the step of creating the tree each time. You can use this one tree for a large number of text strings rather than have separate trees for each string.

This algorithm does not have to be character based. You can just as easily create a tree that contains common words or phrases in addition to individual letters. In this case, a 3-bit code might stand for a whole word, such as "the." If you use a fixed tree for a large amount of text, you can achieve very high compression rates with this technique.

SYSTEM

PROGRAMMING

WITH

TURBO

PASCAL

ascal was designed as a language for demonstrating programming techniques and algorithms in computer science
classes. As a result, it is not well known as a system programming language. Turbo Pascal has several extensions
to standard Pascal that let you access features of the PC and of MS-DOS.
This chapter shows you how to use these features to access the MS-DOS
command line and environment, access special memory areas, and read and
write disk sectors.

Accessing the command line and the MS-DOS environment variables is
easy when you use the Turbo Pascal routines for this purpose. The first section of this chapter shows you how to use these routines. The next section
shows you how to explore the memory of your PC. This section contains
programs to display memory and some information on interesting areas of
memory to look at. The final section shows you how to read and write the
sectors of disks and diskettes. The final program shows you how to get special information from the reserved areas on the disk.

READING THE COMMAND LINE AND ENVIRONMENT WITH TURBO PASCAL

Many programs have a number of optional modes or work with different
data items. One way to tell the program what modes and data to use is to
have the user specify the information interactively as the program runs. This
is not always the most convenient technique, and it makes it impossible to
use the program as part of a batch file.

The solution is to let the user specify options and data on the command line when the program begins. For example, if your program uses different graphics modes, the user can specify the mode as a command-line parameter. Not only is this convenient, since the user does not have to wait for a question, but it also allows the program to be invoked from a batch file.

Passing options and data on the command line can become tedious when many options must be specified every time the program is run. One way to solve this problem is to use an environment variable to hold the options and data. A good example is the PATH environment variable, which holds a list of directories that MS-DOS searches to find programs the user wants to run. You can see other environment variables that your system uses by typing SET at the MS-DOS command line. This section shows you how to make your program look at environment variables and the command line.

5.1   How do I...

Read the command line in a Turbo Pascal program?

Description
MS-DOS passes a pointer to the command line in a memory structure called the program segment prefix (PSP). Turbo Pascal reads the command line and puts it into several string type variables. The command line is divided wherever a space occurs.

See Also
5.2   Reading the environment
5.5   Reading the program segment prefix
9.4   Viewing text files

Solution
You need two functions to read the command line. They are ParamCount, which gives the number of strings found, and ParamStr, which returns one of the strings. This simple program shows how to list all of the parameter strings:

```
{Program to display the command line}
program cmndline;

var
  i : integer;

begin
```

```
{Print each part of the command line}
for i := 0 to ParamCount do
    WriteLn( 'Parameter[', i, ']: ', ParamStr( i ));
end.
```

The for loop in this program goes through ParamCount + 1 parameters and calls ParamStr to get each one.

Comments

The file viewer in question 9.4 is a good example of a program that reads the command line. The first parameter specifies the name of the file to view. Many programs use this technique to get the name of a file to edit, compress, read, or manipulate in some other way.

ParamCount is the number of parameters on the command line, excluding the name of the file itself. According to the Turbo Pascal documentation, the first parameter (the filename) is number 1 and comes directly after the name of the program. When the program is running under MS-DOS version 3.1 and later, parameter number 0 is the name of the program.

Enhancements

A useful feature of parameter 0 is that, for MS-DOS 3.0 and newer, it specifies the complete pathname of the program, including the directory that contains the program. There are several reasons why the directory that contains the program is not the default directory. One is that the program is in a directory in the path instead of the default directory. Another way to run a program that is not in the default directory is to give the pathname of the program on the command line. You can use the pathname of the program to determine the directory that holds the program, and possibly, any files that go with the program.

The following program shows how you can extract the path from the filename, then use the path to open associated files:

```
{Program to open a file in the program directory}
program ReadFile;

var
        Path : string;
        FHand : file;

begin
        {Get the name of the program}
        Path := ParamStr( 0 );
        {Erase the filename part of the string}
        while ( Path[Length( Path )] <> '\' ) AND Length( Path ) > 0 do
                Dec( Path[0] );
        {Add the name of the resource file}
```

```
      Path := Path + _\data.dat   );
      {Open the new file}
      Assign( FHand, Path );
      Reset( FHand );
      {Use the file}
      close (F Hand);
end.
```

The first step is to copy the filename to a local variable. The `while` loop determines whether the last character in the name is a backslash (\). If it is not, the string is shortened by one character. This continues until the `Path` variable contains only the path part of the name of the program. Figure 5-1 illustrates this process. Next, the name of the file to open is added to the path, and the resulting filename is assigned to a `file` type variable. Finally, the file is opened. Of course, a more complete program would read the file and take some action according to the data it found there.

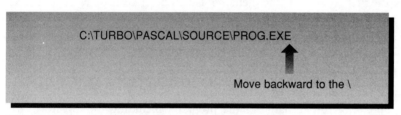

Figure 5-1 Extracting the directory from a path

5.2   How do I...

Read environment variables in Turbo Pascal programs?

Description

MS-DOS keeps a list of strings, called the environment area, that any program can access. MS-DOS itself saves the location of the `command.com` file and the execution path in the environment area. Other programs can use this area to save the path of directories used, commonly used options, or anything else that the programmer thinks is important. Each of the environment strings has two parts: the first is a variable name to identify the string, and the second is the data. These parts are separated by an equal sign (=).

See Also

5.1   Reading the command line

Solution

MS-DOS passes the segment address of the environment in the program segment prefix (PSP) of a program when the program begins. Turbo Pascal reads this value and saves it where it can be used by the three environment functions: `EnvCount`, `EnvStr`, and `GetEnv`. `EnvCount` returns the number of strings in the environment, and `EnvStr` returns one of the strings. These functions are analogous to `ParamCount` and `ParamStr` from question 5.1.

The `GetEnv` function lets you find an environment string for a given variable name. Because the strings can be in any order, this is the best way to find the string that you are looking for.

The program below uses the three environment functions to read the environment:

```
{Program to look at the MS-DOS environment}
program environ;
uses Dos;

var
   i : integer;
   Name : string;

begin
    {Show all of the environment variables}
    for i := 1 to EnvCount do
       WriteLn( 'Env[',i,']: ', EnvStr(i) );
    {Get a variable name}
    Write( 'Enter variable name: ' );
    ReadLn( Name );
    {Look up the variable requested}
    WriteLn( GetEnv( Name ));
    ReadLn;
end.
```

The `for` loop at the beginning of this program uses `EnvCount` to determine how many strings there are and `EnvStr` to print each of the strings. Note that the loop begins with `i := 1`. There is no special value for string number 0, as there is for parameter string 0. After the loop, the program gets a variable name from the user, then uses `GetEnv` to find that variable.

Comments

Compilers or sort routines, which have to save partial results, often save those results in temporary files. These programs often let you set an environment variable specifying the path of the directory to use for the temporary files. This program shows how to open a temporary file in the directory given by the environment variable `TEMP`:

```
{Program to look at the MS-DOS environment}
program environ;
uses Dos;

var
   TempName : string;
   FHand : file;

begin
        {Look up the path for temp variables}
        TempName := GetEnv( 'TEMP' );
        {Make sure that the path ends with a '\'}
        if TempName[Length( TempName )] <> '\' then
                TempName := TempName + '\';
        {Add the name of the temporary file}
        TempName := TempName + 'TEMPFILE.TMP';
        {Open the file}
        Assign( FHand, TempName );
        ReWrite( FHand, 1 );

        {Use the file here}
        Close( FHand );
end.
```

The environment area has a limited amount of space for holding environment strings. Keep this in mind when designing programs that use data from the environment area. Depending on what other programs are doing with the environment area, there may not be enough room for your variables. In this case, your program should have some alternate way of entering the required data.

If you must use a large number of environment variables, you can set up the PC to use a larger environment. Simply add a command like this one to the CONFIG.SYS file:

```
shell = c:\command.com c:\ /p /e:800
```

This command tells MS-DOS to use COMMAND.COM as the user interface shell. The option /e:800 tells COMMAND.COM to use 800 bytes for the environment area. The largest possible environment is 32,767 bytes, and the default size is 160 bytes.

Enhancements

The Turbo Pascal Integrated Development Environment, like many other programs, lets users go to the MS-DOS command line and return to the program just as they left it. Programs do this by running COMMAND.COM as a subprogram. The following program shows how to do this:

```
{Program to execute command.com}
{$M 8192,0,0}
program runcmnd;
uses Dos;

begin
    Exec( GetEnv( _COMSPEC ), _ );
end.
```

The $M directive at the beginning of the program sets the stack to 8,192 bytes and no heap. This gives the subprogram the maximum possible amount of memory. The Exec procedure runs a subprogram. The first argument is the pathname of the program to run; in this case the pathname comes from the COMSPEC environment variable. When MS-DOS is booted, it creates this variable and makes it a pointer to the COMMAND.COM file used. The second argument is the command line to pass to the program; in this case, it is an empty string.

EXAMINING PC MEMORY WITH TURBO PASCAL

Most of the variables in a Turbo Pascal program are contained in the program's data area. Meanwhile, there are literally hundreds of interesting locations scattered through the rest of the PC's memory. This section shows how to use pointer variables to get at these interesting locations. You'll also learn where to look for such things as BIOS tables, MS-DOS configuration information, and all programs running on the computer.

5.3   How do I...

Display blocks of memory with Turbo Pascal?

Description

Much of the information in the PC's memory is undocumented. To find out what is there, you have to make some guesses about what is happening, then look at the memory to see if your theories are correct. The routines given here let you display the contents of memory as blocks of hexadecimal digits.

See Also

3.1   Converting hexadecimal numbers

```
Segment:  40
Offset:   0
Size:     300

0040:0000   F8 03 F8 02 00 00 00 00 78 03 00 00 00 00 00 00   ........x.......
0040:0010   21 44 BF 80 02 00 00 A0 00 00 34 00 34 00 6F 18   !D........4.4.o.
0040:0020   0D 1C 34 05 30 0B 0D 1C 30 0B 0D 1C 33 04 30 0B   ..4.0...0...3.0.
0040:0030   30 0B 0D 1C 0D 1C 74 14 75 16 72 13 62 30 01 00   0.....t.u.r.b0..
0040:0040   FD 00 04 00 00 25 01 04 02 03 50 00 00 10 00 00   .....%....P.....
0040:0050   0B 09 00 00 00 00 00 00 00 00 00 00 00 00 00 00   ................
0040:0060   07 06 00 D4 03 29 30 80 02 00 00 FF 7C DB 15 00   .....)0.....:...
0040:0070   00 80 00 12 00 01 00 00 14 14 14 14 01 01 01 01   ................
0040:0080   1E 00 3E 00 18 00 00 60 09 11 0B 81 50 00 00 07   ..>....`....P...
0040:0090   97 00 00 00 25 00 10 12 00 00 00 00 00 00 00 00   ....%...........
0040:00A0   00 00 00 00 00 00 00 00 00 29 06 00 C0 00 00 00   .........)......
0040:00B0   00 00 00 00 00 00 00 00 00 00 00 00 00 00 00 00   ................
0040:00C0   00 00 00 00 00 00 00 00 00 00 00 00 00 00 00 00   ................
0040:00D0   00 00 00 00 00 00 00 00 00 00 00 00 00 00 00 00   ................
0040:00E0   00 00 00 00 00 00 00 00 00 00 00 00 00 00 00 00   ................
0040:00F0   00 00 00 00 00 00 00 00 00 00 00 00 00 00 00 00   ................
0040:0100   00 00 20 20 00 00 20 20 53 59 53 27 00 00 00 00   ..  ..  SYS'....
0040:0110   00 00 00 00 00 00 01 00 F8 0E 02 00 55 57 00 00   ...........UW..
0040:0120

Press <ENTER> to continue
```

Figure 5-2 Hexadecimal dump of memory at $40:0

Solution

A program that displays memory must first access that memory. You gain
this access by using pointer variables. You can place any address in the computer in a pointer variable and dereference the pointer variable to access the
memory at that address. (See question 1.1 for more information on memory
addresses.) For example, to access the byte at $40:0, use the variable PtrVar,
as shown here:

```
PtrVar := Ptr( $40, 0 );
WriteLn( 'The byte is: ', Byte( PtrVar^ ));
```

Once you can access memory, all you need to do is to print the values in
a useful format. Figure 5-2 shows an example of the hexadecimal dump
format for displaying memory.

The unit below implements the DispMem procedure, which takes a starting address and the number of bytes to display as arguments and writes the
memory indicated to the screen. It uses the HexString and FromHex routines from Chapter 3 to handle hexadecimal strings.

```
{This unit displays memory}
unit ShowMem;
```

```
interface
type
    BytePtr = ^byte;

{visible procedures}
procedure DispMem( Start : BytePtr; Size : integer );
procedure HexString( Number, Size : integer; var Result: string );
function FromHex( Number : string ):integer;

implementation
uses crt;

{Array of Hex digits for printing hex numbers}
const
    Digits = '0123456789ABCDEF';

{Convert Number to a string of Size hex digits}
procedure HexString( Number, Size : integer; var Result: string );
var
    Tmp : integer;
    i : integer;
    Str : string[20];
begin
    {Put digits in a variable}
    Str := Digits;
    {Put digits into the string one at a time}
    for i := 1 to Size do
    begin
        {Get the bits for 1 digit}
        Tmp := Number AND $F;
        {Shift out the bits just used}
        Number := Number SHR 4;
        {Use bits as an index to get the hex digit}
        Result[Size + 1 - i] := Str[Tmp + 1];
    end;
    {Set the size of the string}
    Result[0] := Chr( Size );
end;

{Convert a hexadecimal string to a number}
function FromHex( Number : string ):integer;
var
  i : integer;
  Result : integer;
begin
    Result := 0;
    for i := 1 to Length( Number ) do
    begin
        {Convert the character to upper-case}
        Number[i] := UpCase( Number[i] );
        {See if the character is a digit or a letter}
        if Ord( Number[i] ) >= Ord( 'A' ) then
          Result := Result * 16 + Ord( Number[i] ) - Ord('A') + 10
```

```
            else
                Result := Result * 16 + Ord( Number[i] ) - Ord( '0' );
        end;
        {Return the resulting number}
        FromHex := Result;
end;

{Show a block of memory starting at Start and Size bytes long}
procedure DispMem( Start : BytePtr; Size : integer );
var
    Segment : word;
    Offset : word;
    TmpStr : string;
    DataStr : string;
    i : integer;
    Col : integer;
begin
    {Get the segment and offset of the memory block}
    Segment := Seg( Start^ );
    Offset := Ofs( Start^ );
    {Display the memory segment}
    HexString( Segment, 4, TmpStr );
    Write( TmpStr );
    {Show the offset rounded to the next lower 16-byte boundary}
    HexString( Offset AND $FFF0, 4, TmpStr );
    Write( ':', TmpStr, ' ' );
    {Start the printable characters string}
    DataStr := '';
    Col := 0;
    {Print spaces up to the first byte to display}
    if Offset MOD 16 <> 0 then
    begin
        while Col < ( Offset MOD 16 ) do
        begin
            Write( '   ' );
            DataStr := DataStr + ' ';
            Inc( Col );
        end;
    end;
    {Display the data bytes}
    for i := 1 to Size do
    begin
        {Write the current byte}
        HexString( integer( Start^ ), 2, TmpStr );
        Write( TmpStr, ' ' );
        {See if it is a printable character}
        if ( Start^ >= 32 ) AND ( Start^ < 127 ) then
            DataStr := DataStr + Chr( Start^ )
        else
            DataStr := DataStr + '.';
        {Go to the next byte}
        Inc( Start );
        {Keep track of what column is being printed}
```

```
        Inc( Col );
        {If at the end of the line}
        if Col MOD 16 = 0 then
        begin
            {Write the printable data string}
            WriteLn( ' ', DataStr );
            {Write the next address}
            HexString( Segment, 4, TmpStr );
            Write( TmpStr );
            HexString( Ofs( Start^ ), 4, TmpStr );
            Write( ':', TmpStr, ' ' );
            {Start a new printable string}
            DataStr := '';
        end;
    end;
    {Fill out the last line with spaces}
    if Col MOD 16 <> 0 then
    begin
        while Col MOD 16 <> 0 do
        begin
            Write( '  ' );
            Inc( Col );
        end;
        {Write the last printable string}
        WriteLn( ' ', DataStr );
    end;
end;
end.
```

The first two routines are the hexadecimal conversion routines from Chapter 3. The HexString procedure has been modified to convert byte-sized values in addition to word-sized values. The original routine used 4 as the number of nibbles to print; this routine uses the formal parameter Size, allowing the calling routine to specify the number of nibbles to print.

The FromHex routine is included because programs using this unit are likely to accept hexadecimal values as input.

The DispMem procedure reads memory and formats it into a hexadecimal dump. It begins by separating the starting address into a segment word and an offset word so that the address can be printed on the left side of the screen.

Because the calling program can specify any starting address in memory, the block may not begin on a paragraph (16-byte) boundary. To fix this, the initial offset is rounded down to the previous paragraph boundary, and spaces are printed to fill the line up to the starting byte.

The loop in the middle of the program prints each byte in the block. As it prints each byte, the program checks whether the byte represents a printable character. If so, the program saves the character in the string DataStr; otherwise, it saves a period (.) in the string. This string is printed along the right side of the dump.

The variable `Col` is incremented for each byte displayed. When the value of `Col MOD 16` is 0, the line is complete. The program prints `DataStr`, goes to the next line, prints the current address, and continues displaying data.

When all of the data has been displayed, the program exits the loop and tests `Col` to see if the last line was complete. If not, it prints spaces to fill out the line, then prints `DataStr`.

Comments

To use this unit, you must link it in a `uses` statement to a program. Then the program can show a block of memory by calling `DispMem`. The starting address can be a pointer variable to some memory address, such as this one:

```
DispMem( Ptr( $40, 0 ), 100 );
```

Alternatively, the starting address can be the address of a variable in the program. For example, to see the bytes that make up the array `DataList` use this:

```
DispMem( @DataList, sizeof( DataList ));
```

The following program lets the user enter the address and size of the memory area to display.

```
{Program to dump memory}
program Dump;
uses Crt, ShowMem;

var
   TmpStr : string;
   Segment, Offset : word;
   Size : integer;
   Done : boolean;

begin
    Done := FALSE;
    repeat
      {Show the prompts}
      ClrScr;
      GotoXY( 2, 2 );
      Write( 'Segment:        ' );
      GotoXY( 2, 3 );
      Write( 'Offset:        ' );
      GotoXY( 2, 4 );
```

```
      Write( 'Size:          ' );
      {Get the segment address from the user}
      GotoXY( 11, 2 );
      ReadLn( TmpStr );
      {If string given, get the rest of the fields}
      if Length( TmpStr ) > 0 then
      begin
          {Convert the segment to a number}
          Segment := FromHex( TmpStr );
          {Get the offset}
          GotoXY( 11, 3 );
          ReadLn( TmpStr );
          Offset := FromHex( TmpStr );
          {Get the size}
          GotoXY( 11, 4 );
          ReadLn( TmpStr );
          Size := FromHex( TmpStr );
          {Reduce the size if it would not fit}
          if Size > 288 then
              Size := 288;
          {Show the memory}
          GotoXY( 0, 6 );
          DispMem( Ptr( Segment, Offset ), Size );
          {Wait for the user}
          GotoXY( 2, 25 );
          Write( 'Press <ENTER> to continue' );
          ReadLn;
      end
      else
          Done := TRUE;
    until Done;
end.
```

This program clears the screen and asks the user for the segment, offset, and size of the memory area to display. It uses the `DispMem` routine to show the memory. It keeps asking for new memory blocks until the user enters a blank string for the segment.

Warnings

MS-DOS has no way of protecting itself from programs that modify memory locations. Reading memory, as this program does, is safe. The danger lies in what you might do with the information you discover. You can use this same pointer technique to modify memory locations. If you decide to do this, be very careful. You might make a change that can do great damage, and the results may not be evident for days.

5.4 How do I...

Display the BIOS data area with Turbo Pascal?

Description

BIOS is a program that controls most of the hardware in the PC. Because it is a low-level interface, it stands to reason that if you could find the variables BIOS uses you could get some interesting information about the hardware in the computer. This solution below shows you how to find this low-level information.

See Also

5.3   Displaying memory blocks

Solution

BIOS puts most of its variables in memory starting at location $40:0. *The Waite Group's MS-DOS Developer's Guide, second edition,* contains more information about the BIOS data area. Figure 5-3 shows the layout of memory at this location.

Serial ports	S40:0	Cursor positions	S40:50	Serial timeouts	S40:7C
Parallel ports	S40:8	Cursor shape	S40:60	Key buffer start	S40:80
Equipment list	S40:10	Current video page	S40:62	Key buffer end	S40:82
Reserved		6845 I/O port	S40:63	Screen rows	S40:84
Memory size	S40:13	Mode select register	S40:65	Character height	S40:85
Reserved		Palette value	S40:66	VGA control byte	S40:87
Keyboard shift flags	S40:17	Reset vector	S40:67		
Key buffer tail pointer	S40:1A	Last interrupt	S40:6B		
Key buffer head pointer	S40:1C	Timer count	S40:6C		
Key buffer	S40:1E	Timer rollover flag	S40:70		
Disk status	S40:3E	Ctrl-break flag	S40:71		
Disk timeout count	S40:40	System reset flag	S40:72		
Disk flags	S40:41	Fixed disk status	S40:74		
Current video mode	S40:49	Number of fixed disks	S40:75		
Columns on screen	S40:4A	Fixed disk control	S40:76		
Video page size	S40:4C	Fixed disk port	S40:77		
Video page address	S40:4E	Printer timeouts	S40:78		

Figure 5-3 BIOS data area

The following program uses the information in Figure 5-3 to display a screen of information about the computer that is running the program.

```
{Show information from the BIOS data area}
program BIOSData;
uses Crt, ShowMem;

var
   Words : ^Word;
   Bytes : ^Byte;
   Longs : ^Longint;
   i : integer;
   TmpStr : string;
   PrntCnt, ComCnt, DriveCnt, Misc : integer;

begin
    {Get the equipment list word}
    Words := Ptr( $40, $10 );
    PrntCnt := Words^ SHR 14;
    ComCnt := ( Words^ SHR 9 ) AND $3;
    Misc := Words^ AND $FF;
    Words := Ptr( $40, $0 );
    {Show the I/O port addresses of the installed com ports}
    Write( 'Com port addresses: ' );
    for i := 1 to ComCnt do
    begin
        HexString( Words^, 4, TmpStr );
        Write( TmpStr, ' ' );
        Inc( Words );
    end;
    WriteLn;
    {Show the printer ports}
    Words := Ptr( $40, $8 );
    Write( 'Printer port addresses: ' );
    for i := 1 to PrntCnt do
    begin
        HexString( Words^, 4, TmpStr );
        Write( TmpStr, ' ' );
        Inc( Words );
    end;
    WriteLn;
    {Get the number of drives from the equipment list}
    DriveCnt := Misc SHR 6 + 1;
    WriteLn( 'Diskette drives: ', DriveCnt );
    {Show the initial screen mode}
    case Misc AND $30 of
        $30 : WriteLn( '80X25 BW mode' );
        $20 : WriteLn( '80X25 Color mode' );
        $10 : WriteLn( '40X25 Color mode' );
        $0  : WriteLn( 'EGA mode' );
    end;
    if ( Misc AND 4 ) <> 0 then
      WriteLn( 'Pointing device installed' );
```

```
if ( Misc AND 2 ) <> 0 then
  WriteLn( 'Math processor installed' );
{Get installed memory size}
Words := Ptr( $40, $13 );
WriteLn( 'Installed memory: ', Words^, 'K bytes' );
Bytes := Ptr( $40, $49 );
{Show information about the CRT}
WriteLn( 'Video mode: ', Bytes^ );
Words := Ptr( $40, $4A );
WriteLn( 'Number of columns: ', Words^ );
Words := Ptr( $40, $4C );
WriteLn( 'Video page size: ', Words^ );
Words := Ptr( $40, $4E );
WriteLn( 'Video page address: ', Words^ );
Bytes := Ptr( $40, $62 );
WriteLn( 'Video page number: ', Words^ );
Words := Ptr( $40, $50 + Bytes^ * 2 );
WriteLn( 'Cursor row: ', Words^ SHR 8
          , ' column: ', Words^ AND $FF );
Longs := Ptr( $40, $6C );
WriteLn( 'Ticks since mid-night: ', Longs^ );
Words := Ptr( $40, $75 );
WriteLn( 'Number of fixed disks: ', Words^ );
{These next two may only work for VGAs}
Bytes := Ptr( $40, $84 );
WriteLn( 'Number of rows: ', Bytes^ );
Bytes := Ptr( $40, $85 );
WriteLn( 'Character height: ', Bytes^ );
if DriveCnt > 0 then
begin
    Bytes := Ptr( $40, $90 );
    Write( 'Diskette 1 transfer rate: ' );
    case Bytes^ AND $3F of
        0   : WriteLn( '500 Kbs' );
        $40 : WriteLn( '300 Kbs' );
        $80 : WriteLn( '250 Kbs' );
    else
        WriteLn( 'unknown' );
    end;
    case Bytes^ AND 7 of
        0 : WriteLn( 'Trying 360K disk in 360K drive' );
        1 : WriteLn( 'Trying 360K disk, 1.2 meg drive' );
        2 : WriteLn( 'Trying 1.2 meg disk, 1.2 meg drive' );
        3 : WriteLn( '360K disk in 360K drive' );
        4 : WriteLn( '360K disk in 1.2 meg drive' );
        5 : WriteLn( '1.2 meg disk in 1.2 meg drive' );
        6 : WriteLn( '' );
        7 : WriteLn( '720K or 1.44 meg disk' );
    end;
    Bytes := Ptr( $40, $94 );
    WriteLn( 'Diskette 1 track number: ', Bytes^ );
end;
if DriveCnt > 1 then
begin
```

```
      Bytes := Ptr( $40, $91 );
      Write( 'Diskette 2 transfer rate: ' );
      case Bytes^ AND $3F of
          0   : WriteLn( '500 Kbs' );
          $40 : WriteLn( '300 Kbs' );
          $80 : WriteLn( '250 Kbs' );
      else
          WriteLn( 'unknown' );
      end;
      case Bytes^ AND 7 of
          0 : WriteLn( 'Trying 360K disk in 360K drive' );
          1 : WriteLn( 'Trying 360K disk in 1.2 meg drive' );
          2 : WriteLn( 'Trying 1.2 Meg disk, 1.2 meg drive' );
          3 : WriteLn( '360K disk in 360K drive' );
          4 : WriteLn( '360K disk in 1.2 meg drive' );
          5 : WriteLn( '1.2 meg disk in 1.2 meg drive' );
          6 : WriteLn( '' );
          7 : WriteLn( '720K or 1.44 meg disk' );
      end;
      Bytes := Ptr( $40, $95 );
      WriteLn( 'Diskette 2 track number: ', Bytes^ );
   end;
   ReadLn;
end.
```

```
Com port addresses: 03F8 02F8
Printer port addresses: 0378
Diskette drives: 1
80X25 Color mode
Installed memory: 640K bytes
Video mode: 3
Number of columns: 80
Video page size: 4096
Video page address: 0
Video page number: 0
Cursor row: 12 column: 0
Ticks since mid-night: 1433872
Number of fixed disks: 1
Number of rows: 24
Character height: 16
Diskette 1 transfer rate: unknown
720K or 1.44 meg disk
Diskette 1 track number: 37
```

Figure 5-4 BIOS data area results

The key to reading the memory in the BIOS data area is the definition of three pointer types (BytePtr, WordPtr, LongPtr) at the beginning of the program. When you set one of these pointers to an address, the memory at that address can be used like a variable of the corresponding type. For example, because the equipment list is a word at $40:10, you can use a WordPtr variable to read it. In this case the variable is Words; to read the equipment list, you set Words to $40:10 and then dereference it.

You can read the rest of the variables in the BIOS data area similarly. As each field is read, it is displayed on the screen. The result is a list similar to the one in Figure 5-4.

Comments

The information in the BIOS data area is useful in many programs. If your program does serial I/O, you need to know the I/O addresses of the serial ports installed; if your program displays characters on the screen, you need to know the numbers of rows and columns available; if you use timing loops in your program, you can use the timer count value, and so on. The preceding program gives you the tools you need to to access these values from your programs.

Warnings

Most BIOS areas are the same, but there is no requirement that they be so. The purpose of the BIOS is to shield the operating system from the details of the machine hardware. Some computers, such as Texas Instruments PCs, have unusual hardware. In such cases, the BIOS may be very different from that used by the IBM PC, and you may not find the data you expect in the BIOS data area.

Enhancements

If you intend to use several of the BIOS data area variables in your program, it might be worthwhile to define a structure that gives names to all of the variables. Then you can use the variables like those in any other Turbo Pascal structure. Here is the structure to use:

```
type
     BIOSDataPtr = BIOSData^;
     BIOSData = record
          SerPorts : array [1..4] of word;
          ParPorts : array [1..4] of word;
          EquipList : word;
          Reserved1 : word;
          MemSize : word;
          Reserved2 : word;
          KeyShift : word;
          KeyTail : word;
          KeyHead : word;
          KeyBuffer : array [1..16] of word;
          DiskStatus : word;
          DiskTime : byte;
          DiskCode : byte;
          DiskMisc : array [1..7] of byte;
          VideoMode : bytes;
          VidColumns : bytes;
          VidPageSize : word;
          VidPageAddr : word;
          CursorPos : array [1..8] of word;
          CursorShape : word;
          PageNumber : byte;
```

```
        VideoPort : word;
        ModeRegister : byte;
        PalleteValue : byte;
        ResetVector : pointer;
        LastInterrupt : byte;
        TimerCount : longint;
        Rollover : byte;
        BreakFlag : byte;
        ResetFlag : word;
        FixedDiskStatus : byte;
        FixedDiskCount : byte;
        FixedDiskControl : byte;
        FixedDiskPort : byte;
        PrinterTimes : array[1..4] of byte;
        SerialTimes : array[1..4] of byte;
        KeyBuffStart : word;
        KeyBuffEnd : word;
        ScreenRows : byte;
        CharHeight : byte;
        VGAControl : longint;
        DiskSpeed : byte;
        FixedDiskRegs : array [1..3] of byte;
        DiskInfo : byte;
        MediaType : array [1..2] of byte;
        DiskWork : array [1..2] of byte;
        TrackNumb : array [1..2] of byte;
        KeyBrdStatus : byte;
        KeyLights : byte;
        WaitFlags : array [1..5] of byte;
end;
```

To implement this structure, use a line like this one to assign a value to the structure pointer:

```
BOISDataPtr := Ptr( $40, 0 );
```

5.5   How do I...

Read the MS-DOS PSP of a Turbo Pascal program?

Description
MS-DOS puts a 256-byte memory block at the beginning of each program that is loaded into memory. This block, called the program segment prefix (PSP), contains information such as the command line and address of the environment variables. You can access this information by using the memory-access techniques you've already learned. All that you need is a way to find the address of the PSP.

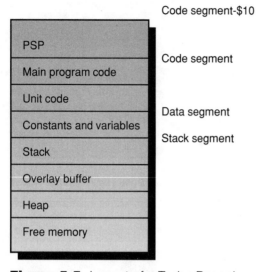

Code segment-$10

Code segment

Data segment

Stack segment

Figure 5-5 Layout of a Turbo Pascal program in memory

See Also

5.1   Reading the command line
5.2   Reading the environment
5.3   Displaying memory blocks

Solution

When an MS-DOS program starts, it finds the segment address of the PSP in the ES register. Unfortunately, Turbo Pascal replaces this address with the address of the data area. All is not lost, however. You can make some assumptions about the layout of a Turbo Pascal program that let you find the address of the PSP. Figure 5-5 shows the layout of a Turbo Pascal program in memory. Note that the PSP occupies the 256 bytes before the beginning of the code segment.

You can find out the segment address of the code segment (the memory segment that contains the executable part of the program). To do so, use the Seg function with any subroutine in your program. To convert this segment to a pointer to the PSP, just subtract $10 from the code segment and make a pointer with the new segment and an offset of 0 (using the Turbo Pascal Ptr function). The following program uses this address and the information in Figure 5-6 to display the data in the PSP:

```
{This program shows the PSP}
program PSP;
uses ShowMem;

var
   PSPSeg : Word;
   Words : ^Word;

procedure Dummy;
begin
end;

begin
    PSPSeg := Seg( Dummy ) - $10;
    DispMem( Ptr( PSPSeg, 0 ), 256 );
    Words := Ptr( PSPSeg, 2 );
    WriteLn( 'Memory used: ', Words^ - PSPSeg, ' Paragraphs' );
    Words := Ptr( PSPSeg, $2C );
    WriteLn( 'Environment segment: ', Words^ );
    ReadLn;
end.
```

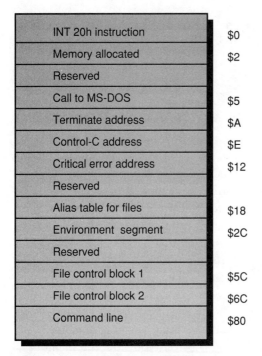

INT 20h instruction	$0
Memory allocated	$2
Reserved	
Call to MS-DOS	$5
Terminate address	$A
Control-C address	$E
Critical error address	$12
Reserved	
Alias table for files	$18
Environment segment	$2C
Reserved	
File control block 1	$5C
File control block 2	$6C
Command line	$80

Figure 5-6 Data in the PSP

The procedure Dummy exists only to provide a symbol that lets you get the code segment in the first line of the program. The program uses the DispMem procedure from question 5.3 to display all of the memory in the PSP. After that, the program shows the amount of memory allocated to the program and the address of the environment segment.

Comments

MS-DOS uses the PSP to hold information about what files a program has open and to pass information to the program at startup. Terminate and stay resident (TSR) programs, which run while other programs are running, must detect when the PSP has been changed and tell MS-DOS what PSP to use when processing file commands.

You have seen how to discover what the PSP segment should be. To find out what PSP MS-DOS is using, you must call the MS-DOS application program interface (API). The MS-DOS API is a set of functions for handling files, devices, and programs. It was designed to be called by assembly-language programs that pass data to and from the API in the CPU registers. Turbo Pascal uses the Intr procedure in the DOS unit to access the API. The Intr procedure copies data from a record to the registers, calls MS-DOS, and copies the registers back to the record. To get the current PSP, put $50 into the AH register, call MS-DOS, and get the PSP address from the BX register. This function shows how to do it:

```
function GetCurrentPSP : word
{Declare the record for passing registers}
vars
      Regs : Registers;
begin
      Regs.ah := $50;              {Setup call to MS-DOS}
      Intr( $21, Regs );           {Call MS-DOS}
      GetCurrentPSP := Regs.BX;{Return the PSP address}
end;
```

To set the PSP to a specified address, set AH to $51 and set BX to the segment of the PSP, as follows:

```
Regs.ah := $51;
Regs.bx := NewPSP;        {The PSP to use}
Intr( $21, Regs );        {Call MS-DOS}
```

5.6   How do I...

Find MS-DOS memory blocks with Turbo Pascal?

Description

MS-DOS allocates memory to hold such things as environment blocks, programs, and data areas required by various programs. When you run a program, MS-DOS allocates memory for the program and a copy of the environment variables. While a program is running, it can call MS-DOS to allocate more memory. In systems that use terminate and stay resident (TSR) programs, such as Sidekick, each program is allocated one or more memory blocks that other programs cannot use. The MS-DOS program CHKDSK shows you how much memory remains, but it does not tell you how the memory is being used. The program in this solution lets you take a look at what is using up memory.

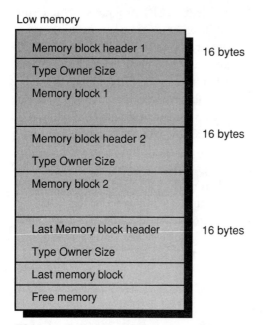

Figure 5-7 MS-DOS memory blocks

See Also

5.3   Displaying memory blocks
5.5   Reading the program segment prefix (PSP)

Solution

Figure 5-7 shows the format of MS-DOS memory blocks. As you can see, the format is very simple. Once you find the first block, it is not difficult to find the rest of the blocks. To find the first block, you must use the undocumented MS-DOS function $52. This function returns an address in ES:BX that points to several variables used by MS-DOS. The variable that gives the segment of the first memory block is at offset -2.

From the information provided, you can discover several things about a memory block. The first is the name of the program that uses the block. The

Address	Parent	Size	Type	Program
09BB	0008	50624	System	
1618	1619	3376	Program	<MS-DOS>
16EC	0000	48	Free space	
16F0	1619	800	Environment	<MS-DOS>
1723	2337	304	Environment	C:\TPHOWTO\MCB.EXE
1737	1738	49120	program	CAPTURE.EXE
2336	2337	510768	Program	C:\TPHOWTO\MCB.EXE
9FEA	1738	320	Environment	CAPTURE.EXE
9FFF	0000	0	Free space	

Figure 5-8 Sample output of memory program

owner field of the memory block contains the segment address of the PSP of the program that owns the memory block. When the owner field indicates the current memory block, you know that the block contains a program. If the owner is 0, the block is unallocated.

When the block is a program, you can look into the PSP at the beginning of the block to find the address of the environment block. MS-DOS makes a copy of the environment and appends the name of the program to this copy. Thus, you can find the name of the program in a program block.

You can also find out the name of the program that owns a data block. Because the owner block is the program that allocated the block, you can look at the PSP of the owner block to find the environment block. Then you can use that environment block to find out the name of the program.

The following program displays a list of the memory blocks. Figure 5-8 shows a typical display.

```
{This is a program to look at MS-DOS memory usage}
program MCB;
uses Dos, ShowMem;

type
  {A record to match the format of a memory header}
  MCBPtr = ^MCBRec;
  MCBRec = record
     MCBType : byte;
     Owner : word;
     Size : word;
  end;
  WordPtr = ^Word;

var
  Regs : registers;
```

```
    Words : WordPtr;
    Bytes : BytePtr;
    CurMCB : MCBPtr;
    EnvMCB : Word;
    TmpStr : string;

begin
    {Call MS-DOS to get the address of the first block}
    Regs.ah := $52;
    Intr( $21, Regs );
    Words := Ptr( Regs.es, Regs.bx - 2 );
    CurMCB := Ptr( Words^, 0 );
    {Write the report header}
    WriteLn;
    WriteLn( 'Address  Parent   Size Type       Program' );
    WriteLn;
    {Go through each memory block found}
    while CurMCB <> Nil do
    begin
        {Show the address of the block}
        HexString( Seg( CurMCB^ ), 4, TmpStr );
        Write( TmpStr );
        {Show the address of the owner}
        Words := Ptr( CurMCB^.Owner, 0 );
        HexString( Words^, 4, TmpStr );
        {Show the size of the file}
        Write( '    ', TmpStr, '  '
            , longint( CurMCB^.Size ) * 16 : 6, ' ' );
        {If it is a system block}
        if CurMCB^.Owner = 8 then
            Write( 'System ' )
        {If it is an unallocated block}
        else if CurMCB^.Owner = 0 then
            Write( 'Free space' )
        else
        begin
                {Get the environment segment of the owner}
                EnvMCB := Word( Ptr( CurMCB^.Owner, $2C )^ );
                {If this is an environment block}
                if EnvMCB = ( Seg ( CurMCB^ ) + 1 ) then
                        Write( 'Environment ' );
                {If it is a program block}
                else if CurMCB^.Owner = ( Seg ( CurMCB^ ) + 1 ) then
                        Write( 'Program    ' )
                else    {It's a data block}
                        Write( 'Data       ' );
                {Look for the end of the environment strings}
                Bytes := Ptr( EnvMCB, 0 );
                repeat
                        while Bytes^ <> 0 do
                        Inc( Bytes );
                        Inc( Bytes );
                until Bytes^ = 0;
```

```
            Inc( Bytes );
            {If it is a special MS-DOS block}
            if Bytes^ = 2 then
                    Write( '<MS-DOS>' )
            {If there is a program name}
            else if Bytes^ = 1 then
            begin
                    {Skip over the block type}
                    Inc( Bytes );
                    Inc( Bytes );
                    {Copy the name to TmpStr}
                    TmpStr := '';
                    while Bytes^ <> 0 do
                    begin
                            TmpStr := TmpStr + Chr( Bytes^ );
                            Inc( Bytes );
                    end;
                    Write( TmpStr );
            end;
        end;
        WriteLn;
        {If this is not the last block in the list}
        if CurMCB^.MCBType <> $5A then
                {Go to the next block}
                CurMCB := Ptr( Seg( CurMCB^ ) + CurMCB^.Size + 1, 0 )
        else    {Otherwise indicate no more blocks}
                CurMCB := Nil;
    end;
    ReadLn;
end.
```

This program begins by calling MS-DOS to get the address of the first memory block. With this address as the starting point, the big while loop goes though each memory block. The first three fields in the output list come directly from the memory block header. Note that the size of the block is given in paragraphs so you must multiply that value by 16 to get the size in bytes. Because the size can be larger than 65,535, you must use longints in the calculation.

The owner field in the memory block header is used to get the type of the block. If the owner is 8, then this is the block that contains MS-DOS itself. If the owner is 0, the block is unallocated. All other blocks contain programs, environment variables, or program data.

If the block is not MS-DOS or a free block, the program uses the PSP of the owner to get the environment block associated with the owner. If this environment block is the same as the current block, the current block is an environment block. If the owner block is the same as the current block, then the block is a program. The last possibility is that the block is a data block.

The owner's environment block, saved in EnvMCB, is used to find the name of the owner program. The environment strings each end in 0, and the last string is followed by two 0s. The `repeat-until` loop uses a `while` loop to skip each string until it finds two 0s in a row. If the word following the two 0s is a 2, then the block is owned by MS-DOS itself; otherwise, the program name follows.

The innermost loop copies the program name from the environment block to the string variable `TmpStr` by adding each byte up to the next 0 to `TmpStr`.

At the end of the main loop, the `type` field from the memory block header is checked to see if it is `$5A` indicating the last block. If not, the size of the block is added to the current block address to get the address of the next block. If it is the last block, the current block pointer is set to `Nil` to make the loop exit.

Comments

This program shows you how much memory fragmentation has occurred. Memory is fragmented when you load and unload TSR programs. Each time you load a TSR program, MS-DOS allocates space for it. When you unload the program, MS-DOS may release the memory. If it was the last program loaded, the released memory becomes part of the large free block at the end of memory. But, if other programs have been loaded, the released memory creates an unallocated "hole" in the middle of memory. This memory can be used only by programs that are small enough to fit in the hole. Some versions of MS-DOS do not even try to put a program there, and this memory is wasted until you reboot.

LOW-LEVEL DISK ACCESS

A disk is divided into concentric cylinders that are in turn divided into tracks. The tracks are in turn divided into sectors (see Figure 5-9). MS-DOS shields you from this complexity by mapping all disk partitions—all of the sectors on all of the tracks in all of the cylinders—to logical sectors. Thus, you can think of the disk as a large array of sectors.

MS-DOS makes disk management even simpler by letting you access a group of sectors as a single file, which you can think of as an array of bytes. MS-DOS does all of the bookkeeping needed to allocate sectors to a file and maintain a database of files (directories).

This simplification of disk usage comes at a price, such as the ability to sort directories or recover from errors in the file database. This section shows you how to read and write directly to the logical sectors of the disk and how to interpret some of the things you find there.

5.7   How do I...

Read and write disk sectors with Turbo Pascal?

Description

For most programs, it is enough to read from and write to files on the disk. In other cases, such as a program that sorts disk directories, or MS-DOS itself, the program needs to read from and write to individual sectors on the disk. This solution shows you how to use MS-DOS functions to read from and write to disks at the sector level.

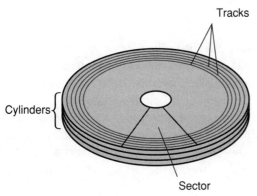

Figure 5-9 A PC disk

See Also

5.3   Displaying memory blocks

5.8   Getting information from
the disk

Solution

You cannot call the MS-DOS functions that read from and write to disk sectors simply by loading some values into a `Registers` structure and using `Intr` to call an interrupt. The problem with this technique is that these MS-DOS functions put an extra word on the stack that must be popped before any other stack operations. When trying to return to your program, the `Intr` procedure checks the stack to get the address to return to. But the stack is wrong, so it jumps to some unknown location. If you are *lucky*, this will simply lock up your computer and you will have to reboot.

The solution is to write a short assembly-language routine. You can link this routine to a Turbo Pascal program that calls MS-DOS to read from and write to the disk. This routine should call MS-DOS and pop the extra word off of the stack before returning. The following routine demonstrates how this is done:

```
; Program name: DISK.ASM
; This program reads the disk sector by sector
        .MODEL TPASCAL
        .CODE
        PUBLIC  ReadSect
ReadSect  PROC  NEAR BuffSeg : WORD, BuffOff : WORD, Drive : WORD, Sect :
WORD
        push  ds                        ; Save the data segment
```

```
         mov   ax, BuffSeg    ; Get the segment of the data
                              ; buffer
         mov   ds, ax         ; Put it in DS
         mov   bx, BuffOff    ; Put the offset in BX
         mov   ax, Drive      ; Put the drive number in AX
         mov   cx, 1          ; Get 1 sector
         mov   dx, Sect       ; Put the sector number in DX
         int   25h            ; Call the read interrupt
         jc    Done           ; If the carry is set, there was
                              ; an error
         popf                 ; Otherwise, pop the flags off
                              ; the stack
Done:
         pop   ds             ; Restore the saved data segment
         ret                  ; Return to the calling program
ReadSect ENDP
end
```

This routine uses some of the features of Turbo Assembler to make it easy to interface with Turbo Pascal. The .MODEL TPASCAL statement at the top of the program invokes these features. The procedure, called ReadSect, uses four parameters to hold the buffer segment, offset, drive number, and sector number. These parameters are copied to the appropriate registers, and interrupt $25 is called to read the disk. MS-DOS sets the carry flag if there was an error. The program jumps, if the carry flag is set, to the label Done and returns to the calling program. If there were no errors, the program pops the flags off the stack before returning.

The program to write sectors is identical except that interrupt $26 is used instead of interrupt $25. To do this, change the int 25h instruction to int 26h. Here is the complete read/write module:

```
; Program name: DISK.ASM
; This program reads and writes the disk sector by sector
         .MODEL TPASCAL
         .CODE
         PUBLIC  ReadSect, WriteSect
ReadSect PROC  NEAR BuffSeg : WORD, BuffOff : WORD
       , Drive : WORD, Sect : WORD
         push  ds             ; Save the data segment
         mov   ax, BuffSeg    ; Get the segment of the data
                              ; buffer
         mov   ds, ax         ; Put it in DS
         mov   bx, BuffOff    ; Put the offset in BX
         mov   ax, Drive      ; Put the drive number in AX
         mov   cx, 1          ; Get 1 sector
         mov   dx, Sect       ; Put the sector number in DX
         int   25h            ; Call the read interrupt
         jc    RDone          ; If the carry is set, there was
                              ; an error
         popf                 ; Otherwise, pop the flags off
                              ; the stack
```

```
RDone:
        pop   ds              ; Restore the saved data segment
        ret                   ; Return to the calling program
ReadSect ENDP

WriteSect  PROC  NEAR BuffSeg : WORD, BuffOff : WORD
        , Drive : WORD, Sect : WORD
        push  ds              ; Save the data segment
        mov   ax, BuffSeg     ; Get the segment of the data
                              ; buffer
        mov   ds, ax          ; Put it in DS
        mov   bx, BuffOff     ; Put the offset in BX
        mov   ax, Drive       ; Put the drive number in AX
        mov   cx, 1           ; Get 1 sector
        mov   dx, Sect        ; Put the sector number in DX
        int   26h             ; Call the write interrupt
        jc    WDone           ; If the carry is set, there was
                              ; an error
        popf                  ; Otherwise, pop the flags off
                              ; the stack
WDone:
        pop   ds              ; Restore the saved data segment
        ret                   ; Return to the calling program
WriteSect ENDP
end
```

Before you can use this routine in a Turbo Pascal program, you must use Borland's TASM assembler to make it an object file. You can enter the source using a text file editor such as the Turbo Pascal IDE (or order the companion disk for this book). Save the source in a file called DISK.ASM, then use this command to assemble it:

```
tasm disk
```

The assembler creates a file called DISK.OBJ that can be linked to a Turbo Pascal program. There are two steps to linking an assembly-language module to a Turbo Pascal program. First, you must put the name of the module in a $L directive. Then you must declare each of the routines in the assembly-language module. This program shows how to link in the DISK module:

```
{This program reads a sector on drive C}
program ReadDisk;
uses dos, showmem;

{Include the read sector routine from the file disk.obj}
{$L DISK}
procedure ReadSect( BuffSeg, BuffOff : word; Disk : word
      ; Sector : word ); external;

var
   SectBuff : array [1..4096] of byte;
```

```
   TmpStr : string;
   SectNumb, Code : integer;
begin
   Write( _Enter the sector to read: _ );
   ReadLn( TmpStr );
   {Convert the string to a number}
   Val( TmpStr, SectNumb, Code );
   ReadSect( Seg( SectBuff ), Ofs( SectBuff ), 2, SectNumb );
   {Show the sector}
   DispMem( @SectBuff, 512 );
   ReadLn;
end.
```

This program asks the user for a sector number to read and calls ReadSect to read the sector from the disk. The DispMem procedure shows the data found. One of the uses of this program is to search through a partially damaged disk to find out what data can be recovered. You can recover the data by using this program to look at each of the sectors until you find all of the data.

Warnings

In general, it is safe to read sectors from the disk. This is not the case for writing. If you write to a sector that has important information used by MS-DOS, you can easily make the disk unusable. Before experimenting with routines that write to the disk, make sure that the entire disk is backed up and that you have a spare boot diskette to use in case of disaster.

5.8   How do I...

Use Turbo Pascal to get detailed disk information?

Description

Everything that MS-DOS needs to know about a disk is stored on the disk itself. All that you need to get this information is the ReadSect routine from question 5.7 and some information about where to look. The solution below shows you how to find this information.

See Also

Logical sector 0

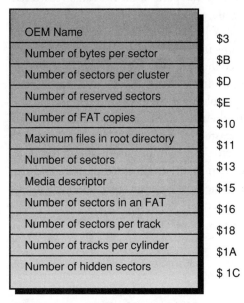

OEM Name	$3
Number of bytes per sector	$B
Number of sectors per cluster	$D
Number of reserved sectors	$E
Number of FAT copies	$10
Maximum files in root directory	$11
Number of sectors	$13
Media descriptor	$15
Number of sectors in an FAT	$16
Number of sectors per track	$18
Number of tracks per cylinder	$1A
Number of hidden sectors	$ 1C

Figure 5-10 The boot sector

Solution

Logical sector 0, the boot sector for the disk, holds a bock of information about the disk (see Figure 5-10). The information in this block includes the size of a sector and the location of the root directory. It also includes a field that gives the cluster size. A cluster is a group of contiguous sectors. MS-DOS allocates disk space on a cluster-by-cluster basis.

Another piece of information in the boot sector is the location of the file allocation table (FAT). The FAT contains information about the contents of every cluster on the disk. It tells what clusters go together in a single file, what sectors are reserved, and what sectors are available. Figure 5-11 shows the layout of a FAT.

When MS-DOS creates a new file, it makes a directory entry that gives the first cluster of the file. This gives the entry point into the FAT. As the file grows, MS-DOS searches the FAT for available clusters and links them into the file chain.

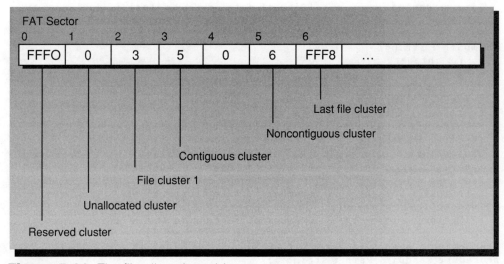

Figure 5-11 The file allocation table

One disadvantage of this technique is that parts of the file can be scattered all over the disk so that, to read the file, the disk heads must move back and forth across the surface of the disk. You can determine the extent of this scattering by looking at the file chains in the FAT.

The smallest amount of disk space that MS-DOS can allocate is a cluster. If the file being saved is not an even multiple of the size of a cluster, the extra space used by the file is wasted. By looking at the FAT and comparing the number of clusters used for files to the total size of all files, you can get an idea of the amount of space being wasted on your disk.

This program reads the boot sector to get information about the disk, then it reads the FAT to get information about allocated clusters and the amount of scattering of file sectors. The final step is to read all of the directory entries to see how much data is actually being used.

```
{This program reads interesting information from the disk}
program DiskInfo;
uses Dos;

{Include the ReadSect routine}
{$L DISK}
procedure ReadSect( BuffSeg, BuffOff : word; Disk : word; Sector : word
); external;

type
    WordPtr = ^Word;
    BytePtr = ^Byte;

var
    Size : longint;             {Size of data used by files}
    SectSize : longint;         {Bytes in allocated sectors}
    Sector : array [1..4096] of byte;
    TmpStr : string;
    i, j : integer;
    Words : WordPtr;
    Bytes : BytePtr;
    BytesSect : integer;        {Number of bytes in a sector}
    ClustSect : integer;        {Sectors in a cluster}
    TotalSect : word;           {Number of sectors available}
    FirstFAT : integer;         {First FAT sector}
    UnusedClust : integer;      {Number of unused clusters}
    ReservedClust : integer;    {Number of reserved clusters}
    BadClust : integer;         {Number of bad clusters}
    FileClust : integer;        {Number of file clusters}
    FraggedClust : integer;     {Number of noncontiguous clusters}
    FATSectors : integer;       {Number of sectors in the FAT}

{Recursively search directories and add up the sizes of each file}
procedure ReadDir( Path : string );
var
    PathLen : integer;
```

```
   DirInfo : SearchRec;
begin
    {Make a pattern to look for}
    PathLen := Length( Path );
    Path := Path + '*.*';
    {Find the first matching file}
    FindFirst( Path, AnyFile, DirInfo );
    {Read the rest of the files in the directory}
    while DosError = 0 do
    begin
        {If it is a subdirectory}
        if (( DirInfo.Attr AND Directory ) <> 0 )
           AND ( DirInfo.Name[1] <> '.') then
        begin
                {Read the files in the subdirectory}
                Path[0] := Chr( PathLen );
                Path := Path + DirInfo.Name + '\';
                ReadDir( Path );
        end;
        {Add in the file size to the total}
        Size := Size + DirInfo.Size;
        {Look for the next file}
        FindNext( DirInfo );
    end;
end;


begin
{Get info about the disk}
    {Read the boot sector}
    ReadSect( Seg( Sector ), Ofs( Sector ), 2, 0 );
    {Get the system ID}
    for i := 1 to 8 do
        TmpStr[i] := Chr( Sector[3 + i] );
    TmpStr[0] := Chr( 8 );
    WriteLn( 'System ID: ', TmpStr );
    {Get disk facts}
    BytesSect := WordPtr( Ptr( Seg( Sector ), Ofs( Sector ) + $B ))^;
    WriteLn( 'Bytes per sector: ', BytesSect );
    ClustSect := BytePtr( Ptr( Seg( Sector ), Ofs( Sector ) + $D ))^;
    WriteLn( 'Sectors per cluster: ', ClustSect );
    FirstFAT := WordPtr( Ptr( Seg( Sector ), Ofs( Sector ) + $E ))^;
    WriteLn( 'Size of reserved area: ', FirstFAT );
    Bytes := Ptr( Seg( Sector ), Ofs( Sector ) + $10 );
    WriteLn( 'Number of FAT copies: ', Bytes^ );
    Words := Ptr( Seg( Sector ), Ofs( Sector ) + $11 );
    WriteLn( 'Maximum number of root directory entries: '
             , Words^ );
    TotalSect := WordPtr( Ptr( Seg( Sector ), Ofs( Sector ) + $13 ))^;
    WriteLn( 'Number of sectors: ', TotalSect );
    Bytes := Ptr( Seg( Sector ), Ofs( Sector ) + $15 );
    WriteLn( 'Media descriptor: ', Bytes^ );
    FATSectors := WordPtr( Ptr( Seg( Sector ), Ofs( Sector ) + $16 ))^;
    WriteLn( 'Number of FAT sectors: ', FATSectors );
```

```
    Words := Ptr( Seg( Sector ), Ofs( Sector ) + $18 );
    WriteLn( 'Number of sectors per track: ', Words^ );
    Words := Ptr( Seg( Sector ), Ofs( Sector ) + $1A );
    WriteLn( 'Number of heads: ', Words^ );
    Words := Ptr( Seg( Sector ), Ofs( Sector ) + $1C );
    WriteLn( 'Number of hidden sectors: ', Words^ );
    {Read the fat sectors}
    UnusedClust := 0;
    ReservedClust := 0;
    BadClust := 0;
    FileClust := 0;
    FraggedClust := 0;
    for i:=1 to FATSectors do
    begin
        ReadSect(Seg( Sector ),Ofs( Sector ),2,FirstFAT + i - 1 );
        {Go through all of the FAT entries}
        for j:=1 to BytesSect do
        begin
                Words := Ptr( Seg( Sector ), Ofs( Sector ) + j );
                {Decide what type of entry it is}
                if Words^ = 0 then
                   Inc( UnusedClust )
                else if ( Words^ >= $FFF0 ) AND ( Words^ <= $FFF6 ) then
                   Inc( ReservedClust )
                else if Words^ = $FFF7 then
                   Inc( BadClust )
                else if Words^ >= $FFF8 then
                   Inc( FileClust )
                else {regular file cluster}
                begin
                   Inc( FileClust );
                   {If the clusters are not contiguous }
                   if Words^ <> j + 1 then
                        Inc( FraggedClust );
                end;
            Inc( j );
        end;
    end;
    {Show the information from the FAT}
    WriteLn( 'Unused clusters: ', UnusedClust );
    WriteLn( 'Reserved clusters: ', ReservedClust );
    WriteLn( 'Bad clusters: ', BadClust );
    WriteLn( 'File clusters: ', FileClust );
    WriteLn( 'Fragmented clusters: ', FraggedClust );
    {Add up the space used by files}
    Size := 0;
    ReadDir( 'c:\' );
    WriteLn( 'Total files size: ', Size );
    {Calculate file space allocated}
    SectSize := longint( FileClust ) * longint( ClustSect )
          * longint( BytesSect );
    WriteLn( 'Slack bytes: ', SectSize - Size );
    ReadLn;
end.
```

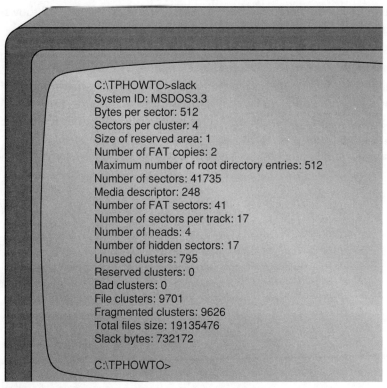

```
C:\TPHOWTO>slack
System ID: MSDOS3.3
Bytes per sector: 512
Sectors per cluster: 4
Size of reserved area: 1
Number of FAT copies: 2
Maximum number of root directory entries: 512
Number of sectors: 41735
Media descriptor: 248
Number of FAT sectors: 41
Number of sectors per track: 17
Number of heads: 4
Number of hidden sectors: 17
Unused clusters: 795
Reserved clusters: 0
Bad clusters: 0
File clusters: 9701
Fragmented clusters: 9626
Total files size: 19135476
Slack bytes: 732172

C:\TPHOWTO>
```

Figure 5-12 The disk information program

The ReadDir procedure uses the techniques discussed in question 2.3 to read all of the directory entries for the disk and add up the total size of all files. This routine recursively calls itself to read any subdirectories it finds. This guarantees that it looks at all of the files on the disk.

The main program begins by calling ReadSect to read the boot sector of the drive. Then it uses the information shown in Figure 5-10 to interpret the data in the boot sector and display the information. It also saves the number of reserved sectors and the number of FAT sectors so that it can read the FAT.

The first FAT sector immediately follows the last reserved sector. The program uses ReadSect to go through all of the FAT sectors on the disk. Each FAT sector is scanned to collect all of the information about the types of clusters used.

After reading all of the FAT sectors, the program prints the information. The last step is to call ReadDir to get the amount of data in files. The total file size is subtracted from the amount of space that the FAT indicates has been used to get the amount of wasted space on the disk. Figure 5-12 shows the output this program produces after checking a 20-megabyte disk.

Warnings

Not all drives are formatted as illustrated here. In particular, network drives almost always use a different format. If this is the case, this program will not give an accurate picture of the disk. This is especially dangerous if you use the disk information you receive to try to write to sectors on the disk. In general, you should not write to network drives on a sector-by-sector basis.

OBJECT-
ORIENTED
PROGRAMMING

6

Version 5.5 of Turbo Pascal brought object-oriented programming to Pascal. Version 6.0 enhanced object-oriented programming by adding more object-oriented features and the Turbo Vision object library. The main features of object-oriented programming are encapsulation, inheritance, and polymorphism. *Encapsulation* means that the data for an object and the routines that manipulate that data are combined into a single unit. *Inheritance* lets you use features of one object as part of another object. Turbo Pascal uses *polymorphism* to allow similar actions to use the same name.

One of the benefits of object-oriented programming is that its routines are more reusable than other routines. Because of encapsulation, you can copy an object from one program to another without having to look at the details of the object itself. After copying an object and its methods, you have the whole object. No extra code is required to initialize or use the data in the object; it is all in the object itself.

Inheritance and polymorphism let you add features to an object without affecting the object itself. If you have an object that is almost what your program needs, you can create a new object that inherits features from the old one. You simply write code for the parts of the object that need to be changed; everything else can be used as is. This keeps the object reusable because you don't clutter it up with special code for each program that uses the object.

An object-oriented language is only a small part of object-oriented programming. You also need to think differently about how to write a program.

What were once familiar routines must be twisted around to fit into the object-oriented mold. This chapter shows some popular routines done in the object-oriented style. The first five solutions are useful objects that you can use in your programs.

Solution 6.1 illustrates how you can use Turbo Pascal objects to represent graphical objects. By making each object correspond to a visible item, you get a visual representation of how objects work. As you use the various object methods, you see the results on the screen.

By making files and directories into objects, you can simplify programs that deal with the file system. Solution 6.2 shows how you can use this technique to make a program that finds files in any subdirectory on the disk.

Solution 6.3 uses encapsulation to make a convenient, reusable object for implementing virtual memory. With this object you can allocate memory on the heap without worrying about running out of heap space. When the heap is used up, parts of it are copied to disk so that the memory can be recycled. If a memory block is on the disk, it is swapped back into the heap before it is used.

Solution 6.4 shows how you can break a complex program into objects. The program uses objects to implement dialog boxes such as those used in the Turbo Pascal IDE.

Solution 6.5 uses objects to implement a database. Objects are used to organize the many routines needed to save and retrieve data. The solution includes a program that reuses the dialog objects from solution 6.4 to retrieve and display data from the database.

Solutions 6.6 and 6.7 show some interesting ways to deal with objects. Solution 6.6 shows how you can save an object in a file. You can use this technique to save that state of a program from one run to another.

Although objects are reusable, it is not convenient to copy them from one program to another every time you want to use one. The way to solve this problem is to put the object in a unit that can be linked with any program. Solution 6.7 gives some pointers on the best ways to do this.

USEFUL OBJECTS

Because objects are reusable, it makes sense to create a library of useful objects. The goal of this library is to provide a framework of objects that might be useful. Programs with simple needs can use the objects directly; those with more complex requirements can inherit objects and fill in the details on a program-by-program basis. If at some point you find that a routine in an object should be improved, you can make improvements without affecting other programs that use the object.

The solutions that follow are intended to get you started on a library of useful objects. The objects handle operations that come up in many applications. Some simple applications are provided to show how to use these objects in real programs.

Create graphical objects with Turbo Pascal?

Description

One way to illustrate the use of objects is to create objects that you can see. In this solution, the objects are pictures. The methods and data required for such objects are fairly obvious. You need to save the location and shape of the object; you also need methods to draw and erase the object.

When you look at these objects, you can easily see what data fields and methods you must add. For example, you can foresee that you may want to change the color of the object. This indicates that you need to save the color of the object. You also need a method that changes that data item.

You can also see how to use polymorphism. All of the graphical objects need to be drawn. This implies that they should each have their own Draw method, while sharing most other methods. From the application program's point of view, all graphical objects are the same. To draw them, call the Draw method. Turbo Pascal makes sure that the correct method for the object is called.

See Also

6.4   Creating dialog boxes
Ch 7   Graphics

Solution

The objects in this solution represent triangles on the screen. Each object includes data that gives the position of the 3 vertices of a triangle. The methods for the object let you draw, erase, and move triangles. Two other methods let you change the shape and color of triangles.

The graphics routines used are from Turbo Pascal's graphics unit. This unit makes it possible to write graphics routines that are portable across a variety of graphics interfaces. For more information on these routines, see Chapter 7.

The following program defines a graphical object class called GraphObj and a triangle-drawing object called TriObj. These objects include a method that moves the object from one location on the screen to another. The main program uses this method to move the triangle from the upper-left corner to the lower-right corner. Note that triangles are only one possibility. Anything that you can draw with a Turbo Pascal program can be derived from the GraphObj class.

```
{Program to use graphics in objects}
uses graph;            {Use Turbo Pascal graphics routines}

type
    {Graphics object class}
    GraphObj = object
        x, y : integer;            {Position of the object}
        Clr : integer;             {Color of the object}
        constructor Init;
        procedure Move( XPos, YPos : integer ); virtual;
        procedure Colorize( Color : word ); virtual;
        procedure Draw; virtual;
        procedure Erase; virtual;
    end;

    {Triangle object}
    TriObj = object( GraphObj )
        x2, y2 : integer;
        x3, y3 : integer;
        procedure Draw; virtual;
        procedure Shape( px1, py1, px2, py2, px3, py3 : integer );
        procedure Erase; virtual;
    end;

{Generic init routine for graphical objects}
constructor GraphObj.Init;
begin
    x := 0;            {Set the location to 0,0}
    y := 0;
    Clr := 1;          {Set the color to color 1}
end;

{Move a graphical object}
procedure GraphObj.Move( XPos, YPos : integer );
begin
    Erase;                     {Erase the object}
    x := XPos;                 {Move it}
    y := YPos;
    Draw;                      {Redraw the object}
end;

{Change the color of an object}
procedure GraphObj.Colorize( Color : word );
```

```
begin
    Clr := Color;
end;

{Generic draw method}
procedure GraphObj.Draw;
begin
    PutPixel( x, y, Clr );   {Draw a point on the screen}
end;

{Erase an object from the screen ( Generic )}
procedure GraphObj.Erase;
begin
    PutPixel( x, y, 0 );      {Draw the pixel in black}
end;

{Methods for triangles}

{Define three points}
procedure TriObj.Shape( px1, py1, px2, py2, px3, py3 : integer );
begin
    x := px1;                 {Copy the first point}
    y := py1;
    x2 := px2 - x;            {Second point is relative to the first}
    y2 := py2 - y;
    x3 := px3 - x;            {Third point is relative to the first}
    y3 := py3 - y;
end;

{Draw the triangle}
procedure TriObj.Draw;
begin
    SetColor( Clr );              {Set the color}
    MoveTo( x, y );              {Move the location point}
    LineTo( x + x2, y + y2 );    {Draw lines to the other two
                                  vertices}
    LineTo( x + x3, y + y3 );
    LineTo( x, y );
end;

{Erase the triangle}
procedure TriObj.Erase;
begin
    SetColor( 0 );               {Set color to black}
    MoveTo( x, y );              {Draw over the triangle}
    LineTo( x + x2, y + y2 );
    LineTo( x + x3, y + y3 );
    LineTo( x, y );
end;

{Variables for the program}
var
  GraphDriver, GraphMode : integer;        {Used by BGI}
```

```
    i : integer;
    Color : integer;
    Pict : TriObj;

begin
    {Initialize graphics}
    GraphDriver := Detect;
    InitGraph( GraphDriver, GraphMode, 'c:\tp' );
    {Initialize the triangle}
    Pict.Init;
    {Set its color}
    Pict.Colorize( 15 );
    {Define the shape}
    Pict.Shape( 0, 0, 100, 100, 200, 30 );
    {Move the triangle across the screen}
    for i := 0 to 70 do
        Pict.Move( i * 5, i * 5 );
end.
```

The GraphObj is as simple as a graphics object can be. It represents a single point on the screen. This point has a location and a color. There are methods to initialize, move, color, draw, and erase the point. This object by itself is not very useful, its real purpose is to be a base class for other objects.

The other object in this program is TriObj, which represents a triangle. This object defines two points besides the location of the object. These points are the other two corners of the triangle. To simplify the Move routine, these two points are specified relative to the first point. Figure 6-1 shows how the Move method works with relative points. The Shape method lets you set these points for the triangle. The six arguments to this method define the three points of the triangle. The points are given in absolute coordinates and converted to relative ones by the Shape method.

Because drawing a triangle is different from drawing a point, the TriObj object requires its own Draw and Erase methods. Both of these methods use the BGI routine LineTo to draw the edges of the triangle. The Erase method draws in black to remove the triangle from the screen.

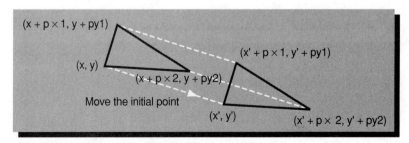

Figure 6-1 Moving the triangle

The main program uses a triangle object called `Pict` for its graphical object. After initializing the graphics and the triangle object, it uses a simple loop to call the `Move` method, which moves the triangle across the screen.

Comments

Once you have defined a graphical object, creating graphics is easy. You should have no trouble using these objects to draw all types of triangles all over the screen. It is also easy to change the program to draw other things. Simply define an object that inherits from `GraphObj`, and you're in business. The only routines you need to write are the methods to draw and erase the object. Some objects also require a method to define the object, as the `Shape` method does for triangles.

Warnings

When creating graphics, you need to be aware of what happens when you get to the edge of the screen. Some drawing routines clip the object at the edge, others wrap the object around to the other side, some even crash the system or have other unpredictable results. There are three ways you can deal with this problem. The simplest is to ignore it and trust that the program will not move the object off the screen, or that nothing bad will come of such a move. A more defensive approach is to add, to the `Draw` and `Erase` methods, code that prevents drawing off the edge of the screen. The code for this varies with each object. Another defensive approach is to add size fields to `GraphObj` and have the `Move` method refuse to move the object off the screen. This technique has some appeal because it works for all objects and you don't need to write extra code for each object.

Enhancements

You can enhance graphical objects in two ways. The first is to add more types of objects. You can follow the trend of the objects defined here and add other polygons such as squares, pentagons, and hexagons. You can also define more complex objects, such as shapes and pictures.

The second way to enhance these objects is to add other methods. For example, you can add a method to see if a point is inside the object. This method is useful for programs that must know when one object touches another. You can add this method to the `GraphObj` object. Add the fields `Xsize` and `Ysize` to the object and use a method like this one:

```
function GraphObj.PointIn( XPoint, YPoint : integer );
begin
        if ( XPoint > x ) AND ( XPoint < x + Xsize )
            AND ( YPoint > y ) AND ( YPoint < y + Ysize ) then
            PointIn := TRUE
```

```
    else
            PointIn := FALSE;
end;
```

The if statement in this method checks whether the x-coordinate is between the left and right edges of the object and the y-coordinate is between the top and bottom edges. If so, then the point is inside the object, and the method returns TRUE. Otherwise, the point is not in the object, and the method returns FALSE. This is a simple way to determine if a point is within a given rectangle. If the object is not rectangular, you can use this test to see if the point is close, then add code to determine if the point touches or not.

6.2 How do I...

Put the MS-DOS file system into a Turbo Pascal object?

Description

The MS-DOS file system lets you organize your files in small groups so that you do not have to look through every file to find the one you want. Unfortunately, if you cannot remember which directory contains the file, the file system makes it harder to search for that file.

See Also

2.5 Using the file manager

Solution

The program below creates objects for all of the files and subdirectories on the disk. Once you create these objects, you can interrogate them to see if they contain a file by a certain name. There is one object type for all of these objects. The object includes the name of the file or subdirectory and a list of subobjects if the object represents a subdirectory.

The Match function returns the pathname of the file if the object represents the file. Otherwise, it returns a directory in the path for the file. For example, if you have a file named fileobj.pas in the directory c:\pascal\source\objects, the Match function returns that path for the following objects:

```
c:\

c:\pascal

c:\pascal\source
```

```
c:\pascal\source\objects

c:\pascal\source\objects\fileobj.pas
```

You could find the file anywhere on the disk by simply calling the `Match` function for the root directory object with the filename as the argument.

```pascal
{File system object}
program Files;
uses Dos;

type
       {Object to hold directory trees}
       TreePtr = ^TreeObj;
       TreeObj = object
            PathName : string;
            SubList : array[0..511] of TreePtr;
            SubCnt : integer;
            FileType : byte;
            constructor Init( IPath : string; IType : byte );
            function Match( Key : string ) : string; virtual;
       end;

{Read files and directories into the tree object}
constructor TreeObj.Init( IPath : string; IType : byte );
var
   Pattern : string;
   DirInfo : SearchRec;
begin
    {Initialize the object variables}
    SubCnt := 0;
    PathName := IPath;
    FileType := IType;
    {If it is a directory read files}
    if FileType = Directory then
    begin
        {Make a pattern to read all files}
        Pattern := IPath + '\*.*';
        {Get the first file in the directory}
        FindFirst( Pattern, AnyFile, DirInfo );
        {Keep reading files until there are no more or
        there is no more room in the array}
        while ( DosError = 0 ) AND ( SubCnt < 512 ) do
        begin
            {If the name starts with a '.' don't include it}
            if DirInfo.Name[1] <> '.' then
            begin
                {Make an object for the file}
                Pattern := IPath + '\' + DirInfo.Name;
                New( SubList[SubCnt]
                    , Init( Pattern, DirInfo.Attr ));
                {Keep track of the number of objects}
                Inc( SubCnt );
```

```
                end;
                {Read the next file}
                FindNext( DirInfo );
            end;
        end;
end;


{See if a file is in an object}
function TreeObj.Match( Key : string ) : string;
var
   i : integer;
   Name : string;
begin
    {Get just the filename part of the pathname}
    i := Length( PathName );
    while ( i > 1 ) AND ( PathName[i] <> '\' ) do
        Dec( i );
    if PathName[i] = '\' then
      Inc( i );
    Name := Copy( PathName, i, Length( PathName ) - i + 1 );
    {If the names match, we are done}
    if Name = Key then
      Match := PathName
    else
    {Otherwise, check all subobjects}
    begin
        i := 0;
        repeat
            Name := SubList[i]^.Match( Key );
            if Length( Name ) = 0 then
              Inc( i );
        until ( i >= SubCnt ) OR ( Length( Name ) > 0 );
        {Return the pathname found, or a zero-length string}
        if i < SubCnt then
          Match := Name
        else
          Match := '';
    end;
end;


{Main program}
var
   CurTree : TreeObj;
   TmpStr : string;
   i : integer;

begin
    {Get the directory for the bottom of the tree from the user}
    Write( 'Enter base directory: ' );
    ReadLn( TmpStr );
    {Make it uppercase}
    for i := 1 to Length( TmpStr ) do
        TmpStr[i] := UpCase( TmpStr[i] );
```

```
    {Use it to initialize the objects}
    CurTree.Init( TmpStr, Directory );
    {Get the file to find from the user}
    Write( 'Enter file to find: ' );
    ReadLn( TmpStr );
    {Make it uppercase}
    for i := 1 to Length( TmpStr ) do
        TmpStr[i] := UpCase( TmpStr[i] );
    {Search for the file}
    WriteLn( 'Path: ', CurTree.Match( TmpStr ));
    ReadLn;
end.
```

TreeObj is an object-oriented directory entry. It contains the name of the file, the type of the file, and, if the file is a subdirectory, the files in that subdirectory. The Init method is responsible for moving the directory information from the disk to TreeObj. It does this by using the Turbo Pascal FindFirst and FindNext procedures. The FindFirst routine looks for the first file that matches the pattern supplied. In this case, the pattern is the name of the directory for the object followed by "*.*"—a "wild card" character that matches all of the files in the directory. FindNext looks for the next file that matches in the same directory. Both of these routines store returned values in the SearchRec structure.

When a file is found, the Init routine creates an object and adds a pointer to this object to the list of objects for the current directory. Init uses the Turbo Pascal New procedure to allocate space for and initialize the new object. This procedure has been enhanced to work with objects. In addition to the name of the object to be created, you also pass the name and arguments of the constructor of the object. The New procedure allocates enough space for the object, then calls the constructor to initialize the object. In this case the constructor is the Init method. Do not worry about this being a recursive call; Turbo Pascal takes care of that, just as it would with a regular function or procedure.

The Init routine keeps looking for files and subdirectories until the FindNext procedure reports that there are no more matching files or there is no more room in the array. At this point, if no errors have occurred, the entire directory structure is in memory. Now you can use the Match method to find files.

The Match method begins by extracting the filename from the pathname in the current object. It does this by scanning the pathname backward until it finds a backslash (\). The text to the right of the backslash is compared to the name of the file you are looking for. If it matches, the search is over, and the Match method returns the pathname. Otherwise, it checks whether any of the subobjects contain the file. It does this by looping through the list of subobjects, calling the `Match` method for each one. If the file is found during one of these calls, the path returned is passed up to the calling function. If it is not found, an empty string is returned.

The main program prompts the user for a directory name and a filename. The directory name is used to initialize a `TreeObj`, and the filename is used as the argument for the `Match` method. Note that both of these strings are converted to uppercase. The filename must be uppercase to match the results of `FindFirst` and `FindNext` procedures. The directory is converted for aesthetic reasons, so that the whole pathname is uppercase.

Comments

Initializing the directory structure can be a long process. Fortunately, you do not need to initialize it every time you want to look for a file. You can call `Match` as often as you like with as many different filenames as you need.

Warnings

These objects are not very memory-efficient. Searching even a moderate sized disk can overfill the available memory. When this happens, you get a run-time error that stops the program. You can use a virtual-memory technique to increase the amount of space available, or you can modify the `TreeObj` object so that it does not require as much memory. One way to do this is to save only directories in objects. If you do this, you need to modify the `Match` routine to go to the disk to read the actual files each time you look for a file.

Enhancements

The `Match` routine is OK for finding a file hidden deep in the directory structure, but it won't tell you if that is the only copy of the file or, if not, where other copies are. You can fix this by adding a method to look for successive files. For this job, you need to add a variable to the `TreeObj` object. This variable keeps track of where the last search ended. Call the variable `LastSearch` and use it instead of `i` in the search loop in `Match`. The `MatchNext` method, shown below, finds other files with the name supplied:

```
function TreeObj.MatchNext( Key : string ) : string;
var
        i : integer;
        Name : string;
begin
    {Get just the filename part of the pathname}
    i := Length( PathName );
    while ( i > 1 ) AND ( PathName[i] <> '\' ) do
        Dec( i );
    if PathName[i] = '\' then
```

```
        Inc( i );
Name := Copy( PathName, i, Length( PathName ) - i + 1 );
    if Name = Key then
            MatchNext := PathName
    else
    begin
        if LastSearch <= SubCnt then
            Inc( LastSearch );
        while ( LastSearch <= SubCnt) AND ( Length( Name )>0 ) do
        begin
            Name := SubList[LastSearch]^.MatchNext( Key );
            if Length( Name ) = 0 then
                Inc( LastSearch );
        end;
    end;
    {Return the pathname found, or a zero-length string}
    if i < SubCnt then
        MatchNext := Name
    else
        MatchNext := _ ;
end;
```

This routine is very similar to the Match function. The difference is that instead of beginning at the head of the list of subobjects, it begins at the last file found. If the file is not found, it places the pointer past the end of the list to indicate that no searching is required.

6.3   How do I...

Use Turbo Pascal objects to make virtual memory?

Description

Virtual memory is memory that is not really in your computer. Instead, the data that should be in that memory is saved on the disk. When your program needs to look at the data, it transfers to disk some other data that is currently in memory and reads in the data the program needs. The overall effect is that the program has a very large amount of slow memory.

See Also

2.8   Creating database files

Solution

This solution uses an object to represent a block of virtual memory. The object itself must always be in memory, but the data that it represents can be in physical memory or on the disk. When you call on the object to allocate memory, it actually reserves space in a data file. To use the space, you must lock the memory. During this step the program checks if the block is already in physical memory; if not, it allocates space in memory for the data. If the memory cannot be allocated, the program searches the memory objects to find one occupying enough memory to accommodate the new block. It copies the old block to disk, freeing its memory space. Now there is enough memory for the new block, and the data in the disk file is read. When the program does not need the block anymore, it unlocks it. This does not free the memory used; it just sets a flag that indicates that the block can be freed if required.

Using virtual memory is similar to using the heap, with two important steps added. The familiar steps of allocating and freeing memory blocks remain the same: allocate the block to get the space, and free it to return the space to the heap. Typically you allocate memory in a set-up routine and free the memory before the program or module finishes. The new steps fall between these operations. Just before you actually use the memory, you must lock it to get it into memory. Then, when you do not need it for awhile, you unlock it so that it can be swapped out to make room for some other block. This program illustrates the process:

```
{Objects to handle memory allocations}
program mem;
uses RandFile;

type
    MemPtr = ^MemObj;
    MemObj = object
        Locked : boolean;
        InMemory : boolean;
        RecNumb : integer;
        MemoryAddr : ^byte;
        DataSize : integer;
        PrevObj : MemPtr;
        NextObj : MemPtr;
        constructor Allocate( ISize : integer );
        function Lock : pointer;
        procedure UnLock;
        procedure SwapOut;
        procedure Release;
    end;

var
    DataFile : VariableFile;
    BaseMemObj : MemPtr;

{Make heap errors return a nil pointer}
function HeapFunc( Size : word ) : integer; far;
begin
    HeapFunc := 1;
```

```pascal
end;

constructor MemObj.Allocate( ISize : integer );
begin
    {Initialize data fields}
    Locked := False;
    InMemory := False;
    DataSize := ISize;
    MemoryAddr := Nil;
    {Make space in the data file}
    RecNumb := DataFile.AddRec( Self, ISize );
    {Set up the pointers}
        PrevObj := BaseMemObj;
    NextObj := Nil;
        if PrevObj <> Nil then
        PrevObj^.NextObj := @Self
    else
        BaseMemObj := @Self;
end;

{Lock a block in memory}
function MemObj.Lock : pointer;
var
    TestMemObj : MemPtr;
begin
    if NOT InMemory then
    begin
        repeat
            {Allocate space for the block}
            GetMem( MemoryAddr, DataSize );
            if MemoryAddr <> Nil then
            begin
                Locked := True;
                DataFile.ReadRec( MemoryAddr^, RecNumb );
                InMemory := TRUE;
            end
            else {Release a block to make room}
                begin
                TestMemObj := BaseMemObj;
                {Find a block that is in memory
                , unlocked and big enough}
                while ( TestMemObj <> Nil )
                    AND (( TestMemObj^.DataSize < DataSize )
                    OR ( TestMemObj^.Locked = True )
                    OR ( TestMemObj^.InMemory = False )) do
                    TestMemObj := TestMemObj^.NextObj;
                if TestMemObj <> Nil then
                    TestMemObj^.SwapOut;
                end;
        until MemoryAddr <> Nil;
    end;
    Lock := MemoryAddr;
end;
```

```pascal
procedure MemObj.Unlock;
begin
    Locked := False;
end;

procedure MemObj.SwapOut;
begin
    if InMemory AND NOT Locked then
    begin
        DataFile.WriteRec( MemoryAddr^, RecNumb );
        FreeMem( MemoryAddr, DataSize );
        InMemory := False;
    end;
end;

procedure MemObj.Release;
begin
    if InMemory then
      FreeMem( MemoryAddr, DataSize );
    DataFile.DelRec( RecNumb );
    if PrevObj <> Nil then
      PrevObj^.NextObj := NextObj
    else
       BaseMemObj := NextObj;
    if NextObj <> Nil then
      NextObj^.PrevObj := PrevObj;
    Dispose( @Self );
end;

var
  i, j : integer;
  MemList : array[1..100] of MemPtr;
  DataPtr : ^byte;
  Line : string;

begin
    {Open the file}
    DataFile.Init( 'memory.dat' );
    {Initialize everything}
    BaseMemObj := nil;
    {Allocate a number of memory blocks}
    for i := 1 to 50 do
    begin
        New( MemList[i], Allocate( 25 ));
    end;
    {Do something with the memory}
    Line := 'Test';
    for i := 1 to 50 do
    begin
        DataPtr := MemList[i]^.Lock;
        DataPtr^ := byte( Length( Line ) + 2 );
        Inc( DataPtr );
        for j :=1 to Length( Line ) do
```

```
    begin
        DataPtr^ := byte( Line[j] );
        Inc( DataPtr );
    end;
    DataPtr^ := byte( i DIV 10 + $30 );
    Inc( DataPtr );
    DataPtr^ := byte( i MOD 10 + $30 );
    MemList[i]^.UnLock;
end;
{Show the list}
for i := 1 to 50 do
begin
    DataPtr := MemList[i]^.Lock;
    for j := 0 to 25 do
    begin
        Line[j] := Chr( DataPtr^ );
        Inc( DataPtr );
    end;
    WriteLn( 'Line[', i, ']: ', Line );
    MemList[i]^.UnLock;
end;
DataFile.Done;
ReadLn;
end.
```

The RandFile unit in this program contains the VariableFile object described in question 2.8. The first procedure in the program tells the Turbo Pascal heap routines what to do when no memory is available. The default action of the heap routines is to abort with a run-time error. Making the HeapError variable a pointer to HeapFunc in the main program causes the heap function to call HeapFunc when there is an error. HeapFunc returns 1 to indicate that the heap function should return a Nil pointer, signaling an error. This value is used later to determine when memory blocks must be freed to load another block.

The first MemObj method is Allocate, which creates a new memory block. It sets the flags to indicate that the block is not in memory and not locked. Then, it creates a new record in the file by calling the AddRec method. After saving the record number and the size of the block, it places the block in the linked list of memory blocks. Figure 6-2 shows how the links work. The PrevObj link points to the last block allocated, and the NextObj is set to Nil. When a new block is allocated, the NextObj field points to the new block. The program uses the NextObj links to search the list of blocks for one to swap out when more memory is needed. The PrevObj link is used to simplify the deletion of a memory block.

The next method is Lock, which makes sure that the block is in memory, sets the locked flag, and returns the address of the block. If the block is not in memory, Lock allocates space, and the block reads from the data file. After

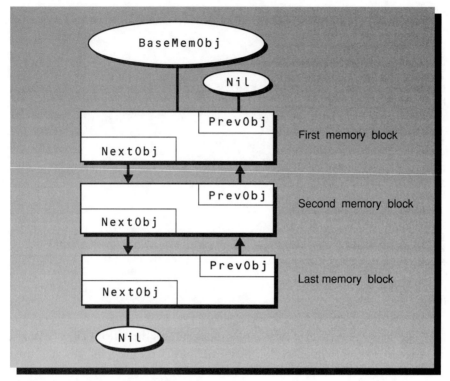

Figure 6-2 Memory object links

calling GetMem, Lock checks if the pointer is Nil. If so, it searches the linked list of blocks, looking for one that is in memory, is not locked, and occupies enough memory to hold the new block. When the block is found, it is freed, and the Lock function tries again to allocate memory for the new block.

The Unlock method is very simple; it simply sets the Locked flag to FALSE. This is so that the Lock method can free the block if the space is needed. Because the block stays in memory, the Allocate method does not need to reload the block if the program needs it again.

When Allocate needs more memory, it calls the SwapOut method for the appropriate memory object. The SwapOut method begins by writing the data for the memory block to the data file. This is so that it can be read in the next time the block is locked. Once the data is written, the memory for the block is freed, the InMemory flag is set to FALSE and the method returns to Allocate.

The Release method lets the program get rid of a memory block when it is no longer needed. The first step is to free the memory block if it is in memory. Then it deletes the record from the data file. Finally, it adjusts the links for the previous and next memory objects to go around the object being deleted.

The main program exercises these routines by allocating 50 memory blocks, storing a string in each one, and displaying the strings. Note that each block is locked only while it is being accessed. When the program is ready to go to the next block, it unlocks the current block so that its memory is available.

Comments

For programs that use only a small amount of data, this object is overkill. It does not take long, however, for even a simple program to grow to the point where the heap just cannot hold all of the data required. (See the file system object in question 6.2 for a good example.) When you are out of memory, the MemObj is a simple alternative to either letting the program crash or developing complex algorithms that let the program "forget" some things.

Warnings

The MemObj object does not guarantee that you will never run out of memory. It is possible to fragment the available memory into several small blocks scattered throughout the memory space. When this happens, you cannot allocate a block that is larger than the spaces between allocated blocks. Figure 6-3 illustrates this problem.

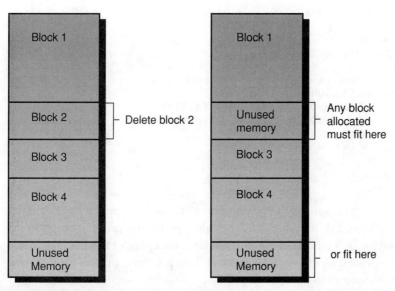

Figure 6-3 Fragmented memory

To keep this from happening, you should keep as few blocks locked as possible. This lets the `Lock` method swap out more blocks until enough consecutive blocks are freed to hold the block being locked.

Enhancements

When the `Lock` method swaps out memory blocks, it looks for the first block that is large enough and calls `SwapOut`. This can cause a problem called "thrashing," in which blocks are swapped in and out because they happen to be at the beginning of the list. One way to get around this is to change the loop that searches for a block to swap so that it looks for the least recently used (LRU) block. The idea is that a recently used block is likely to be used again. If a block has not been used for awhile, it is likely that it will not be used for a while longer.

To implement the LRU algorithm you need to add another field, called `LRUNumb`, to `MemObj`. This integer variable is assigned a new value every time the block is locked. The block with the lowest `LRUNumb` is the most recently used block. The easiest way to assign these numbers is to keep a global variable that contains the next number to use. Each time the global variable is used, it is incremented to get the next number. These two lines show how:

```
LRUNumb := GlobalLRU;
Inc( GlobalLRU );
```

Now you need to change the loop that searches for the block to be swapped out so that it finds the least recently used block.

```
{Make pointers to an object and the oldest object}
TestMemObj := BaseMemObj;
OldMemObj := BasMemObj;
while TestMemObj <> Nil do
begin
        {See if the block is eligible and older}
        if ( TestMemObj^.Locked = FALSE )
                AND ( TestMemObj^.InMemory = FALSE )
                AND ( TestMemObj^.LRUNumb < OldMemObj^.LRUNumb ) then
                OldMemObj := TestMemObj;
        TestMemObj := TestMemObj^.NextObj;
end;
{Free the old object found}
OldMemObj^.SwapOut;
```

This loop goes through every object in the list, keeping track of the oldest object. When the loop is done, `OldMemObj` points to the oldest object in the list and swaps it out. If the block is not large enough, `GetMem` fails again, and the next-oldest block gets swapped out. This process continues until there is enough memory to hold the new block.

Create a dialog box object in Turbo Pascal?

Description

An important part of modern user interfaces are dialog boxes that provide a simple, consistent way for the user to enter data into a program. A dialog box contains different controls, such as text-entry fields and buttons. Each control has a recognizable appearance and behaves in a predictable way. Dialog boxes spare users the time and trouble of learning to enter data; they already know the data-entry procedures from having used other programs. This leaves users free to spend their time learning the more important aspects of the program.

If you have used the Turbo Pascal IDE, you know how dialog boxes are used to get information from the user. When you select a menu command (such as an Open File command) that cannot be completed without more information, Turbo Pascal presents a dialog box in which you specify that information (for example, you select a filename from a list or type the name of the file). The dialog boxes in the Turbo Pascal IDE were created with Turbo Vision, which is described in Chapter 10. This solution shows how you can program your own dialog boxes without using Turbo Vision.

See Also

1.4   Drawing boxes on the screen
1.19   Handling numeric data entry
1.20   Making formatted text entry
6.7   Putting objects in units

Solution

In this solution each dialog box control is described by a Turbo Pascal object. The dialog box itself is an object that contains pointers to the controls used in that dialog box. The methods for the dialog box (such as Draw) call methods in the control objects to complete the drawing of the dialog box. The dialog box object also keeps track of what control object should be getting input and calls the appropriate method.

This unit defines dialog box objects and several control objects used in them:

```
{Screen objects unit}
unit Entry;

Interface
type
        Proc = function : integer;
```

```pascal
{Object for all screen objects to inherit}
ScrnPtr = ^ScrnObj;
ScrnObj = object
     Row, Col : integer;
     Attr : byte;
     Id : integer;
     constructor Init( IRow,ICol: integer; IAttr: byte );
     procedure Draw; virtual;
     function Input : integer; virtual;
     function Match( key : integer ) : boolean; virtual;
end;

{This object is for the whole dialog}
DialogObj = object( ScrnObj )
     Hght, Width : integer;
     SubObj : array[1..50] of ScrnPtr;
     SubCnt : integer;
     TextData : string;
     constructor Init( IRow, ICol, IHght, IWidth : integer;
         IAttr : byte; IText : string );
     procedure Draw; virtual;
     function Input : integer; virtual;
     procedure AddObj( ObjPtr : ScrnPtr );
end;

{Static text objects}
StaticLit = object( ScrnObj )
     TextData : string;
     constructor Init( IRow, ICol : integer
         ; IText : string; IAttr : byte );
     procedure Draw; virtual;
end;

{Text entry field objects}
TextObj = object( ScrnObj )
     TextData : string;
     Width : integer;
     constructor Init( IRow, ICol, IWidth : integer
         ; IText : string; IAttr : byte );
     procedure Draw; virtual;
     function Input : integer; virtual;
end;

{Button control objects}
ButtonObj = object( ScrnObj )
     Hght, Width : integer;
     TextData : string;
     ButtFunc : Proc;
     constructor Init( IRow, ICol, IHght, IWidth : integer;
         IText : string; IAttr : byte; Doit : Proc;
         IID : integer );
     procedure Draw; virtual;
     function Input : integer; virtual;
```

```
end;

implementation
uses Crt;

{Generic routines}
constructor ScrnObj.Init( IRow, ICol : integer; IAttr : byte );
begin
    {Copy parameters to the object}
    Row := IRow;
    Col := ICol;
    Attr := IAttr;
    {Set the default ID}
    Id := -1;
end;

{Do-nothing draw routine}
procedure ScrnObj.Draw;
begin
end;

{Do-nothing input routine}
function ScrnObj.Input : integer;
begin
    Input := 9;
end;

{See if the key matches the ID}
function ScrnObj.Match( key : integer ) : boolean;
begin
    if key = Id then
                Match := True
    else
                Match := False;
end;

{Static text object routines}
constructor StaticLit.Init( IRow, ICol : integer
            ; IText : string; IAttr : byte );
begin
    Row := IRow;
    Col := ICol;
    TextData := IText;
    Attr := IAttr;
end;

procedure StaticLit.Draw;
begin
    TextAttr := Attr;
    GotoXY( Col, Row );
    Write( TextData );
end;
```

```
{Text data routines}
constructor TextObj.Init( IRow, ICol, IWidth : integer
            ; IText : string; IAttr : byte );
begin
    Row := IRow;
    Col := ICol;
    Width := IWidth;
    TextData := IText;
    Attr := IAttr;
end;

procedure TextObj.Draw;
var
   TmpStr : string;
begin
    {Fill the text field with the text data and spaces}
    TmpStr := TextData;
    while Length( TmpStr ) < Width do
        TmpStr := TmpStr + ' ';
    {Set the attribute for this control}
    TextAttr := Attr;
    {Write the text at the saved position}
    GotoXY( Col, Row );
    Write( TmpStr );
    {Put the cursor at the end of the data}
    GotoXY( Col + Length( TextData ), Row );
end;

{Get text input}
function TextObj.Input : integer;
var
   ch : integer;
   SaveAttr : byte;
begin
    SaveAttr := Attr;
    Attr := $70;
    repeat
        {Draw the text}
        Draw;
        {Get a key from the user}
        ch := Ord( ReadKey );
        if ch = 8 then {Backspace}
            Dec( TextData[0] )
        {See if storable character}
        else if ( ch <> 13 ) AND ( ch <> 9 ) AND ( ch <> 27 )
            AND ( ch <> 0 ) AND ( Length( TextData ) < Width ) then
                TextData := TextData + Chr( ch );
    {Check for Enter, Tab, or Escape}
    until ( ch = 13 ) OR ( ch = 9 ) OR ( ch = 27 ) OR ( ch = 0 );
    {Handle function keys}
    if ch = 0 then
        ch := 256 + Ord( ReadKey );
    Attr := SaveAttr;
```

```
        Self.Draw;
        Input := ch;
end;


{Dialog routines}
constructor DialogObj.Init( IRow, ICol, IHght, IWidth : integer;
                    IAttr : byte; IText : string );
begin
        SubCnt := 0;
        Row := IRow;
        Col := ICol;
        Hght := IHght;
        Width := IWidth;
        Attr := IAttr;
        TextData := IText;
end;

procedure DialogObj.AddObj( ObjPtr : ScrnPtr );
begin
        Inc( SubCnt );
        SubObj[SubCnt] := ObjPtr;
end;

procedure DialogObj.Draw;
var
    r, c : integer;
begin
        TextAttr := Attr;
        GotoXY( Col, Row );                      {Do the upper-left corner}
        Write( Chr( 201 ));
        for c := 1 to Width - 2 do               {Then the top line}
            Write( Chr( 205 ));
        Write( Chr( 187 ));                      {And the upper-right corner}
        for r := 1 to Hght - 2 do
        begin
            GotoXY( Col, Row + r );              {The left side}
            Write( Chr( 186 ));
            for c := 1 to Width - 2 do           {Clear the interior of}
                Write( ' ' );                    {The box}
            Write( Chr( 186 ));                  {The right side}
        end;
        GotoXY( Col, Row + Hght - 1 );           {Do lower-left corner}
        Write( Chr( 200 ));
        for c := 1 to Width - 2 do               {Then the bottom line}
            Write( Chr( 205 ));
        Write( Chr( 188 ));                      {And the lower-right corner}
        {Put the title on the box}
        GotoXY( Col + ( Width - Length( TextData )) DIV 2, Row );
        Write( TextData );
        {Draw all of the objects in the dialog}
        for r := 1 to SubCnt do
            SubObj[r]^.Draw;
end;
```

```
{Get input from dialog box controls}
function DialogObj.Input : integer;
var
   CurrentFld : integer;
   ResCode : integer;
begin
    CurrentFld := 1;
       repeat
          {Do input for the current field}
           ResCode := SubObj[CurrentFld]^.Input;
          {Check the result code}
          if ResCode = 13 then        {Enter, move ahead one field}
          CurrentFld := CurrentFld + 1
          else if ResCode = 27 then {ESC exit}
          CurrentFld := SubCnt + 1
           else if ResCode = 9 then {TAB ahead one and wrap if at
          the end}
          CurrentFld := CurrentFld MOD SubCnt + 1
          else
          begin                        {Otherwise, check for a matching ID}
              CurrentFld := 1;
              while ( CurrentFld <= SubCnt )
              AND NOT SubObj[CurrentFld]^.Match do
              Inc( CurrentFld );
          end;
{Keep getting input until field is outside the dialog box}
 until CurrentFld > SubCnt;
end;

{Button routines}
constructor ButtonObj.Init( IRow, ICol, IHght, IWidth : integer;
                 IText : string; IAttr : byte; Doit : Proc;
                IID : integer );
begin
    Row := IRow;
    Col := ICol;
    Hght := IHght;
    Width := IWidth;
    TextData := IText;
    Attr := IAttr;
    ButtFunc := Doit;
    Id := IID;
end;

procedure ButtonObj.Draw;
var
  r, c : integer;
begin
    {Set the attribute}
    TextAttr := Attr;
    {Position cursor at the upper-left corner}
    GotoXY( Col, Row );
    {Draw the top line}
    Write( Chr( 201 ));
```

```
        for c := 1 to Width - 2 do
            Write( Chr( 205 ));
        Write( Chr( 187 ));
        {Draw the sides of the button}
        for r := 1 to Hght - 2 do
        begin
            GotoXY( Col, Row + r );
            Write( Chr( 186 ));
            for c := 1 to Width - 2 do
                Write( ' ' );
            Write( Chr( 186 ));
        end;
        {Draw the bottom line}
        GotoXY( Col, Row + Hght - 1 );
        Write( Chr( 200 ));
        for c := 1 to Width - 2 do
            Write( Chr( 205 ));
        Write( Chr( 188 ));
        {Put the text into the button}
        GotoXY( Col + ( Width - Length( TextData )) DIV 2, Row + 1 );
        Write( TextData );
end;

{See if the button is pressed}
function ButtonObj.Input : integer;
var
    SaveAttr : byte;
    ch : integer;
begin
    SaveAttr := Attr;
    Attr := $70;
    Self.Draw;
    repeat
        ch := Ord(ReadKey);
        if (ch = Ord( ' ' )) OR ( ch =  13 ) then
            ch := ButtFunc;
    until ( ch = 13 ) OR ( ch = 9 ) OR ( ch = 27 ) OR ( ch = 0 );
    if ch = 0 then
        ch := 256 + Ord( ReadKey );
    Attr := SaveAttr;
    Self.Draw;
    Input := ch;
end;

end.
```

The interface portion of this unit defines the five objects in the unit. The first (ScrnObj) is the object from which all other screen objects are descended. ScrnObj contains data and methods that all screen objects have in common, such as location, ID, and the attribute. The ID identifies a particular object in a dialog box. The methods are mostly do-nothing routines that exist just to make sure that the methods are defined for all screen objects. Note the type `ScrnPtr`, which is a pointer to a screen object. This pointer can be used for any of the descendant objects of `ScrnObj`. Turbo Pascal uses a feature called *late binding* to sort out what kind of object `ScrnPtr` points to. This is used in the dialog box object, which must keep a list of all of its controls. The `ScrnPtr` type lets the dialog box put the controls into an array.

The next object (`DialogObj`) defines the dialog box object. In addition to the data used in `ScrnObj`, it defines the height, width, and title of the dialog box. It also includes an array of `ScrnPtr` to hold pointers to the objects that appear in the dialog box. None of the methods in `ScrnObj` are suitable for dialog boxes, so they are all *overloaded* with methods specific to dialog boxes. Overloading is the term used in object-oriented programming to describe what happens when an object has a virtual method with the same name as the object it inherits. In these objects, methods such as `Draw` are overloaded; so, instead of using the `Draw` method in `ScrnObj`, the program uses the `Draw` method in the `DialogObj` (or whatever other object overloads `Draw`). There is also a method to add objects to the object list.

The `StaticLit` and `TextObj` objects are for text fields. The difference between them is that `TextObj` accepts user input and `StaticLit` does not. This is accomplished by letting the `StaticLit` object use the do-nothing input method from `ScrnObj`, whereas the `TextObj` object uses a specialized text-input routine.

The last object is `ButtonObj`, which defines buttons. Buttons have height, width, text, and an action to perform. By selecting the button, the user calls the action routine specified.

The methods for the screen objects are in the implementation section of the unit. As mentioned before, the methods for the `ScrnObj` are simple do-nothing routines. The `Init` method copies parameters to the object; the `Draw` method does nothing at all; the `Input` method tells the caller to go to the next field. The `Match` method is the only useful method in the object; it tests the key provided to see if it matches the `ID` field. This object type is not intended to be used; it is just an anchor to tie screen objects together.

The methods for the `DialogObj` object are much more interesting. The `Init` method fills in the extra fields required by a dialog box and initializes the list of subobjects. To add items to this list, use the `AddObj` method. This method puts an object into the `SubObj` array and increments the counter `SubCnt`.

The `Draw` method borrows the box-drawing routine from Chapter 1 to draw the box itself. Once that is drawn, the dialog box `Draw` method calls the `Draw` methods for all of the objects in the `SubObj` array. The final result is that the dialog box, with all of its controls, appears on the screen.

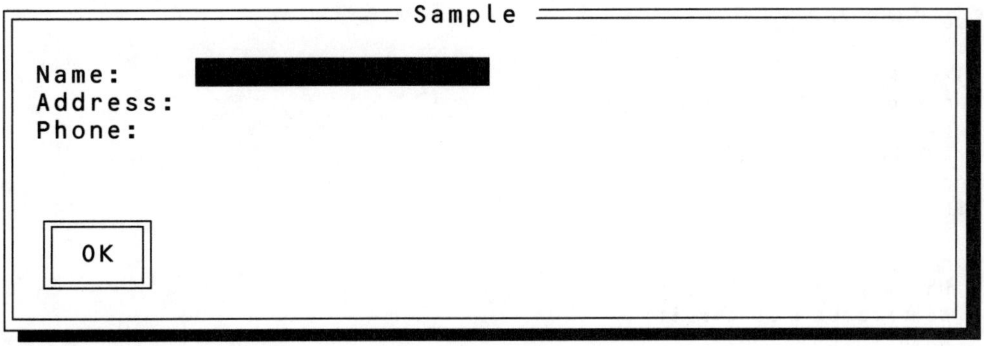

```
┌══════════════════════ Sample ══════════════════════┐
│                                                       │
│  Name:        ███████████████████                    │
│  Address:                                             │
│  Phone:                                               │
│                                                       │
│                                                       │
│  ┌─────────┐                                          │
│  │  OK     │                                          │
│  └─────────┘                                          │
│                                                       │
└───────────────────────────────────────────────────┘
```

Figure 6-4   A sample dialog box

The `Input` method for dialog box objects calls the `Input` method for the object in the `SubObj` array indicated by the `CurrentFld` variable. The input methods must return a value that tells the dialog object which field to activate next. This value is 9, 13, 27, or the second byte of one of the function key codes plus 256. A value of 9 (Tab) or 13 (Enter) indicates that the user wants to select the next field. A value of 27 (Esc) indicates that the user wants to exit the dialog box. Any other value is compared to the IDs of the dialog box objects to determine which field to activate next.

The methods for static and text objects are similar to the text-input routines presented in Chapter 1. `StaticLit` objects do not allow input. Instead, the `Input` method inherited from `ScrnObj` returns a 9, so the dialog input method selects the next field.

The `Init` and `Draw` methods for buttons are similar to those for dialog boxes. One difference is that buttons do not have a list of subobjects. The title text for a button appears inside the box instead of on the top line. Another difference is that buttons are associated with a function that should be called when the user presses the button. This function is called by the button `Input` method when the user selects the button and presses Enter. The function should return a value that the dialog `Input` method can use as a result code.

Comments

You must take several important steps to use the screen objects in this unit. This program illustrates the procedure by creating a dialog box similar to the one in Figure 6-4.

```
{This is a program to show off the dialog box class}
program dialog;
```

```pascal
uses crt, Entry;

{$F+}
function QuitDialog : integer;
begin
    QuitDialog := 27;
end;
{$F-}

var
   WhatsUp : DialogObj;
   NamePrompt : StaticLit;
   NameFld : TextObj;
   AddrPrompt : StaticLit;
   AddrFld : TextObj;
   PhonePrompt : StaticLit;
   PhoneFld : TextObj;
   OKButt : ButtonObj;
   Ch : integer;

begin
    TextAttr := $10;
    ClrScr;
    {Make the dialog boxes and the controls}
    WhatsUp.Init( 5, 10, 12, 60, $24, 'Sample' );
    NamePrompt.Init( 7, 12, 'Name:', $24 );
    AddrPrompt.Init( 8, 12, 'Address:', $24 );
    PhonePrompt.Init( 9, 12, 'Phone:', $24 );
    NameFld.Init( 7, 21, 20, '', $25 );
    AddrFld.Init( 8, 21, 40, '', $25 );
    PhoneFld.Init( 9, 21, 15, '', $25 );
    OKButt.Init( 12, 13, 3, 8, 'OK', $34, QuitDialog );
    {Add the controls to the dialog box}
    WhatsUp.AddObj( @NamePrompt );
    WhatsUp.AddObj( @AddrPrompt );
    WhatsUp.AddObj( @PhonePrompt );
    WhatsUp.AddObj( @NameFld );
    WhatsUp.AddObj( @AddrFld );
    WhatsUp.AddObj( @PhoneFld );
    WhatsUp.AddObj( @OKButt );
    WhatsUp.Draw;
    Ch := WhatsUp.Input;
end.
```

First, this program includes the screen objects unit (Entry) in the uses statement. Next, the program defines functions used by any buttons in the dialog. In this case, the only button function is QuitDialog. Note that the directives {$F+} and {$F-} surround the function. They are required so that a pointer to the function can be saved in the button object (see questions 9.1 and 9.2).

The variable section of this program includes a variable for each field in the dialog. For small dialog boxes, this approach is OK; for dialog boxes with many items, you can create an array of pointers to hold the screen objects.

Most of the program simply initializes the objects and adds them to the dialog box object. After that you simply call the dialog box Draw and Init methods; they do all the rest.

Enhancements

You may have noticed that these dialog boxes do not have the visual appeal of those in professional programs. The reason is that those programs use high-resolution graphics instead of the simple text graphics used here.

This is where inheritance can come in handy. All that you need to do is to create an object that inherits all but the Draw method. The new Draw method can draw whatever fancy graphics are required. See question 6.1 for how to draw graphical objects.

6.5   How do I...

Reuse objects to make a database of names and addresses?

Description

One advantage of using objects is the ease with which you can use them in other programs. This solution uses the database objects defined in Chapter 2 to handle files and the dialog box objects from question 6.4 to interact with the user. The final result is a program that lets you add, change, and delete records in a database of names and addresses.

See Also

6.4   Creating dialog boxes
2.8   Creating database files

Solution

Most of the program for this solution has already been written. See the code for dialog box objects in question 6.4 and the code for file objects in question 2.8. All that is left is some code to define the dialog box and the actions corresponding to the buttons in it. Figure 6-5 shows the dialog box used in this program.

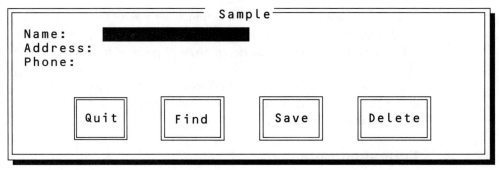

Figure 6-5 The address book dialog box

This program implements the database:

```
{Object oriented database program}
program dbase;
uses Crt, Entry, RandFile;

type
    {Record for the data collected by the dialog}
    AddrBook = record
            Name : string[20];
            Address : string[40];
            Phone : string[15];
    end;

var
    DataFile : VariableFile;
    IndxFile : BTree;
    MyBook : AddrBook;
    WhatsUp : DialogObj;
    NamePrompt : StaticLit;
    NameFld : TextObj;
    AddrPrompt : StaticLit;
    AddrFld : TextObj;
    PhonePrompt : StaticLit;
    PhoneFld : TextObj;
    DoneButt : ButtonObj;
    FindButt : ButtonObj;
    SaveButt : ButtonObj;
    DeleteButt : ButtonObj;
    Ch : integer;

{$F+}
{These functions are called when the
 corresponding button is pressed}

{Exit the program}
function QuitDialog : integer;
begin
```

```
    {Return an ESC code}
    QuitDialog := 27;
end;

{Save the record in the dialog box}
function SaveRec : integer;
var
   RecNo : longint;
begin
    {Copy the data from the dialog controls to
     the address record}
    MyBook.Name := NameFld.TextData;
    MyBook.Address := AddrFld.TextData;
    MyBook.Phone := PhoneFld.TextData;
    {See if the record exists}
    RecNo := IndxFile.LookUp( MyBook.Name );
    if RecNo > 0 then {The record already exists}
        DataFile.WriteRec( MyBook, RecNo )
    else {The record does not exist}
    begin
        {Create a new record}
        RecNo := DataFile.AddRec( MyBook, SizeOf( MyBook ));
        {Save the key}
        IndxFile.AddKey( MyBook.Name, RecNo );
    end;
    SaveRec := 287;
end;

{Find a record with the name in the dialog box}
function FindRec : integer;
var
   RecNo : longint;
begin
    {Load the record}
    RecNo := IndxFile.LookUp( NameFld.TextData );
    if RecNo > 0 then
    begin
        {Read the record}
        DataFile.ReadRec( MyBook, RecNo );
        {Copy it to the dialog box}
        NameFld.TextData := MyBook.Name;
        AddrFld.TextData := MyBook.Address;
        PhoneFld.TextData := MyBook.Phone;
    end
    else
    begin
        AddrFld.TextData := '';
        PhoneFld.TextData := '';
    end;
    WhatsUp.Draw;
    FindRec := 289;
end;
```

```
{Delete the current record}
function DeleteRec : integer;
var
   RecNo : longint;
begin
    {Find the record}
    RecNo := IndxFile.LookUp( NameFld.TextData );
    {Delete the record}
    DataFile.DelRec( RecNo );
    {Delete the key}
    IndxFile.DelKey( NameFld.TextData );
    {Clear out the dialog data}
    NameFld.TextData := '';
    AddrFld.TextData := '';
    PhoneFld.TextData := '';
    WhatsUp.Draw;
    DeleteRec := 288;
end;
{$F-}

begin
    {Open the data file and index}
    DataFile.Init( 'address.dat' );
    IndxFile.Init( @DataFile, 20 );
    TextAttr := $10;
    ClrScr;
    {Initialize the controls}
    WhatsUp.Init( 5, 10, 11, 53, $24, 'Sample' );
    NamePrompt.Init( 7, 12, 'Name:', $24 );
    AddrPrompt.Init( 8, 12, 'Address:', $24 );
    PhonePrompt.Init( 9, 12, 'Phone:', $24 );
    NameFld.Init( 7, 21, 20, '', $25 );
    AddrFld.Init( 8, 21, 40, '', $25 );
    PhoneFld.Init( 9, 21, 15, '', $25 );
    DoneButt.Init( 12, 15, 3, 8,'Quit', $34, QuitDialog, 272 );
    FindButt.Init( 12, 26, 3, 8,'Find', $34, FindRec, 289 );
    SaveButt.Init( 12, 37, 3, 8,'Save', $34, SaveRec, 287 );
    DeleteButt.Init( 12,48,3,10,'Delete', $34, DeleteRec, 288 );
    {Add them to the dialog}
    WhatsUp.AddObj( @NamePrompt );
    WhatsUp.AddObj( @AddrPrompt );
    WhatsUp.AddObj( @PhonePrompt );
    WhatsUp.AddObj( @NameFld );
    WhatsUp.AddObj( @AddrFld );
    WhatsUp.AddObj( @PhoneFld );
    WhatsUp.AddObj( @DoneButt );
    WhatsUp.AddObj( @FindButt );
    WhatsUp.AddObj( @SaveButt );
    WhatsUp.AddObj( @DeleteButt );
    {Draw the dialog}
    WhatsUp.Draw;
    {Get user input}
    Ch := WhatsUp.Input;
    {Close the file}
```

```
    DataFile.Done;
end.
```

This program use the units `Entry` and `RandFile`, which contain the dialog and data file object definitions. Dialog box objects are used to create the dialog box shown in Figure 6-5. A data file object holds the data entered by the user. Most of the main program is used to initialize the dialog box. The actual work of this program is done by the functions corresponding to the buttons in the dialog box.

The buttons in the dialog let you quit the program, save the information on the screen, find an address, or delete an address. The QuitDialog function returns an Esc code, which tells the dialog box object that there is no more input. The SaveRec function gets the name field from the screen and uses it as a key into the database, either to find a record by the same name or to create a new record. The FindRec function uses the name on the screen to look up a record in the database. If the record is found, it is displayed in the dialog box. The `DeleteRec` function also looks up the name in the database. If the record is found, it deletes the record from the database.

Enhancements

Most of the main program is devoted to setting up the dialog box. One thing you can do to reduce the amount of code in this part is to save information about the dialog box in a file. This technique is demonstrated in question 6.6.

ADVANCED OBJECTS

The next two solutions demonstrate some useful techniques for working with objects. Solution 6.6 shows you how to save objects in a file so that you can restore and reuse them later. Solution 6.7 describes how to put an object in a unit. You've seen this technique before, but this solution shows you how to encapsulate an object in a unit to make convenient object libraries.

6.6 / How do I...

Save a Turbo Pascal object to a file?

Description

The data for objects defines the state of the object. The methods use this data to determine object behavior under various circumstances. Because the object is stored in memory, everything about the object disappears when the program ends. Sometimes it is convenient to save an object to a file so that

Memory

```
Sample = Object
    Param1 : integer;
    Param2 : string[10];
    Param3 : real;
    Constructor Init;
    procedure DoSomething; virtual;
    Destructor Done;
end;
```

Figure 6-6 Memory format of an object

users can reload it the next time they run the program. By saving the objects, you can make the program pick up where the user left off.

See Also

2.8   Creating database files

9.3   Making a dialog editor

Solution

Figure 6-6 shows the format of an object in memory. All of the data for an object is grouped together as if the object were a Turbo Pascal record. You can read and write object data as if it were a record with procedures such as BlockRead and BlockWrite.

If you look closely at Figure 6-6, you'll see a field in the object data that was not defined in the object. This field is the pointer to the object's virtual method table (VMT), which Turbo Pascal uses to figure out what methods to call for an object.

Every type of object has a unique VMT. The dialog box objects in question 6.4 use the VMT to determine the type of the object. The dialog box object uses an array of pointers to screen objects to define the items in the dialog box. When the time comes to call one of the methods for these objects, Turbo Pascal looks in the VMT to determine the method to use. The result is that although each object uses the same variable type, they are, in fact, different.

You can use this feature when you are saving objects to a file. You can, for example, save the objects that define a dialog box in the file, then read all of the objects into memory when the dialog box is needed. The VMTs for each object ensure that the object is handled correctly. This program shows you how:

```
{Program to save dialog objects}
program Savediag;
uses Entry, Crt, Dos;

var
   Cmnd : string;
   Name : string;
   Xpos, Ypos, XLen, YLen : integer;
   Attr : byte;
   Diag : ^DialogObj;
   SText : ^StaticLit;
   FHand : file;

begin
    Diag := Nil;
    repeat
        {Clear the screen with blue spaces}
        TextAttr := $17;
        ClrScr;
        {If a dialog box is defined, draw it}
        if Diag <> Nil then
          Diag^.Draw;
        {Get the user command}
        TextAttr := $24;
        GotoXY( 1, 1 );
        ClrEol;
        Write( 'Enter command: ' );
        ReadLn( Cmnd );
        if Cmnd = 'cd' then {create dialog command}
        begin
            GotoXY( 1, 1 );
            ClrEol;
            Write( 'Enter dialog name: ' );
            ReadLn( Name );
            GotoXY( 1, 1 );
            ClrEol;
            Write( 'Enter coordinates: ' );
            ReadLn( Ypos, Xpos, YLen, XLen );
            GotoXY( 1, 1 );
            ClrEol;
            Write( 'Enter attribute: ' );
            ReadLn( Attr );
            {Create the dialog box}
            New(Diag, Init( Ypos, Xpos, YLen, XLen, Attr, Name ));
        end
        else if Cmnd = 'cs' then {Create a static text field}
        begin
            GotoXY( 1, 1 );
            ClrEol;
            Write( 'Enter static text: ' );
            ReadLn( Name );
            GotoXY( 1, 1 );
            ClrEol;
```

```
            Write( 'Enter position: ' );
            ReadLn( YPos, XPos );
            GotoXY( 1, 1 );
            ClrEol;
            Write( 'Enter attribute: ' );
            ReadLn( Attr );
            {Create the text control}
            New( SText, Init( Ypos, Xpos, Name, Attr ));
            {Add it to the dialog box}
            Diag^.AddObj( SText );
        end
        else if Cmnd = 'n' then {Erase old dialog}
        begin
            Dispose( Diag, Done );
            Diag := Nil;
        end
        else if Cmnd = 's' then {Save the dialog}
        begin
            GotoXY( 1, 1 );
            ClrEol;
            Write( 'Enter filename: ' );
            ReadLn( Name );
            {Open the file for writing}
            Assign( FHand, Name );
            ReWrite( FHand, 1 );
            Diag^.Save( FHand );
            Close( FHand );
        end
        else if Cmnd = 'r' then {Read the dialog}
        begin
            GotoXY( 1, 1 );
            ClrEol;
            Write( 'Enter filename: ' );
            ReadLn( Name );
            {Open the file for reading}
            Assign( FHand, Name );
            Reset( FHand, 1 );
            New( Diag, Init( 0, 0, 0, 0, 0, '' ));
            Diag^.Load( FHand );
            Close( FHand );
        end;
    until Cmnd = 'q';
end.
```

This program waits for the user to enter a command, asks the user for some information, then carries out the command. The user gives the command "cd" to create a new dialog box. The user enters the location, attribute, and title for the dialog box, then the program uses the Turbo Pascal procedure New to allocate memory for the object and call the dialog box Init method. The command "cs" is similar, except that the object created is a static text string. After the object is created, the program calls the dialog box AddObj method to add the text to the dialog box. You can add commands to create other controls by following the example of the "cs" command.

The commands "n" (New), "s" (Save), and "r" (Load) use new methods in the screen objects unit. The "n" command uses the Turbo Pascal Dispose procedure to free the memory used by previously defined objects. The Dispose procedure calls the Done method for the object, being freed. For most screen objects, this method does nothing. You can handle the method by adding it to the ScrnObj object, making it available to all objects. The Done method for dialog boxes has to free all of the memory used by controls in that dialog. This method shows how:

```
destructor DialogObj.Done;
var
   i : integer;
begin
   {Free the member objects}
   for i := 1 to SubCnt do
      Dispose( SubObj[i], Done );
end;
```

The "s" command saves all of the objects defined. For most objects, the method to do this looks like this:

```
procedure ScrnObj.Save( var FHand : file );
var
   Size : integer;
begin
   {Save the size of the object}
   Size := SizeOf( Self );
   BlockWrite( FHand, Size, SizeOf( integer ));
   {Save the object}
   BlockWrite( FHand, Self, Size );
end;
```

The dialog box object needs to save itself and all of the control objects in the dialog. This method looks like this:

```
procedure DialogObj.Save( var FHand : file );
var
   i : integer;
begin
   {Save the dialog}
   ScrnObj.Save( FHand );
   {Save the member objects}
   for i := 1 to SubCnt do
      SubObj[i]^.Save( FHand );
end;
```

The last command is "r", which loads the dialog box into memory. This is done by calling the `Load` method in the dialog box object, as follows:

```
procedure DialogObj.Load( var FHand : file );
var
   i : integer;
   ObjPtr : ^ScrnObj;
   Size : integer;
begin
   {Read the dialog box object}
   BlockRead( FHand, Size, SizeOf( integer ));
   BlockRead( FHand, Self, Size );
   {Read the control objects}
   for i := 1 to SubCnt do
   begin
       BlockRead( FHand, Size, SizeOf( integer ));
       GetMem( SubObj[i], Size );
       BlockRead( FHand, SubObj[i]^, Size );
   end;
end;
```

Enhancements

Typing in the coordinates, attributes, and other information for each control is not the easiest way to define a dialog box. Another drawback to the program in this solution is that you cannot change the data once you have entered it. Solution 9.3 is a program that lets you create and edit dialog boxes with simple menu commands. This makes it easier to try different layouts for the dialog before you save it to the file.

6.7 How do I...

Put Turbo Pascal objects in units?

Description

Encapsulation means hiding the details of an object from the rest of the program. The only way for a program to use the encapsulated object is by calling the object's methods. Programs cannot use the object in unforeseen ways, because the program cannot access the details of the object. Turbo Pascal objects are not completely encapsulated. A program can access any field in an object as easily as it can access a field in a record. One way to solve this problem is to put the object in a unit and mark fields that the program should not be able to change as `private`. Putting an object in a unit has the added advantage of making it easy to use the object in other programs. Rather that cutting and pasting the code from one program to another, you simply include the unit in a `uses` statement.

See Also

6.4   Creating dialog boxes

Solution

The differences between a Turbo Pascal program and a Turbo Pascal unit begin with the very first command. In a program, you use a `program` command; in a unit, you use a `unit` command. These commands are followed by the name of the program or unit, respectively.

The next thing that you do in a program is to define the types, variables, functions, and procedures it uses. In a unit, you must divide the module into two parts. The first part is the `interface`, in which you define all of the data and procedures accessible by programs that include the unit. The second part is the `implementation` part, which contains private data, and code for the functions and procedures used in the unit. Figure 6-7 shows the parts of a unit.

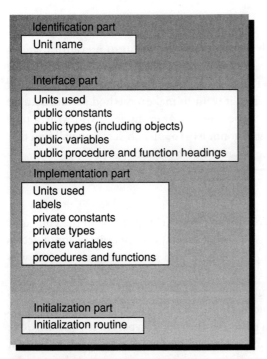

The simplest way to put an object in a unit is to use the technique used in question 6.4 for the dialog unit. In this case, the type definitions for the objects go in the `interface` part of the unit, and the methods themselves go in the `implementation` part. Once you have done this you can include the object in any program by putting a `uses` statement at the beginning.

Figure 6-7 The parts of a unit

You get some encapsulation with this technique, because the `implementation` part contains functions and data that cannot be accessed by the program using the unit. The object is not truly encapsulated, however, because the program can still access the fields in the objects since they are in the `interface` portion. Turbo Pascal lets you get around the problem by creating a `private` section. Any field or method in the `private` section of an object cannot be used by programs outside of the unit.

In the case of the `Dialog unit`, all of the data fields can go in the `private section`, since the program does not need to access the fields. To see what this looks like, look at this example of the `DialogObj` object using a `private` section:

```
DialogObj = object( ScrnObj )
   {Visible methods}
   constructor Init( IRow, ICol, IHght, IWidth : integer;
             IAttr : byte; IText : string );
   procedure Draw; virtual;
   function Input : integer; virtual;
   procedure AddObj( ObjPtr : ScrnPtr );
private        {Private data fields}
   Hght, Width : integer;
   SubObj : array[1..50] of ScrnPtr;
   SubCnt : integer;
   TextData : string;
end;
```

You can also put methods in the `private` section to prevent programs from accessing them. You may want to do this for functions, such as the `Draw` procedure in the `TextObj` object, that are called only from other methods. In most cases, you do not want to make a method private because doing so limits the usability of the object. For example, if you write a program that uses `TextObj` objects but not `DialogObj` objects, you will find that you cannot draw text because the method is private.

Warnings

A major drawback to having a `private` section in an object is that any object that inherits from an object with private fields must be in the same unit as the parent object. The reason is that the inheriting object cannot access the private fields if it is in another source, and so it cannot change the way these fields are used.

This drawback does not make inheritance impossible, just inconvenient. For instance, to add new objects to the dialog unit, you must put them in that unit, not in the program that uses the special type. After you have done this for several programs, the unit may become very crowded, making it difficult to find particular parts of the unit when you need to make changes.

7

GRAPHICS

urbo Pascal comes with an easy-to-use graphics unit that handles the details of displaying pixels. This chapter shows you how to use this unit to draw polygons, polyhedrons, and images. The first section includes programs to handle polygons. It shows you not only how to store and draw polygons but also how to fill them and find their areas. The next section adds another dimension: it shows you how to draw three-dimensional objects. The final section shows how to enhance and modify images.

In addition to demonstrating the graphics capabilities of Turbo Pascal, this chapter includes some more examples of object-oriented programming. Each of the programs inherits features from the `GraphObj` object you saw in Chapter 6. This is a good example of the power of object-oriented programming. Any programs written for use with the simple graphical objects from Chapter 6 can also be used with the more complex objects in this chapter. Without object-oriented programming, you would have to rewrite your program to handle the new graphics images.

TWO-DIMENSIONAL OBJECTS

By using a large number of short edges, you can create very detailed polygons such as the one in Figure 7-1. Solution 7.1 shows how to display and store such polygons. With polygons like the one in Figure 7-1, it is difficult to determine which points lie inside and which lie outside. Solution 7.2 shows how to determine the status of points on the screen. When you use

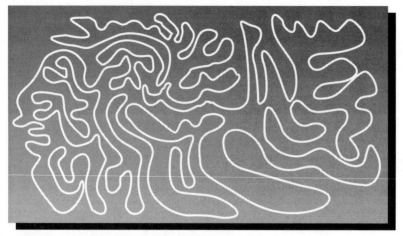

Figure 7-1 A detailed polygon

Figure 7-2 A cycloid curve

polygons to represent objects in the real world, you may need to know how much area the polygon takes up. This question is answered in solution 7.3.

You can use Turbo Pascal to draw other things besides polygons. Solution 7.4 shows how to draw graphs of the results of mathematical equations. In this case, the equations describe cycloid curves that show the path of the edge of a circle as it moves around another circle. The results make interesting patterns, such as the one in Figure 7-2.

7.1 How do I...

Draw polygons using Turbo Pascal?

Description

The graphical object in Chapter 6 shows how to draw the simplest polygon, the triangle. This solution shows how to draw polygons with up to 8192 sides.

See Also

Solution

You can store polygons in memory as a list of points that represent the vertices of the polygon. The usual way to make this list in Turbo Pascal is to define an array, as follows:

```
Points = record
    x, y : integer;
end;
PointLst = array [1..8192] of Points;
```

The problem with this is that you must set aside 32,768 bytes for this array even if the polygon uses less than 8192 vertices. This kind of memory usage severely limits the number of polygons that your program can use. The answer to this problem is to adjust the array size and use the heap to store the list.

When you allocate memory for a `PointLst` type variable, Turbo Pascal tries to allocate the whole 32,768 bytes. To allocate a memory block of a different size, you must use the `GetMem` procedure and assign the result to a pointer. The declaration for the pointer type looks like this:

```
PointLstPtr = ^PointLst;
```

If you define a variable of type `PointLstPtr`, called `PntList`, you can allocate a ten-element array with this statement:

```
GetMem( PntList, Sizeof( Point ) * 10 );
```

To access an element in the array, dereference the pointer and treat the result as a normal array, as follows:

```
PntList^[2].x; {Get the X value of the second element}
```

Once you have defined this memory structure, simply write a routine to draw the polygon and package everything up in an object that inherits features from the `GraphObj` described in Chapter 6. To draw the polygon, use the `MoveTo` procedure to move to the first point, then use `LineTo` to draw lines from one point to the next.

The following program reads mouse positions to define the sides of a polygon. To simplify the listing, the `GraphObj` from Chapter 6 has been moved to its own unit.

```
{Program to use graphics in objects}
uses Dos, Graph, GrafBase;

type
       {Define types used to make a list of vertices}
```

```
        Point = record
            x, y : integer;
        end;
        PointLstPtr = ^PointLst;
        PointLst = array [1..8192] of Point;

        {Define the polygon object}
        PolyObj = object( GraphObj )
            Vertices : PointLstPtr;    {Array of vertices}
            VCount : integer;          {Number of vertices}
            VSpace : integer;          {Space for vertices}
            constructor Init;
            procedure AddVertex( XPos, YPos : integer );
            procedure Draw; virtual;
            procedure Erase; virtual;
        end;

{Initialize a polygon object}
constructor PolyObj.Init;
begin
    {Put the object in the upper left corner of the screen}
    x := 0;
    y := 0;
    {Make it white}
    Clr := 15;
    {Allocate space for 10 points}
    VSpace := 10;
    VCount := 0;
    GetMem( Vertices, VSpace * sizeof( Point ));
end;

{Add a vertex to the object}
procedure PolyObj.AddVertex( XPos, YPos : integer );
var
   pl : PointLstPtr;
begin
    {If there is not enough space allocated}
    if VCount = VSpace then
    begin
       {Allocate more space}
       GetMem( pl, ( VSpace + 10 ) * sizeof( Point ));
       {Copy the data to the new space}
       Move( Vertices^, pl^, VSpace * sizeof( Point ));
       {Free the old space}
       FreeMem( Vertices, VSpace * sizeof( Point ));
       Vertices := pl;
       VSpace := VSpace + 10;
    end;
    {Add the new point to the list}
    Vertices^[VCount + 1].x := XPos;
    Vertices^[VCount + 1].y := YPos;
    Inc( VCount );
end;
```

```
{Draw the polygon}
procedure PolyObj.Draw;
var
   i : integer;
begin
    {Set the polygon color}
    SetColor( Clr );
    {Go to the first point for the polygon}
    MoveTo( x, y );
    {Draw all of the edges of the polygon}
    for i := 1 to VCount do
        LineTo( Vertices^[i].x + x, Vertices^[i].y + y );
    {Draw the last edge}
    LineTo( x, y );
end;

{Erase the polygon}
procedure PolyObj.Erase;
var
   i : integer;
begin
    {Set the color to black}
    SetColor( 0 );
    {Undraw with the same commands as for draw}
    MoveTo( x, y );
    for i := 1 to VCount do
        LineTo( Vertices^[i].x + x, Vertices^[i].y + y );
    LineTo( x, y );
end;

var
   GraphDriver, GraphMode : integer;
   Pict : PolyObj;
   Regs : Registers;
   Buttons : word;
   FirstTime : boolean;

begin
    {Initialize BGI graphics}
    GraphDriver := Detect;
    InitGraph( GraphDriver, GraphMode, _c:\tp  );
    {Initialize the mouse driver}
    Regs.ax := 0;
    Intr( $33, Regs );
    if Regs.ax = 0 then
        WriteLn( _Mouse not installed  );
    Regs.ax := 1;     {Show the cursor}
    Intr( $33, Regs );
    {Initialize the polygon object}
    Pict.Init;
    FirstTime := FALSE;
    repeat
```

```
            {Get mouse position and button status}
            Regs.ax := 3;
            Intr( $33, Regs );
            Buttons := Regs.bx;
            {If the left button is down}
            if Buttons = 1 then
            begin
                {Hide mouse cursor}
                Regs.ax := 2;
                Intr( $33, Regs );
                {If this is the first point}
                if FirstTime then
                begin
                    {Move the polygon to the indicated point}
                    Pict.MoveIt( Regs.cx, Regs.dx );
                    FirstTime := FALSE;
                end
                else {Not the first point}
                begin
                    {Erase the old polygon}
                    Pict.Erase;
                    {Add the indicated point}
                    Pict.AddVertex( Regs.cx - Pict.x
                                    ,Regs.dx - Pict.y );
                    {Draw the new polygon}
                    Pict.Draw;
                end;
                {Show the cursor}
                Regs.ax := 1;
                Intr( $33, Regs );
            end;
        {Repeat until the right button is pressed}
        until Buttons = 2;
        ReadLn;
end.
```

At the beginning of the program are the data definitions required to make a variable-length list of points. Following that is the definition of the polygon object. This object includes a list of vertices, the number of vertices in the list, and the number of points that can fit in the amount of memory currently allocated. The space available does not equal the number of points because of the way new space is allocated when a vertex is added.

The AddVertex method begins by checking whether there is room for a new point. If not, it allocates a new list of points that is ten points larger than the previous list. Then it copies the old list to the new list and frees the old list. If it allocated space one point at a time, the program would spend most of its time allocating memory. This way, it allocates memory only every ten points, vastly improving performance.

Function	Description
0	Reset the mouse Input: **A X** = 0 Output: **A X** = Status 　　　　 **B X** = Type of mouse
1	Show the mouse pointer Input: **A X** = 1
2	Hide the mouse pointer Input: **A X** = 2
3	Get mouse data Input: **A X** = 3 Output: **B X** = Button status (bit 0 = left, bit 1 = right) 　　　　 **C X** = Pointer column 　　　　 **D X** = Pointer row
4	Move mouse pointer Input: **A X** = 4 　　　　 **B X** = Pointer column 　　　　 **C X** = Pointer row
5	Get button press status Input: **A X** = 5 　　　　 **B X** = Button (0 = left, 1 = right) Output: **A X** = Status flag 　　　　 **B X** = Number of times pressed since last call 　　　　 **C X** = Column of last press 　　　　 **D X** = Row of last press
6	Get button release status Input: **A X** = 6 　　　　 **B X** = Button (0 = left, 1 = right) Output: **A X** = Status flag 　　　　 **B X** = Number of times released 　　　　 **C X** = Column of last release 　　　　 **D X** = Row of last release
7	Set horizontal limits Input: **A X** = 7 　　　　 **B X** = Minimum limit 　　　　 **C X** = Maximum limit
8	Set vertical limits Input: **A X** = 8 　　　　 **B X** = Minimum limit 　　　　 **C X** = Maximum limit
9	Set graphics cursor bitmap Input: **A X** = 9 　　　　 **B X** = column of hot spot 　　　　 **C X** = row of hot spot **D S : D X** = Pointer to bitmap

Table 7-1 Mouse functions

The Draw and Erase methods both work by using MoveTo to move to the first point of the polygon and LineTo to drawn each of the edges. When lines have been drawn to each of the points in the list, a final line is draw from the last point back to the first to complete the polygon.

The first two statements in the main program initialize the Turbo Pascal graphics system. These statements work with any supported graphics hardware such as CGA, EGA, VGA, and MCGA. The next step is to initialize the mouse driver. All mouse commands are issued by putting values into registers and using software interrupt number $33. Table 7-1 shows how to set up the registers for several of the available mouse commands.

After initializing Pict, the polygon object, the program goes into the draw loop. This loop reads the mouse status and, if the left button is pressed, adds the current mouse position to the polygon as a new vertex. Notice that before any drawing is done, the mouse pointer is made invisible. This ensures that the mouse driver has complete data when it tries to move the mouse. If you do not do this, the mouse driver erases parts of the screen as the mouse pointer moves.

Comments

The preceding program uses the mouse to enter the vertices of the polygon. Using a mouse makes it easy to enter a large number of graphics coordinates. Other ways to make vertices are to use mathematical formulas or to read data from a file. One interesting way to generate polygons is to use random numbers. Figure 7-3 shows how random numbers can be converted to coordinates that make a polygon.

```
var
        Angle, Radius : real;

begin
    {Initialize graphics driver}
    GraphDriver := Detect;
    InitGraph( GraphDriver, GraphMode, _c:\tp  );
    {Initialize random-number generator}
    Randomize;
    {Initialize the polygon}
    Pict.Init;
    Pict.Colorize( 15 );
    Pict.MoveIt( 300, 200 );
    {Move around in a circle to generate vertices}
    Angle := 0.0;
    repeat
        {Get a radius}
        Radius := Random( 100 ) + 20.0;
        {Add the new vertex}
        Pict.AddVertex( Round( Cos( Angle ) * Radius )
```

```
            , Round( Sin( Angle ) * Radius) );
         {Move around the circle by a random interval}
         Angle := Angle + Random( 7 ) / 20.0;
      until Angle > 2.0 * Pi;
      {Draw the polygon}
      Pict.Draw;
      ReadLn;
   end.
```

The `repeat-while` loop in this program moves around the polygon by accumulating random intervals in `Angle`. At each vertex, it gets a random radius. This radius, along with the angle, determines the vertex. The coordinates of the vertex are calculated according to the trigonometric principle

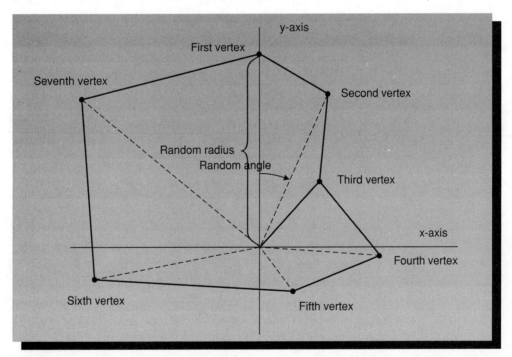

Figure 7-3 Generating random vertices

that the x part is equal to the radius times the cosine of the angle and the y part is equal to the radius times the sine of the angle. After the point is added to the polygon, the angle is increased by a random amount. The loop ends when the angle is greater than 2 * pi radians (a complete circle).

Warnings

An important feature of Pascal is the run-time bounds checking that it does. Each time that your program accesses an array, Pascal checks to make sure that the index is within the specified limits for that array (Turbo Pascal allows you to turn this feature off to speed up your program). The technique used in this program to put arrays on the heap makes the array bounds checking invalid. The check makes sure that the index is between 1 and 8192 but the actual length of the array is something less that 8192 points. The problem is that Turbo Pascal does not know how much space has been allocated.

When you write programs that use this type of array, make sure that you do not go beyond the limits of the array. In the `AddVertex` method the amount of space is checked before adding a point, to make sure that there is enough space. The other methods are written in such a way that they never need to go beyond the array limit.

Enhancements

The `MoveIt` method in `GraphObj` is an example of a graphical translation. It causes all of the points in the object to move on the screen. Another way of changing the object is called *transformation*, which modifies the shape of the polygon. For example, you can implement a simple transformation that makes the polygon taller or shorter, as follows:

```
procedure PolyObj.StretchHeight( Factor : real );
var
        i : integer;
begin
        for i := 1 to VCount do
                Vertices^[i].y := Round( Vertices^[i].y * Factor );
end;
```

Each point in the polygon is scaled by `Factor` in the `for` loop. If the value of `Factor` is between 0 and 1, the object will be shorter. If the value of `Factor` is greater than 1, the object will be taller.

Another transformation is the rotation of the object:

```
procedure PolyObj.Rotate( Angle : real );
var
        i, x, y : integer;
        SinAngle, CosAngle : real;
begin
        SinAngle := Sin( Angle );
        CosAngle := Cos( Angle );
        for i := 1 to VCount do
        begin
                x := Vertices^[i].x;
                y := Vertices^[i].y;
```

```
        Vertices^[i].x := Round( x * CosAngle - y * SinAngle );
        Vertices^[i].y := Round( x * SinAngle + y * CosAngle );
    end;
end;
```

This transform uses a bit of trigonometry to rotate each point in the object around its initial point. The sine and cosine of the angle are computed outside of the loop to save time. Because these routines require extensive computation, they should be called as infrequently as possible. The variables x and y hold the old values of the coordinates while they are being transformed.

7.2   How do I...

Fill the interior of a polygon using Turbo Pascal graphics routines?

Description
The Turbo Pascal graphics library includes two procedures for filling shapes on the screen. The FillPoly routine fills in polygons, but it imposes strict requirements about the format of the polygon vertex array. The FloodFill procedure can fill any object on the screen, but you must first find a point inside the polygon. The solution below shows how the computer can determine if a point is inside a polygon so that you can fill it with FloodFill.

See Also
7.1   Drawing polygon objects

Solution
The basic principle in determining if a point is inside or outside a polygon is to draw a line from a point that is known to be outside the polygon and count the number of times that the line crosses the edge of the polygon. As you can see in Figure 7-4, if the line crosses the edge an even number of times, the point is outside the polygon. If the count is odd, the point is inside the polygon.

The algorithm that uses this principle has two steps. The first is to find a point that must be outside the polygon; a line is drawn from that point to the point being tested. The second is to determine how many times the resulting line crosses an edge of the polygon. The following method assumes that the left edge of the screen is outside the polygon. This means that you can find a horizontal line between the point to be tested and the edge of the screen. Using a horizontal line simplifies the test.

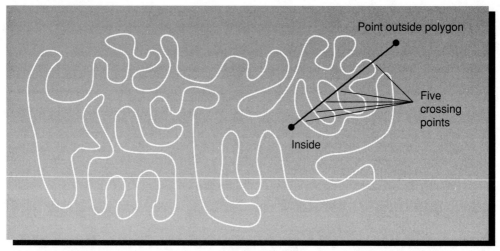

Figure 7-4 Determining whether a point is inside a polygon

A horizontal line crosses an edge whenever the y-coordinate of one end of the edge is above the line and the other end is below the line. Only edges that are to the left of the test point should be tested.

The following method uses the techniques described to determine if a point is inside or outside of the polygon:

```
function PolyObj.Intest( xPos, yPos : integer ) : boolean;
var
        i : integer;
        Count : integer;
begin
        Count := 0;
        for i := 2 to VCount do
        begin
                {See if the edge is left of the point}
                if Vertices^[i - 1].x < xPos then
                begin
                        {See if the edge straddles the line}
                        if (( Vertices^[i - 1].y >= yPos )
                                AND ( Vertices^[i].y < yPos ))
                                OR (( Vertices^[i - 1].y <= yPos )
                                AND ( Vertices^[i].y > yPos )) then
                                Inc( Count );
                end;
        end;
        {See if the count is even}
        if ( Count MOD 2 ) = 0 then
                Intest := FALSE
        else
                Intest := TRUE;
end;
```

This method loops through each of the points, checking the edge between the vertex and the previous vertex in the polygon. First it tests whether the edge is to the left of the test point. If so, the next test determines if the test line crosses the edge. If the current point is above the line and the previous point is below, the line crosses the edge. Also, if the current point is below the line and the previous point is above, the line crosses the edge. The variable `Count` keeps track of the number of crossings. At the end of the routine, the `MOD` operator is used to test whether `Count` is odd or even. If it is even, the routine returns `TRUE`; otherwise, it returns `FALSE`.

To fill a polygon with the `FloodFill` routine, you need to find a point that is inside the polygon. You can try points all over the screen until you stumble on one that is inside, or you can use the following routine to calculate the point:

```
procedure PolyObj.FillPoly;
var
   MinXVertex : integer;
   i : integer;
begin
   MinXVertex := 1;
   {Search for the leftmost vertex}
   for i := 1 to VCount do
   begin
       if Vertices^[i].x < Vertices^[MinXVertex].x then
          MinXVertex := i;
   end;
   SetColor( Clr );
   FloodFill( Vertices^[MinXVertex].x + x + 1
      , Vertices^[MinXVertex].y + y, Clr );
end;
```

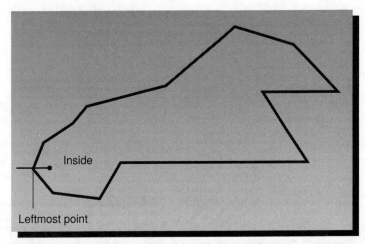

Inside

Leftmost point

Figure 7-5 Finding a point inside the polygon

This routine searches for the leftmost point in the polygon and assumes that the point to the right of the vertex is inside. Figure 7-5 shows how this works. This point must be inside the polygon because a line drawn from the left edge of the screen to the point passes through only one edge (the one that includes the vertex).

Warnings

These routines require that the edges of the polygon do not cross each other. As soon as an edge crosses another, the concept of inside and outside no longer applies. Also, you cannot fill a polygon in which a vertex touches another edge. The `FloodFill` routine considers the closure point as the edge of the area to fill and stops there.

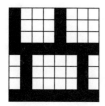

Figure 7-6
A fill pattern

Enhancements

The color that you use to fill the polygon does not have to be the same as the color of the edges.

The `SetFillPattern` and `SetFillStyle` procedures let you set the color and pattern used to fill an area. To use `SetFill-Pattern`, you must design a pattern to use and store it in a `FillPatternType` variable. To set up the pattern in Figure 7-6, use the following:

```
const
     Bricks : FillPatternType =
          ($88, $88, $88, $FF, $22, $22, $22, $FF);
```

Once the pattern is defined, use it in `SetFillPattern`, as follows:

```
SetFillPattern( Bricks, PolyColor );
```

The `SetFillStyle` procedure is similar to `SetFillPattern`, except that it fills the polygon with a predefined pattern. Figure 7-7 shows the patterns available.

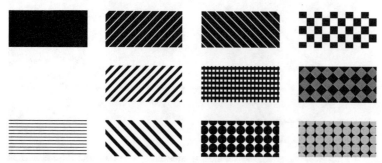

Figure 7-7 Predefined fill patterns

7.3   How do I...

Determine the area of a polygon using Turbo Pascal?

Description

Finding the area of some polygons is simply a matter of filling in a formula. For example, the area of a rectangle is the product of the lengths of two adjacent sides, and the area of a triangle is half the base length times the height. Similar formulas exist for many other shapes, such as circles, rhombuses, and trapezoids. The solution given here demonstrates a technique for finding the area of the more complex polygons shown in this chapter.

See Also

7.1   Drawing polygon objects

Solution

The brute-force solution is to test every point on the screen to see if it is inside or outside the polygon. The number of points inside the polygon is the area. A better solution is to find a way to break down the polygon into shapes whose areas you can determine by a simple formula.

The shape used in this solution is a four-sided figure called a trapezoid, which has at least two parallel sides. The formula for the area of a trapezoid is the sum of the lengths of the parallel sides times the distance between the parallel sides divided by two.

As Figure 7-8 shows, a trapezoid is formed by each edge of the polygon and its projection on the bottom edge of the screen. If you add the areas of all of the trapezoids projected from the top side of the polygon, you get the area of the polygon plus the area below the polygon. If you add the areas of the trapezoids projected from the bottom side of the polygon, you get the area below the polygon. Subtract the second area from the first to get the area of the polygon itself.

To tell the difference between trapezoids projected from the top and bottom sides, enter the points for the polygon in a clockwise direction. Thus, all the edges that move to the right are top edges, and all the edges that move to the left are bottom edges.

The following routine uses this principle to find the area of a polygon:

```
{Find the area of a polygon}
function PolyObj.Area : longint;
var
   Total : longint;
   i : integer;
begin
```

```
{Get the area of the first trapezoid}
Total := (x - ( Vertices^[1].x + x )) * ( Vertices^[1].y + 2 * y ) DIV 2;
{Go through all of the edges}
for i := 1 to VCount - 1 do
    {Add or subtract the area of the trapezoid}
    Total := Total + ( Vertices^[i].x - Vertices^[i + 1].x )
        * (( Vertices^[i].y + Vertices^[i + 1].y ) DIV 2 + y );
{Add in the last trapezoid}
Total := Total + ( Vertices^[i].x ) * ( Vertices^[i].y DIV 2 + y );
Area := Total;
end;
```

This routine loops through each of the edges, finding the area of the trapezoid under the edge. When it calculates the distance between the parallel sides, it subtracts the second y-coordinate from the first. The result of this subtraction is positive for edges that move right and negative for edges that move left. This makes the whole area positive or negative according to whether the trapezoid is projected from the top or bottom edge, respectively. Thus, no special logic is required to decide if the area should be added or subtracted.

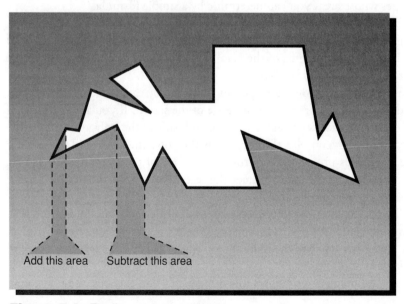

Add this area   Subtract this area

Figure 7-8 Finding polygon areas

7.4   How do I...

Plot mathematical functions using Turbo Pascal?

Description
Many mathematical expressions are used to model real life events. For example, the voltage in alternating current moves up and down in a sine wave. You can model this event with a single mathematical expression, as follows:

```
Voltage = Sine( Time );
```

This may explain everything to a mathematician, but for the rest of us it doesn't help much. The graph in Figure 7-9 makes the idea behind this equation much clearer.

You can use the computer to plot simple curves such as sine waves or parabolas. You loop through values for the x-axis, then plug the *x* value into the equation to get the *y* value for each point in the curve. This solution is fine for mathematical functions that have only one *y* value for each *x* value. This next solution shows how to plot a more complex curve called a cycloid. To create a cycloid you must evaluate separate equations to get the x- and y-coordinates of a point on the curve.

```
x = ( a+b ) * cos( Theta ) - b * cos( ( a+b ) / b * Theta );
y = ( a+b ) * sin( Theta ) - b * sin( ( a+b ) / b * Theta );
```

When plotted, these equations make interesting curves, such as the one in Figure 7-2.

See Also
6.1   Creating graphical objects

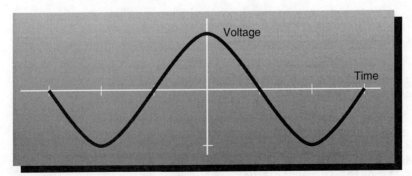

Figure 7-9 Graph of Voltage = Sine(Time)

Solution

The equations for cycloids are called parametric equations. That means that the coordinates are calculated relative to a third parameter. In this case, the parameter is the angle `Theta`. The variables `a` and `b` are constant for any given cycloid curve. Changing them changes the basic shape of the curve.

To generate all of the points in the curve, start with an angle of 0 degrees and increment the angle by a small amount until the current point is the same as the first point plotted. This program defines an object that is a plot of a cycloid curve:

```
{Program to draw epicycloids}
program Cycloid;
uses Graph, GrafBase;

type
        {Define the cycloid object}
        CycloidObj = object( GraphObj )
            BigRadius : real;
            LittleRadius : real;
            InOutFlag : integer;
         constructor Init( BR, LR : real; IO : integer );
         procedure Draw; virtual;
         procedure Erase; virtual;
    end;

{Initialize the constants in the equation}
constructor CycloidObj.Init( BR, LR : real; IO : integer );
begin
    x := 0;
    y := 0;
    Clr := 15;
    BigRadius := BR;
    LittleRadius := LR;
    InOutFlag := IO;
end;

{Draw the curve}
procedure CycloidObj.Draw;
var
  Angle : real;
  XPart, YPart : real;
  XPart1 : real;
  RadSum : real;
begin
    SetColor( Clr );
    {Calculate a + b}
    RadSum := BigRadius + LittleRadius;
    {Calculate the point for Angle = 0}
    XPart1 := RadSum - LittleRadius * InOutFlag;
    MoveTo( Round( XPart1 ) + x, y );
    {Move the angle 1/10 of a radian}
```

```
    Angle := 0.1;
    repeat
        {Evaluate the parametric equations}
        XPart := RadSum * Cos( Angle )
            - LittleRadius * Cos( RadSum / LittleRadius * Angle )
            * InOutFlag;
        YPart := RadSum * Sin( Angle )
        - LittleRadius * Sin( RadSum / LittleRadius * Angle );
        {Draw a line from the last point}
        LineTo( Round( XPart ) + x, Round( YPart ) + y );
        {Increment the angle}
        Angle := Angle + 0.1;
        {Keep looping until close to the original point}
    until ( Abs( XPart - XPart1 ) < 0.7 ) AND ( Abs( YPart ) < 0.7 );
end;

{Draw a square over the top of the object}
procedure CycloidObj.Erase;
var
    Box : array[1..4] of PointType;
    Dist : word;
begin
    {Set the color to black}
    SetColor( 0 );
    {Set the fill style to solid}
    SetFillStyle( SolidFill, 0 );
    {Figure out how large a square to draw}
    Dist := Round( BigRadius + LittleRadius * 2.0 ) + 1;
    {Make an array of the corners for the square}
    Box[1].X := x - Dist;
    Box[1].Y := y - Dist;
    Box[2].X := x + Dist;
    Box[2].Y := y - Dist;
    Box[3].X := x + Dist;
    Box[3].Y := y + Dist;
    Box[4].X := x - Dist;
    Box[4].Y := y + Dist;
    {Fill the square}
    FillPoly( 4, Box );
end;

var
    GraphDriver, GraphMode : integer;
    Pict : CycloidObj;

begin
    {Initialize graphics}
    GraphDriver := Detect;
    InitGraph( GraphDriver, GraphMode, _c:\tp  );
    {Initialize the curve}
    Pict.Init( 70.0, 45.0, -1 );
    {Put the curve in the center of the screen}
    Pict.MoveIt( 320, 200 );
```

```
    {Draw the curve}
    Pict.Draw;
    {Wait for ENTER}
    ReadLn;
    {Erase the object}
    Pict.Erase;
    ReadLn;
end.
```

This program is a simple case of an object that inherits from the `GraphObj` class. The `Init` method sets the usual defaults for `GraphObj` objects, then it sets the constant values used to draw the object.

The `Draw` method does the work of evaluating the parametric equations and plotting the points generated. The variable `Angle` is the angle in the equation. It is incremented by 1/10th of a radian for each point. This is not quite small enough to make the points plot next to each other. To fill in the gaps, the points are plotted by drawing a line from the last point. The angle interval is also not small enough to make the last point generated match the first point exactly. Therefore, the test for the end of the loop checks whether the last point is close to the first point.

Erasing the curve by redrawing it in black is inefficient. You can erase it easily by drawing a black square over the whole thing. The `Erase` method is a good example of using the `PolyFill` routine from question 7.2.

Comments

Once the object is drawn, it is easier to see that this curve describes the path followed by a point on the edge of a circle as it goes around another circle. The `InOutFlag` field in the object determines whether the first circle goes around the inside or the outside of the second circle.

THREE-DIMENSIONAL OBJECTS

One of the most useful capabilities of the computer is the ability to create a model of something so that it can be studied. For example, instead of building an airplane to see if it will fly, you can create a computer model of the airplane and examine it to see how it performs. One aspect of computer modeling is drawing a picture of the object. To do this, you need to draw three-dimensional objects on a two-dimensional computer screen. You also need to turn the object so you can examine it from all sides. The programs in this section show one way to solve these problems.

Draw 3-D objects with Turbo Pascal?

Description
Not all things can be represented by a two-dimensional polygon. To get the full view of the object, you need a way to represent it in three dimensions. This solution shows a simple technique for displaying three-dimensional objects.

See Also
6.1   Creating graphical objects

Solution
The first thing you must do to make 3-D objects is to expand the definition of a point. You must add a z-coordinate to the x- and y-coordinates. The z-coordinate represents the distance in front of or behind the center of the object.

In a 3-D object, each vertex is connected to a number of other vertices in the object. To define the edges, you need a table that indicates which points should be connected. The edges array is a variable-length array similar to the one used to hold vertices. Each edge contains an index into the list of vertices for each end of the edge.

The simplest way to draw a 3-D object is to draw each of the edges, ignoring the z-coordinate. This rendition is accurate but, depending on what side of the object is facing the viewer, can be confusing. You can turn a real object around until you see exactly what it is. The computer can use trigonometry to rotate the object mathematically, allowing you to see different sides.

This program draws an icosahedron (20-sided figure) and lets the user turn it around to see it from different angles:

```
{Program to draw 3-D objects}
uses Dos, Graph, GrafBase, Crt;

type
      {Define the point type}
      Point = record
        x, y, z: integer;
      end;
      PointLstPtr = ^PointLst;
      PointLst = array [1..8192] of Point;
      {Define the edge type}
      PointPair = record
        p1, p2 : integer;
```

```
            end;
            EdgeLstPtr = ^EdgeLst;
            EdgeLst = array [1..8192] of PointPair;

            SolidObj = object( GraphObj )
               Vertices : PointLstPtr;    {Array of corners}
               VCount : integer;          {Number of corners}
               VSpace : integer;          {Space for corners}
               Edges : EdgeLstPtr;        {Array of edges}
               ECount : integer;          {Number of edges}
               ESpace : integer;          {Space for edges}
               constructor Init;
               procedure AddVertex( XPos, YPos, ZPos : integer );
               procedure AddEdge( Point1, Point2 : integer );
               procedure Draw; virtual;
               procedure Erase; virtual;
               procedure Rotate( Pitch, Yaw, Roll : real ); virtual;
         end;

{Initialize the object}
constructor SolidObj.Init;
begin
     x := 0;
     y := 0;
     Clr := 1;
     VSpace := 10;
     VCount := 0;
     GetMem( Vertices, VSpace * sizeof( Point ));
     ESpace := 10;
     ECount := 0;
     GetMem( Edges, ESpace * sizeof( PointPair ));
end;

{Add a vertex to the object}
procedure SolidObj.AddVertex( XPos, YPos, ZPos : integer );
var
   pl : PointLstPtr;
begin
     {See if there is enough space for the vertex}
     if VCount = VSpace then
     begin
         GetMem( pl, ( VSpace + 10 ) * sizeof( Point ));
         Move( Vertices^, pl^, VSpace * sizeof( Point ));
         FreeMem( Vertices, VSpace * sizeof( Point ));
         Vertices := pl;
         VSpace := VSpace + 10;
     end;
     {Add the new vertex}
     Inc( VCount );
     Vertices^[VCount].x := XPos;
     Vertices^[VCount].y := YPos;
     Vertices^[VCount].z := ZPos;
end;
```

```
{Add an edge}
procedure SolidObj.AddEdge( Point1, Point2 : integer );
var
   el : EdgeLstPtr;
begin
    {See if there is enough space for the new edge}
    if ECount = ESpace then
    begin
        GetMem( el, ( ESpace + 10 ) * sizeof( PointPair ));
        Move( Edges^, el^, ESpace * sizeof( PointPair ));
        FreeMem( Edges, ESpace * sizeof( PointPair ));
        Edges := el;
        ESpace := ESpace + 10;
    end;
    {Add the new edge}
    Inc( ECount );
    Edges^[ECount].p1 := Point1;
    Edges^[ECount].p2 := Point2;
end;

{Draw the object}
procedure SolidObj.Draw;
var
   i : integer;
begin
    SetColor( Clr );
    {Draw each edge}
    for i := 1 to ECount do
    begin
        MoveTo( Vertices^[Edges^[i].p1].x + x
            , Vertices^[Edges^[i].p1].y + y );
        LineTo( Vertices^[Edges^[i].p2].x + x
            , Vertices^[Edges^[i].p2].y + y );
    end;
end;

{Erase the object}
procedure SolidObj.Erase;
var
   i : integer;
begin
    {Set the color to black}
    SetColor( 0 );
    {Undraw each edge}
    for i := 1 to ECount do
    begin
        MoveTo( Vertices^[Edges^[i].p1].x + x
            , Vertices^[Edges^[i].p1].y + y );
        LineTo( Vertices^[Edges^[i].p2].x + x
            , Vertices^[Edges^[i].p2].y + y );
    end;
end;
```

```pascal
{Rotate the object}
procedure SolidObj.Rotate( Pitch, Yaw, Roll : real );
var
   i, Tmp : integer;
   CosAngle, SinAngle : real;
begin
    {Do x rotation}
    if Pitch <> 0.0 then
    begin
        {Calculate the cosine and sine of the pitch angle}
        CosAngle := Cos( Pitch );
        SinAngle := Sin( Pitch );
        {Transform all of the points}
        for i := 1 to VCount do
        begin
            Tmp := Round( CosAngle * Vertices^[i].y )
                - Round( SinAngle * Vertices^[i].z );
            Vertices^[i].z := Round( SinAngle * Vertices^[i].y )
                + Round( CosAngle * Vertices^[i].z );
            Vertices^[i].y := Tmp;
        end;
    end;
    {Do z rotation}
    if Yaw <> 0.0 then
    begin
        CosAngle := Cos( Yaw );
        SinAngle := Sin( Yaw );
        for i := 1 to VCount do
        begin
            Tmp := Round( CosAngle * Vertices^[i].x )
                + Round( SinAngle * Vertices^[i].z );
            Vertices^[i].z := Round( CosAngle * Vertices^[i].z)
                - Round( SinAngle * Vertices^[i].x );
            Vertices^[i].x := Tmp;
        end;
    end;
    {Do y rotation}
    if Roll <> 0.0 then
    begin
        CosAngle := Cos( Roll );
        SinAngle := Sin( Roll );
        for i := 1 to VCount do
        begin
            Tmp := Round( CosAngle * Vertices^[i].x )
                - Round( SinAngle * Vertices^[i].y );
            Vertices^[i].y := Round( SinAngle * Vertices^[i].x)
                + Round( CosAngle * Vertices^[i].y );
            Vertices^[i].x := Tmp;
        end;
    end;
end;

var
```

```
    GraphDriver, GraphMode : integer;
    Pict : SolidObj;
    Ch : char;

begin
    {Initialize graphics}
    GraphDriver := Detect;
    InitGraph( GraphDriver, GraphMode, _c:\tp  );
    {Initialize the object}
    Pict.Init;
    Pict.Colorize( 15 );
    Pict.MoveIt( 300, 200 );
    {Define the vertices}
    Pict.AddVertex( -50, 0, 81 );   {Point 1}
    Pict.AddVertex( -81, 50, 0 );   {Point 2}
    Pict.AddVertex( -50, 0, -81 );  {Point 3}
    Pict.AddVertex( 50, 0, -81 );   {Point 4}
    Pict.AddVertex( 81, -50, 0 );   {Point 5}
    Pict.AddVertex( 50, 0, 81 );    {Point 6}
    Pict.AddVertex( 0, 81, 50 );    {Point 7}
    Pict.AddVertex( 0, 81, -50 );   {Point 8}
    Pict.AddVertex( 81, 50, 0 );    {Point 9}
    Pict.AddVertex( -81, -50, 0 );  {Point 10}
    Pict.AddVertex( 0, -81, -50 );  {Point 11}
    Pict.AddVertex( 0, -81, 50 );   {Point 12}
    {Define the edges}
    Pict.AddEdge( 1, 2 );
    Pict.AddEdge( 1, 7 );
    Pict.AddEdge( 2, 7 );
    Pict.AddEdge( 1, 6 );
    Pict.AddEdge( 7, 6 );
    Pict.AddEdge( 6, 9 );
    Pict.AddEdge( 7, 9 );
    Pict.AddEdge( 6, 5 );
    Pict.AddEdge( 5, 9 );
    Pict.AddEdge( 12, 5 );
    Pict.AddEdge( 6, 12 );
    Pict.AddEdge( 1, 12 );
    Pict.AddEdge( 1, 10 );
    Pict.AddEdge( 2, 10 );
    Pict.AddEdge( 12, 10 );
    Pict.AddEdge( 2, 8 );
    Pict.AddEdge( 2, 3 );
    Pict.AddEdge( 7, 8 );
    Pict.AddEdge( 5, 11 );
    Pict.AddEdge( 5, 4 );
    Pict.AddEdge( 11, 4 );
    Pict.AddEdge( 11, 3 );
    Pict.AddEdge( 3, 4 );
    Pict.AddEdge( 3, 8 );
    Pict.AddEdge( 8, 9 );
    Pict.AddEdge( 8, 4 );
    Pict.AddEdge( 9, 4 );
```

```
    Pict.AddEdge( 12, 11 );
    Pict.AddEdge( 11, 10 );
    Pict.AddEdge( 10, 3 );
    {Draw the object}
    Pict.Draw;
    repeat
        {Get a key command}
        Ch := ReadKey;
        Pict.Erase;
        {Decide what kind of rotation to do}
        case Ch of
            _8  : Pict.Rotate( 2.0 * Pi / 30.0, 0.0, 0.0 );
            _2  : Pict.Rotate( -2.0 * Pi / 30.0, 0.0, 0.0 );
            _7  : Pict.Rotate( 0.0, 0.0, 2.0 * Pi / 30.0 );
            _3  : Pict.Rotate( 0.0, 0.0, -2.0 * Pi / 30.0 );
            _4  : Pict.Rotate( 0.0, 2.0 * Pi / 30.0, 0.0 );
            _6  : Pict.Rotate( 0.0, -2.0 * Pi / 30.0, 0.0 );
            _c  : Pict.Colorize( Pict.Clr MOD 16 + 1 )
        end;
        Pict.Draw;
    until Ch = Chr( 27 );
end.
```

Much of this program is similar to the program for drawing polygons. The first difference you may notice is that there are two lists, one for vertices and one for edges. Both of these lists have variables in the object to hold the number of items, the amount of space available for items, and a pointer to the list of items. Both lists also have a method for adding items to the list, AddVertex for vertices and AddEdge for edges.

To draw or erase the object, the Draw and Erase methods go through the list of edges, drawing each one. To find the location of the end points of each line, the routine must get the index of the starting vertex from the edge array. This index is used to get the point from the vertices array. The same thing is done to get the other end of the edge, and a line is drawn between the two points.

The Rotate method transforms the points in the vertices list, using the formulas for rotating polygons from question 7.1. The difference is that there are three rotations, one for each axis. The edges array does not need to be changed, because when the vertices move the edges also move.

The main program loads the coordinates of each of the edges and the edges that connect them. Then it loops, waiting for a keypress. Pressing various keys on the numeric keypad causes a rotation in the corresponding direction. Pressing the Esc key exits the loop and stops the program.

Comments

The easiest way to get a sense of what the icosahedron really looks like is to hold down the "4" key. As the icosahedron rotates, you can see which lines are the front of the object. Figure 7-10 shows the object with the foreground lines emphasized.

Warnings

You do not need to do one rotation at a time. The `Rotate` method lets you supply all three angles at the same time. When you do this, pay attention to the order in which you give the angles. Rotating an object on the x-axis and then the z-axis does not give the same final result as rotating the object in

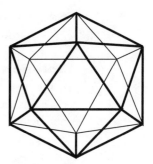

Figure 7-10
An icosahedron

the z-axis and then the x-axis. This is easy enough to demonstrate; tilt this book back 90 degrees around the x-axis, then spin it 90 degrees clockwise around the z-axis. The pages should be facing your right (difficult to read that way!). Now start from the same position and spin the book 90 degrees clockwise around the z-axis, then tilt it back 90 degrees around the x-axis. Now the pages are facing up.

Enhancements

The object would be much easier to make out if you did not have to look at the lines at the back of the object. Solution 7.6 shows how to remove these lines.

7.6 How do I...

Remove hidden lines from a 3-D object with Turbo Pascal?

Description

Many of the edges in a physical 3-D object are behind the object and therefore cannot be seen. With a computer-drawn object, the trick is to let the computer to know which edges are in the back so that it won't draw them. Getting a computer to remove these hidden lines is not as simple as it sounds. The surfaces of real-world objects can overlap in many ways, each of which must be tested by the drawing program. As the number of faces on the surface increases, the time required to do all of the required computations also increases.

This solution shows how to draw certain objects with the hidden lines removed. By limiting the types of objects, you can use much simpler programs.

See Also

7.5   Drawing 3-D objects

Solution

If the object to draw is convex, the only edges that can be seen make up polygons that face the viewer. Try mentally eliminating the triangles that are not facing you in the icosahedron from question 7.5. So, for convex objects, all the program needs to do is determine which triangles are facing the viewer.

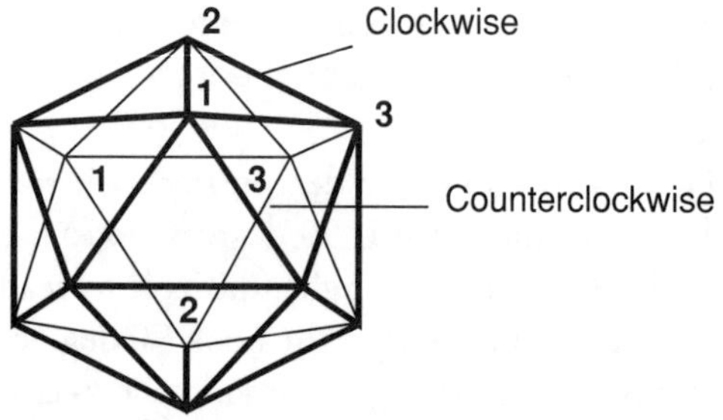

Look at the triangles that are visible and assign a number to each of the corners of each triangle. Make sure that the corners are numbered in a clockwise order. Turn the object around and number each of the triangles this way. Notice that in the triangles facing away from you (the hidden ones) the corners are numbered counterclockwise. You will find that no matter what you do, all of the visible triangles go clockwise and all of the invisible triangles go counterclockwise (see Figure 7-11).

Figure 7-11 Clockwise and counterclockwise triangles

To use this feature, you must group vertices into triangles instead of into edges. The triangle list is just like the edge list with one extra number added per item for the third corner of the triangle. If you simply add this list and a method to add triangles to the existing 3-D object, you can continue to use most of the existing 3-D code. Here is the first part of the program with the new type added:

```
{Program to draw 3-D objects}
uses Dos, Graph, GrafBase, Crt;

type
   Point = record
       x, y, z: integer;
   end;
   PointLstPtr = ^PointLst;
   PointLst = array [1..8192] of Point;
   PointPair = record
       p1, p2 : integer;
   end;
   EdgeLstPtr = ^EdgeLst;
   TriPoint = record
       p1, p2, p3 : integer;
   end;
   EdgeLst = array [1..8192] of PointPair;
```

```
PolyLstPtr = ^PolyLst;
PolyLst = array [1..8192] of TriPoint;

SolidObj = object( GraphObj )
        Vertices : PointLstPtr;    {Array of corners}
        VCount : integer;          {Number of corners}
        VSpace : integer;          {Space for corners}
        Edges : EdgeLstPtr;        {Array of edges}
        ECount : integer;          {Number of edges}
        ESpace : integer;          {Space for edges}
        Poly : PolyLstPtr;
        PCount : integer;
        PSpace : integer;
        constructor Init;
        procedure AddVertex( XPos, YPos, ZPos : integer );
        procedure AddEdge( Point1, Point2 : integer );
        procedure AddPoly( Point1, Point2, Point3 : integer );
        procedure Draw; virtual;
        procedure Erase; virtual;
        procedure HideLines; virtual;
        procedure Rotate( Pitch, Yaw, Roll : real ); virtual;
    end;
```

The Poly field holds the list of polygons, and the PCount and PSpace variables hold the number of polygons and space available for polygons. The AddPoly method lets you add polygons to the list.

```
procedure SolidObj.AddPoly( Point1, Point2, Point3 : integer );
var
   pl : PolyLstPtr;
begin
    if PCount = PSpace then
    begin
        GetMem( pl, ( PSpace + 10 ) * sizeof( TriPoint ));
        Move( Poly^, pl^, PSpace * sizeof( TriPoint ));
        FreeMem( Poly, PSpace * sizeof( TriPoint ));
        Poly := pl;
        PSpace := PSpace + 10;
    end;
    Inc( PCount );
    Poly^[PCount].p1 := Point1;
    Poly^[PCount].p2 := Point2;
    Poly^[PCount].p3 := Point3;
end;
```

The HideLines method looks through the list of polygons for clockwise triangles, which it draws:

```
procedure SolidObj.HideLines;
var
   i : integer;
   DeltaX, DeltaY : integer;
```

```
   DrawOK : boolean;
   Slope : real;
   Intercept : integer;
begin
   SetColor( Clr );
   {Look at each polygon}
   for i := 1 to PCount do
   begin
      {Compute the directions from the first point to the second}
      DeltaX := Vertices^[Poly^[i].p2].x
            - Vertices^[Poly^[i].p1].x;
      DeltaY := Vertices^[Poly^[i].p2].y
            - Vertices^[Poly^[i].p1].y;
      {Assume the triangle will not be drawn}
      DrawOK := FALSE;
      {If the first side is vertical}
      if ( DeltaY = 0 ) then
      begin
            {If the third point is to the left}
            if Vertices^[Poly^[i].p3].y
              < Vertices^[Poly^[i].p1].y then
            begin
                  {If the second point is below the first}
                  if DeltaX < 0 then
                        DrawOK := TRUE;
            end
            else   {The third point is to the right}
            begin
                  {If the second point is above the first}
                  if DeltaX > 0 then
                        DrawOK := TRUE;
            end;
      end
      {If the first side is horizontal}
      else if ( DeltaX = 0 ) then
      begin
          {If the third point is above}
          if Vertices^[Poly^[i].p3].x
              <Vertices^[Poly^[i].p1].x then
          begin
              {If the second point is left of the first}
              if DeltaY < 0 then
                    DrawOK := TRUE;
          end
          else {The third point is below}
          begin
              {If the second point is right of the first}
              if DeltaY > 0 then
                    DrawOK := TRUE;
          end;
      end
      else
```

```
    begin
            {Calculate the slope and intercept for a line
             passing through the first two points}
            Slope := DeltaY / DeltaX;
            Intercept := Vertices^[Poly^[i].p1].y
                    - Round( Slope * Vertices^[Poly^[i].p1].x );
            {If the third point is right of the line}
            if ( Vertices^[Poly^[i].p3].y - Intercept ) / Slope
                < Vertices^[Poly^[i].p3].x then
            begin
                {If the first point is above the second}
                if Vertices^[Poly^[i].p1].y
                    > Vertices^[Poly^[i].p2].y then
                    DrawOK := TRUE;
            end
            else      {The third point is left of the line}
            begin
                {If the first point is below the second}
                if Vertices^[Poly^[i].p1].y
                        < Vertices^[Poly^[i].p2].y then
                        DrawOK := TRUE;
            end;
        end;
        {If the polygon goes clockwise}
        if DrawOK then
        begin
            MoveTo( Vertices^[Poly^[i].p1].x + x
                , Vertices^[Poly^[i].p1].y + y );
            LineTo( Vertices^[Poly^[i].p2].x + x
                , Vertices^[Poly^[i].p2].y + y );
            LineTo( Vertices^[Poly^[i].p3].x + x
                , Vertices^[Poly^[i].p3].y + y );
            LineTo( Vertices^[Poly^[i].p1].x + x
                , Vertices^[Poly^[i].p1].y + y );
        end;
    end;
end;
```

Most of the routine determines if the polygon goes clockwise or counter-clockwise. The first step is to draw a line that passes through the first two points of the triangle. Three cases must be examined: the line is sloped, vertical, or horizontal. Figure 7-12 shows these three cases; in each case, the figure shows where the third point must be for the triangle to be considered a clockwise one.

If the triangle is clockwise, lines are drawn between each of the vertices. When all of the triangles have been examined, the object is drawn except for the hidden lines.

To use these routines, you must update the main program to set up the polygons. Here are the statements required:

```
{Define Polygons}
Pict.AddPoly( 1, 7, 2 );
Pict.AddPoly( 1, 6, 7 );
Pict.AddPoly( 6, 9, 7 );
Pict.AddPoly( 6, 5, 9 );
Pict.AddPoly( 6, 12, 5 );
Pict.AddPoly( 1, 12, 6 );
Pict.AddPoly( 1, 2, 10 );
Pict.AddPoly( 1, 10, 12 );
Pict.AddPoly( 2, 7, 8 );
Pict.AddPoly( 7, 9, 8 );
Pict.AddPoly( 2, 8, 3 );
Pict.AddPoly( 2, 3, 10 );
Pict.AddPoly( 10, 3, 11 );
Pict.AddPoly( 10, 11, 12 );
Pict.AddPoly( 12, 11, 5 );
Pict.AddPoly( 5, 9, 4 );
Pict.AddPoly( 5, 11, 4 );
Pict.AddPoly( 9, 4, 8 );
Pict.AddPoly( 8, 4, 3 );
Pict.AddPoly( 3, 4, 11 );
```

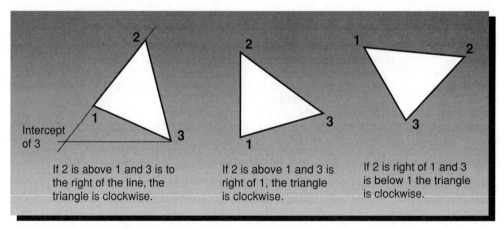

If 2 is above 1 and 3 is to the right of the line, the triangle is clockwise.

If 2 is above 1 and 3 is right of 1, the triangle is clockwise.

If 2 is right of 1 and 3 is below 1 the triangle is clockwise.

Figure 7-12 Checking for clockwise triangles

Comments

Now, when you hold down one of the rotation keys, the object turns, revealing some triangles and hiding others. It is very clear what the true shape of the object is.

Warnings

This technique works only for convex objects. If the object has concave areas, one of the polygons may be partially visible. This algorithm has no way of determining what part of the polygon is visible, so it draws the whole polygon. The result is that some hidden lines do not remain hidden.

ENHANCING IMAGES

It is popular these days to "colorize" old movies and remove scratches from the film. The programs used to do this are called *image-enhancers*. Solution 7.7 shows how to clean up a picture by removing pixels that do not appear to belong in the image. Solution 7.8 uses a similar technique to remove all of the pixels except the edges of objects in the image. Once you define the edges of an object, you can change the color of that object by using the Turbo Pascal `FloodFill` routine.

Solution 7.9 shows how to get more colors on the screen by combining pixels of two different colors. This technique, called *dithering*, lets you make colorful images using only the 16 colors available on EGA cards.

7.7   How do I...

Remove "noise" from an image?

Description

Some of the sources for graphics images include video cameras, scanners, or data links to the Hubble telescope. The problem with these sources is the possibility of noise in the image. Figure 7-13 shows how noise in the image can distort a page of scanned text. This solution shows how to find and remove pixels that do not belong in the image.

See Also

7.8   Finding edges of images

Figure 7-13 An image with noise

Solution

The key to this solution is to test each pixel by counting the number of surrounding pixels of a different color. If all of the surrounding pixels are different from the test pixel, then the pixel is noise. If some of the surrounding pixels are different, the number of different pixels determines if the test pixel is noise. You can experiment with different counts to find the one that works best for your image.

This routine reads all of the pixels on the screen, checks neighboring pixels, and writes changed pixels back to the screen.

```pascal
type
        LinePtr = ^LineArray;
        LineArray = array [0..639] of byte;

procedure Enhance;
var
        Line1, Line2, Line3 : LineArray;
        LPtr1, LPtr2, LPtr3 : LinePtr;
        x, y, i : integer;
        ColorList : array [0..15] of byte;
        Popular : integer;
begin
        {Load the first three lines}
        for x := 0 to GetMaxX do
        begin
                Line1[x] := GetPixel( x, 0 );
                Line2[x] := GetPixel( x, 1 );
                Line3[x] := GetPixel( x, 2 );
        end;
        LPtr1 := @Line1;
        LPtr2 := @Line2;
        LPtr3 := @Line3;
        {Enhance each line of the image}
        for y := 1 to GetMaxY - 1 do
        begin
                for x := 1 to GetMaxX - 1 do
                begin
                        {Clear the color list}
                        for i := 0 to 15
                                ColorList[i] := 0;
                        {Look at nine pixels}
                        Inc( ColorList[LPtr1^[x - 1]] );
                        Inc( ColorList[LPtr1^[x]] );
                        Inc( ColorList[LPtr1^[x + 1]] );
                        Inc( ColorList[LPtr2^[x - 1]] );
                        Inc( ColorList[LPtr2^[x]] );
                        Inc( ColorList[LPtr2^[x + 1]] );
                        Inc( ColorList[LPtr3^[x - 1]] );
                        Inc( ColorList[LPtr3^[x]] );
                        Inc( ColorList[LPtr3^[x + 1]] );
                        {Find the most popular}
```

```
            Popular := 0;
            for i := 0 to 15 do
                    if ColorList[Popular] < ColorList[i] then
                            Popular := i;
            {See if color is over the threshold}
            if ColorList[Popular] > 4 then
            begin
                    SetColor( Popular )
                    PutPixel( x, y );
            end;
            end;
    {Go to the next line}
    LPtr1      := LPtr2;
    LPtr2      := LPtr3;
    LPtr3      := LPtr1;
    for x      := 0 to GetMaxX do
            LPtr3^[x] := GetPixel( x, y + 1 );
        end;
end;
```

This routine looks at the image nine pixels at a time to determine the color of the center pixel. To save time, three lines of pixels are held in memory at all times. The variables Line1, Line2, and Line3 hold the lines. The first for loop goes through all of the lines on the screen, and the inner for loop goes through each of the columns on the current line.

The array ColorList keeps track of the number of pixels of each possible color in the nine-pixel block being examined. After the nine Inc procedure calls, each element of ColorList contains the number of times that color appears in the block. Next, ColorList is searched for the most-used color. The variable Popular contains the result of that search. The decision to change the current pixel is based on how many times the most popular color is used. If there are more than four pixels of the color in the block, the current pixel is set to that color.

Once the whole line has been processed, the outer loop moves on to the next line. Rather than copy the data in the line buffers from one line to another, pointer variables are used to keep track of what buffer goes with what line. Because the pointers are changed, the data for the second line goes to the first line, the data for the third line goes to the second line, and the data for the first line goes to the third line. Since the first line (now in the third line) is no longer needed, a new line of pixels can be read into the buffer.

Comments

To use this routine, you must have a program that can display an image on the screen, then call Enhance to clean up the image. Most PC images come from files created by the driver for the device that captured the image (scanner, video frame grabber, satellite link, and so on). You will have to contact the manufacturer of the device to get the format of the file used.

Enhancements

You can get many interesting effects by experimenting with the `Enhance` routine. An easy experiment is to see how different threshold values affect the image. You can also try using a larger block of pixels, say 5-by-5 blocks. Use odd numbers to ensure that there is a center pixel.

If you have an EGA or VGA card, you can adjust the palette so that you use only shades of a single color. With this palette, you can average the values of all of the surrounding pixels to get the value of the center pixel. A variation of this technique is to multiply certain pixels in the block by some special factor before averaging all of the pixels. This is the basis for the edge-finding routine in question 7.8.

7.8 How do I...

Find the edges of an image in Turbo Pascal programs?

Description

To add color to a black-and-white picture, you have to specify what part of the picture should be a given color. One way to do this is to draw a border around the area to color with a pointing device such as a mouse. This technique is labor-intensive and prone to error. This solution shows you how to get the computer to look for edges in an image.

See Also

7.7   Removing "noise" from images

Solution

The solution for finding the edge of an image is similar to the solution for removing noise. The secret is to look at a small portion of the screen at a time. Instead of counting up all of the pixels in the nine-pixel block, you compute the average color for both the right and left half of the pixel block. If the two values computed are different, then the center pixel is part of an edge and should be set to the line color. This routine shows the technique:

```
type
    LinePtr = ^LineArray;
    LineArray = array [0..639] of byte;
```

```
procedure Edges;
var
        Line1, Line2, Line3 : LineArray;
        LPtr1, LPtr2, LPtr3 : LinePtr;
        x, y, i : integer;
        Ave1, Ave2 : integer;
begin
        {Load the first three lines}
        for x := 0 to GetMaxX do
        begin
                Line1[x] := GetPixel( x, 0 );
                Line2[x] := GetPixel( x, 1 );
                Line3[x] := GetPixel( x, 2 );
        end;
        LPtr1 := @Line1;
        LPtr2 := @Line2;
        LPtr3 := @Line3;
        {Enhance each line of the image}
        for y := 1 to GetMaxY - 1 do
        begin
                for x := 1 to GetMaxX - 1 do
                begin
                        {Look at Left side}
                        Ave1:=( LPtr1^[x - 1] + LPtr2^[x - 1] + LPtr3^[x - 1]
                                ) DIV 3;
                        {Look at Right side}
                        Ave2:=( LPtr1^[x + 1] + LPtr2^[x + 1] + LPtr3^[x + 1]
                                ) DIV 3;
                        {See if this is an edge}
                        if Abs( Ave1 - Ave2 ) > 3 then
                        begin
                                SetColor( White )
                                PutPixel( x, y );
                        end;
                end;
                {Go to the next line}
                LPtr1 := LPtr2;
                LPtr2 := LPtr3;
                LPtr3 := LPtr1;
                for x := 0 to GetMaxX do
                        LPtr3^[x] := GetPixel( x, y + 1 );
        end;
end;
```

Notice that the basic structure of this routine is identical to the routine used in question 7.7. The difference is in the inner loop. Instead of counting each color, it computes the average for each half of the pixel block. If the two averages are different by more than three, the center pixel is set.

Comments

You need to incorporate this routine in a program that displays an image on the screen, for instance, the same one you used for question 7.7. This routine works best when most of the lines in the image are *not* horizontal. If the image has many horizontal lines, you can count pixels in the top and bottom halves instead of the left and right halves (see the enhancement section). The lines in most images can be found by using the top and bottom or the left and right techniques. For some images, you may want to run both routines and combine the results to see all of the lines.

Enhancements

You can get an interesting variety of effects by experimenting with this routine. For example, instead of averaging values from the left and right halves of the image, you can average the top and bottom halves, as follows:

```
{Look at Top}
Ave1:=( LPtr1^[x - 1] + LPtr1^[x] + LPtr1^[x + 1] ) DIV 3;
{Look at Bottom}
Ave2:=( LPtr3^[x - 1] + LPtr3^[x] + LPtr3^[x + 1] ) DIV 3;
```

This emphasizes horizontal lines instead of vertical lines.

Noise interferes with the ability of this routine to find edges. If this is a problem, you may want to run the Enhance routine on the image before running the Edges routine.

7.9 How do I...

Use dithering to get more colors?

Description

The 16 colors of an EGA graphics adapter may not be enough to show a particular image. Fortunately, it is possible to get the effect of having many more colors by blending two or more of the available colors. The process, called dithering, is demonstrated in this solution.

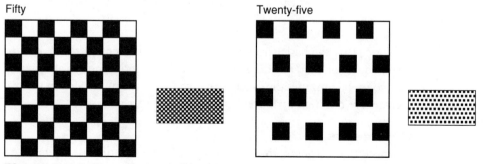

Fifty   Twenty-five

Figure 7-14 The effects of dithering

See Also

Solution

A color TV has only three colors to work with. You have the illusion of seeing many colors because the pixels of the TV screen are so small that you cannot see each one. Instead, your eye combines several of them together, blending the colors into one.

This same principle can be used in computer-generated images. When you change the number of pixels of a certain color, the overall color of the image appears to change (see Figure 7-14).

This program uses different patterns with the `FloodFill` routine to paint areas of different colors on the screen:

```
{Program to test fill stuff}
uses Graph;

{Define fill patterns for dithering}
const
    Fifty : FillPatternType =
        ( $AA, $55, $AA, $55, $AA, $55, $AA, $55 );
    Forty : FillPatternType =
        ( $92, $24, $49, $92, $49, $24, $92, $24 );
    TwentyFive : FillPatternType =
        ( $AA, $00, $55, $00, $AA, $00, $55, $00 );

{Graphics library variables}
var
   Gd, Gm : Integer;

begin
    {Initialize graphics}
    Gd := Detect;
    InitGraph( Gd, Gm, _c:\tp   );
    {Set the standard colors}
    SetColor( White );
    SetBkColor( Blue );
    {Clear the screen}
    ClearViewPort;
    {Draw the first circle and fill it}
    Circle( 200, 200, 50 );
    SetFillPattern( Fifty, Red );
    FloodFill( 200, 200, White );
    {Draw the second circle and fill it}
    Circle( 100, 100, 50 );
    SetFillPattern( TwentyFive, Red );
    FloodFill( 100, 100, White );
    {Draw the last circle and fill it}
    Circle( 300, 110, 50 );
```

```
      SetFillPattern( Forty, Red );
      FloodFill( 300, 110, White );
      ReadLn;
end.
```

This program draws three circles and fills them with different patterns. The three patterns used are named for the percentage of pixels that are set in each. This program uses a blue background and fills the circles with red patterns. The result is three shades of purple.

Comments

The FloodFill routine is used because it is a quick way to set a large number of pixels. This lets you combine two colors to make a third. By changing the pattern, you can adjust the amount of each of these colors to get just the color you want.

You may be surprised by the colors generated by some combinations. For example, blue and green make yellow. This is because combining light sources is different from combining pigments. A good text on optics can explain what is occurring, or you can experiment with different combinations until you figure out what is going on.

Warnings

There is a price to pay for the larger number of colors. Since you are, in effect, combining several pixels into one, you reduce the screen resolution. For many images, this is not a problem, but if you need sharp edges (for instance, for displaying text), you may find the image quality unsatisfactory.

8

ROUTINES FROM COMPUTER SCIENCE

8

hrough the years, computer scientists have discovered programming techniques and algorithms that make the
programmer's job much easier. The Pascal language itself
is the product of computer science. Savvy programmers
noticed how this bit of computer science could make their jobs easier, and
Pascal was quickly adopted.

Although you cannot keep track of all of the developments in computer
science, an understanding of some of the basic concepts can improve your
programs. For example, how do you make the best use of memory to hold a
variable sized list of data items? Any beginning computer science text shows
that the linked list is a good way to handle this problem. It is also the first
solution in this chapter. The other basic data structures shown in this
chapter are queues and stacks.

Computer scientists often draw on the work of other mathematicians.
For example, astronomers have several formulas for computing the number
of days between two dates. Computer scientists can use these formulas to
store dates efficiently. This formula is shown in solution 8.4. Two other
formulas demonstrate how to compute compound interest and verify that
data is correct.

Computer science's greatest contribution to programming is high-level
languages. High-level languages allow programmers to concentrate more
on what the program should do than on how to implement the program.
The last two solutions in this chapter are a peek inside a compiler. They
show how to evaluate mathematical expressions and parse commands.

DATA STRUCTURES

The first three solutions in this section show three different ways of addressing data stored in memory. Solution 8.1 shows how to store information in a linked list. This is a structure in which related data items are connected by pointers. Linked lists allow you to use noncontiguous records and change the order of records easily.

Solutions 8.2 and 8.3 are different ways of getting data in and out of arrays. The queue lets you put data into the array and get it back out in the same order. Programs that use one module to generate data and another to process it can use a queue to send the data from one module to another. You can use stacks to store data temporarily. The last item put on the stack is the first item read from the stack. You can use a stack to save the state of global variables when one routine calls another. Solution 8.8 shows how to use stacks.

8.1	How do I...

Make a linked list in Turbo Pascal?

Description

Linked lists are a good way of associating data items. The items in the list can be anywhere in memory and in any order; the links put the items in order. This solution shows how to make a linked-list object that other objects can inherit. In this way any object type can reap the benefits of linked lists.

See Also

8.2   Making queues

8.3   Making stacks

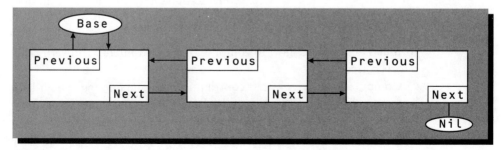

Figure 8-1 A linked list

Solution

Figure 8-1 shows the structure of a linked list. Notice that there are links to move forward and backward. Because two links are associated with every item, this structure is sometimes called a *doubly-linked list*. The following routine is a unit containing the linked-list object

```
{Linked list object}
unit LINK;
interface

type
   LLPtr = ^LinkList;
   LinkList = object
       NextItem : LLPtr;    {Pointer to the next item}
       PrevItem : LLPtr;    {Pointer to the previous item}
       Constructor Init( ListBase : LLPtr );
       Destructor  Done;
   end;

implementation

{Add an item to the linked list}
Constructor LinkList.Init( ListBase : LLPtr );
var
   Hunt : LLPtr;
begin
   Hunt := ListBase;
   {Find the last item}
   while Hunt^.NextItem <> Nil do
      Hunt := Hunt^.NextItem;
   {Point back at the old last item}
   PrevItem := Hunt;
   {Make the old last item point at the current item}
   Hunt^.NextItem := @Self;
   {Indicate that this is the last item}
   NextItem := Nil;
end;

{Undo the links}
Destructor LinkList.Done;
begin
   {Make the item before this point to the item after}
   PrevItem^.NextItem := NextItem;
   {If there is a next item, make it point at the previous item}
   if NextItem <> Nil then
      NextItem^.PrevItem := PrevItem;
end;
end.
```

The linked-list object is very simple. The only data items are the pointers to the next and previous objects. Presumably, the object that inherits this object would have other fields to hold information about the item.

The two methods are the constructor, Init, and the destructor, Done. Init starts by searching the linked list to find the item at the end. Different linked list constructors perform this search differently. For example, if the list is sorted in ascending order, the search stops when the constructor finds an item that is greater than the item being inserted. If the order of the list is not important, the new item can be inserted at the beginning, saving the time it would take to search. Once the location for the item is found, the links are changed to put the new item in place. In this case, the next item pointer for the last object is set to point to the new object, and the previous pointer of the new object is set to point to the old last object. Finally, Init puts Nil in the next item pointer for the new item.

The Done method removes an item from the linked list by making all of the relevant links bypass the item to be deleted (see Figure 8-2). Done changes the next item pointer of the previous item so that it points to the item after the one to be deleted. Then it tests the next item pointer to see if there is really an item there. If so, it changes the previous item pointer of the next item so that it points to the item before the one being deleted.

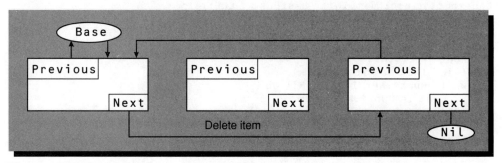

Figure 8-2 Removing an item from a linked list

Comments

The linked-list object has been set up so that it is easy to use with the Turbo Pascal routines New and Dispose. These routines allocate and free up space on the heap. You can call a constructor with the New routine and a destructor with the Dispose routine. When you use these routines with linked-list objects, new objects are automatically linked and unlinked as they are created. The following program, which allocates and frees 20 linked objects, shows you how to do this:

```
{Demonstrate linked lists}
program demo;
uses LINK;
```

```
type
        MyObject = Object( LinkList )
                Data : string;
        end;

var
        FirstOne : MyObject;
        p : ^MyObject;
        i : integer;

begin
        {Initialize the first item}
        FirstOne.NextItem := Nil;
        FirstOne.PrevItem := Nil;
        {Create objects}
        for i := 1 to 20 do
                New( p, Init( FirstOne ));
        {Delete objects}
        for i := 1 to 20 do
                Dispose( FirstOne.NextItem, Done );
end.
```

MyObject is an object that inherits from the linked-list object. The variable FirstOne is the only instance of MyObject; all other instances are allocated on the heap and can be accessed by searching the linked list. FirstOne serves as an anchor that gets you into the linked list at some known location. Because the Init method uses this anchor, it cannot be initialized in the normal fashion. Fortunately, the initialization is simply a matter of setting the pointers equal to Nil.

The variable p is used to give New some place to put the pointer it generates. Because the location of the item is saved in the linked list, there is no need to keep this information. Thus, you can reuse p each time an object is created.

The last loop in the program gets rid of all of the objects. The pointer for the Dispose routine comes from the NextItem field in FirstOne. Each time an item is deleted, the NextItem field is updated to point to the next object. If you did not know how many objects had been allocated, you could keep freeing objects until this field becomes Nil.

Warnings

Linked lists are a very fragile data structure. The links can point to anywhere in memory, and you have no way of knowing if the indicated location is really an other item or a random memory location. An error in the program may change some of the links in the list. This type of error is difficult to find because the location of the error may have nothing to do with any symptoms you may see.

8.2   How do I...

Make a queue in Turbo Pascal?

Description
Queues are an important way for one module of a program to communicate with another module. Data comes out of a queue in the same order it went in; thus the module taking data from the queue and the module putting it in observe the same order. This is important in multitasking systems, where the module that put the information in the queue may have moved on to something else by the time the other module reads the queue.

See Also
2.11   Serial device driver

Solution
Figure 8-3 shows how a queue works. The head index points to the next available location in the queue, and the tail index points to the next item to read from the queue. Each of these indexes moves through the array until it reaches the end. At this point, the index wraps back to the beginning of the array.

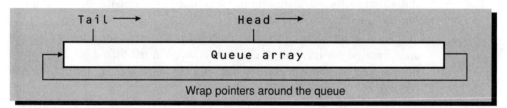

Figure 8-3 A queue

This unit defines a queue object you can use to implement queues in your programs:

```
{Define a queue object}
unit QUEUE;
interface
type
   Queue = object
       Items : array [0..1023] of integer;
       Head, Tail : integer;
       Constructor Init;
```

```
        procedure AddItem( Itm : integer );
        function GetItem : integer;
        function QueueSize : integer;
    end;

implementation

{Queue methods}
Constructor Queue.Init;
begin
    {Set both head and tail to the beginning of the array}
    Head := 0;
    Tail := 0;
end;

procedure Queue.AddItem( Itm : integer );
begin
    {Store the data}
    Items[Head] := Itm;
    {Advance head and wrap if necessary}
    Head := ( Head + 1 ) MOD 1024;
end;

function Queue.GetItem : integer;
begin
    {Get the data}
    GetItem := Items[Tail];
    {Advance tail and wrap if necessary}
    Tail := ( Tail + 1 ) MOD 1024;
end;

function Queue.QueueSize : integer;
begin
    {If head is past tail the size is the difference}
    if Head >= Tail then
        QueueSize := Head - Tail
    else {Otherwise head has wrapped so use everything but the
            bytes between the pointers}
        QueueSize := Head - Tail + 1024;
end;
end.
```

The data for the queue object includes an array to hold the data and the head and tail indexes. The methods initialize the queue, add items, remove items, and give the number of items in the queue. The Init method initializes the queue by setting both the head and tail indexes to 0. The AddItem method puts a number in the queue. After storing the number in the array, it increments Head and wraps it if needed. (Computing the Head + 1 modulo 1024 has the effect of wrapping the index.) GetItem works in a similar fashion, but it uses the index Tail instead of Head.

Comment

The serial device driver in question 2.11 contains a good example of a queue. When the program detects data from the serial port, it puts the data in the queue with the `Head` pointer. When the program wants the data, it gets the data from the queue with the `Tail` pointer.

Warnings

If the queue is not large enough, the head index wraps around the buffer and passes the tail index. Your program cannot detect that this has happened. The tail index continues forward, reading data that has been overwritten, until it catches up with the head index. The result is that all of the data in the queue seems to disappear. The solution to this problem is to improve the performance of the routine that reads the queue so that the head cannot get too far ahead, or to increase the size of the queue so that there is enough room for the possible data. In the latter case, the assumption is that at some time the head index will move slowly for awhile, so that the tail can catch up.

8.3   How do I...

Make a stack in Turbo Pascal?

Description

Whether you know it or not, you have been using stacks in your programs already. Turbo Pascal uses a stack to provide storage for local variables and return addresses of functions and procedures. Because this stack usage is a built-in feature of Turbo Pascal, you have not had to pay much attention to how it works. This solution shows how you can implement stacks and use them to save temporary values in your programs.

See Also

8.7   Evaluating expressions

Solution

A stack is an array with a single index called the *stack pointer* (see Figure 8-4). The stack pointer is initialized to point to the last item in the array. Data is added to the stack at the location indicated by the stack pointer. Then the stack pointer is decremented to point to the next available location. To recover the data from the stack, the stack pointer is incremented, and the data is read at the indicated location.

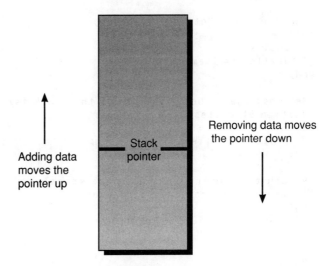

Figure 8-4 A stack

This unit shows how to do this with Turbo Pascal:

```
{STACK object definition}
unit STACK;
interface
type
    Stack = object
        Items : array [0..1023] of integer;
        StkPtr : integer;
        Constructor Init;
        procedure AddItem( Itm : integer );
        function GetItem : integer;
        function StackSize : integer;
        function TestItem : integer;
    end;

implementation

{Stack methods}
Constructor Stack.Init;
begin
    {Set the stack pointer to the end of the array}
    StkPtr := 1023;
end;

{Add an integer to the stack}
procedure Stack.AddItem( Itm : integer );
begin
    Items[StkPtr] := Itm;
    Dec( StkPtr );
end;

{Get an integer off the stack}
```

```
function Stack.GetItem : integer;
begin
    Inc( StkPtr );
    GetItem := Items[StkPtr];
end;

{See what the value on the top of the stack is}
function Stack.TestItem : integer;
begin
    TestItem := Items[StkPtr + 1];
end;

{Return the number of items in the stack}
function Stack.StackSize : integer;
begin
    StackSize := 1023 - StkPtr;
end;

end.
```

The data for the stack object includes an array to hold items and an integer to be used as a stack pointer. The methods allow programs to initialize the stack, add data, get data, and query the status of the stack. The beauty of stacks is their simplicity. Each of the methods does one simple task. The `Init` method sets the stack pointer to the last item in the array; the `AddItem` method puts an integer on the stack; and `GetItem` gets it back from the stack. The next two methods give information about the stack. `TestItem` looks at the item on the top of the stack without changing the stack pointer. Finally, `StackSize` returns the number of items on the stack.

Comments

Take a look at solution 8.7 (evaluating expressions) for an example of how stacks are used to store temporary values. The stack holds partial results of the expression as it is evaluated.

For most programs, the Turbo Pascal stack is all you need. One disadvantage of using the Turbo Pascal stack is that your program cannot tell how much stack space is available. This is a problem for recursive routines that run until they are done or the stack overflows, crashing the program. There is no way for the routine to determine when the amount of stack space is too small to support further recursion.

You can change any recursive routine to a nonrecursive one by using the stack object. Figure 8-5 illustrates how to convert a recursive routine to a nonrecursive one. First, determine which variables must be saved from one recursive call to the next. Then, replace all of the recursive calls with code that pushes the variables onto the stack and then jumps to the beginning of the routine. Finally, add code that pops the variables off the stack and jumps to the location after the old recursive call. If there are no variables on the stack at the end of the routine, the routine is finished and should exit. Now you can add code to check how much stack space is available and take some action before pushing variables on the stack.

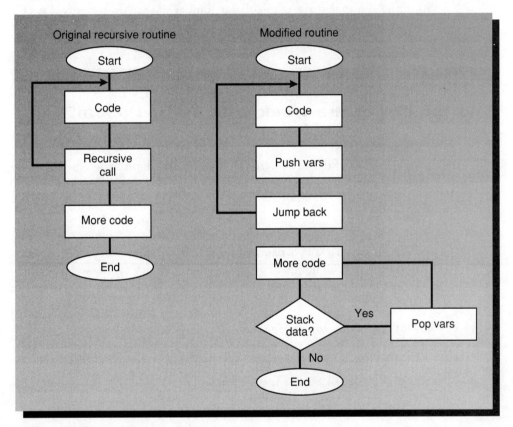

Figure 8-5 Unrolling recursive routines

Warnings

These routines rely on Turbo Pascal's built-in range checking to detect when the stack pointer goes beyond the ends of the stack array. For this reason, when range checking is in effect, you get a run-time error if the stack pointer goes out of range. If range checking is not in effect, the stack overwrites neighboring data items, possibly causing errors later in your program.

You should carefully analyze the needs of your program, then run some tests with range checking on until you are sure that the stack array is large enough.

FORMULAS

The formulas in the next three solutions show how research in mathematics can be applied in computer programs. Solution 8.4 uses a formula from an astronomy text to calculate the day of the week for any date. Solution 8.5 uses a formula from numerical analysis to compute compound interest. Solution 8.6 uses statistics to calculate a number you can use to verify that a file contains correct data.

8.4   How do I...

Find the day of the week with Turbo Pascal?

Description

On what day of the week were you born? If you don't know, the computer can tell you.

Solution

The way to find the day of the week for any date is to compute the number of days between a known date and the date in question then use that number modulo 7 to get a number corresponding to the day of the week. The program below computes the number of days since January 1, 0 A.D. (a Wednesday):

```
{Find the day of the week for any date}
program dates;

const
    DayList : array [0..6] of string[15] = (
        'Sunday', 'Monday', 'Tuesday', 'Wednesday'
        , 'Thursday', 'Friday', 'Saturday' );
var
  Month, Day, Year, Tmp1 : longint;
  Code : integer;
  TmpStr : string;

begin
  Write( 'Enter month ( 1-12 ): ' );
  ReadLn( TmpStr );
  Val( TmpStr, Month, Code );
  Write( 'Enter Day: ' );
  ReadLn( TmpStr );
  Val( TmpStr, Day, Code );
  Write( 'Enter year: ' );
  ReadLn( TmpStr );
  Val( TmpStr, Year, Code );
```

```
{Deal with February}
if Month <= 2 then
begin
    Dec( Year );
    Month := Month + 12;
end;
{Compute the number of days since 1/1/0}
Tmp1 := ( 1461 * Year ) DIV 4 - Year DIV 400
    + (306001 * ( Month + 1 )) DIV 10000
    + Day - 64;
WriteLn( 'Julian: ', Tmp1 );
WriteLn( 'Weekday: ', DayList[(Tmp1 + 3) MOD 7] );
ReadLn;
end.
```

After getting the month, day, and year from the user, this program adjusts the month so that it ranges from 3 to 15. The reason for this is to get February at the end of the year, where its unusual length will not affect the equation. In the equation the year is multiplied by 365.25 and the month by 30.6001. These floating-point operations are done with long integers: the year is multiplied by 4 and the month by 10,000, then these factors are divided out.

The output of the program is the number of days since January 1, 0 A.D. and the day of the week.

Comments

You can use this routine to print formatted date strings such as:

`Friday, the 13th of June, 1991`

The day, month, and year come directly from the supplied date, but the day of the week must be computed with the above routine.

Warnings

This formula uses 365.25 as the number of days in a year; the fractional part accounts for leap years. The problem with this is that the year is not exactly 365.25 days long. This problem was noted several centuries ago, and the calendar was modified to account for the difference: every 400 years there is no leap year. Because the formula used in this solution takes this special leap year into account, it is not accurate for dates that precede calendar reform. The actual date of calendar reform varies from country to country, so you should do some careful research before using this program for old dates.

Enhancements

You need 9 bytes to store dates as a string in the mm/dd/yy format. If you use the formula in this solution to convert the date to a long integer, you need only 4 bytes to save it. However, you need a way to convert the date back to mm/dd/yy format. This program does the job:

```
{Program to convert Julian dates back to mm/dd/yy format}
program JDATE;

var
   TmpStr : string;
   Julian : longint;
   Code : integer;
   Year, Month : longint;

begin
   Write( 'Enter Julian date: ' );
   ReadLn( TmpStr );
   Val( TmpStr,Julian,Code );
   Julian := Julian + 64;
   Year := ( Julian * 4 ) DIV 1461;
   Julian := Julian - (( 1461 * Year) DIV 4 - Year DIV 400 );
   Month := ( Julian * 10000 ) DIV 306001 - 1;
   Julian := Julian - (306001 * ( Month + 1 ) DIV 10000 );
   if Month <= 2 then
   begin
     Julian := Julian - 3;
     if Julian = 0 then
     begin
         Month := 1;
         Julian := 31;
     end;
   end;
   WriteLn( 'Month: ',Month,' Day: ',Julian,' Year: ',Year );
   ReadLn;
end.
```

This program works the Julian date equation backward. After getting the Julian date from the user, it divides by 365.25 to get the year. Then it subtracts the number of days to the beginning of that year from the original Julian date. It divides the result by 30.6001 to get the month; the remainder of this division is the day. If the day is in January or February, some adjustments must be made to the month and day.

8.5   How do I...

Calculate compound interest with Turbo Pascal?

Description
You calculate simple interest by multiplying the principal times the interest rate. Unfortunately, simple interest is rarely used in the real world. Most interest is compounded at periodic intervals, and interest is added to previ-

ous interest. This solution shows how to compute compound interest. It also shows how to figure out what payment is required to amortize a loan over a given time period.

Solution

Table 8-1 shows the effect of compounding interest. Each month a portion of the interest is added to the principal, and this value is used to compute the interest for the next month.

Beginning principal: **$2,500.00**
Yearly interest rate: **12.30%**

Month	Principal	Simple interest	Compound interest
1	$2,500.00	$25.63	$25.63
2	$2,525.63	$25.63	$25.89
3	$2,551.52	$25.63	$26.15
4	$2,577.67	$25.63	$26.42
5	$2,604.09	$25.63	$26.69
6	$2,630.78	$25.63	$26.97
7	$2,657.75	$25.63	$27.24
8	$2,684.99	$25.63	$27.52
9	$2,712.51	$25.63	$27.80
10	$2,740.31	$25.63	$28.09
11	$2,768.40	$25.63	$28.38
12	$2,796.78	$25.63	$28.67

Table 8-1 Compound interest

You can compute the effective interest rate over any given period by using the *net present value* equation:

```
Effective rate = (1 + Interest rate / 12)^Term
```

The following program uses the net present value equation to find the total payback on a loan over a given period. Divide this value by the term of the loan to find out the payment required to amortize the loan in the given time.

```
{Program to amortize a loan}
program amort;
```

```
var
   Principal : real;
   Interest : real;
   Term : integer;
   PayBack, Payment : real;
   Code : integer;
   TmpStr : string;
   i : integer;

begin
    Write( 'Enter the principal: ' );
    ReadLn( TmpStr );
    Val( TmpStr, Principal, Code );
    Write( 'Enter the interest rate ( Yearly ): ' );
    ReadLn( TmpStr );
    Val( TmpStr, Interest, Code );
    Write( 'Enter the term (Months): ' );
    ReadLn( TmpStr );
    Val( TmpStr, Term, Code );
    {Compute the total payback of the period of the loan}
    PayBack := Principal * Exp( Ln( 1.0 + Interest / 12.0 ) * Term );
    {Compute the payment}
    Payment := PayBack / Term;
    WriteLn( 'Payback: ', PayBack : 10 : 2 );
    WriteLn( 'Payment: ', Payment : 10 : 2 );
    WriteLn( 'Remaining principal   Interest    Principal' );
    {Show the first year}
    for i := 1 to 12 do
    begin
        WriteLn( Principal * ( 1.0 + Interest / 12.0 ) - Payment : 10 : 2
              , '            ', Principal * Interest / 12.0 : 10 : 2
              , '  ', Payment-Principal * Interest / 12.0:10:2 );
        Principal := Principal * ( 1.0 + Interest / 12.0) - Payment;
    end;
    ReadLn;
end.
```

The program asks the user for the beginning principal, interest rate, and term. Then, the net present value equation is used to compute the amount that must be paid back, and the result is stored in the variable PayBack. PayBack is divided by the term to get Payment, which is the monthly payment for the loan.

The loop at the end of the program computes the first twelve months of payments and their effect on the principal. The principal is increased by the amount of interest and decreased by the payment amount.

Comments

This program is very useful in planning your personal finances. Before you purchase a new car or a house, you can look at the effects of various terms and interest rates to figure out just what you can afford.

This program is also useful in planning investments. When you trade bonds, you must calculate the value of the bond to see if you are getting a good deal. For example, how much should you pay for a $1000 bond with an 8.2% interest rate that comes due in 5 years? When solved for initial principal, the net present value formula gives $674.31. If you pay less than this, you are getting a higher interest rate; if you pay more, you are getting a lower interest rate.

Warnings

This program is prone to rounding-off errors. Each time you multiply by the interest rate you get a fractional number of cents. Just as the interest rate is compounded, so is the round-off error. The longer the loan the greater the error.

8.6   How do I...

Verify data with Turbo Pascal?

Description

You risk losing data when you move it from place to place. Some connections are more reliable than others. For example, the connection to a hard drive is very reliable, and a modem connection is very error prone. Whenever you suspect that data may be corrupted, you should check it. One way of checking is to compare each byte of the source with each byte of the destination. However, in addition to being very time-consuming, this method is prone to the same errors that may have corrupted the data in the first place. A better approach is to compute a number that can tell you if the data is the same at both ends of the connection. This solution shows how to compute such a number.

Solution

The key to checking the file is to devise a computation that can be done to the data at both ends of the connection. You can then compare the results to find out if the data is different. The simplest computation is to add all of the bytes in the data together. This check shows any single-byte errors in the data and some multiple-byte errors. If more than one byte is incorrect, however, the errors may offset each other, and you may miss the errors.

Mathematicians working on this problem have devised a statistical check to detect multiple errors. The key to this technique is to consider the data as one large number used to evaluate a polynomial. For example, if the data is the string "The data," the initial number is $5468652064617461. This number is used as the input to a specially selected polynomial, then the result is divided by a prime number. The remainder after this division, called the Cyclical Redundancy Check (CRC), is the final result. CRC computations provide high reliability in finding errors.

For the CRC to work properly, you must choose your polynomial and prime number carefully. If you do not have a good background in mathematics, you should select a polynomial that is known to work.

Once you have a polynomial, you are faced with the task of evaluating it with a number that may be hundreds of bytes long. You can make the job much easier by creating a table that gives a partial result for each possible byte that can appear in the file. The following program uses this technique to compute the CRC for a file:

```pascal
{Calculate CRC}

{The table of CRC values}
const
    CRCTab : array[0..255] of word = (
    $0000, $1021, $2042, $3063, $4084, $50A5, $60C6, $70E7,
    $8108, $9129, $A14A, $B16B, $C18C, $D1AD, $E1CE, $F1EF,
    $1231, $0210, $3273, $2252, $52B5, $4294, $72F7, $62D6,
    $9339, $8318, $B37B, $A35A, $D3BD, $C39C, $F3FF, $E3DE,
    $2462, $3443, $0420, $1401, $64E6, $74C7, $44A4, $5485,
    $A56A, $B54B, $8528, $9509, $E5EE, $F5CF, $C5AC, $D58D,
    $3653, $2672, $1611, $0630, $76D7, $66F6, $5695, $46B4,
    $B75B, $A77A, $9719, $8738, $F7DF, $E7FE, $D79D, $C7BC,
    $48C4, $58E5, $6886, $78A7, $0840, $1861, $2802, $3823,
    $C9CC, $D9ED, $E98E, $F9AF, $8948, $9969, $A90A, $B92B,
    $5AF5, $4AD4, $7AB7, $6A96, $1A71, $0A50, $3A33, $2A12,
    $DBFD, $CBDC, $FBBF, $EB9E, $9B79, $8B58, $BB3B, $AB1A,
    $6CA6, $7C87, $4CE4, $5CC5, $2C22, $3C03, $0C60, $1C41,
    $EDAE, $FD8F, $CDEC, $DDCD, $AD2A, $BD0B, $8D68, $9D49,
    $7E97, $6EB6, $5ED5, $4EF4, $3E13, $2E32, $1E51, $0E70,
    $FF9F, $EFBE, $DFDD, $CFFC, $BF1B, $AF3A, $9F59, $8F78,
    $9188, $81A9, $B1CA, $A1EB, $D10C, $C12D, $F14E, $E16F,
    $1080, $00A1, $30C2, $20E3, $5004, $4025, $7046, $6067,
    $83B9, $9398, $A3FB, $B3DA, $C33D, $D31C, $E37F, $F35E,
    $02B1, $1290, $22F3, $32D2, $4235, $5214, $6277, $7256,
    $B5EA, $A5CB, $95A8, $8589, $F56E, $E54F, $D52C, $C50D,
    $34E2, $24C3, $14A0, $0481, $7466, $6447, $5424, $4405,
    $A7DB, $B7FA, $8799, $97B8, $E75F, $F77E, $C71D, $D73C,
    $26D3, $36F2, $0691, $16B0, $6657, $7676, $4615, $5634,
    $D94C, $C96D, $F90E, $E92F, $99C8, $89E9, $B98A, $A9AB,
    $5844, $4865, $7806, $6827, $18C0, $08E1, $3882, $28A3,
    $CB7D, $DB5C, $EB3F, $FB1E, $8BF9, $9BD8, $ABBB, $BB9A,
    $4A75, $5A54, $6A37, $7A16, $0AF1, $1AD0, $2AB3, $3A92,
    $FD2E, $ED0F, $DD6C, $CD4D, $BDAA, $AD8B, $9DE8, $8DC9,
    $7C26, $6C07, $5C64, $4C45, $3CA2, $2C83, $1CE0, $0CC1,
    $EF1F, $FF3E, $CF5D, $DF7C, $AF9B, $BFBA, $8FD9, $9FF8,
    $6E17, $7E36, $4E55, $5E74, $2E93, $3EB2, $0ED1, $1EF0
    );
```

```
{Compute the next part of the CRC}
function CalcCRC( CRC : word; Data : byte ) : word;
begin
    CalcCRC := CRCTab[( CRC SHR 8 ) AND $FF] XOR ( CRC SHL 8 ) XOR Data;
end;

var
  CRC : word;
  F : file;
  Buffer : array [1..1024] of byte;
  BuffCnt, i : integer;

begin
    {Open a file}
    Assign( F, ParamStr( 1 ));
    Reset( F, 1 );
    {Start the CRC at 0}
    CRC := 0;
    {Read all of the bytes in the file and use them
     to make a CRC}
    repeat
        BlockRead( F, Buffer, 1024, BuffCnt );
        for i := 1 to BuffCnt do
            CRC := CalcCRC( CRC, Buffer[i] );
    until BuffCnt <> 1024;
    {Close the file}
    Close( F );
    {Show the CRC}
    WriteLn( 'CRC: ', CRC );
end.
```

The function CalcCRC uses the table CRCTab to combine the previous CRC with the next byte to get a new CRC. When all of the bytes have been sent to CalcCRC, the final result is the CRC for all of the data. The main program starts by opening the file specified on the command line. Then, the file is read 1024 bytes at a time, and each byte is sent to CalcCRC to make the CRC. When all of the file has been read, the program closes the file and writes the CRC on the screen.

Comments

This program can help protect you from viruses. Viruses are programs that are part of other programs passed around by computer users. The virus usually waits for some specific event and then prints a message or does something more destructive to the infected system. Viruses work by attaching themselves to programs that you run often, such as COMMAND.COM. You can protect yourself from viruses by periodically checking whether programs and files on your system have been changed. You can make this check very quickly by looking at the checksum for each file. If the program has been changed, it may contain a virus, and you should recopy the program from a backup as soon as possible.

Warnings

Because the CRC is a word, it can have only one of 65,536 possible values. Obviously, some files might share the same CRC, and so the CRC check is not foolproof. The check usually works because errors should affect only part of the file, leaving most of it unchanged. The polynomial is designed so that only very different files will have the same CRC. If there is any question that a file is correct, you should not only check the CRC but also examine the data to see if they match. If the CRCs match, you should need to make only a few spot checks to see if the files are different.

PARSING

These last two solutions give you a peek at how a compiler such as Turbo Pascal works. Solution 8.7 shows how to evaluate a mathematical expression. The program correctly reads mathematical expressions such as 4 + 3 * 2, performing multiplication and division before addition and subtraction.

Solution 8.8 shows how to parse program statements. The program reads a file of commands and interprets each command. The commands let you create and modify variables and print the results.

| 8.7 | How do I... |

Evaluate expressions with Turbo Pascal?

Description

When you evaluate an algebraic equation, you perform the calculations in a set order: begin by evaluating terms in parentheses, then working left to right, perform exponentiation first, then multiplication and division, and then addition and subtraction. This solution shows how to "teach" your Turbo Pascal programs the order of arithmetic.

See Also

8.8   Parsing statements

Solution

You begin the evaluation of an expression by breaking the expression down into numbers and operators. In general, a number begins with a digit and ends when something other than a digit is found. Operators are symbols such as '+', '*', '/', and '–'. A typical expression begins with a number followed by an operator and another number. If there are no more symbols, you have reached the end of the expression; otherwise, the next two symbols are an operator and another number. One exception is the minus sign before negative numbers.

If there were no operator precedence, your program could simply read the first number into a variable, then read operator-number pairs, doing each operation, until the end of the expression. Because you must take operator precedence into account, you need to save partial results somewhere while you do higher-precedence operations. Figure 8-6 shows how to use stack objects to save these partial results.

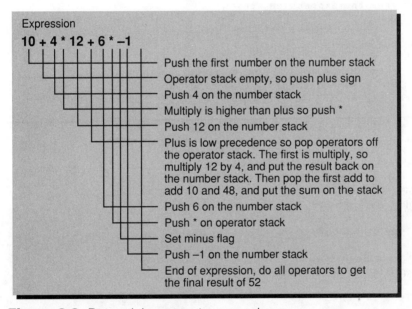

Figure 8-6 Determining operator precedence

This program gets an expression from the command line, evaluates it, and prints the result:

```
{Evaluate an expression}
program Eval;
uses Struct;

const
    Number = 0;
```

```
      TokError = 1;
      Plus = 2;
      Minus = 3;
      Times = 4;
      Divide = 5;

var
   Expression : string;
   i, Code : integer;
   TokenPos : integer;
   Token : String;
   TokenType : integer;
   Numbers : Stack;
   Operators : Stack;
   MinusFlag : boolean;
   Arg1, Arg2 : integer;

{Get one token from the expression string}
procedure GetToken;
begin
    {Clear the token string}
    Token := '';
    {If the expression has a digit, it is a number}
    if ( Ord( Expression[TokenPos] ) >= Ord('0' ))
       AND ( Ord( Expression[TokenPos] ) <= Ord( '9' )) then
    begin
        {Keep getting digits}
        repeat
            Token := Token + Expression[TokenPos];
            Inc( TokenPos );
        until ( Ord( Expression[TokenPos] ) < Ord( '0' ))
            OR ( Ord(Expression[TokenPos] ) > Ord( '9') )
            OR ( TokenPos > Length( Expression ));
        {Mark the token type as a number}
        TokenType := Number;
    end
    {See if it is a plus sign}
    else if Expression[TokenPos] = '+' then
    begin
        TokenType := Plus;
        Inc( TokenPos );
    end
    {See if it is a minus sign}
    else if Expression[TokenPos] = '-' then
    begin
        TokenType := Minus;
        Inc( TokenPos );
    end
    {See if it is a multiply sign}
    else if Expression[TokenPos] = '*' then
    begin
        TokenType := Times;
        Inc( TokenPos );
```

```
        end
        {See if it is a divide}
        else if Expression[TokenPos] = '/' then
        begin
            TokenType := Divide;
            Inc( TokenPos );
        end
        {Otherwise it is just junk}
        else
            TokenType := TokError;
    end;

begin
    {Initialize the number and operator stacks}
    Numbers.Init;
    Operators.Init;
    {Clear the expression}
    Expression := '';
    {Put the arguments into expression}
    for i := 1 to ParamCount do
        Expression := Expression + ParamStr( i );
    {Start TokenPos at the beginning of the expression}
    TokenPos := 1;
    {While there are more tokens in the string}
    while TokenPos <= Length( Expression ) do
    begin
        {Get a token}
        GetToken;
        {Check for negative number}
        if TokenType = Minus then
        begin
            MinusFlag := TRUE;
            GetToken;
        end
        else
            MinusFlag := FALSE;
        {The first token should be a number}
        if TokenType = Number then
        begin
                Val( Token, i, Code );
                if MinusFlag then
                    i := -i;
                {Put the number on the stack}
                Numbers.AddItem( i );
                {See if at the end of the expression}
                if TokenPos <= Length( Expression ) then
                begin
                    {Get the operator}
                    GetToken;
                    {Do any higher precedence operations
                     from the stack}
                    if Operators.StackSize <> 0 then
                        while ( Operators.StackSize<>0 )
```

```
                         AND (( Operators.TestItem DIV 2 )
                         > ( TokenType DIV 2 )) do
              begin
                         Arg1 := Numbers.GetItem;
                         Arg2 := Numbers.GetItem;
                         case Operators.GetItem of
                           Plus :
                              Numbers.AddItem( Arg2 + Arg1 );
                           Minus :
                              Numbers.AddItem( Arg2 - Arg1 );
                           Times :
                              Numbers.AddItem( Arg2 * Arg1 );
                           Divide :
                              Numbers.AddItem( Arg2 DIV Arg2 ) ;
                         end;
              end;
              Operators.AddItem(TokenType);
              end
              else {At the end clean up}
              begin
                         {Do all operations on the stack}
                         while Operators.StackSize > 0 do
                         begin
                           Arg1 := Numbers.GetItem;
                           Arg2 := Numbers.GetItem;
                           case Operators.GetItem of
                              Plus : Numbers.AddItem( Arg2 + Arg1 );
                              Minus : Numbers.AddItem( Arg2 - Arg1 );
                              Times : Numbers.AddItem( Arg2 * Arg1 );
                              Divide : Numbers.AddItem( Arg2 DIV Arg2 );
                           end;
                         end;
                  end;
        end
        else
           TokenType := TokError;
        if TokenType = TokError then
        begin
           WriteLn( 'Syntax Error' );
           TokenPos := Length( Expression ) + 1;
           Numbers.AddItem( 0 );
        end;
     end;
     WriteLn( 'Result: ', Numbers.GetItem );
     ReadLn;
end.
```

The GetToken function at the beginning of this program reads one token from the expression and puts it in the variable Token. In addition it sets TokenType to indicate what kind of token it found. The variable TokenPos is an index into the expression to keep track of the first character in the next token to read.

The main program begins by setting up two stacks, one for numbers and the other for operators. Then it reads the command line arguments and concatenates them to make the expression. The main loop calls `GetToken` repeatedly to get all of the tokens in the expression.

The first token read is tested to see if it is a minus sign. If it is, the minus flag is set, and a new token is read. Then the token is tested to see if it is a number. If it is, the number is pushed on to the number stack, and another token is read. This next token should be an operator. Operators on the stack that have higher precedence than the current operator are executed until the stack is empty or the operator on top of the stack has lower precedence than the current operator.

When the entire expression has been read, any operators remaining on the operator stack are executed to get the final result, which is on top of the number stack. Before exiting, the program pops the result off the number stack and writes it to the screen.

Comments

This program can be used as a simple integer calculator. Just type the name of the program followed by the expression to evaluate, like this

```
eval   28 * 5 + 13 - 12
```

The program will evaluate this and quickly print the result (141).

Warnings

The user can enter any string, not just expressions, on the command line. This program does only minimal checking for correct syntax and no checking for values out of range. Carefully check any results from this program to see if they make sense before you accept them as correct.

Enhancements

Adding more operators is simply a matter of adding the symbol to the list of symbols that `GetToken` looks for, assigning a constant to the operator, and adding another statement to the case statement that evaluates operators in the main program. The constant used determines the precedence of the operator; a higher number indicates higher precedence. Note that when the program tests for precedence, it divides the number by 2 so that two operators, for example plus and minus, can share the same precedence.

One change that is not so simple is having the program evaluate subexpressions in parentheses. To implement parentheses, you have to add two new tokens to `GetToken` and make several changes to the main program. This program shows the modifications:

```
{Evaluate an expression}
program Eval;
uses Struct;

const
    Number = 0;
    TokError = 1;
    Plus = 2;
    Minus = 3;
    Times = 4;
    Divide = 5;
    LParen = 6;
    RParen = 7;

var
  Expression : string;
  i, Code : integer;
  TokenPos : integer;
  Token : String;
  TokenType : integer;
  Numbers : Stack;
  Operators : Stack;
  MinusFlag : boolean;
  Arg1, Arg2 : integer;

procedure GetToken;
begin
    Token := '';
    if ( Ord( Expression[TokenPos] ) >= Ord( '0' ))
      AND ( Ord( Expression[TokenPos] ) <= Ord( '9' )) then
    begin
        repeat
            Token := Token + Expression[TokenPos];
            Inc( TokenPos );
        until ( Ord( Expression[TokenPos] ) < Ord( '0' ))
            OR ( Ord( Expression[TokenPos] ) > Ord( '9' ))
            OR ( TokenPos > Length( Expression ));
        TokenType := Number;
    end
    else if Expression[TokenPos] = '+' then
    begin
        TokenType := Plus;
        Inc( TokenPos );
    end
    else if Expression[TokenPos] = '-' then
    begin
        TokenType := Minus;
        Inc( TokenPos );
    end
    else if Expression[TokenPos] = '*' then
    begin
        TokenType := Times;
        Inc( TokenPos );
```

```
        end
    else if Expression[TokenPos] = '/' then
    begin
        TokenType := Divide;
        Inc( TokenPos );
    end
    else if Expression[TokenPos] = '(' then
    begin
        TokenType := LParen;
        Inc( TokenPos );
    end
    else if Expression[TokenPos] = ')' then
    begin
        TokenType := RParen;
        Inc( TokenPos );
    end
    else
        TokenType := TokError;
end;

begin
    Numbers.Init;
    Operators.Init;
    {Make sure that there is something on the operator stack}
    Operators.AddItem( LParen );
    Expression := '';
    for i := 1 to ParamCount do
        Expression := Expression + ParamStr( i );
    TokenPos := 1;
    while TokenPos <= Length( Expression ) do
    begin
        GetToken;
        {Check for opening parens}
        while TokenType = LParen do
        begin
            Operators.AddItem( LParen );
            GetToken;
        end;
        {Check for negative number}
        if TokenType = Minus then
        begin
            MinusFlag := TRUE;
            GetToken;
        end
        else
            MinusFlag := FALSE;
        if TokenType = Number then
        begin
          Val( Token, i, Code );
          if MinusFlag then
              i := -i;
          Numbers.AddItem( i );
          {See if at the end of the expression}
```

```
          if TokenPos <= Length( Expression ) then
          begin
              {Get the operator}
              repeat
                  GetToken;
                  if Operators.TestItem <> LParen then
                      {Do operations of higher precedence up
                       to the left paren}
                      while ( Operators.TestItem <> LParen )
                      AND ((( Operators.TestItem DIV 2 )
                      >= ( TokenType DIV 2 ))
                      OR ( TokenType = RParen)) do
                      begin
                          Arg1 := Numbers.GetItem;
                          Arg2 := Numbers.GetItem;
                          case Operators.GetItem of
                              Plus :
                                  Numbers.AddItem( Arg2 + Arg1 );
                              Minus :
                                  Numbers.AddItem( Arg2 - Arg1 );
                              Times :
                                  Numbers.AddItem( Arg2 * Arg1 );
                              Divide :
                                  Numbers.AddItem( Arg2 DIV Arg2 );
                          end;
                      end;
                  if TokenType = RParen then
                      i := Operators.GetItem;
              until ( TokenType <> RParen )
                  OR ( TokenPos >= Length( Expression ));
              Operators.AddItem( TokenType );
          end
      end
      else
          TokenType := TokError;
      if TokenType = TokError then
      begin
          WriteLn( 'Syntax Error' );
          TokenPos := Length( Expression ) + 1;
          Numbers.AddItem( 0 );
      end;
  end;
  while Operators.StackSize > 1 do
  begin
      Arg1 := Numbers.GetItem;
      Arg2 := Numbers.GetItem;
      repeat
          i := Operators.GetItem;
      until ( i <> LParen ) AND ( i <>RParen );
      case i of
          Plus : Numbers.AddItem( Arg2 + Arg1 );
          Minus : Numbers.AddItem( Arg2 - Arg1 );
```

```
        Times : Numbers.AddItem( Arg2 * Arg1 );
        Divide : Numbers.AddItem( Arg2 DIV Arg2 );
      end;
    end;
    WriteLn( 'Result: ', Numbers.GetItem );
    ReadLn;
end.
```

The difference between this program and the previous one is that this one uses left parentheses to mark the bottom of the stack, instead of looking for the bottom of the stack. Extra logic has been added that recognizes right parentheses and uses them to indicate when it is OK to pop a left parenthesis off the stack.

8.8   How do I...

Parse statements with Turbo Pascal?

Description

A command parser must find commands and recognize variations of commands. For example, a language may include a PRINT command for printing literal strings or the contents of string variables. The parser must not only recognize the PRINT command but also check whether the argument is a variable or a string. This solution shows how to implement this type of parsing.

See Also

8.7   Evaluating expressions

Solution

For a command parser to work, the syntax of the commands must let the parser recognize different token types. In most languages, for example, variables must begin with a letter and must not include characters that might be interpreted as some other operator. These rules help the parser to recognize a variable and distinguish it from other tokens, such as strings and operators.

The format of a parser is similar to that used in question 8.7 for evaluating expressions. The first step is to break the input strings down into tokens. Then the type of each token is used to determine what commands to execute. Each token found determines the possible tokens that follow. For example, in some languages the first token must be a command, then the next token must be something that makes sense for that command. The token following a PRINT command might be limited to strings or variables; you would not expect to find an operator or another command in this location.

Here is a short program in the language to interpret:

```
Test = "This is a test"
PRINT Test
PRINT "Another line"
```

This program puts the string "This is a test" in the variable Test, then prints Test. It also prints the literal string, "Another line". As you can see, this is not a very useful computer language, but it gives you a good idea of how a language interpreter works.

The program below interprets a simple language that lets you assign strings to variables and print strings or variables:

```
{Evaluate an expression}
program Eval;
uses Struct;

type
    {Define an entry in the symbol table}
    SymEntry = record
        Name : string[20];    {Name of the symbol}
        Value : string;       {The data represented}
    end;

const
    {Define token types}
    Number = 0;
    TokError = 1;
    StringTok = 2;
    Symbol = 3;
    PrintCmnd = 4;
    EOL = 5;
    Equals = 6;

var
    Expression : string;
    i, j, Code : integer;
    TokenPos : integer;
    Token : String;
    TokenType : integer;
    F : Text;
    SymTable : array [1..20] of SymEntry;
    SymCnt : integer;

{Get tokens, determine command type}
procedure GetToken;
begin
    {Skip white space}
    while (( Expression[TokenPos] = ' ' )
```

```
          OR ( Expression[TokenPos] = Chr( 9 )))
          AND ( TokenPos <= Length( Expression )) do
          Inc( TokenPos );
   Token := '';
   if TokenPos > Length( Expression ) then
      TokenType := EOL
   {Is the token a number?}
   else if ( Ord(Expression[TokenPos] ) >= Ord( '0' ))
      AND ( Ord(Expression[TokenPos] ) <= Ord( '9' )) then
   begin
      repeat
         Token := Token + Expression[TokenPos];
         Inc( TokenPos );
      until ( Ord( Expression[TokenPos] ) < Ord( '0' ))
         OR ( Ord(Expression[TokenPos] ) > Ord( '9' ))
         OR ( TokenPos > Length( Expression ));
      TokenType := Number;
   end
   {Is the token a string?}
   else if Expression[TokenPos] = '"' then
   begin
      Inc( TokenPos );
      while Expression[TokenPos] <> '"' do
      begin
         Token := Token + Expression[TokenPos];
         Inc( TokenPos );
      end;
      TokenType := StringTok;
   end
   {Is the token an equal sign?}
   else if Expression[TokenPos] = '=' then
   begin
      Inc( TokenPos );
      TokenType := Equals;
   end
   {Is the token a command or symbol?}
   else
   begin
      {Get the whole symbol}
      while ( Expression[TokenPos] > ' ' )
         AND ( Expression[TokenPos] <> '=' )
         AND ( TokenPos <= Length(Expression )) do
      begin
         Token := Token + Expression[TokenPos];
         Inc( TokenPos );
      end;
      {See if it is the print command}
      if Token = 'PRINT' then
         TokenType := PrintCmnd
      else
         TokenType := Symbol;
   end;
end;
```

```
begin
    {Initialize variable count}
    SymCnt := 0;
    {Open the command file}
    Assign( F, ParamStr( 1 ));
    Reset( F );
    {Read each line from the file and interpret it}
    repeat
        {Read a line from the file}
        ReadLn( F, Expression );
        TokenPos := 1;
        {Get the first token}
        GetToken;
        {If the token is a variable, this is an assignment}
        if TokenType = Symbol then
        begin
            {Look up the variable in the symbol table}
            i := 1;
            while ( i <= SymCnt ) AND ( Token <> SymTable[i].Name ) do
                Inc(i);
            {If it does not exist, create an entry for it}
            if i > SymCnt then
            begin
                Inc( SymCnt );
                SymTable[i].Name := Token;
            end;
            {Get the equals sign}
            GetToken;
            if TokenType = Equals then
            begin
                {Get the data to assign to the variable}
                GetToken;
                {If it is a string, copy it to the variable}
                if TokenType = StringTok then
                    SymTable[i].Value := Token
                else
                begin
                    {Look up the source variable}
                    j := 1;
                    while ( j <= SymCnt )
                        AND ( Token <> SymTable[j].Name ) do
                        Inc( j );
                    {If the variable exists, copy it}
                    if j <= SymCnt then
                        SymTable[i].Value
                            := SymTable[j].Value;
                end;
            end;
        end
        {See if the token is the print command}
        else if TokenType = PrintCmnd then
        begin
```

```
          {Get the item to print}
          GetToken;
          {If it is a string print it}
          if TokenType = StringTok then
            WriteLn( Token )
          else
          {If it is a variable look it up}
          begin
              i := 1;
              while ( i <= SymCnt )
                    AND(Token <> SymTable[i].Name ) do
                    Inc( i );
              {If the variable exists, print the contents}
              if i <= SymCnt then
                WriteLn( SymTable[i].Value );
          end;
       end;
    until Eof( F );
    Close( F );
    ReadLn;
end.
```

The GetToken routine for this program finds numbers, strings, equal signs, variables, and commands. Numbers are defined as anything that starts with a digit and contains only digits. Strings begin and end with double quotes ("). Anything that begins with a letter up to the next space or equal sign is a command or a variable. The only possible command is PRINT, so anything else must be a variable. The GetToken routine does not check whether the variable is defined.

The main program opens a file and reads each line, processing the commands found. There are two possibilities for the first token. It can be a variable, or the PRINT command. If it is a variable, the program assumes that you want to assign a value to the variable. First, it checks if the variable is already defined by searching the list of defined variables. If the variable is not in the list, the program adds it to the list. In any case the variable i is the index to the variable in the list. Next, the program checks for an equal sign, which confirms that this is an assignment statement. The token after the equal sign is the data to assign to the variable. There are two possibilities here. The first is that the token is a string, which can be copied directly to the variable. The second possibility is that the token is a variable. In this case, the variable must be looked up in the symbol table and its contents copied to the first variable.

If the first token is a PRINT command, the next token is either a string or a variable. This is the same case as for the right side of an assignment statement, so similar code is used. The difference is that instead of copying the result to a variable, the program prints the result on the screen.

Warnings

This program takes no special action for lines that contain syntax errors. At best, it ignores a command that it cannot figure out. A proper parser would include code to display diagnostic messages when a syntax error is found. It would also try to get back to a known state, so that one syntax error does not appear to create a whole screen of errors.

9

UTILITY PROGRAMS AND UNITS

9

his chapter contains units and programs that you can use
while programming or as part of your own applications.
The interactive nature of Turbo Pascal makes it ideal for
quickly developing user interface units and utilities such as
those found here. Solutions 9.1 and 9.2 show two different approaches to
menus, Lotus-style menus and pull-down menus. With these units you can
add menus to a program by simply including the unit and initializing the
menu objects.

Popular interfaces such as Turbo Vision and Microsoft Windows use dialog boxes for user input. Solution 6.4 shows how to implement dialog boxes
by using objects. If you experimented with that solution, you may have noticed how difficult it is to create good-looking dialog boxes. The problem is
that you cannot see the dialog box until the program is written. If the dialog
box does not look good, you have to rewrite portions of the program. Then
you retest and do it all over again. Solution 9.3 solves this problem by letting
you see the dialog as you edit it.

Solution 9.4 is a program that makes it easy to look at text files. It displays
the file, along with information about the file, one screenful at a time. Solutions 9.5 through 9.7 are also programs that help you work with files. They
let you sort the lines in large files, search several files, and compress files to
save disk space.

SCREEN UTILITIES

Some programs do only one or two simple tasks, so they don't need much in the way of a user interface. Other programs have options that must be set, data fields to fill in, and a number of commands to choose from. The next three solutions are for that latter type of program. The first two solutions show different types of menu you can use in your programs. The first is the menu style used by Lotus 1-2-3. The menu shows a list of options on one line and a brief description of the command on another line. The second type is the pull-down menu. It shows a list of submenus that you can expand into a list of commands.

Solution 9.3 takes care of the problem of getting data into the program. It shows you how to design dialog boxes for use with the dialog object routines in question 6.4.

9.1   How do I...

Create Lotus-style menus with Turbo Pascal?

Description

The menu system of Lotus 1-2-3 and similar products makes it easy for users to enter commands. The menu shows a list of possible commands and a line explaining the selected command. The selected command appears in inverse video. Figure 9-1 shows a sample Lotus-style menu. The user can press the arrow keys to move from one command to another. As the user selects commands, the explanation line changes to match the new selected command. To execute the command the user presses the Enter key.

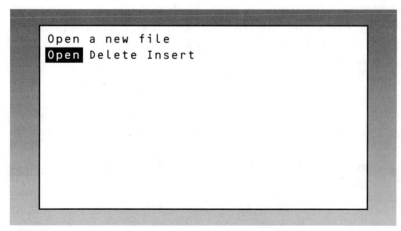

```
Open a new file
Open Delete Insert
```

Figure 9-1 A Lotus-style menu

See Also

8.1   Button objects

9.2   Making pull-down menus

Solution

This solution implements menus as objects in a separately compiled unit. This makes it easy to add menus to any Turbo Pascal program. Two objects that make up the menu: the first holds the menu selection, and the second holds the whole menu. These objects work closely together to display the menu, get user input, and execute the selected routines.

This unit implements the objects:

```
{This unit implements a Lotus-style menu using objects}
unit LMenu;
interface

type
   Proc = procedure;

{This is the object for each menu item}
type
      MenuItem = object
      X, Y : Byte;            {Item location}
      KeyWord : String;          {Text for menu line}
      Descrpt : String;       {Text for description line}
      DoThis : Proc;          {Procedure to execute when chosen}
      procedure Init( NewX, NewY : Byte; KeyW, Dscrpt : String; Doit : Proc);
      procedure Show;
      procedure Select;
      function IsMatch( ch : char ) : boolean;
      procedure ExecItem;
   end;

{This is the object for the whole menu }
type
  MenuObj = object
      Line : Byte;            {Menu line}
      LastX : Byte;           {Last column for the menu}
      ItemCnt : integer;   {Number of choices}
      CurItem : integer;   {Selected item}
      Items : array [1..20] of MenuItem;
      procedure Init( WhatLine : Byte );
      procedure AddItem( Key, Desc : String; Doit : Proc );
      procedure GoLeft;
      procedure GoRight;
      procedure MatchChar( ch : char );
      procedure Exec;
      end;

implementation
uses Crt;
```

```
{Initialize a menu item}
procedure
MenuItem.Init( NewX, NewY : Byte; KeyW, Dscrpt : String; Doit : Proc );
begin
    X := NewX;
    Y := NewY;
    KeyWord := KeyW;
    Descrpt := Dscrpt;
    DoThis := Doit;
end;

{Print plain menu item}
procedure MenuItem.Show;
begin
    TextColor( White );
    TextBackground( Black );
    GotoXY( X, Y );
    write( KeyWord );
end;

{Show the item as selected}
procedure MenuItem.Select;
begin
    {Write the item in inverse video}
    TextColor( Black );
    TextBackground( White );
    GotoXY( X, Y );
    write( KeyWord );
    {Write the description}
    TextColor( White );
    TextBackground( Black );
    GotoXY( 1, Y - 1 );
    write( Descrpt );
    ClrEol;
end;

{See if the character matches the first letter of the item}
function MenuItem.IsMatch( ch : char ) : boolean;
begin
    if ch = KeyWord[1] then
        IsMatch := TRUE
    else
        IsMatch := FALSE;
end;

{Execute the procedure that goes with this item}
procedure MenuItem.ExecItem;
begin
    DoThis;
end;

{Initialize a menu}
procedure MenuObj.Init( WhatLine : Byte );
```

```
begin
    Line := WhatLine;
    ItemCnt := 0;
    LastX := 1;
    CurItem := 1;
end;

{Add a menu item to the menu}
procedure MenuObj.AddItem( Key, Desc : String; Doit : Proc );
begin
        {Increment the item count}
        Inc( ItemCnt );
        {Initialize the item}
        Items[ItemCnt].Init( LastX, Line + 1, Key, Desc, Doit );
        {Move the last column past the new item}
        LastX := LastX + Ord( Key[0] ) + 1;
        {Show the item}
        if ItemCnt = CurItem then
            Items[ItemCnt].Select
        else
            Items[ItemCnt].Show;
end;

{Handle a right-arrow key}
procedure MenuObj.GoRight;
begin
    if CurItem + 1 <= ItemCnt then
    begin
        {Deselect the current item}
        Items[CurItem].Show;
        {Go to the next item}
        Inc( CurItem );
        {Show the new selected item}
        Items[CurItem].Select;
    end;
end;

{Handle left arrow}
procedure MenuObj.GoLeft;
begin
    if CurItem > 1 then
    begin
        {Deselect the current item}
        Items[CurItem].Show;
        {Go to the previous item}
        Dec( Curitem );
        {Select the new item}
        Items[CurItem].Select;
    end;
end;

{Find an item that matches the current key character}
procedure MenuObj.MatchChar( ch : Char );
```

```pascal
var
   i : integer;
begin
    {Make the char uppercase}
    ch := UpCase( ch );
    {Try each of the items}
    for i := 1 to ItemCnt do
    begin
        {If it matches, select the item}
        if Items[i].IsMatch( ch ) then
        begin
            Items[CurItem].Show;
            CurItem := i;
            Items[CurItem].Select;
        end;
    end;
end;

{Execute the currently selected item}
procedure MenuObj.Exec;
begin
    Items[CurItem].ExecItem;
end;

end.
```

The MenuItem object defines each item on the menu line. It contains data fields for the location of the item, the text for the command and description, and the address of the procedure to execute. The methods allow the object to be initialized, printed, and selected, and the command to be executed. This object is not directly used by programs; instead, it is used by the MenuObj object that represents the entire menu.

The data for MenuObj includes the line on which to show the menu, the length of the menu line, an array of items, the number of items in the array, and the currently selected item. The methods are for initializing the object, adding items to the menu, and handling various keys.

A program that uses this unit begins by initializing a MenuObj object. This sets the menu line to the passed value and sets the item count to 0. Next, the program adds the menu items by calling the AddItem method, which computes the position of the new item and calls the Init method for a menu item. After adding all of the items to the menu, the program can use the GoLeft, GoRight, and MatchChar methods to select different items in the menu. To execute the procedure for the currently selected item, it calls the Exec method.

Comments

To use the menu unit, you must define the functions for each menu item and initialize the menu using these functions. This program shows how this works:

```
{This program demonstrates Lotus-style menus}
program menu;
uses Crt, LMenus;

{These procedures do nothing more than print a message. They
 illustrate how menus work}
{$F+}
procedure ExecOpen;
begin
    GotoXY( 10, 10 );
    write( 'Open the file' );
    ClrEol;
end;

procedure ExecDelete;
begin
    GotoXY( 10, 10 );
    write( 'Delete data' );
    ClrEol;
end;

procedure ExecInsert;
begin
    GotoXY( 10, 10 );
    write( 'Insert data' );
    ClrEol;
end;
{$F-}

{This procedure handles the cursor keys. It is called when the main key
parser hits an extended key}
procedure DoFuncKey;
var ch : char;
begin
    {Get the second byte of the key code}
    ch := ReadKey;
    case ch of
        {Right-arrow key}
        chr( 77 ) : MainMenu.GoRight;
        {Left-arrow key}
        chr( 75 ) : MainMenu.GoLeft;
        {Home key}
        chr ( 71 ) : MainMenu.GoHome;
        {End key}
        chr( 79 ) : MainMenu.GoEnd;
    end;
end;

{This is the main program}
var
        Running : boolean;          {True while the main loop is
                                     running}
        ch : char;                  {Character from the keyboard}
        MainMenu : MenuObj;
```

```
begin
    MainMenu.Init( 1 );      {Initialize a menu on line 1}
    {Initialize the first item}
    MainMenu.AddItem( 'Open', 'Open a new file', ExecOpen );
    {And the second item}
    MainMenu.AddItem( 'Delete', 'Delete text at the cursor',
        ExecDelete );
    {And the third item}
    MainMenu.AddItem( 'Insert', 'Insert text at the cursor',
        ExecInsert );
    Running := TRUE;         {Indicate that the main loop is running}
    while Running do
    begin
        ch := ReadKey;       {Get a key}
        case ch of
            {Exit if the key is X or Esc}
            'X','x', Chr(27) : Running := FALSE;
            {Go to DoFuncKey for extended keys }
            Chr( 0 ) : DoFuncKey;
            {Do the command for the Enter key}
            Chr( 13 ) : MainMenu.Exec;
        else
            {For all other keys, see if they match a menu item}
            MainMenu.MatchChar( ch );
        end;
    end;
end.
```

This program creates three menu items that print different messages. Note that the procedures for the menu items are between {F+} and {F-} directives. This is required to allow the program to store pointers to these procedures in the MenuItem objects. After initializing the menu and menu items, the program gets keystrokes from the user. The program takes different actions according to which key the user pressed. If the key is X or Esc, the program exits. If it is a function key, the program checks whether the next character is a Right-Arrow or Left-Arrow key, which change the selected item. The Enter key executes the currently selected item. Any other key is tested to see if it matches the first character of a menu item, in which case that item is selected.

Enhancements

Because these routines are object-oriented, they are easy to modify. For example, you can change the menu routines to allow multiple-line menu commands or explanations without affecting the code that uses the menus. You can also modify the IsMatch routine so that the user's keypress matches some letter other than the first one in a menu item. This would give you more flexibility in choosing names of menu commands, because not all items would have to begin with different first letters.

9.2   How do I...

Make pull-down menus in Turbo Pascal?

Description

The main drawback to Lotus-style menus is that they allow only one line of commands per menu. Pull-down menus overcome this problem because each item represents a list of commands. Each list can have as many commands as there are lines on the screen, greatly increasing the number of available commands. Figure 9-2 shows the pull-down menus used with Turbo Pascal.

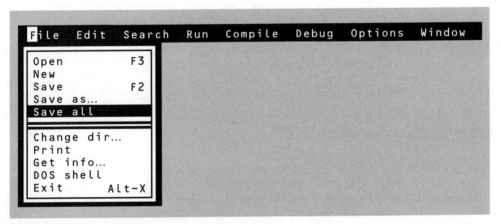

Figure 9-2 Turbo Pascal pull-down menus

See Also

1.4   Drawing boxes on the screen

6.4   Creating dialog boxes

9.1   Creating Lotus-style menus

Solution

Each pull-down menu has two display states, open or closed. When the menu is closed, it appears as a heading at the top of the screen. When opened, it is a box full of commands. After the menu is opened, the program gets keyboard input from the user to select a command and run it. When closed, the menu simply waits for an open command.

This unit defines an object for a pull-down menu:

```
{Pull-down menu object}
unit PullMenu;
```

```
interface
type
    proc = function : boolean;
    MenuItem = record
        Text : string[80];
        Attr : byte;
        DoThis : proc;
        Key : word;
    end;

    SubMenu = object
        Title : string[80];
        List : array [1..25] of MenuItem;
        Count : integer;
        Left : integer;
        Width : integer;
        Attr : byte;
        CursorAttr : byte;
        Key : word;
        procedure Init( Ttle : string; Ky : word
                ; Lft, Wid : integer; At1, At2 : byte );
        procedure AddItem( Text : string; Ky : word
                ; At : byte; DoIt : proc );
        procedure DrawTitle;
        procedure Open( Ky : word );
    end;

implementation
uses Crt;
{Initialize a submenu}
procedure SubMenu.Init( Ttle : string; Ky : word
        ; Lft, Wid : integer; At1, At2 : byte );
begin
    {Copy parameters to the object fields}
    Title := Ttle;
    Count := 0;
    Left := Lft;
    Width := Wid;
    Attr := At1;
    CursorAttr := At2;
    Key := Ky;
end;

{Add an item to the submenu}
procedure SubMenu.AddItem( Text : string; Ky : word
        ; At : byte; DoIt : proc );
begin
    Inc( Count );
    List[Count].Text := Text;
    List[Count].Attr := At;
    List[Count].DoThis := DoIt;
    List[Count].Key := Ky;
end;
```

```
{Write the title on the screen}
procedure SubMenu.DrawTitle;
begin
    TextAttr := Attr;
    GotoXY( Left + ( Width - Length( Title )) DIV 2, 1 );
    Write( Title );
end;

{Move the selected item}
function NewCur( Cur, Change, Max : integer ) : integer;
var
   i : integer;
begin
    i := Cur + Change;
    if i > Max then
         i := Max
    else if i < 1 then
         i := 1;
    NewCur := i;
end;

{Open up the submenu}
procedure SubMenu.Open( Ky : word );
var
   i, j : integer;
   Ch : char;
   UserKey : word;
   Done : boolean;
   CurItem : integer;
begin
    if Ky = Key then
    begin
        TextAttr := Attr;
        {Draw a box}
        GotoXY( Left, 1 );
        Write( Chr( 201 ) );
        GotoXY( Left + Width, 1 );
        Write( Chr( 187 ));
        for i := 1 to Count do
        begin
            GotoXY( Left, i + 1 );
            Write( Chr( 186 ), ' ', List[i].Text );
            for j := Length( List[i].Text ) + 3 to Width do
                Write( ' ' );
            Write( Chr( 186 ));
        end;
        GotoXY( Left, Count + 2 );
        Write( Chr( 200 ));
        for i := 1 to Width - 1 do
            Write( Chr( 205 ));
        Write( Chr( 188 ));
        CurItem := 1;
        Done := FALSE;
```

```
        while NOT Done do
        begin
            {Draw the cursor}
            TextAttr := CursorAttr;
            GotoXY( Left + 1, CurItem + 1 );
            Write( ' ', List[CurItem].Text );
            for i := Length( List[CurItem].Text ) + 3 to Width do
                Write( ' ' );
            {Get a key from the user}
            Ch := ReadKey;
            if Ord( Ch ) = 0 then
                UserKey := Ord( ReadKey ) * 256
            else
                UserKey := Ord( Ch );
            {Erase the cursor}
            TextAttr := Attr;
            GotoXY( Left + 1, CurItem + 1 );
            Write( ' ', List[CurItem].Text );
            for i := Length( List[CurItem].Text ) + 3 to Width do
                Write( ' ' );
            Case UserKey of
                {On ESC close the menu}
                27 : Done := TRUE;
                {Move cursor down}
                20480 : CurItem := NewCur( CurItem, 1, Count );
                {Move cursor up}
                18432 : CurItem := NewCur(CurItem, -1, Count );
                13 : Done := List[CurItem].DoThis;
            else
                for i := 1 to Count do
                    if UserKey = List[i].Key then
                        Done := List[i].DoThis;
            end;
        end;
    end;
end;

end.
```

In this unit, the type proc is defined as a function returning a Boolean value, allowing menu commands to indicate success or failure. Menu items are a record (instead of an object, as in the LMenu unit) because the SubMenu object actually does all of the work. The fields for a SubMenu object include the title of the submenu, a list of menu items, the position of the submenu, and attributes to use when drawing the submenu. These fields are filled in by the Init and AddItem methods.

The Init and AddItem methods simply copy their parameters to the corresponding fields in the object. The AddItem method uses the field Count to keep track of the number of items in the menu. The next method, DrawTitle, simply draws the title at the top of the screen.

The Open method lets the user manipulate the opened submenu. It begins by testing the key passed to it to see if the menu really should be opened. It opens the menu by drawing a box large enough to hold all of the menu items. The variable CurItem holds the number of the selected menu item, which is displayed in the cursor color for the submenu. Once the menu is displayed, the Open method gets keys from the keyboard to move the cursor around or select an item to run. The user can move the cursor up and down by pressing the arrow keys, exit the menu, run the selected item, or directly run any of the items by pressing the key associated with that item in the AddItem method.

Comments
To create pull-down menus you must first declare a SubMenu object for each submenu used in the program. Next you should initialize the submenu and add the menu items. To let the user activate the menus, you must pass any keystrokes to each of the submenus. See question 9.3 for a good example of pull-down menus put to use.

9.3   How do I...

Make a dialog editor in Turbo Pascal?

Description
It is hard to get a dialog box to look just right. You must run the program, look at the dialog box, make some changes, and run the program again. You repeat the process until the dialog box looks good enough. This solution takes some of the work out of this chore by letting you look at dialog boxes as you create them.

See Also
8.1   Creating dialog boxes
9.2   Making pull-down menus

Solution
Figure 9-3 shows the initial dialog editor screen. Across the top is the menu, in the upper-right corner are some statistics, and in the middle is a dialog box to edit.

The Done menu contains the Quit command, which lets you exit the dialog editor. The Edit menu contains commands to change the characteristics of a screen object, such as position, text, and size. The Add Objects menu commands are for creating new objects. Each type of screen object is represented by a command in this menu that creates an object of that type. The last menu, Select, lets you choose the current screen object. All editing applies to the current object, so you need a way to select different objects. As objects are created, they are assigned an object number that appears in the upper-right corner of the screen. The Select menu lets you move to the previous or next object in the list of objects.

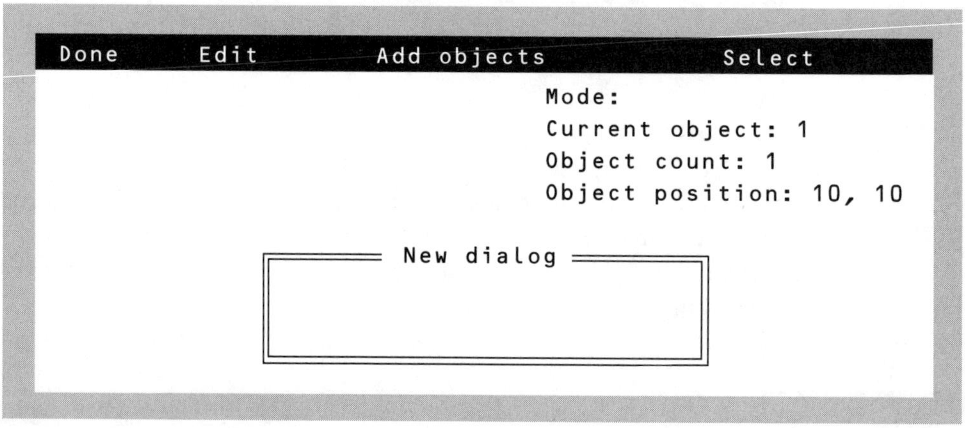

Figure 9-3 The dialog box editor

Here is the source code for the dialog editor:

```
{Dialog box editor}
program de;
uses PullMenu, Crt, Entry;

var
   Menu1 : SubMenu;
   Menu2 : SubMenu;
   Menu3 : SubMenu;
   Menu4 : SubMenu;
   TmpStr : String;
   Ch : char;
   Key : word;
   Done : boolean;
   FileName : string;
   UserObjects : array [1..50] of ScrnPtr;
   DlgDummy : ^DialogObj;
   StatDummy : ^StaticLit;
   TextDummy : ^TextObj;
   ButtonDummy : ^ButtonObj;
   UserCount, UserCurrent : integer;
   Moving, Sizing : boolean;
```

```pascal
{Paint the screen}
procedure PaintScreen;
var
   i : integer;
begin
   {Clear the screen}
   TextAttr := $17;
   ClrScr;
   GotoXY( 0, 0 );
   {Draw the menu bar}
   FillChar( TmpStr, sizeof( TmpStr ), ' ' );
   TmpStr[0] := Chr( 80 );
   TextAttr := $70;
   Write( TmpStr );
   {Fill in the menu headings}
   Menu1.DrawTitle;
   Menu2.DrawTitle;
   Menu3.DrawTitle;
   Menu4.DrawTitle;
   {Write the status information}
   TextAttr := $17;
   GotoXY( 50, 2 );
   Write( 'Mode: ' );
   if Moving then
      Write( 'Moving ' );
   if Sizing then
      Write( 'Resizing' );
   GotoXY( 50, 3 );
   Write( 'Current object: ', UserCurrent );
   ClrEol;
   GotoXY( 50, 4 );
   Write( 'Object count: ', UserCount );
   ClrEol;
   GotoXY( 50, 5 );
   Write( 'Object position: '
       , UserObjects[UserCurrent]^.Col, ', '
       , UserObjects[UserCurrent]^.Row );
   ClrEol;
   i := 1;
   while i <= UserCount do
   begin
       UserObjects[i]^.Draw;
       Inc( i );
   end;
end;


{$F+}
{Do-nothing function for buttons}
function DullButton : integer;
begin
   DullButton := 0;
end;
```

```
function Quit : boolean;
begin
    Done := TRUE;
    Quit := TRUE;
end;

function StartMove : boolean;
begin
    Moving := TRUE;
    Sizing := FALSE;
    StartMove := TRUE;
end;

function StartSize : boolean;
begin
    Moving := FALSE;
    Sizing := TRUE;
    StartSize := TRUE;
end;

function EditText : boolean;
var
   STDiag : DialogObj;
   STPrompt : StaticLit;
   STData : TextObj;
   Result : integer;
   F : file;
begin
    {Make dialog to get the new text}
    STDiag.Init( 5, 10, 3, 35, $24, 'New text' );
    STPrompt.Init( 6, 12, 'Text:', $24 );
    STData.Init( 6, 23, 20, '', $25 );
    STDiag.AddObj( @STPrompt );
    STDiag.AddObj( @STData );
    STDiag.Draw;
    Result := STDiag.Input;
    {Get the text from the dialog box}
    UserObjects[UserCurrent]^.SetText( STData.TextData );
    EditText := TRUE;
end;

function NextObj : boolean;
begin
    if UserCurrent < UserCount then
       Inc( UserCurrent );
    NextObj := TRUE;
end;

function PrevObj : boolean;
begin
    if UserCurrent > 1 then
       Dec( UserCurrent );
```

```
        PrevObj := TRUE;
end;

{Add a static text object}
function AddStatic : boolean;
begin
    New( StatDummy, Init( 2, 1, 'Static', $24 ));
    Inc( UserCount );
    UserObjects[UserCount] := StatDummy;
    UserCurrent := UserCount;
    AddStatic := TRUE;
end;

{Add a dialog box object}
function AddDialog : boolean;
begin
    New( DlgDummy, Init( 2, 1, 5, 40, $24, 'New dialog' ));
    Inc( UserCount );
    UserObjects[UserCount] := DlgDummy;
    UserCurrent := UserCount;
    AddDialog := TRUE;
end;

{Add a text field object}
function AddTxtFld : boolean;
begin
    New( TextDummy, Init( 2, 1, 20, 'Entry field', $42 ));
    Inc( UserCount );
    UserObjects[UserCount] := TextDummy;
    UserCurrent := UserCount;
    AddTxtFld := TRUE;
end;

{Add a button object}
function AddButton : boolean;
begin
    New( ButtonDummy, Init( 2,1,3,8,'Button',$24,DullButton,0 ));
    Inc( UserCount );
    UserObjects[UserCount] := ButtonDummy;
    UserCurrent := UserCount;
    AddButton := TRUE;
end;
{$F-}

begin
    FileName := '';
    Menu1.Init( 'Done', 8192, 1, 10, $74, $24 );
    Menu1.AddItem( 'Quit', 4096, $74, Quit );
    Menu2.Init( 'Edit', 4608, 12, 20, $74, $24 );
    Menu2.AddItem( 'Move object', 12800, $74, StartMove );
    Menu2.AddItem( 'Resize item', 4864, $74, StartSize );
    Menu2.AddItem( 'Change text', 11776, $74, EditText );
```

```
Menu3.Init( 'Add objects', 7680, 35, 20, $74, $24 );
Menu3.AddItem( 'Dialog', 8192, $74, AddDialog );
Menu3.AddItem( 'Static text', 7936, $74, AddStatic );
Menu3.AddItem( 'Text entry', 5120, $74, AddTxtFld );
Menu3.AddItem( 'Button', 12288, $74, AddButton );
Menu4.Init( 'Select', 7936, 57, 20, $74, $24 );
Menu4.AddItem( 'Next object', 12544, $74, NextObj );
Menu4.AddItem( 'Previous object', 6400, $74, PrevObj );
{Make the first object}
New( DlgDummy, Init( 10, 10, 5, 40, $24, 'New dialog' ));
UserObjects[1] := DlgDummy;
UserCount := 1;
UserCurrent := 1;
Moving := FALSE;
Sizing := FALSE;
Done := FALSE;
while NOT Done do
begin
    {Show the main screen}
    PaintScreen;
    {Get a key from the user}
    Ch := ReadKey;
    if Ord( Ch ) = 0 then
      Key := Ord( ReadKey ) * 256
    else
       Key := Ord( Ch );
    if Key = 20480 then  {Check for Down arrow}
    begin
        if Moving then
          UserObjects[UserCurrent]^.Move( 0, 1 )
        else if Sizing then
            UserObjects[UserCurrent]^.Resize( 0, 1 );
    end
    else if Key = 18432 then {Check for Up arrow}
    begin
        if Moving then
          UserObjects[UserCurrent]^.Move( 0, -1 )
        else if Sizing then
            UserObjects[UserCurrent]^.Resize( 0, -1 );
    end
    else if Key = 19712 then {Check for Right arrow}
    begin
        if Moving then
          UserObjects[UserCurrent]^.Move( 1, 0 )
        else
            UserObjects[UserCurrent]^.Resize( 1, 0 );
    end
    else if Key = 19200 then {Check for Left arrow}
    begin
        if Moving then
          UserObjects[UserCurrent]^.Move( -1, 0 )
        else
            UserObjects[UserCurrent]^.Resize( -1, 0 );
```

```
        end
        else if Key = 27 then {Check for Esc}
        begin
            Moving := FALSE;
            Sizing := FALSE;
        end
        else
        begin
            {See if the key opens menu 1}
            Menu1.Open( Key );
            {Try menu 2}
            Menu2.Open( Key );
            Menu3.Open( Key );
            Menu4.Open( Key );
        end;
    end;
end.
```

This program uses the PullMenu unit from question 9.2 and the Entry unit from question 6.4. The variables Menu1, Menu2, Menu3, and Menu4 are the four pull-down menus. Screen objects are stored in the array UserObjects. UserCount is the number of objects defined, and UserCurrent is the number of the current object.

The first procedure, PaintScreen, draws the screen. First it clears the screen and draws the menu. Next it draws the status information in the upper-right corner of the screen. Finally, it draws all of the screen objects created by the user. Note that none of the objects are added to the dialog object, so they must all be explicitly drawn.

The rest of the functions in the program are for the various menu commands. Most of these functions set flags to control modes such as moving and resizing. The EditText function is interesting because it brings up a dialog box to get the new text for the current object. Because it uses local variables to hold the objects for this dialog box, the dialog box is separate from the rest of the program.

The main program begins by initializing the menus. Next, it creates a dialog box that is the first object to be edited. After everything is initialized, the program goes into a large loop that handles user interaction. The first job of the loop is to paint the screen. Because most commands change the screen somehow, the screen is repainted before the user's keypress is accepted.

The loop checks whether the user pressed an arrow key and, if so, whether the current item should be moved or resized. If the user did not press an arrow key, the keypress is passed to each of the menus to determine whether one of them should be opened. This process is repeated until the user selects the Quit item in the Done menu, which sets the Done flag, causing the loop to terminate.

Comments

When you run this program, you see a dialog box that you can change by moving, resizing, and adding items. When the dialog box looks just right, look at the status information for each item. Record the coordinates so that you can reproduce the dialog box in your program.

Enhancements

A useful enhancement is to add commands to save dialog boxes in a file. Then, your program can read the file to initialize the dialog box. Do not use the object-saving technique described in question 6.6 because there is no guarantee that the VMT (Virtual Method Table) for the dialog editor is the same as the VMT for your application. Instead, you should write special save methods for each screen object type. Include code to save the type of object and size at the beginning of each object so that the file can be decoded.

FILE UTILITIES

One of the main reasons people use computers is to store information. On the PC, this information is stored in disk files created and maintained by programs such as word processors and databases. The utilities in this section help you manage files by letting you look at the contents of a file, search for files that contain certain strings, sort the lines in very large files, and compress files.

The basic principles used in these utilities have been discussed in previous solutions. Here, these principles have been applied to simple utility programs to show you some practical uses for the solutions.

9.4   How do I...

View text files with Turbo Pascal?

Description

When you want to take a quick look at a file, you may not want to wait for your word processor to load. You might use the MS-DOS `type` command to look at the file, but more often than not, the part of the file you want to look at scrolls by quickly before you can stop the listing. This solution is a program that shows a test file one screen at a time.

See Also

1.5   Using the file manager

Solution

The MS-DOS `type` command simply reads lines from the file and displays them on the screen until it reaches the end of the file. This solution, by contrast, counts the number of lines it prints, and stops every 23 lines to get a key from the user. Figure 9-4 shows the output of this program.

```
File: view.pas
{Program to view text files}
uses DOS, Crt;

var
    F : text;
    OneLine : string;
    LineNumber : integer
    Ch : char;

begin
    {If there is a file name on the command line}
    if ParamCount = 1 then
    begin
        {Open the file}
        Assign( F, ParamStr( 1 ));
        Reset( F );
        {Initialize the line number)
        LineNumber := 1;
        Ch := ' ';
        {Make sure that the cursor is on the left edge}
        WriteLn;
        {Show the filename}
        TextAttr := $70;
    More? (y/n)
```

Figure 9-4 Output of the file view program

```
{Program to view text files}
uses Dos, Crt;

var
  F : text;
  OneLine : string;
  LineNumber : integer;
  Ch : char;

begin
    {If there is a filename on the command line}
    if ParamCount = 1 then
    begin
        {Open the file}
        Assign( F, ParamStr( 1 ));
```

```
Reset( F );
{Initialize the line number}
LineNumber := 1;
Ch := ' ';
{Make sure that the cursor is on the left edge}
WriteLn;
{Show the filename}
TextAttr := $70;
Write( 'File: ', ParamStr( 1 ));
ClrEol;
TextAttr := $7;
WriteLn;
{Show the file}
repeat
    ReadLn( F, OneLine );
    WriteLn( OneLine );
    Inc( LineNumber );
    {Every 24 lines, wait for a key}
    if LineNumber = 24 then
    begin
        {Print footer}
        TextAttr := $70;
        Write( 'More? (y/n)' );
        ClrEol;
        {Get a key}
        Ch := ReadKey;
        LineNumber := 1;
        {If the key is not an 'n' , write a new header}
        if Ch <> 'n' then
        begin
            Write( Chr( 13 ), 'File: ', ParamStr( 1 ));
            ClrEol;
        end;
        TextAttr := $7;
        WriteLn;
    end;
{Keep it up until the end of the file, or user command}
until Eof( F ) OR ( Ch = 'n' );
Close( F );
{If the user did not exit, show the EOF footer}
if Ch <> 'n' then
begin
    {Go down to the bottom of the screen}
    while LineNumber < 24 do
    begin
        WriteLn;
        Inc( LineNumber );
    end;
    TextAttr := $70;
    Write( 'End of file' );
    ClrEol;
    Ch := ReadKey;
end;
```

```
    end;
end.
```

This program begins by opening the file to display. The name of the file should be the first parameter on the command line. After opening the file, this program prints the name of the file in inverse video. Next, the program reads each line of the file and prints it on the screen. Every 23 lines the program prints a prompt at the bottom of the screen and waits for the user to press a key.

If the user does not press "n," the program keeps printing lines. The `repeat-until` loop exits when it reaches the end of the file or when the user presses "n." When the loop exits, the program closes the file. If the loop reached the end of the file, the program displays a message to this effect at the bottom of the screen and waits for the user to press a key.

Comments

This utility is designed to work from the command line. You should use the Alt-F9 command in the Turbo Pascal IDE to make this an executable program. To use the program, type the program name followed by the name of the file to view, as follows:

```
view source.pas
```

Warnings

This program does not check whether the file is really a text file. If you try to view a binary file, such as an executable file, the screen is filled with gibberish.

9.5   How do I...

Sort a large file with Turbo Pascal?

Description

Sort programs rely on the ability of the program to swap records until the records are in order. The fastest way to do this is to read the records into memory and sort them there. The trouble with this technique is that a file may not fit into the available memory. This solution uses an algorithm called *sort-merge* to sort files of any size.

See Also

4.2   Sorting strings

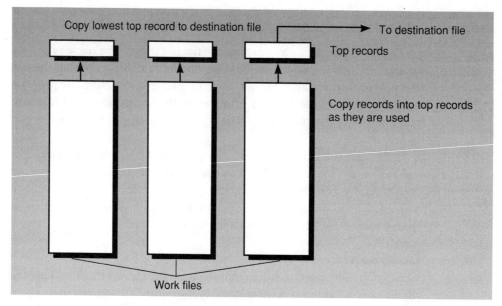

Copy lowest top record to destination file → To destination file

Top records

Copy records into top records as they are used

Work files

Figure 9-5 The merge phase of a sort-merge

Solution

A sort-merge works by dividing the file into pieces that fit into memory, sorting each piece and writing it to a work file, then combining the work files to make the final sorted file. The first step in a sort-merge is to read as much of the file into memory as will fit. The next step is to sort the records in memory. This solution uses the shell sort shown in solution 4.2 during the sort phase. Next, the sorted records are written to a work file. The process is repeated until the entire source file has been read.

The last step is to merge the work files. The first step of the merge is to read a record from each of the work files. These records are checked to find the lowest. The lowest record is written to the destination file, and a new record is read from the corresponding work file. The program keeps moving the lowest record to the destination file, reading new records from the work files, until all of the records have been copied from all of the work files. Figure 9-5 shows how the merge phase works.

To reduce the number of work files, this program performs the merge phase as soon as there are three work files. The resulting file becomes the first work file for the next batch of work files. The process is repeated until all of the records have been read. This technique simplifies the merge because the program must merge only three records at a time.

This program performs the sort-merge:

```
{Program to sort lines}
program sort;

var
   SourceFile : Text;
   WorkFiles : array [1..3] of Text;
   FileCnt : integer;
   FileNumber : integer;
   StrList : array [1..320] of string[100];
   StrCnt : integer;
   FileName : string;
   i, j : integer;

{Shell sort the strings in memory}
procedure SortLines;
var
   i, j, h : integer;
   v : string[100];
begin
    {Shell sort the fields}
    h := 1;
    repeat
        h := 3 * h + 1;
    until h > StrCnt;
    repeat
        h := h DIV 3;
        for i := h + 1 to StrCnt do
        begin
            v := StrList[i];
            j := i;
            while ( StrList[j - h] > v ) AND ( j > h ) do
            begin
                StrList[j] := StrList[j - h];
                j := j - h;
            end;
            StrList[j] := v;
        end
    until h = 1;
end;

{Merge all of the work files into one}
procedure MergeWorkFiles;
var
   MergedFile : Text;
   DoneFlags : array [1..3] of boolean;
   DoneCnt : integer;
   TopStrings : array [1..3] of string[100];
   Min : integer;
begin
    DoneCnt := 0;
    {Get to the beginning of all of the workfiles}
    for i := 1 to FileCnt do
    begin
```

```
    {Set up work files for reading}
    Close( WorkFiles[i] );
    Reset( WorkFiles[i] );
    {Read the first string, or indicate done}
    if NOT Eof( WorkFiles[i] ) then
    begin
        DoneFlags[i] := FALSE;
        ReadLn( WorkFiles[i], TopStrings[i] );
     end
     else
     begin
        DoneFlags[i] := TRUE;
        Inc( DoneCnt );
     end;
end;
{Open the file to merge to}
FileName := 'workfile.   ';
j := FileNumber;
for i := 1 to 3 do
begin
    FileName[13 - i] := Chr( Ord( '0' ) + ( j MOD 10 ) );
    j := j DIV 10;
end;
Inc( FileNumber );
Assign( MergedFile, FileName );
Rewrite( MergedFile );
{While there are files with records}
while DoneCnt < FileCnt do
begin
    {Find the lowest top string}
    Min := 1;
    while DoneFlags[Min] do
        Inc( Min );
    i := 1;
    while i <= FileCnt do
    begin
        if ( NOT DoneFlags[i] )
          AND ( TopStrings[Min] > TopStrings[i] ) then
          Min := i;
        Inc( i );
    end;
    {Write the string}
    WriteLn( MergedFile, TopStrings[Min] );
    {Read a new one from the file used}
    if Eof( WorkFiles[Min] ) then
    begin
        DoneFlags[Min] := TRUE;
        Inc( DoneCnt );
    end
    else
        ReadLn( WorkFiles[Min], TopStrings[Min] );
end;
{Close all of the work files}
```

```
        for i := 1 to FileCnt do
            Close( WorkFiles[i] );
        {Close the merge file}
        Close( MergedFile );
        {Reopen the merge file as a work file}
        Assign( WorkFiles[1], FileName );
        Reset( WorkFiles[1] );
        FileCnt := 1;
end;

begin
    Assign( SourceFile, ParamStr( 1 ));
    Reset( SourceFile );
    FileCnt := 0;
    StrCnt := 0;
    FileNumber := 0;
    repeat
        {Read strings into memory}
        Inc( StrCnt );
        ReadLn( SourceFile, StrList[StrCnt] );
        {See if buffer is full}
        if ( StrCnt = 320 ) OR Eof( SourceFile ) then
        begin
            {Do in memory sort}
            SortLines;
            {Open a work file}
            FileName := 'workfile.   ';
            j := FileNumber;
            for i := 1 to 3 do
            begin
                FileName[13 - i] := Chr( Ord( '0 ') + ( j MOD 10 ));
                j := j DIV 10;
            end;
            Inc( FileNumber );
            Inc( FileCnt );
            Assign( WorkFiles[FileCnt], FileName );
            Rewrite( WorkFiles[FileCnt] );
            {Write the sorted section to a workfile}
            for i := 1 to StrCnt do
                WriteLn( WorkFiles[FileCnt], StrList[i] );
            {If 3 workfiles in use, merge them}
            if FileCnt = 3 then
                MergeWorkFiles;
            StrCnt := 0;
        end;
    until Eof( SourceFile );
    {Close the source}
    Close( SourceFile );
    {Do the final merge}
    MergeWorkFiles;
    {Sorted data is in the first merge file}
    Close( WorkFiles[1] );
    Reset( WorkFiles[1] );
```

```
      {display the sorted records}
      repeat
        ReadLn( WorkFiles[1], StrList[1] );
        WriteLn( StrList[1] );
    until Eof( WorkFiles[1] );
end.
```

The first procedure is the shell sort routine from question 4.2. It has been set up to sort the strings in the array StrList. The next procedure merges the three work files and makes the merged file the first work file.

MergeWorkFiles keeps the first line from each work file in the array TopStrings. It also keeps an array of flags that tell if a given work file has been completely read. When all of the files have been completely read, the merge is done. The last step is to close the merged file and reopen it as the first work file.

The main program reads the lines of the source file, stopping to sort every 320 lines. When it has a sorted list of lines, it writes them to a work file. The name of the work file is computed by concatenating the string "workfile" with a unique number converted to a three-character string. This ensures that no work file is overwritten by a later work file.

When the program has three work files, it calls MergeWorkFiles to merge the work files into a single file. This process continues until there are no more records in the source file. After all of the source records are read, the program does a final merge. This puts the sorted file into the first merge file, which is printed.

Comments

Like the view program in question 9.4, this program is designed to be a command line utility. You should compile it with the Alt-F9 command in the Turbo Pascal IDE. To use it, type the name of the program followed by the name of the file to sort. You will see the sorted file on the screen. You can put the sorted results into a file by using the MS-DOS redirection operator, like this:

```
sort textfile.txt > sorted.txt
```

Warnings

This program requires extra disk space to hold the work files while it is sorting. You must have at least enough free space to accommodate the size of the file being sorted. If the program runs out of disk space, it generates a run-time error and halts.

Search for text with Turbo Pascal?

Description

The directories and subdirectories of the MS-DOS file system make it easy to organize your files into various categories, keeping related files together. It also makes it easy to lose a file in a maze of obscure pathnames. Knowing the name of the file you are looking for helps, but what do you do if you cannot remember the name of the file? This solution helps you find a file by searching all of the files for a text string.

See Also

2.3   Listing files

4.3   Searching for strings

Solution

The first step in searching for files containing a string is to list all of the files on the disk. You solved this problem in question 2.3 by using the Turbo Pascal FindFirst and FindNext routines. Next you need to search the file to see if the string is in it. A brute-force technique would take too long for all of the files on a large hard disk, so it is better to use the Boyer-Moore search from question 4.1.

This program combines solutions 2.3 and 4.1 to make a disk- search utility:

```
{This program searches for files containing a string}
program findtext;
uses Dos;

var
   PathName : string;
   SearchStr : string;
   HomeDir : string;
   Skip : array[0..127] of byte;     {Number of chars to skip}

{Make the skip array for Boyer-Moore search}
procedure MakeArray( Pattern : string );
var
   StrLen : integer;
   i : integer;
begin
    StrLen := Length( Pattern );
```

```
    {Initialize the entire array}
    for i := 0 to 127 do
        Skip[i] := StrLen;
    {Mark the characters that occur in the pattern string}
    for i := 1 to StrLen do
        Skip[Ord( Pattern[i] )] := StrLen - i;
end;

{Use the current Boyer-Moore array to check text}
function Search( Text, Pattern : string ) : integer;
var
  i, j : integer;
  TxtLen, PatLen : integer;
begin
      {Initialize variables}
      PatLen := Length( Pattern );
      TxtLen := Length( Text );
      i := PatLen;
      j := PatLen;
      repeat
              {If the current characters match, back up}
              if Text[i] = Pattern[j] then
              begin
                      i := i - 1;
                      j := j -1;
              end
              else {Characters do not match}
              begin
              {Advance based on values in the skip array}
              if PatLen - j + 1 > Skip[Ord( Text[i] )] then
                      i := i + PatLen - j + 1
              else
                      i := i + Skip[Ord( Text[i] )];
              j := PatLen;
         end;
      until (j < 1) or ( i > TxtLen );
      {Indicate success or failure}
      Search := i + 1;
end;

{Read a file and search each line}
procedure SearchFile( FileName : string );
var
  F : Text;
  TmpStr : string;
  LineNumber : integer;
begin
      {Open the file}
      Assign( F, FileName );
      Reset( F );
      {Keep track of the line number}
      LineNumber := 1;
      repeat
```

```
              {Read a line}
              ReadLn( F, TmpStr );
              {See if it contains the pattern}
              if Search( TmpStr, SearchStr ) < Length( TmpStr ) then
                  {If matched, print the name of the file and the
                   line number}
                  WriteLn( 'File: ',FileName,' Line: ',LineNumber );
              Inc( LineNumber );
      until Eof( F );
      Close( F );
end;

{Recursive routine to get all of the files on the disk}
procedure GetFiles;
var
   Len : integer;
   FileRec : SearchRec;
begin
      {Save the length of the pathname}
      Len := Length( PathName );
      {Go to test directory}
      if Len <> 1 then
              Dec( PathName[0] );
      ChDir( PathName );
      {Write the name of the directory so the user knows the
       program is working}
      WriteLn( 'Directory: ', PathName );
      if Len <> 1 then
              Inc( PathName[0] );
      {Get the first file in the directory}
      PathName := PathName + '*.*';
      FindFirst( PathName, Directory, FileRec );
      while DosError = 0 do
      begin
              {If the file is a directory, get its files}
              if FileRec.Attr = Directory then
              begin
                  if FileRec.Name[1] <> '.' then
                  begin
                     PathName[0] := Chr( Len );
                     PathName := PathName + FileRec.Name + '\';
                     GetFiles;
                     PathName[0] := Chr( Len );
                     if Len <> 1 then
                         Dec( PathName[0] );
                     ChDir( PathName );
                     if Len <> 1 then
                         Inc( PathName[0] );
                  end;
              end
              else {If regular file, search it}
                  SearchFile( FileRec.Name );
          {Get the next file in the current directory}
```

```
        FindNext( FileRec );
    end;
end;

begin
        {Get the string to find from the command line}
        SearchStr := ParamStr( 1 );
        {Make a Boyer-Moore array from the string}
        MakeArray( SearchStr );
        {Start the search for files}
        PathName := '\';
        GetDir( 0, HomeDir );
        GetFiles;
        {Go back to the original directory}
        ChDir( HomeDir );
        ReadLn;
end.
```

The routines MakeArray and Search implement the Boyer-Moore algorithm described in question 4.1. Because the string to look for does not change, you need to call the MakeArray routine only once at the beginning of the program. The Search routine uses the array created by MakeArray to look at each line of every file to find matches.

The SearchFile routine searches a file by reading each line from the file and calling Search. If there is a match, SearchFile prints the name of the file and the line number that contains the match. The entire file is searched to find all matching lines.

The GetFiles procedure finds filenames and passes them to SearchFile. GetFiles uses the Turbo Pascal FindFirst and FindNext routines to search directories, as described in question 2.3. When GetFiles finds a directory name, it adjusts the PathName variable to include the new directory, then calls itself to read the new directory. GetFiles changes the current directory to the directory being searched. The reason is that MS-DOS can open a file in the current directory much faster than it can open a file in some other directory. If the name found is that of a regular file, GetFiles calls SearchFile to find any matches.

The main program gets the string to find from the command line and passes it to MakeArray to get ready for the Boyer-Moore search. Next, the program gets the pathname of the current directory so that it can return to it after searching the rest of the disk. After saving the current directory, the program calls GetFiles to begin the search. The last step is to restore the current directory and exit.

Comments

To use this utility, you should compile it into an executable program. Then type the name of the program followed by the text to search for. Note that because of the way that the command line is parsed, you cannot search for strings that include spaces. If you want to allow searches that include spaces, see solution 5.1 for how to read such strings from the command line.

Warnings
Whenever you use recursive routines, such as `GetFiles`, you run the risk of overflowing the stack. This program is vulnerable if you have deeply nested subdirectories. If you are having trouble searching a disk, try increasing the stack size of the program by using the memory command in the options menu of the Turbo Pascal IDE.

9.7   How do I...

Compress and restore files with Turbo Pascal?

Description
A corollary to Parkinson's law is that the amount of data you have to save expands to overfill the available disk space. Before you rush out and pay money for another hard drive, you should look into the possibility of compressing the files so that they take up less space. This solution shows how to use Huffman encoding to compress and restore files.

See Also
4.8   Compressing strings with Huffman encoding

Solution
In solution 4.8, you learned how to use Huffman encoding to compress a string. This solution goes a step further and compresses an entire file. If you review solution 4.8, you'll remember that you need a table of character frequencies to build the tree that gives the Huffman codes for each character. To restore a compressed file properly, you must have this table, so it is stored in the compressed file.

This solution includes two programs: one to compress the file and one to restore it. Here is the program that compresses the file:

```
{Compress a file}
program compress;

type
    Node = record
        Freq : integer;
        Parent : integer;
```

```
        Left : integer;
        Right : integer;
    end;


var
   Tree : Array[0..511] of Node;
   List : Array[0..255] of integer;

{Sort the list of indexes based on frequency}
procedure SortList;
var
   i, j, h : integer;
   Tmp : integer;
begin
    h := 364;
    repeat
        h := h DIV 3;
        for i := h + 1 to 256 do
        begin
            Tmp := List[i - 1];
            j := i;
            while ( Tree[List[j - h - 1]].Freq < Tree[Tmp].Freq )
                AND (j > h) do
            begin
                List[j - 1] := List[j - h - 1];
                j := j - h;
            end;
            List[j - 1] := Tmp;
        end
    until h = 1;
end;

{Compute frequencies and make the Huffman tree}
procedure MakeTree( var F : file );
var
   i, j : integer;
   ListCnt : integer;
   TreeCnt : integer;
   NewFreq : integer;
   Buffer : array [0..1023] of byte;
   Count : integer;
begin
    for i := 0 to 255 do
    begin
        Tree[i].Freq := 0;
        Tree[i].Parent := -1;
        List[i] := i;
    end;
    {Read source file to calculate frequencies}
    repeat
        BlockRead( F, Buffer, 1024, Count );
        for i := 0 to Count - 1 do
```

```
            begin
                Inc( Tree[Buffer[i]].Freq );
                {If a value gets above 255 scale all values down}
                if Tree[Buffer[i]].Freq = 255 then
                for j := 0 to Count - 1 do
                    Tree[Buffer[i]].Freq
                        := ( Tree[Buffer[i]].Freq + 1) DIV 2;
            end;
        until Eof( F );
        SortList;
        ListCnt := 255;
        {Back up to nonzero frequency}
        while ( ListCnt > 0) AND ( Tree[List[ListCnt]].Freq = 0 ) do
            Dec( ListCnt );
        {Create the tree}
        TreeCnt := 255;
        while ListCnt > 0 do
        begin
            {Make a new tree node}
            Inc( TreeCnt );
            {Combine the top two frequencies}
            NewFreq := Tree[List[ListCnt]].Freq
                    + Tree[List[ListCnt - 1]].Freq;
            Tree[TreeCnt].Freq := NewFreq;
            Tree[TreeCnt].Parent := -1;
            {Make the children of the new node the old top two}
            Tree[TreeCnt].Left := List[ListCnt];
            Tree[TreeCnt].Right := List[ListCnt - 1];
            {Make the children point back}
            Tree[List[ListCnt - 1]].Parent := -TreeCnt;
            Tree[List[ListCnt]].Parent := TreeCnt;
            Dec( ListCnt );
            i := ListCnt;
            {Sort the new node into the list}
            while ( i > 0 ) AND (NewFreq > Tree[List[i - 1]].Freq ) do
            begin
                List[i] := List[i - 1];
                Dec( i );
            end;
            List[i] := TreeCnt;
        end;
end;

{Read and convert the source file}
procedure Encode( var SFile, DFile : file );
var
    i : integer;
    NodeNumb : integer;
    InBuff, OutBuff : array [0..1023] of byte;
    ICount, OCount : integer;
    BitNumb : byte;
    Code : longint;
    CodeBit : byte;
```

```
begin
        {Initialize index and mask for output data}
        OCount := 0;
        BitNumb := 7;
        OutBuff[0] := 0;
        repeat
                {Read 1024 bytes from the source file}
                BlockRead( SFile, InBuff, 1024, ICount );
                {Compress each byte in the source file}
                for i := 0 to ICount - 1 do
                begin
                        {Go to the node that corresponds to the
                        source byte being encoded}
                        NodeNumb := InBuff[i];
                        CodeBit := 0;
                        {Code will be the encoded value}
                        Code := 0;
                        {Go until you get to the root node}
                        while NodeNumb <> List[0] do
                        begin
                                {Set a bit if the node is a right child}
                                if Tree[NodeNumb].Parent > 0 then
                                    Code := Code OR ( 1 SHL CodeBit );
                                Inc( CodeBit );
                                {Go to the parent node}
                                NodeNumb := Abs( Tree[NodeNumb].Parent );
                        end;
                        {Copy bits from Code to the output file}
                        while CodeBit > 0 do
                        begin
                                Dec( CodeBit );
                                if (Code AND ( 1 SHL CodeBit )) <> 0 then
                                    OutBuff[OCount]
                                        := Ord(OutBuff[OCount])
                                        OR( 1 SHL BitNumb );
                                {Dec BitNumb until all eight bits
                                 are copied}
                                if BitNumb > 0 then
                                    Dec( BitNumb )
                                else
                                begin
                                    {If the output buffer is full,
                                     write the block}
                                    if OCount = 1023 then
                                    begin
                                        BlockWrite( DFile,OutBuff
                                                ,1024,OCount );
                                        OCount := 0;
                                    end
                                else {Otherwise go to the next byte}
                                    Inc( OCount );
                                    BitNumb := 7;
                                    OutBuff[OCount] := 0;
```

```
                        end;
                    end;
                end;
        until Eof( SFile );
        {Write any left over data}
        if BitNumb <> 7 then
            Inc( OCount );
        if OCount > 0 then
            BlockWrite( DFile, OutBuff, OCount, i );
    end;

var
    SourceFile : file;
    DestFile : file;
    DestName : string;
    i : integer;
    Count : integer;

begin
    {Open the source file}
    Assign( SourceFile, ParamStr( 1 ));
    Reset( SourceFile, 1 );
    MakeTree( SourceFile );
    {Go back to the beginning of the source file}
    Seek( SourceFile, 0 );
    {Create the destination filename}
    DestName := ParamStr( 1 );
    for i := 1 to Length( DestName) do
        if DestName[i] = '.' then
            DestName[0] := Chr( i - 1 );
    DestName := DestName + '.cmp';
    {Open the destination file}
    Assign( DestFile, DestName );
    Rewrite( DestFile, 1 );
    {Write the frequencies to the file}
    for i := 0 to 255 do
        BlockWrite( DestFile, Tree[i].Freq, 1, Count );
    {Read the file and compress}
    Encode( SourceFile, DestFile );
    {Close the files}
    Close( DestFile );
    Close( SourceFile );
end.
```

The Huffman tree algorithm requires that the array of frequencies be in sorted order. This is the reason for the SortList procedure. Because other routines in the program require the character array to be in character order, SortList actually sorts the array List, which is a list of pointers to the first 256 elements of Tree.

The next procedure, MakeTree, reads the source file, counting each byte found, then sorts the frequencies and creates a Huffman tree (see question

4.8 for details on this routine). In the compressed file, each character in the frequency list occupies 1 byte. If there are more than 255 of any byte in the source file, `MakeArray` divides all of the values in the frequency list in half to ensure that all of the values will fit in a single byte.

The third procedure is the `Encode` routine, which converts the source file to a compressed file. The routine in question 4.8 has been modified slightly so that it reads from a source file and writes to another file. Each of the two files has a 1024-byte buffer that acts as a window into the file. When the buffer from the source file has been processed, the next block is read from the file. Also, when the compressed file buffer is full, it is written to the compressed file.

The main program opens the source file and calls `MakeTree` to get the frequencies. Next, it creates the filename for the compressed file by changing the extension to ".cmp". After opening the file, the program writes the frequencies to the compressed file. The only job left is calling `Encode` to compress the data.

The second program decompresses the compressed file by reading the frequencies in the file and building a Huffman tree from them.

```
{Decompress a file}
program restore;

type
   Node = record
       Freq : integer;
       Parent : integer;
       Left : integer;
       Right : integer;
   end;

var
   Tree : Array[0..511] of Node;
   List : Array[0..255] of integer;

{Sort the list of indexes based on frequency}
procedure SortList;
var
   i, j, h : integer;
   Tmp : integer;
begin
    h := 364;
    repeat
        h := h DIV 3;
        for i := h + 1 to 256 do
        begin
            Tmp := List[i - 1];
            j := i;
            while ( Tree[List[j - h - 1]].Freq < Tree[Tmp].Freq )
```

```
                AND (j > h) do
            begin
                List[j - 1] := List[j - h - 1];
                j := j - h;
            end;
            List[j - 1] := Tmp;
        end
    until h = 1;
end;

{Make a Huffman tree from the frequencies found in the
 compressed file}
procedure MakeTree( var F : file );
var
  i, j : integer;
  ListCnt : integer;
  TreeCnt : integer;
  NewFreq : integer;
  Buffer : array [0..1023] of byte;
  Count : integer;
begin
    {Read the frequencies from the compressed file}
    for i := 0 to 255 do
    begin
        Tree[i].Freq := 0;
        BlockRead( F, Tree[i].Freq, 1, Count );
        Tree[i].Parent := -1;
        List[i] := i;
    end;
    {This is the same as for the compress program}
    SortList;
    ListCnt := 255;
    {Back up to nonzero frequency}
    while ( ListCnt > 0) AND ( Tree[List[ListCnt]].Freq = 0 ) do
        Dec( ListCnt );
    TreeCnt := 255;
    while ListCnt > 0 do
    begin
        Inc( TreeCnt );
        NewFreq := Tree[List[ListCnt]].Freq
              + Tree[List[ListCnt - 1]].Freq;
        Tree[TreeCnt].Freq := NewFreq;
        Tree[TreeCnt].Parent := -1;
        Tree[TreeCnt].Left := List[ListCnt];
        Tree[TreeCnt].Right := List[ListCnt - 1];
        Tree[List[ListCnt - 1]].Parent := -TreeCnt;
        Tree[List[ListCnt]].Parent := TreeCnt;
        Dec( ListCnt );
        i := ListCnt;
        while ( i > 0 ) AND ( NewFreq > Tree[List[i - 1]].Freq ) do
        begin
            List[i] := List[i - 1];
            Dec( i );
```

```
            end;
         List[i] := TreeCnt;
      end;
end;

{Convert Huffman codes back to bytes}
procedure Decode( var SFile, DFile : file );
var
   CharNumb : integer;
   BitNumb : byte;
   NodeNumb : integer;
   Buffer : array [0..1023] of byte;
   Count : integer;
   OutBuff : array [0..1023] of byte;
   OutPoint, OCount : integer;
begin
   BitNumb := 7;
   OutPoint := 0;
   repeat
      {Read a block from the compressed file}
      BlockRead( SFile, Buffer, 1024, Count );
      CharNumb := 0;
      {Do all of the bytes in the buffer one bit at a time}
      while CharNumb < Count do
      begin
           NodeNumb := List[0];  {Start at the root}
           {Search to a final node}
           while NodeNumb > 255 do
           begin
               {Use the bit to decide to go left or right}
               if ( Ord( Buffer[CharNumb] )
                   AND ( 1 SHL BitNumb )) = 0 then
                   NodeNumb := Tree[NodeNumb].Right
               else
                   NodeNumb := Tree[NodeNumb].Left;
               {Decrement through the bits}
               if BitNumb > 0 then
                   Dec( BitNumb )
               else
               begin
                   {If all bits used, go to the next byte}
                   Inc( CharNumb );
                   {See if done with the buffer}
                   if CharNumb >= Count then
                   begin
                       if Eof( SFile ) then
                         NodeNumb := -1
                       else
                       begin
                          {Read the next buffer}
                          BlockRead( SFile,Buffer
                                    ,1024,Count );
                          CharNumb := 0;
```

```
                            end;
                        end;
                        BitNumb := 7;
                    end;
                end;
                {If not the end of the file store the result}
                if NodeNumb >= 0 then
                begin
                    OutBuff[OutPoint] := NodeNumb;
                    Inc( OutPoint );
                    {If the buffer is full, write it}
                    if OutPoint = 1024 then
                    begin
                        BlockWrite( DFile, OutBuff
                        , 1024, OCount );
                        OutPoint := 0;
                    end;
                end;
            end;
        until Eof( SFile );
        {Write any left over buffer}
        if OutPoint > 0 then
            BlockWrite( DFile, OutBuff, OutPoint, OCount );
end;

var
    SourceFile : file;
    DestFile : file;
    SourceName : string;
    i : integer;
    Count : integer;

begin
    {Create the source filename}
    SourceName := ParamStr( 1 );
    for i := 1 to Length(SourceName) do
        if SourceName[i] = '.' then
            SourceName[0] := Chr( i - 1 );
    SourceName := SourceName + '.cmp';
    {Open the source file}
    Assign( SourceFile, SourceName );
    Reset( SourceFile, 1 );
    {Read the frequencies and build a tree}
    MakeTree( SourceFile );
    {Open the destination file}
    Assign( DestFile, ParamStr( 1 ));
    Rewrite( DestFile, 1 );
    {Read the file and uncompress}
    Decode( SourceFile, DestFile );
    {Close the files}
    Close( DestFile );
    Close( SourceFile );
end
```

The first difference between this program and the compress program is the way the `MakeTree` routine works. Instead of reading the whole source file to count the frequencies, it gets the frequencies by reading the first 256 bytes from the compressed file. Once the frequencies are in `Tree`, the rest of `MakeTree` is the same as for the compress program.

The next difference is that the `Encode` routine is replaced by the `Decode` routine. This routine is the same as the one in question 4.8 except for changes to read the compressed file and write to a destination file.

The main program is also similar to the compress program. Instead of creating the name of the destination file it creates the name of the compressed file.

Comments

To use these programs, you should compile them to executable programs. Each of these programs requires a filename argument on the command line, as follows:

```
compress test.txt
```

This command creates a file called `test.cmp`. To restore the original file, use this:

```
restore test.txt
```

This command reads `test.cmp` and creates `test.txt`. Note that you can restore a compressed file to a new file with a different extension.

Warnings

One of the drawbacks of the Huffman compression routine is the possibility that the compressed file will be larger than the original file. This happens when most of the 256 possible bytes occur with nearly even frequency in the file.

10

USING

TURBO VISION

AND

TURBO PASCAL

FOR

WINDOWS

10

uch of the time spent writing a major application is devoted to the user interface. Because users work directly with the interface, it shapes their impressions of the program. A bad user interface taints the entire program. Because so much effort goes into the user interface, anything that simplifies the writing of interfaces improves programs and reduces programming time. Turbo Pascal version 6.0 and Turbo Pascal for Windows are two good tools for developing user interfaces. Turbo Pascal version 6.0 includes Turbo Vision, an object-oriented library of routines that handles interface events. Turbo Pascal for Windows lets you write programs for Microsoft Windows, a graphically oriented computing environment.

The objects in Turbo Vision define such things as pull-down menus, dialog boxes, and windows. Turbo Vision can handle input from both the keyboard and the mouse. Because it is object-oriented, your program need only describe the differences between your program and the default action. For example, the default window-drawing action is to fill it with blanks. To put text in the window, just make an object that inherits from the basic window object but includes its own virtual `draw` method.

Turbo Pascal for Windows makes programs that are compatible with Microsoft Windows. It includes functions and procedures that call Windows routines for creating pull-down menus, dialog boxes, and sophisticated graphics. Turbo Pascal for Windows uses object-oriented techniques to simplify many aspects of Windows programming. To write Windows applications with Turbo Pascal, simply establish the appropriate inheritance of objects and add the virtual methods that define your unique application.

Turbo Vision and Turbo Pascal for Windows are event-driven programming environments. That means that routines run in response to some event, such as a keypress, a mouse action, or a menu command. Turbo Vision programs run on MS-DOS computers in text mode, whereas Turbo Pascal programs run on systems running Microsoft Windows in graphics modes.

When you write event-driven programs, you must adopt a new way of thinking about program design. The solutions in this chapter show you how to design event-driven programs using the objects of Turbo Vision and Turbo Pascal for Windows. Solution 10.1 shows the basic structure of an event-driven program. Other solutions show how to set up and respond to different events.

CREATING TURBO VISION AND TURBO PASCAL FOR WINDOWS APPLICATIONS

All Turbo Vision and Turbo Pascal for Windows programs have the same structure. Solution 10.1 shows the simplest possible program. You can create other applications by modifying the objects in the basic program. For example, solution 10.2 shows you how to modify the initialization of the application object to include a menu. Once you have a menu, you have events to handle, so solution 10.2 also shows how to respond to an event.

Turbo Vision and Turbo Pascal for Windows programs direct output to windows. Solution 10.3 shows how to modify the window object to make it do what you want.

One important type of window is the dialog box, which contains controls such as text-entry fields, list boxes, and buttons. Filling in a field or pressing a button generates an event. Programs must define the fields of the dialog box and respond to the events to use dialog boxes. Solution 10.4 shows how to display dialog boxes and respond to the events generated.

Graphics are an important part of Turbo Pascal for Windows. Most programs use graphics to enhance the user interface in some way. Solution 10.5 shows you how to create graphics and retain them so that images are automatically redrawn when the user changes the window.

It is possible to separate an application from its dialog boxes, menus, and windows. You can put these features into a separate resource file where you can edit them to meet the changing user interface needs of the program without affecting the core of the application. This technique is often used to create versions of the program in different languages. Solution 10.6 shows how to use resource files in your programs.

10.1   How do I...

Create a basic Turbo Vision or Turbo Pascal application for Windows programs

Description
The main code of a Turbo Vision or Turbo Pascal for Windows program always remains the same. The main code uses an object type called TApplication to do its job. Different applications make different modifications to parts of TApplication to do their jobs. This solution shows the simplest possible application. All other applications begin with this one.

See Also
10.2   Adding menus

10.3   Creating windows

10.4   Using dialog boxes

Solution
The first step in creating a Turbo Vision application is declaring an instance of an object derived from the object TApplication. The program code calls three methods for this object: Init, Run, and Done. The Init method initializes and draws the object. The Run method handles events. The Done method closes the application in preparation for returning to MS-DOS.

```
{This is a test T-Vision program}
program TTest;
uses App;

type
    {Derive an application object}
    TMyApp = Object( TApplication )
    end;

var
  MyApp : TMyApp;

begin
    {Initialize the object}
    MyApp.Init;
    {Handle events}
    MyApp.Run;
    {Clean up before exiting}
    MyApp.Done;
end.
```

The most important statement in this program is uses App. The App unit contains the objects used by Turbo Vision. Without it, the program is just like any other Turbo Pascal program.

The TApplication object in this program is MyApp. The main program initializes, runs, and closes MyApp. Figure 10-1 shows the screen for this program. It is similar in form to the Turbo Pascal IDE screen because the IDE was written using Turbo Vision.

An application for Turbo Pascal for Windows looks similar to the one for Turbo Vision. The differences are in the uses statement and the Init method.

```
{This is a test Windows program}
program WTest;
uses WObjects;

type
    {Derive an application object}
    TMyApp = Object( TApplication )
    end;

var
    MyApp : TMyApp;

begin
    {Initialize the object}
    MyApp.Init( 'TestProg' );
    {Handle events}
    MyApp.Run;
    {Clean up before exiting}
    MyApp.Done;
end.
```

This program uses the WObjects unit instead of App, and the Init method takes an argument that sets the application name.

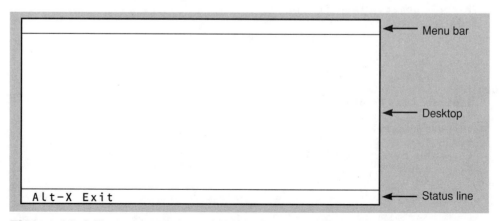

Figure 10-1 The screen output of simple Turbo Vision program

Enhancements

This program is not much by itself, but it is the basis of all Turbo Vision and Turbo Pascal for Windows programs. The TApplication object MyApp represents this simple application. As with any other object, you can create an object that inherits features from this one. That is exactly how you expand this simple program into a complete application. Table 10-1 shows some of the fields and methods that make up a Turbo Pascal for Windows TApplication object. By overloading these methods with methods of your own, you can change the behavior of the application.

Name	Description
KBHandlerWnd	Pointer to the window that is currently getting input from the keyboard.
MainWindow	Pointer to the main window for the application.
Init	Constructor method for the application. If you overload this method, be sure to call the default method from your method.
Done	Destructor method for the object.
ExecDialog	Method to execute a dialog object.
InitApplication	Called during the first instance of the program.
InitInstance	If the program is started while another copy of the program is running, this method is called instead of InitApplication.
InitMainWindow	Creates the main window for the application. Overload this method to create specialized main windows.

Table 10-1 Methods and fields for TApplication objects

The next program shows how to create an object that inherits the TApplication object. It overloads the InitMainWindow method to create a new application window when the program is started.

```
{A simple Windows program}
program Win1;
uses WObjects;

type
   MyApp = Object( TApplication )
             procedure InitMainWindow; virtual;
   end;

{Initialize the main application window}
procedure MyApp.InitMainWindow;
```

```
begin
      MainWindow := New( PWindow
            , Init( nil, 'First Windows Program' ));
end;

var
  MyApp : TMyApp;

begin
    MyApp.Init( 'TestProg' );
    MyApp.Run;
    MyApp.Done;
end.
```

10.2   How do I...

Add menus to a Turbo Vision or Turbo Pascal for Windows program?

Description

Turbo Vision and Turbo Pascal for Windows programs use pull-down menus to let the user enter commands. To generate menus, you add menu objects to the TApplication object. The user's selection of a menu item generates an event that you tell the program how to handle.

See Also

9.2   Making pull-down menus

10.1   Creating a basic application for Windows programs

10.2   Creating windows

10.6   Using resources

Solution

Adding a menu to a Turbo Vision program is a two-step process. The first step is initializing the menu objects; the second is handling the events generated by the menu. The TApplication object contains a variable MenuBar, which is a pointer to a MenuBar object that defines the menu. This variable is set up by the InitMenuBar method in the TApplication object. To change the menu, you change this method.

The HandleEvent method handles application events. Each event is described in a TEvent variable of this structure:

```
TEvent = record
        What : Word;                           {Tells what type of event}
        case Word of
```

```
        evNothing : ();              {A do-nothing event}
        evMouse : (                  {A mouse event}
             Buttons : Byte;         {Button state}
             Double : boolean;       {Double-click flag}
             Where : TPoint );       {Location of the cursor}
        evKeyDown : (                {A keyboard event}
             case Integer of
                 0 : ( KeyCode : word);  {What key}
                 1 : ( CharCode : char;  {ASCII character}
                     ScanCode : byte )); {Keyboard scan code}
        evMessage : (
             Command : Word;         {Type of command}
             case Word of            {Command info}
                 0 : ( InfoPtr : Pointer );
                 1 : ( InfoLong : Longint );
                 2 : ( InfoWord : Word );
                 3 : ( InfoInt : Integer );
                 4 : ( InfoByte : Byte );
                 5 : ( InfoChar : Char );
```

When handling an event, the program first checks the What field to determine the type of the event. Events that result from menu selections are evMessage events. When there is an evMessage event, you need to check Command to determine what command to execute. The next program shows how to set up the menu and handle the events it generates:

```
{This is a test T-Vision program with menus}
program TMenu;
uses App, Objects, Menus, Drivers, Views, Crt;

type
   TMyApp = Object( TApplication )
        procedure InitMenuBar; virtual;
        procedure HandleEvent( var Event : TEvent ); virtual;
   end;

{Define event numbers}
const
   cmMyEvent = 1000;

{Replacement method to initialize menus}
procedure TMyApp.InitMenuBar;
var
  Rect : TRect;
begin
   {Get the dimensions of the screen}
   GetExtent( Rect );
   {Make a one-line box for the menu bar}
   Rect.B.Y := Rect.A.Y + 1;
   {Fill in the menu bar}
   MenuBar := New( PMenuBar, Init( Rect, NewMenu(
      NewSubMenu( '~F~ile', hcNoContext, NewMenu(
          NewItem( '~O~pen','F3',kbF3,cmMyEvent, hcNoContext,
```

```
                NewItem( '~N~ew', 'F4',kbF4,cmQuit, hcNoContext,
                NewLine(
                NewItem( '~Q~uit','F3',kbF3,cmQuit, hcNoContext,
                nil ))))),
        NewSubMenu( '~E~dit', hcNoContext, NewMenu(
                NewItem( '~C~ut', '',kbNoKey, cmQuit, hcNoContext,
                NewItem( 'Cop~y~','',kbNoKey, cmQuit, hcNoContext,
                NewItem( '~P~aste','',kbNoKey, cmQuit, hcNoContext,
                nil )))),
        nil )))));
end;

{Procedure to make a noise}
procedure Beep;
begin
    Sound( 220 );
    Delay( 200 );
    NoSound;
end;

{Replacement method to handle events}
procedure TMyApp.HandleEvent( var Event : TEvent );
begin
    {Do default event handling}
    TApplication.HandleEvent( Event );
    {See if the event is a command}
    if Event.What = evCommand then
    begin
        case Event.Command of
            cmMyEvent : Beep;
        else
            exit;
        end;
        ClearEvent( Event );
    end;
end;

var
   MyApp : TMyApp;

begin
    MyApp.Init;
    MyApp.Run;
    MyApp.Done;
end.
```

Notice that several new units (Objects, Menus, Drivers, and Views, all at the beginning of the program) are required to run this program. These units contain the various objects required to create menus and handle events. Also notice that two methods for TApplication objects have been added. The first is InitMenuBar, which sets up the menu.

The first step in setting up the menu bar is determining the size and location of the window that contains the menu bar. The first two statements in the `InitMenuBar` method compute a one-line rectangle at the top of the screen. Next, the method uses the `New` function to allocate a `MenuBar` object on the heap. To see what is happening in the `Init` routine, you need to dissect the statement that returns the pointer for `MenuBar`. The format of the `Init` method is

```
Init( Rectangle, NewMenus );
```

where `Rectangle` is the rectangle for the menu bar and `NewMenus` is a pointer to the first submenu. The `NewMenu` function, which returns the pointer, gets a pointer from the `NewSubMenu` function, which has this format:

```
NewSubMenu( Name, HelpContext, SubMenu, NextMenu );
```

Here, `Name` is the name of the submenu, `HelpContext` is a number that can be used to display help information, `SubMenu` is a pointer to a list of menu items, and `NextMenu` is a pointer to the next pull-down menu. Each new pull-down menu goes into the previous menu's `NextMenu` field. The last menu has nil in this field. The `SubMenu` pointer comes from a call to `NewItem` which looks like this:

```
NewItem( Name, KeyPrompt, KeyNo, Command, HelpContext
    , NextItem )
```

Here, `Name` is the name of the menu item, `KeyPrompt` is the text for the hot key for this item, `KeyNo` is the code for the hot key, `Command` is the number of the command message, `HelpContext` is the help section number, and `NextItem` is a pointer to the next item in the menu.

Nesting the calls to `NewItem`, `NewSubMenu`, and `NewMenu` makes it easier to see how the menus relate to each other.

In the calls to `NewItem` most of the items use `cmQuit` in the command field. This command, which is automatically handled by the event handler, causes the program to exit. The command for the `Open` item is `cmMyEvent`. This constant, declared in the `const` sections, identifies the event. Some event numbers are reserved for use by Turbo Vision and should not be used. The available numbers are from 100 to 255 and 1000 to 65535.

The `HandleEvent` method is called in response to an event, such as the user selecting a menu item. It begins by calling the parent event handler, which handles most events. Next it checks the `What` field of the event record to see if the event is a command. If so, the method checks the `Command` field to see what kind of command it is. If the command is `cmMyEvent`, `HandleEvent` calls the `Beep` procedure, which generates a noise.

Turbo Pascal for Windows handles menus and events in a different way. Windows menus are stored as resources that are bound to the program's executable file. This simplifies the program, because loading the menu is just a matter of including the resource file and loading the menu resource. It does complicate the programming process because you need to use some other utility to create a resource file.

Events are also handled differently. Instead of using one method to sort out all of the events, Turbo Pascal for Windows uses a special method referred to by a number instead of a name. This means that each event has its own method.

The event methods are part of TWindow objects, which represent windows in the program. Everything that the user does or the program displays is mediated by a window object. To create special-purpose windows, you can create an object that inherits from the TWindow object and overloads methods. Table 10-2 lists some of the fields and methods in TWindow objects.

Name	Description
Scroller	Pointer to the window's scroll bar object.
Init	Constructor for new windows.
InitResource	Constructor for a resource window.
Done	Destructor for the window.
DefWndProc	Calls the default message handler.
GetID	Get the window identifier.
GetWindowClass	Gets the window class.
Paint	Draws on the window.
WMActivate	Called when the window gets or loses the keyboard focus.
WMCreate	Called when the window is created.
WMDestroy	Called when the window is being destroyed.
WMSize	Called when the window size is changed.

Table 10-2 The TWindow object

Turbo Pascal for Windows comes with the resource file STDWNDS.RES, which contains resources for standard dialog boxes and menus. The following sample program uses a menu from the STDWNDS.RES resource file to demonstrate the use of menus in Windows programs:

```
{This is a Windows program with menus}
program WMenus;
```

```
uses WObjects, WinTypes, WinProcs;

{$R STDWNDS.RES}
type
        {Define the application object}
        TMyApp = Object( TApplication )
                procedure InitMainWindow; Virtual;
        end;
        {Define a window object}
        AWindowPtr = ^AWindow;
        AWindow = Object( TWindow )
                constructor Init( TheParent:PWindowsObject
                        ; TheTitle:PChar );
                {Method for menu event}
                procedure ShowText( Var Msg : TMessage )
                        ; virtual cm_First + 24327;
        end;

{Method to initialize the application}
procedure TMyApp.InitMainWindow;
begin
     MainWindow := New( AWindowPtr,Init( nil,'Windows Program' ));
end;

{Method for initializing the window}
constructor AWindow.Init( TheParent : PWindowsObject
        ; TheTitle : PChar );
begin
        {Do the default init stuff}
        TWindow.Init( TheParent, TheTitle );
        {Load the menu from the resources}
        Attr.Menu := LoadMenu( HInstance, 'FILECOMMANDS' );
end;

{Respond to the "Open" command}
procedure AWindow.ShowText( var Msg : TMessage );
var
        TmpDC : HDC;
begin
        {Get a device context}
        TmpDC := GetDC( HWindow );
        {Write a text string}
        TextOut( TmpDC, 100, 100, 'Event occurred', 13 );
end;

var
  MyApp : TMyApp;

begin
    MyApp.Init( 'TestProg' );
    MyApp.Run;
    MyApp.Done;
end.
```

The {$R} directive at the beginning of the program tells the compiler to link in resources from the file STDWNDS.RES. After compiling the program, Turbo Pascal copies the resources from STDWNDS.RES to the end of the .EXE file. The program reads resources from this file as needed. Question 10.6 gives more information on resources.

The AWindow object represents the main window of the program. This object is the parent of the menu object loaded in the window's Init method. The procedure for loading a menu is called LoadMenu. The arguments for this procedure are HInstance, which is an inherited field for windows, and the name of the menu resource to load.

The definition of the AWindow method ShowText shows how events are handled in Turbo Pascal for Windows. The expression after the virtual keyword defines the event to be handled. In this case, the event is 24327, which is the command number for the Open menu selection in the STDWNDS.RES file. When the Open command is executed, Windows puts event number 24327 in the queue, which calls the ShowText method. ShowText writes a string to the window to show that something happened.

Comments

Question 10.6 discusses some ways to make resource files with different menus for Windows programs. Part of the process of defining menus is to assign command numbers to each menu selection. This number defines the methods that execute the command. You may want to define constants for each command number in the const section of your program to make it easy to remember what number goes with what command.

10.3   How do I...

Create windows using Turbo Vision or Turbo Pascal for Windows?

Description

Turbo Vision and Turbo Pascal for Windows programs send all output to windows. Things get complicated when there is more than one window on the screen. In this case, your program must know what window to write to. A further complication is that one window may cover another. The drawing routines automatically handle writing to a covered window. When you uncover the window, however, it should display everything it contains.

See Also

Solution

In a Turbo Vision application, you must first create the window to hold the data. Your program can create the window in response to an event or as part of the normal startup. When you create the window object, you must also create a TView object for the interior of the window. This interior object is the one you use when you want to write text. The interior object includes a method called Draw, which draws the window text on the screen. The application object calls this method as needed to display the window.

The following program creates a window as part of the menu initialization routine:

```
{This is a T-Vision program to show a window}
program TDialog;
uses App, Objects, Menus, Drivers, Views, Crt;

type
      {Application object}
      TMyApp = Object( TApplication )
            procedure InitMenuBar; virtual;
      end;
      {Object for the window}
      AWindowPtr = ^AWindow;
      AWindow = object( TWindow )
            constructor Init( Rect:TRect; DlgHead:String
                        ; Numb:integer );
      end;
      {Object for the interior of the window}
      AInteriorPtr = ^AInterior;
      AInterior = object( TView )
            constructor Init( var Rect:TRect );
            procedure Draw; virtual;
      end;

{Initialize the window when the program starts}
procedure TMyApp.InitMenuBar;
var
   Window : AWindowPtr;
   Rect : TRect;
begin
      {Do the default menu initialization}
      TApplication.InitMenuBar;
      {Create the window}
      Rect.Assign( 10, 10, 50, 20 );
      Window := New( AWindowPtr, Init( Rect,'Sample window', 1 ));
      DeskTop^.Insert( Window );
end;
```

```
{Initialize the interior}
constructor AInterior.Init( var Rect : TRect );
begin
        {Do the default initialization}
        TView.Init( Rect );
        {Set the grow mode flag to follow the window}
        GrowMode := gfGrowHiX + gfGrowHiY;
end;

{Draw the interior of the window}
procedure AInterior.Draw;
begin
        {Do default drawing}
        TView.Draw;
        {Write the text}
        WriteStr( 4, 2, 'A Text String', 1 );
end;

{Initialize the window}
constructor AWindow.Init( Rect:TRect; DlgHead:String
        ; Numb:integer );
var
   Interior : AInteriorPtr;
begin
        {Do default initialization}
        TWindow.Init( Rect, DlgHead, Numb );
        {Get the window rectangle}
        GetClipRect( Rect );
        {Shrink inside of the border}
        Rect.Grow( -1, -1 );
        {Create the interior object}
        Interior := New( AInteriorPtr, Init( Rect ));
        Insert( Interior );
end;

var
   MyApp : TMyApp;

begin
        MyApp.Init;
        MyApp.Run;
        MyApp.Done;
end.
```

The two new objects in this program are AWindow and AInterior, which represent the window to be drawn. There is no special method for creating initial windows in Turbo Vision programs, so this program uses the InitMenuBar method. This method begins by calling the default menu bar method to create a blank menu bar. Next InitMenuBar initializes the rectangle object, Rect, which is used in creating the window Window. The last statement adds the new window to the desktop.

When the new window is created, the program calls the `AWindow.Init` method. This method initializes the window and then creates a rectangle that fits inside it. This rectangle is used to create the interior object.

The `AInterior.Init` method initializes the interior object. After calling the default initialization, the method sets the `GrowMode` field. This field determines what happens to the interior object when the user resizes the window object. In this case, the interior object always fills the window by moving the right and bottom edges as required.

As part of the default initialization of the interior object, `AInterior.Init` calls the `Draw` method. This method calls the default draw routine, which fills the window with blanks. Next, the method uses the `WriteStr` procedure to write text in the window. Figure 10-2 shows the result of running the program.

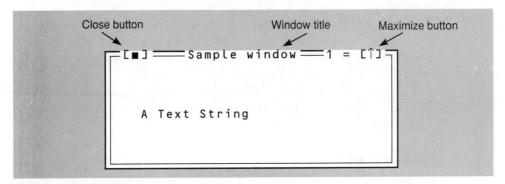

Figure 10-2 A Turbo Vision window

In Windows you can write to the window itself instead of a separate interior window. This, combined with the fact that the default procedures do more of the work, makes the program much shorter.

```
{Program to show windows}
program WWind;
uses WObjects, WinTypes, WinProcs;

type
        TMyApp = Object( TApplication )
        procedure InitMainWindow; Virtual;
        end;
        AWindowPtr = ^AWindow;
        AWindow = Object( TWindow )
                procedure Paint( PaintDC:HDC
                        ; var PaintInfo:TPaintStruct ); virtual;
        end;
```

```
procedure TMyApp.InitMainWindow;
begin
        MainWindow := New( AWindowPtr,Init( nil,'Windows Program' ));
end;

procedure AWindow.Paint( PaintDC : HDC; var PaintInfo : TPaintStruct );
begin
        TextOut( PaintDC, 10, 10, 'This is sample text', 19 );
end;

var
  MyApp : TMyApp;

begin
        MyApp.Init( 'TestProg' );
        MyApp.Run;
        MyApp.Done;
end.
```

Only two methods are required, one to initialize the application object (TMyApp.InitMainWindow) and another to repaint the window (AWindow.Paint). The InitMainWindow method makes sure that the MainWindow object is an AWindow object. This is important, because when Windows needs to repaint the window, it must call the paint routine in AWindow. The Paint method uses the TextOut procedure to put the text on the screen.

Comments

Because Windows applications work in graphics modes, routines such as TextOut specify screen locations in pixel units instead of character units. If you run the sample Windows program, you may notice that the text is very close to the upper-left corner of the window. If the screen units were character cells, the text, which should be printed at location 10, 10, would be much lower and to the right. Figure 10-3 shows how screen locations are numbered.

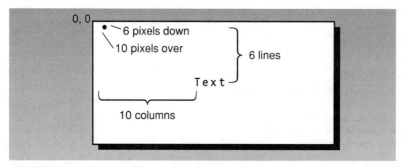

Figure 10-3 Text and graphics screen locations

Use dialog boxes in Turbo Vision or Turbo Pascal for Windows?

Description
Dialog boxes are the best way of getting user input in Turbo Vision and Turbo Pascal for Windows programs. Dialog boxes provide a consistent, easy-to-use interface. This solution shows how to implement dialog boxes in both Turbo Vision and Turbo Pascal for Windows.

See Also
6.4   Creating dialog boxes
10.1   Creating a basic application for Windows programs

Solution
The problem of using dialog boxes has two parts. The first is displaying the dialog box and interacting with the user. The second is putting the user's data into variables that the program can access. In Turbo Vision programs, you create a dialog object by creating each of the controls used in the dialog box and adding them to a window object. When the time comes to display the dialog box, you can choose between making the dialog modal or nonmodal. A modal dialog box takes over the I/O; you cannot place any other windows on the screen until you close the modal dialog box. A nonmodal dialog box lets you access other windows while it is on the screen. Nonmodal dialog boxes are often used to show program status while you do something else in another window.

All the controls that elicit data, such as text-entry fields and checkboxes, put the data into a single record that you can access with the methods `SetData` and `GetData`. Typically, you use `SetData` to set default values when the dialog box is displayed and `GetData` to retrieve the data from the dialog box when the user is finished.

The next program creates a sample dialog box when you select an `Open dialog` menu command:

```
{This is a T-Vision program with menus and dialogs and controls}
program TVDlg;
uses App, Objects, Menus, Drivers, Views, Dialogs;


type
   TMyApp = Object( TApplication )
        procedure InitMenuBar; virtual;
        procedure HandleEvent( var Event : TEvent ); virtual;
        procedure NewDialog; virtual;
```

```
    end;
    {Data for the dialog box}
    DlgData = record
          Color : word;
          Choices : word;
          Line : string[128];
    end;

const
    cmMyEvent = 1000;

{Create the menu}
procedure TMyApp.InitMenuBar;
var
   Rect : TRect;
begin
    GetExtent( Rect );
    Rect.B.Y := Rect.A.Y + 1;
        MenuBar := New( PMenuBar, Init( Rect, NewMenu(
        NewSubMenu( '~M~enu', hcNoContext, NewMenu(
        NewItem( '~O~pen dialog', 'F3', kbF3
            , cmMyEvent, hcNoContext,
            NewLine(
                NewItem( '~Q~uit', 'F4', kbF4
                    , cmQuit, hcNoContext,
                nil )))),
            nil ))));
end;

{Create and execute the dialog box}
procedure TMyApp.NewDialog;
var
   Dialog : PDialog;
   Rect : TRect;
   Control : word;
   MiscViews : PView;
   Info : DlgData;
begin
    Rect.Assign( 10, 7, 50, 20 );
    Dialog := New( PDialog, Init( Rect, 'Sample dialog' ));
    {Create check boxes}
    Rect.Assign( 2, 2, 14, 5 );
    MiscViews := New(PCheckBoxes, Init( Rect,
            NewSItem( '~R~ed',
            NewSItem( '~G~reen',
            NewSItem( '~B~lue',
            Nil )))));
    Dialog^.Insert( MiscViews );
    {Create radio buttons}
    Rect.Assign( 16, 2, 35, 5 );
    MiscViews := New( PRadioButtons, Init( Rect,
            NewSItem( '~F~irst choice',
            NewSItem( '~S~econd choice',
```

```
                    NewSItem( '~T~hird choice',
                    Nil )))));
    Dialog^.Insert( MiscViews );
    {Create an input field}
    Rect.Assign( 3, 7, 30, 8 );
    MiscViews := New( PInputLine, Init( Rect, 128 ));
    Dialog^.Insert( MiscViews );
    {Create a label}
    Rect.Assign( 2, 6, 30, 7 );
    Dialog^.Insert( New( PLabel
            , Init( Rect, 'Enter data here:', MiscViews )));
    {Create buttons}
    Rect.Assign( 2, 10, 15, 12 );
    Dialog^.Insert( New( PButton
            , Init(Rect, '~O~K', cmOK, bfDefault )));
    Rect.Assign( 18, 10, 31, 12 );
    Dialog^.Insert( New( PButton
            , Init( Rect, '~C~ancel', cmCancel, bfNormal )));
    {Make default values}
    Info.Color := 1;
    Info.Choices := 1;
    Info.Line := 'String';
    {Send the defaults to the dialog}
    Dialog^.SetData( Info );
    {Do the modal dialog}
    Control := DeskTop^.ExecView( Dialog );
    {If OK button pressed, get the data}
    if Control = cmOK then
        Dialog^.GetData( Info );
end;

{Handle menu event}
procedure TMyApp.HandleEvent( var Event : TEvent );
begin
    {Do default handling}
    TApplication.HandleEvent( Event );
    {See what kind of event}
    if Event.What = evCommand then
    begin
        case Event.Command of
            cmMyEvent : NewDialog;
        else
           exit;
        end;
        ClearEvent( Event );
    end;
end;

var
   MyApp : TMyApp;

begin
    MyApp.Init;
```

```
    MyApp.Run;
    MyApp.Done;
end.
```

This program uses the menu code from question 10.2. Instead of beeping when the user selects the menu command, this program creates and runs the dialog box in Figure 10-4. Each of the four controls in this dialog is represented by an object that is added to the dialog box with the `Insert` method.

The first control is a list of checkboxes. The items in this control can be individually selected by the user. The data field for this type of control is a `word` in which each bit corresponds to an item in the control.

The next control is a list of radio buttons. Only one of the items in the control can be selected at a time. The data field for this control is a word representing the number of the selected item in the list. The first item in the list is number 0.

The third control lets the user enter a text string. The data field for this control is a 128-byte string. The last control is the label that accompanies the text field. Because this label is static text, there is no data to pass in the data structure.

The `DlgData` type structure called `Info` combines data for all the dialog controls. After the program defines all of the controls and inserts them into the dialog box, the fields of `Info` are initialized and the structure is sent to the dialog with the `SetData` method.

The `ExecView` method displays the dialog box and gets all user input for it. It returns the command number of the button that was pressed to end the dialog. It is the use of the `ExecView` method that makes a dialog box modal. To make a nonmodal dialog box, use the `Insert` method instead of the `ExecView` method.

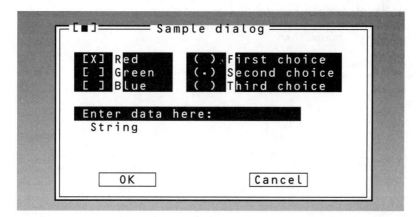

Figure 10-4 A sample dialog box

If the return value for the ExecView method is cmOK, indicating that the OK button was pressed, the program reads the data entered by the GetData method.

The procedure for handling dialog boxes in Windows programs is very different. First, the dialog box is read from a resource file rather than created by the program. Next, there is no data structure to hold the data for the controls. You set the initial data values by sending messages to the control. To get the data, you send messages to the control asking what its current data is.

The following program gets a dialog box from the STDDLGS.RES resource file and executes it when the user selects a menu command:

```
{This is a Windows program with a dialog box}
program WDialog;
uses WObjects, WinTypes, WinProcs;

{$R STDWNDS.RES}
{$R STDDLGS.RES}

type
    TMyApp = Object( TApplication )
            procedure InitMainWindow; Virtual;
    end;
    ADialogPtr = ^ADialog;
    ADialog = Object( TDialog )
            constructor Init( AParent:PWindowsObject; AName:PChar );
    end;
    AWindowPtr = ^AWindow;
    AWindow = Object( TWindow )
            ADlg : ADialogPtr;
            constructor Init( TheParent : PWindowsObject
                    ; TheTitle : PChar );
            procedure FileNew( var Msg : TMessage )
                    ; virtual cm_First + 24327;
    end;

{Initialize the application}
procedure TMyApp.InitMainWindow;
begin
        MainWindow := New( AWindowPtr,Init( nil,'Windows Program' ));
end;

{Initialize the window}
constructor AWindow.Init( TheParent : PWindowsObject
        ; TheTitle : PChar );
begin
        TWindow.Init( TheParent, TheTitle );
        Attr.Menu := LoadMenu( HInstance, 'FILECOMMANDS' );
end;
```

```
{Do the dialog}
procedure AWindow.FileNew( var Msg : TMessage );
var
        ComboData : array [1..20] of char;
        i : integer;
        SelectData : array [1..20] of char;
begin
        {Read the dialog from the resources}
        ADlg := New( ADialogPtr, Init( @Self, PChar( 16383 )));
        {Do the dialog and see if button is OK}
        if ADlg^.Execute <> 0 then
        begin
                {Get the text from the combo box}
                ADlg^.GetDlgItemText( HWindow, 501, ComboData, 20 );
                {Get the selection from the list box}
                i := ADlg^.SendDlgItemMsg( 502, lb_GetCurSel, 0,
                        longint( 0 ));
                ADlg^.SendDlgItemMsg( 502, lb_GetText, i,
                        longint( SelectData ));
        end;
        Dispose( ADlg, Done );
end;

{Initialize the dialog}
constructor ADialog.Init( AParent: PWindowsObject
        ; AName: PChar );
var
        Line : PChar;
begin
        {Do default initialization}
        TDialog.Init( AParent, AName );
        {Add a string to the combo box}
        SetDlgItemText( HWindow, 501, 'Test string' );
        {Add items to the list box}
        Line := 'List item 1';
        SendDlgItemMsg( 502, lb_AddString, 0, longint( Line ));
        Line := 'List item 2';
        SendDlgItemMsg( 502, lb_AddString, 0, longint( Line ));
end;

var
   MyApp : TMyApp;

begin
    MyApp.Init( 'TestProg' );
    MyApp.Run;
    MyApp.Done;
end.
```

This program is similar to the Windows program in question 10.3. Instead of writing text to the window, the "Open" menu command brings up a dialog from the STDDLGS.RES resource file (see Figure 10-5). The method that does this is the `AWindow.FileNew` method. It uses the `ADlg.Init` method to read the dialog box from the resource file. The controls in this dialog box include a combo-box, which is a combination of a text-entry field and a list box, and a list box, which is a list of items from which the user can choose.

The `ADlg.Execute` method runs the dialog. If `ADlg.Execute` returns a number other than 0, the OK button was pressed and there is data in the control objects. The `GetDlgItemText` gets data from the combo-box control. To read the list box data, the program first gets the number of the selected item in the list. It uses this number to get the selected text from the list.

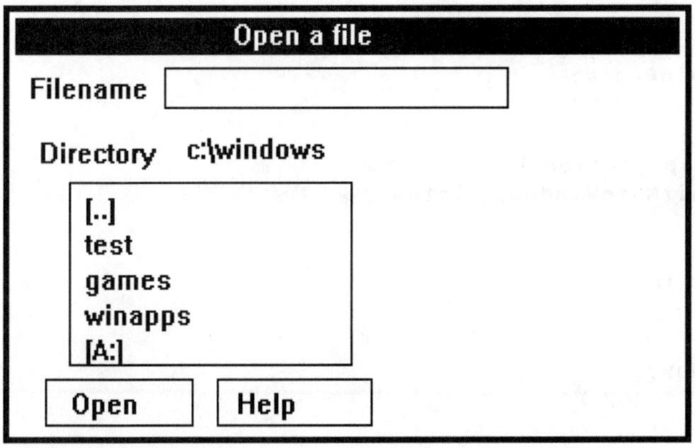

Figure 10-5 A sample Windows dialog box

Comments

Turbo Pascal for Windows comes with the Whitewater Resource Toolkit for editing such resources as dialog boxes and menus. This is the easiest way to create dialog boxes for Windows programs.

10.5 How do I...

Use graphics in Turbo Pascal for Windows?

Description

For many people, graphics are the reason for using Windows. The heart of the Windows interface is its various buttons, windows, and icons. Because everything in the interface is graphical, an application that only uses text seems bland. This solution shows how to draw in a window.

See Also

10.1 Creating a basic application for Windows programs
10.6 Using resources

Solution

Whenever you draw in a window, you must get a *device context* from Windows. The device context is a variable that Windows uses to identify the window that the program is drawing. The `Paint` method automatically supplies a device context, but you must ask Windows for a device context when you use other methods.

Because your window can be covered or uncovered at any time, the `Paint` method must be prepared to redraw the window. To do this you need to store the image in memory, where the `Paint` method can find it. The next program draws lines according to mouse movements. In addition to drawing, it also saves the vertices of the drawing in an array that the `Paint` method can use.

```
{Windows drawing program}
program WGraph;
uses WObjects, WinTypes, WinProcs;

type
        TMyApp = Object( TApplication )
                procedure InitMainWindow; Virtual;
        end;
        APointPtr = ^APoint;
        APoint = object( TObject )
                X, Y : integer;
        end;
        AWindowPtr = ^AWindow;
        AWindow = Object( TWindow )
                DrawDC : HDC;
                ButtonDown : boolean;
                PointColl : PCollection;
                constructor Init( TheParent : PWindowsObject
                        ; TheTitle : PChar );
                procedure WMLButtonDown( var Msg : TMessage )
                        ; virtual wm_First + wm_LButtonDown;
                procedure WMMouseMove( var Msg : TMessage )
                        ; virtual wm_First + wm_MouseMove;
                procedure WMLButtonUp( var Msg : TMessage )
                        ; virtual wm_First + wm_LButtonUp;
                procedure Paint( PaintDC:HDC
                        ; var PaintInfo:TPaintStruct ); virtual;
                destructor Done; virtual;
        end;

{Initialize the application}
procedure TMyApp.InitMainWindow;
begin
        MainWindow := New( AWindowPtr, Init( nil, 'Draw' ));
end;

{Initialize the window}
constructor AWindow.Init( TheParent : PWindowsObject
        ; TheTitle : PChar );
begin
        TWindow.Init( TheParent, TheTitle );
```

```
        {Make a point collection}
        PointColl := New( PCollection, Init( 50, 50 ));
        {Initialize the button state}
        ButtonDown := False;
end;

{Get rid of the point collection on exit}
destructor AWindow.Done;
begin
        TWindow.Done;
        Dispose( PointColl, Done );
end;

{Handle left button press event}
procedure AWindow.WMLButtonDown( var Msg : TMessage );
var
        APnt : APoint;
begin
        {Get rid of all of the collected points}
        PointColl^.DeleteAll;
        {Mark the window as invalid so it will be repainted}
        InvalidateRect( HWindow, nil, True );
        {If the button is not already pressed }
        if not ButtonDown then
        begin
                {Mark the button as pressed}
                ButtonDown := True;
                {Set mouse capture to this window}
                SetCapture( HWindow );
                {Get a device context}
                DrawDC := GetDC( HWindow );
                {Move the graphics cursor}
                MoveTo( DrawDC, Msg.lParamLo, Msg.lParamHi );
                {Record the point in the collection}
                APnt.X := Msg.lParamLo;
                APnt.Y := Msg.lParamHi;
                PointColl^.Insert( @APnt );
        end;
end;

{Handle mouse move events}
procedure AWindow.WMMouseMove( var Msg : TMessage );
var
        APnt : APoint;
begin
        {If the button is down}
        if ButtonDown then
        begin
                {Draw a line to the current point}
                LineTo( DrawDC, Msg.lParamLo, Msg.lParamHi );
                {Record the point in the collection}
                APnt.X := Msg.lParamLo;
                APnt.Y := Msg.lParamHi;
```

```
                        PointColl^.Insert( @APnt );
                end;
        end;

{Handle left button up events}
procedure AWindow.WMLButtonUp( var Msg : TMessage );
begin
        {If the button is pressed}
        if ButtonDown then
        begin
                {Mark it as released}
                ButtonDown := False;
                {Release the mouse capture}
                ReleaseCapture;
                {Release the device context}
                ReleaseDC( HWindow, DrawDC );
        end;
end;

{Repaint the entire drawing}
procedure AWindow.Paint( PaintDC : HDC; var PaintInfo : TPaintStruct );
var
        CurPt : APointPtr;
        i : integer;
begin
        {If there are points in the collection}
        if PointColl^.Count > 0 then
        begin
                {Get the first point}
                CurPt := PointColl^.At( 0 );
                {Move the graphics cursor}
                MoveTo( PaintDC, CurPt^.X, CurPt^.Y );
                {Draw lines to the rest of the points}
                for i := 1 to PointColl^.Count - 1 do
                begin
                        CurPt := PointColl^.At( i );
                        LineTo( PaintDC, CurPt^.X, CurPt^.Y );
                end;
        end;
end;

var
   MyApp : TMyApp;

begin
    MyApp.Init( 'TestProg' );
    MyApp.Run;
    MyApp.Done;
end.
```

The AWindow.Init method in this program initializes an object called PointColl, which stores the vertices of the drawing. The TCollection object type comes from the Turbo Pascal for Windows libraries. It works like a variable-length array of objects.

The WMLButtonDown, WMMouseMove, and WMLButtonUp methods handle mouse events. When the user presses the left mouse button, Windows calls the WMLButtonDown method. Its first job is to tell Windows to send all mouse events to the window. This ensures that all mouse messages are sent to this program, even if the mouse is over another window. Its next job is to use the GetDC routine to get a device context from Windows. It saves the device context in the window object so that other mouse-event methods cannot use it. After getting the device context, the method uses it to move the graphics cursor to the location of the mouse cursor. The last step is to save this point in the point-collection object.

The WMMouseMove method is called whenever the user moves the mouse. If the left button is pressed, the method draws a line to the current mouse location and saves the point in the point-collection object. The drawing is finished when the user releases the left mouse button. Windows calls the WMLButtonUp method to tell this program of the event. The method releases mouse capturing, so that other windows can receive mouse messages. Then the method releases the device context so that Windows knows that the drawing is finished.

The Paint method reads the points from the point-collection object to reconstruct the drawing. It moves the graphics cursor to the first point, then draws lines to the rest of the points in the collection.

Comments

Collections are a versatile way to store the image on the screen. You can use collections to store any object that is descended from a TObject type. For example, your program could use objects for text, lines, circles, and bitmaps when drawing the screen. As each object is created, it is added to the point-collection object, where the Paint method can find it when it is needed to redraw the window.

10.6   How do I...

Use resources in Turbo Pascal for Windows programs?

Description

In Turbo Vision programs, objects such as dialog boxes and menus must be created in the program that uses the object. For its menus and dialog boxes,

Turbo Pascal for Windows uses resources created independently from the rest of the program.

In questions 10.2 and 10.4 the Windows programs used resources to define menus and dialog boxes. Windows resources are not limited to these items; they can also be bitmaps, strings, accelerators, icons, and cursors. This solution shows how to use each of these resources in Windows programs.

See Also
10.1   Creating a basic application for Windows programs
10.2   Adding menus
10.4   Using dialog boxes

Solution
There are five types of resources in addition to menus and dialog boxes. You can define text resources, called strings, to put lines of text in the resource file. If you convert all the strings used in your program into resources, it is easy to modify the text, for example, to translate the program for use in another country. Another resource type is the accelerator table, which is a list of keys and command event numbers. When an accelerator table is loaded and the user presses one of the accelerator keys, Windows performs the corresponding event.

The last three resource types are the graphics resources. The first type, bitmaps, are simply pictures that can be displayed in windows. The second type is an icon, which is a bitmap that represents the application in the program manager window or on the desktop. The last graphics resource is a cursor. A cursor resource defines the shape of the cursor.

The first step in using resources is to create a resource file. Turbo Pascal adds the resource file to the end of the executable program where it can be read when the program needs a resource. Turbo Pascal comes with a program called the Whitewater Resource Toolkit for creating and editing resource files. This program is a Windows application that includes editors for graphics, text, menus, and dialog boxes. You can save the items you create in separate files or combine them into resource files.

Each resource in a resource file can be identified by a name or resource number. When you save a resource in the resource file, the resource toolkit asks you for the name or number of the resource. Be sure to note whatever name or number you use so that you can use it when you load the resource.

Once you have a resource file, you need to make it part of your program. The {$R} directive tells the compiler to include a resource file in the compiled version of the program. Next, you need to add code to the program to load the resource into memory. Questions 10.2 and 10.4 show how to do this for menus and dialog boxes. The next program shows how to load and use other resources:

```
{Windows program that uses resources}
program WWind;
uses WObjects, WinTypes, WinProcs;

{$R RESFILE.RES}

type
        TMyApp = Object( TApplication )
                procedure InitInstance; virtual;
                procedure InitMainWindow; virtual;
        end;
        AWindowPtr = ^AWindow;
        AWindow = Object( TWindow )
                procedure Paint( PaintDC:HDC
                        ; var PaintInfo:TPaintStruct ); virtual;
                procedure GetWindowClass( var AWndClass:TWndClass )
                        ; virtual;
        end;

{Load the accelerator table when the program starts}
procedure TMyApp.InitInstance;
begin
        TApplication.InitInstance;
        HAccTable := LoadAccelerators( HInstance, 'Accel' );
end;

{Create a main window}
procedure TMyApp.InitMainWindow;
begin
    MainWindow := New( AWindowPtr, Init( nil,'Windows Program' ));
end;

{Paint a bit map on the main window}
procedure AWindow.Paint( PaintDC : HDC; var PaintInfo : TPaintStruct );
var
        ABitMap : hBitMap;
        MemDC : HDC;
begin
        ABitMap := LoadBitmap( HInstance, 'BMAP' );
        MemDC := CreateCompatibleDC( PaintDC );
        SelectObject( MemDC, ABitMap );
        BitBlt( PaintDC,0,0,64,64,MemDC,0,0,SrcCopy );
        DeleteDC( MemDC );
        DeleteObject( ABitMap );
end;

{Set the icon for the program and the cursor used in the window}
procedure AWindow.GetWindowClass(var AWndClass : TWndClass );
```

```
begin
      TWindow.GetWindowClass( AWndClass );
      AWndClass.hCursor := LoadCursor( HInstance, 'Curse' );
      AWndClass.hIcon := LoadIcon( HInstance, 'Icon' );
end;

var
   MyApp : TMyApp;

begin
    MyApp.Init( 'TestProg' );
    MyApp.Run;
    MyApp.Done;
end.
```

The directive {$R RESFILE.RES} at the beginning of the program tells the compiler to load the resource file, which must already exist and be in either the current directory or in one of the directories in Turbo Pascal's resource file path.

Windows calls the first method in this program, InitInstance, when the program begins. In this program, the InitInstance method loads an accelerator table (named Accel) from the resources. This table can hold any number of keys, each of which can cause any command event. For example, if you bind the Alt-X key to the cmQuit event, pressing Alt-X ends the program.

The rest of the resources in this program are loaded in the methods for AWindow. In the Paint method, the program loads a bitmap resource named Bitmap and displays it in the window. After the bitmap is displayed, the program deletes it, which leaves the image of the bitmap on the screen but removes the object from memory. It is important to delete any bitmap objects that your program uses because they continue to use up memory even after the program ends.

The Paint method draws the bitmap in several steps. The first step is to create a memory device context (MemDC). A memory device context is a variable that the BitBlt procedure can use to access the memory that holds the bitmap. The SelectObject routine associates the memory device context with the bitmap. The BitBlt procedure uses the memory device context to copy the bitmap from memory to the screen. The last step is to delete the memory device context and the bitmap.

The GetWindowClass method is called as part of the setup of the AWindow object. In this program it loads an icon and a cursor resource.

Warnings

Every resource that you load takes up memory. Be sure to delete the object for each resource that you load. This is especially important in methods such as `Paint`, which are called several times while the program is running. The memory used by most objects is automatically freed at the end of the program. This is not the case with bitmaps; they stay in memory until they are deleted even if the program that loaded them has ended.

INDEX

Three-dimensional objects, *334*
  drawing, *335-341*
  removing hidden lines from, *341-347*
Timer interrupt, *66*
Transformation, *324*
Transpose procedure, *180-181*
TSR (terminate and stay resident) programs,
    253-254, 258
Two-dimensional objects, *315-316*
Type fonts, *135*

U

Units, *310-312*
Unit statement, *67*
Unlock procedure, *288*
UpCase function, *217-218*
Uses statement, *67, 72, 84, 310-311*

V

Variable-length records, *111-119*
Variables, file copying
  CopyOK, *85*
  destination, *84*
  source, *84*
Video BIOS, *37*
Video card, *5*
Video mode, *5*

Video RAM, *5*
Virtual memory, *283-290*
Virtual Method Table (VMT), *306, 412*
Virus protection, *375-376*

W

WhereX variable, *5*
WhereY variable, *5*
Wildcard characters, *89, 281*
Windows
  overlapping, *11-18*
  text-mode, *19-26*
Windows applications, *439-442*
  dialog boxes in, *453-459*
  graphics in, *459-463*
  menus for, *442-448*
  mouse events in, *463*
  window creation, *448-452*
Word pointer, *10*
Word wrap, *134*
WriteLine procedure, *108*
Write procedure, *131*
WriteRec procedure, *117*
WriteSect procedure, *261*

Z

Zero, division by, *172, 183*

COLOPHON

Production for this book was done using desktop publishing techniques and every phase of the book involved the use of computer technology. Never did production have to use traditional typesetting, photostats, or photos, and everything for this book, from the illustrations to the text, was saved on disk. Only the cover painting was created in the traditional manner.

The text was written in Microsoft Word 5.0 for DOS on a 386-SX computer. The source code files were written in Turbo Pascal 5.0, 6.0, and Turbo Pascal for Windows, and imported into Word using Word's Text In feature. The Word files were transferred to a Macintosh directly on a 3.5 inch diskette, using Insignia's Access PC. These text files were then opened directly in Microsoft Word 4 for the Macintosh.

The book's design and all page formatting was done in Aldus PageMaker 4.01 on a Mac IIci and a Mac IIsi, using the imported Microsoft Word files. Adobe and Monotype fonts were used. Design elements were created in Adobe Photoshop 1.0 and Adobe Illustrator 3.01.

Figures were produced on a Mac IIcx using Adobe Illustrator and saved as EPS files for placement in PageMaker. PC screen captures were saved as .BMP files and ultimately saved as PCX files using Microsoft Windows Paintbrush. Inset Systems' Hijack was used to translate the PCX files into TIFF files. The PC TIFF files were transferred to the Macintosh, again on a 3.5-inch disk opened under Access PC, and converted to Macintosh TIFF files directly in Adobe Photoshop. Backmatter figures were done on a Macintosh IIfx using Freehand.

The cover was created as a traditional airbrush painting and was traditionally separated. Quark Express 3.0 was used for four-color cover type and layout.

Final files were sent on a SyQuest 44 Mb disk cartridge to Alpha-Graphics, where they were directly imposed to film through a Macintosh IIfx and Linotronic 530 phototypesetting machine. Plates were then made from the film.

The Waite Group's Master C: *Let the PC Teach You C*
Mitchell Waite, Stephen Prata, Rex Woollard

The programming language known as C has become one of the languages of choice among programmers, due to its enormous range and flexibility which allows it to be used in simple applications as well as advanced operating systems. *Master C: Let the PC Teach You C* is a revolutionary new book/disk package designed to use the power and speed of the IBM PC to provide the fastest, most effective way to learn C. The *Master C* CBT has features not found in books. It automatically guides the user through C topics, notices problems, and recommends action. Sophisticated answer judgment accepts rough responses (even misspellings). "Remediation paths" send the user to review material not understood. All in all, there is no better or faster way to learn C today than with *Master C.*

256 Pages, 7 × 9, 3 5.25" Disks, Softbound   **ISBN: 1-878739-00-X, $44.95**

Fractal Creations
Tim Wegner, Mark Peterson

If the magic place between science and art strikes your fancy—if you enjoy mixing special effects, meditation, and, say, a little mathematics—then take a look at *The Waite Group's Fractal Creations*, a creative new book/disk package. Fractals are the mathematical patterns that underlie many futuristic ideas in science. FRACTINT, the program that comes with the book, turns an IBM PC into an exciting "Fractal Processor" for exploring fractal images. You can zoom in on any of FRACTINT's 68 fractal images; then you can rotate, colorize, or color cycle the images for the most beautiful animated patterns imaginable. The program also converts them to 3-D, and creates 3-D mountain ranges, clouds, ferns, or landscapes—a pair of 3-D glasses is included. The book that accompanies the software is an illustrated tutorial on fractals, a reference manual for FRACTINT, and a bible of all the built-in fractals and how they work. A large fold-out color poster features some of the most beautiful fractals created by FRACTINT users. Check out the future with *The Waite Group's Fractal Creations*.

350 Pages , 7 × 9, 560K 5.25" Disk, Softbound   **ISBN: 1-878739-05-0, $34.95**

The Waite Group's WordPerfect Bible
Joseph Speaks, Rob Weinstein

Until now, WordPerfect has been a difficult product to learn, let alone master: its over 165 powerful text control commands are non-intuitive and difficult to remember. Indeed, WordPerfect is especially hard on people new to computers.

The Waite Group's WordPerfect Bible brings an end to this confusion. It's an exciting reference and tutorial to all WordPerfect commands with a specially designed "idea-in-a-block" format that makes it accessible to first-time users as well as power users. Every one of the beautifully designed command spreads in *WordPerfect Bible* contains blocks for purpose, usage techniques, keyboard shortcuts, mouse selection, an example, deeper details, tips, warning, variations, macros, related commands, and a compatibility box. You waste no time reading large tracts of irrelevant text. This book is The Waite Group at its best—for fast and easy lookup, quick and complete alphabetical and by-task "jump tables" of all WordPerfect commands and concepts are featured on the inside covers. Everyone needs *The Waite Group's WordPerfect Bible* next to their computer. Toss out all of your WordPerfect books—this is the only one you'll ever need.

546 Pages, 7 × 9, Softbound   **ISBN: 1-878739-01-8, $26.95**

WAITE GROUP® PRESS
call 1-800-368-9369

The Waite Group's C++ Primer Plus
Stephen Prata

Computer mavens expect the new programming language C++ to eventually displace C from its position of near-universal preference. An extension of C, C++ treats data and functions as objects (hence the term object-oriented programming or OOP), making it possible to clone, modify, and build upon them. Unlike existing books on the subject, *C++ Primer Plus* is addressed to those without an extensive programming background. It provides a simple introduction to the standard 2.0 AT&T implementations of C++ while also covering the essential concepts of C. It teaches the basics of OOP and shows how to build programs that are flexible and readily modified.

In the friendly, easy-to-follow style of *C Primer Plus* (the author's best-selling work), *C++ Primer Plus* illustrates the language's fundamentals with short sample programs that are easy to key in and experiment with. A companion disk (available through the order card included with the book) contains all the sample programs and projects. The book is compatible with any AT&T Version 2.0 compliant compiler and works under Unix, Borland, Turbo, Zortec, and Sun C++.

744 Pages, 7 × 9, Softbound   **ISBN: 1-878739-02-6, $26.95**

The Waite Group's Object-Oriented Programming in Turbo C++
Robert Lafore

Object-oriented programming (OOP) is the most dramatic—and potentially confusing—innovation in software development since the dawn of the computer age. Based on the idea of treating functions and data as objects, OOP results in programs that are more flexible, more easily maintained, and on the whole, more powerful. *Object-Oriented Programming in Turbo C++* focuses on C as a separate language, distinct from C, and assumes no prior experience with C. Step by step lessons teach Turbo C++, Borland C++, and the basics of OOP at the same time. Suitable for students, hackers, and enthusiasts, *Object-Oriented Programming in Turbo C++* is written by Robert Lafore, author of the best-selling *The Waite Group's Turbo C Programming for the IBM* (over 200,000 copies in print). You'll find details on Turbo C++ graphics and the DOS file system, project chapters enhance your understanding of object-oriented design with a game of life, a program that simulates a town's water distribution system, and a fractal generator, and more. No experience required for this hands-on book.

768 Pages, 7 × 9, Softbound   **ISBN: 1-878739-06-9, $26.95**

The Waite Group's Turbo Pascal How-To
Gary Syck

Turbo Pascal How-To is a working programmer's dream: hundreds of typical programming problems, with creative ways to solve them, in an easy-to-use reference format. The solutions provided are designed to work with the latest, object-oriented Version 6.0 of Turbo Pascal, as well as earlier versions and Turbo Pascal for Windows. Experienced programmers will appreciate the ease of incorporating these solutions, which will allow them to concentrate on their program's unique characteristics and not waste time solving problems. At the same time, novice programmers will find they can quickly begin creating functional programs just by building on the modular examples provided here. Borland's new Turbo Vision interface system is covered too.

The Waite Group's *Turbo Pascal How-To* answers the most practical questions any programmer has, such as: "How do I put information in a window? How do I build a fancy pull-down menu system? How do I scroll the screen? Create a directory? Save memory?" And more. In short, this book has everything readers need to know to write professional Turbo Pascal programs.

496 Pages, 7 × 9, Softbound   **ISBN: 1-878739-04-2, $24.95**

Disk Order Form

Filling out this order form may change your life, help you impress friends, and perhaps even influence people.

The companion disk for *The Waite Group's Turbo Pascal How-To* includes all of the Turbo Pascal program listings contained in this book, organized by chapter, and pre-tested and debugged. Note that some programs require Turbo Pascal for Windows or Turbo Pascal 6 with Turbo Vision.

The Waite Group's Master C is a disk-based training system that turns your IBM PC into a C instructor. Master C uses modern computer-based techniques including sophisticated answer judgement to teach C, from fundamentals through advanced concepts. It presents information, gives quizzes, keeps score, notices problems, recommends action, and even lets you chart your own C course.

To order by phone, call 800-368-9369 or 415-331-1075 (FAX)
or send to The Waite Group, 100 Shoreline Highway, Suite A-285, Mill Valley, CA 94941

Name

Company

Address
Street Address Only, No P.O. Box

City ___ State ___ ZIP ___ — ___

Daytime Phone

Quantity and Type

Name	Item #	Quantity	Price	
Turbo Pascal How-To companion disk	WGP-CD11	☐	x $19.95 =	
Master C training system	CBT-1	☐	x $44.95 =	

Sales Tax—California addresses add 7.25% sales tax.
Shipping—Add $5 USA, $10 Canada, or $30 Foreign for shipping and handling. Standard shipping is UPS Ground. Allow 3 to 4 weeks. Prices subject to change. Purchase orders subject to credit approval, and verbal purchase orders will not be accepted.

Sales Tax ___

Shipping ___

Total Due ___

Disk Type: ☐ 5.25-inch ☐ 3.5-inch

Method of Payment

Checks or money orders, payable to The Waite Group. To pay by credit card, complete the following:

☐ Visa ☐ MasterCard   Card Number ___

Cardholder's Name _____   Exp. Date ___

Cardholder's Signature _____

AS A PUBLISHER AND WRITER WITH OVER 360,000 BOOKS SOLD EACH YEAR, IT CAME AS A GREAT SHOCK TO DISCOVER THAT OUR RAIN FORESTS, HOME FOR HALF OF ALL LIVING THINGS ON EARTH, ARE BEING DESTROYED AT THE RATE OF 50 ACRES PER MINUTE ☙ AT THIS RATE THE RAIN FORESTS WILL COMPLETELY DISAPPEAR IN JUST 50 YEARS ☙ BOOKS HAVE A LARGE INFLUENCE ON THIS RAMPANT DESTRUCTION ☙ FOR EXAMPLE, SINCE IT TAKES 17 TREES TO PRODUCE ONE TON OF PAPER, A FIRST PRINTING OF 30,000 COPIES OF A TYPICAL 480 PAGE BOOK CONSUMES 108,000 POUNDS OF PAPER WHICH WILL REQUIRE 918 TREES. TO HELP OFFSET THIS LOSS, WAITE GROUP PRESS WILL PLANT TWO TREES FOR EVERY TREE FELLED FOR PRODUCTION OF THIS BOOK ☙ THE DONATION WILL BE MADE TO RAINFOREST ACTION NETWORK (THE BASIC FOUNDATION, P.O. BOX 47012, ST. PETERSBURG, FL 33743), WHICH CAN PLANT 1,000 TREES FOR $250.

Disk Order Form

Filling out this order form may change your life, help you impress friends, and perhaps even influence people.

The companion disk for *The Waite Group's Turbo Pascal How-To* includes all of the Turbo Pascal program listings contained in this book, organized by chapter, and pre-tested and debugged. Note that some programs require Turbo Pascal for Windows or Turbo Pascal 6 with Turbo Vision.

The Waite Group's Master C is a disk-based training system that turns your IBM PC into a C instructor. Master C uses modern computer-based techniques including sophisticated answer judgement to teach C, from fundamentals through advanced concepts. It presents information, gives quizzes, keeps score, notices problems, recommends action, and even lets you chart your own C course.

To order by phone, call 800-368-9369 or 415-331-1075 (FAX)
or send to The Waite Group, 100 Shoreline Highway, Suite A-285, Mill Valley, CA 94941

Name

Company

Address
Street Address Only, No P.O. Box

City   State   ZIP   —

Daytime Phone

Quantity and Type

Name	Item #	Quantity	Price	
Turbo Pascal How-To companion disk	WGP-CD11		x $19.95 =	
Master C training system	CBT-1		x $44.95 =	

Sales Tax—California addresses add 7.25% sales tax.
Shipping—Add $5 USA, $10 Canada, or $30 Foreign for shipping and handling. Standard shipping is UPS Ground. Allow 3 to 4 weeks. Prices subject to change. Purchase orders subject to credit approval, and verbal purchase orders will not be accepted.

Sales Tax

Shipping

Total Due

Disk Type: ☐ 5.25-inch   ☐ 3.5-inch

Method of Payment

Checks or money orders, payable to The Waite Group. To pay by credit card, complete the following:

☐ Visa   ☐ MasterCard   Card Number

Cardholder's Name _____   Exp. Date

Cardholder's Signature _____

NO POSTAGE
NECESSARY
IF MAILED
IN THE
UNITED STATES

BUSINESS REPLY MAIL
FIRST CLASS MAIL   PERMIT NO. 33   MILL VALLEY, CA

POSTAGE WILL BE PAID BY ADDRESSEE

ATTENTION: DISK ORDERS
WAITE GROUP PRESS, INC.
100 SHORELINE HIGHWAY, SUITE A-285
MILL VALLEY, CA 94941-9840

- **FOLD HERE** -

Waite Group Satisfaction Report Card

Please fill out this card if you wish to know of future updates to *The Waite Group's Turbo Pascal How-To*, or to receive our catalog.

Company Name: _____

Division: _____   Mail Stop: _____

Last Name: _____   First Name: _____   Middle Initial: _____

Street Address: _____

City: _____   State: _____   Zip: _____

Daytime telephone: (_____) _____

Date product was acquired: Month _____ Day _____ Year _____   Your Occupation: _____

Overall, how would you rate *The Waite Group's Turbo Pascal How-To*?

☐ Excellent   ☐ Very Good   ☐ Good
☐ Fair   ☐ Below Average ☐ Poor

What did you like MOST about this book? _____
_____
_____

What did you like LEAST about this book? _____
_____
_____

How do you use this book (problem solver, tutorial, reference ...) _
_____
_____

What version of Turbo Pascal are you using? _____

Do you use Turbo Pascal for Windows? _____

What is your experience with object-oriented programming? _____
_____
_____

What computer languages are you familiar with? _____

What level of Turbo Pascal programmer are you?

☐ New   ☐ Dabbler   ☐ Hacker
☐ Power user   ☐ Know other language ☐ Experienced professional

Where did you buy this book?

☐ Bookstore (name) _____
☐ Discount store (name) _____
☐ Computer store (name) _____
☐ Catalog (name) _____
☐ Direct from WGP   ☐ Other _____

What price did you pay for this book? _____

What influenced your purchase of this book?

☐ Recommendation   ☐ Mailing
☐ Advertisement   ☐ Book's format
☐ Magazine review   ☐ Reputation of The Waite Group
☐ Store display   ☐ Other _____

How many computer books do you buy each year? _____

How many other Waite Group books do you own? _____

What is your favorite Waite Group book? _____
_____

Is there any program or subject you would like to see the Waite Group cover in a similar approach? _____
_____

Any other comments? _____
_____

☐ Check here for free Waite Group catalog

Waite Group Press, Inc.
Attention: *Turbo Pascal How-To*
100 Shoreline Highway, Suite A-285
Mill Valley, CA 94941

— — — — — — — — — — — — — — — — — **FOLD HERE** — — — — — — — — — — — — — — — —